D0891395

Creating the
American Mind

American Intellectual Culture

Series Editors: Jean Bethke Elshtain, University of Chicago,
Ted V. McAllister, Pepperdine University,
Wilfred M. McClay, University of Tennessee at Chattanooga

Creating the American Mind

Intellect and Politics
in the Colonial Colleges

J. David Hoeveler

ROWMAN & LITTLEFIELD PUBLISHERS, INC.
Lanham • Boulder • New York • Oxford

ROWMAN & LITTLEFIELD PUBLISHERS, INC.

Published in the United States of America
by Rowman & Littlefield Publishers, Inc.
A Member of the Rowman & Littlefield Publishing Group
4720 Boston Way, Lanham, Maryland 20706
www.rowmanlittlefield.com

PO Box 317, Oxford, OX2 9RU, United Kingdom

British Library Cataloguing in Publication Information Available

Library of Congress Cataloging-in-Publication Data
Hoeveler, J. David, 1943–
  Creating the American mind : intellect and politics in the Colonial
colleges / J. David Hoeveler.
    p. cm.—(American intellectual culture)
Includes bibliographical references and index.
  ISBN 0-8476-8830-5 (cloth : alk. paper)
  1. Universities and colleges—United States—History—17th century.
2. Universities and colleges—United States—History—18th century. 3.
Education, Higher—United States—History—17th century. 4. Education,
Higher—United States—History—18th century. 5. United
States—History—Colonial period, ca. 1600–1775. I. Title. II. Series.
  LA227 .H64 2002
  378.73'09'032—dc21
                                                          2002006101

Printed in the United States of America

♾™ The paper used in this publication meets the minimum requirements of American
National Standard for Information Sciences—Permanence of Paper
for Printed Library Materials, ANSI/NISO Z39.48–1992.

For Wint

Contents

Preface

Nine colleges existed in the British colonies of North America at the time of the American Revolution. This book studies those institutions. It has some specific purposes in view and some strategies designed to pursue them.

American intellectual culture is the general subject of the series to which this book belongs. Hence this study examines the colonial colleges with a large interest in how they expressed, advanced, and challenged the intellectual systems in which they functioned. Much in view is the public nature of the schools—their interconnections with the apparatus of the colonies or Crown that incorporated them, the religious denominations that sponsored them, and above all the expansive literature of religious dogmatics and disputation that played so important a role in defining and differentiating the institutions in question.

We often idealize our institutions of higher learning. We like to think that the intellectual world of colleges and universities must thrive within an autonomy essential to the disinterested pursuit of truth. And yet we know that higher education in our time has come under sustained attack for taking on a political ideology. References to the "culture wars" describe a scene of contest, where the campuses, and especially the college curricula, reinforce the ideological warfare that rages beyond. The label "politically correct," which critics apply to the partisan agenda of putatively leftist-oriented universities, signifies to them a betrayal of intellectual neutrality or objectivity. Conservative detractors see a one-dimensional habit of mind that tolerates no dissent and casts out those who interrogate the official coda.

This book recovers an era in which colleges were political to the core. One will learn of a college president who spent time in prison for his political transgressions, of a faculty member who became a British spy, of college leaders who preached revolution, and of college leaders who did all they could to prevent it. One will see college graduates who emerged from their institutions armed with a thinking that carried them into revolution and, in some cases, into the highest offices of the United States. But I mean by "political" something more than these familiar expressions of the word, and something more important. I mean the politics of intellect. For in the era studied here intellect meant politics. A college's very identity embraced a position often painstakingly secured through elaborate argumentation, within an array of religious opinion, theological discourse, and denominational prescriptions that proliferated in the seventeenth and eighteenth centuries. It mattered that one college had a Calvinist identity, and it mattered if it seemed that a college was losing that identity. It mattered that one understood baptism properly to mean antipaedobaptism, and it mattered that one understood Scripture as giving a plenary sanction for the institutions of bishops. It mattered that one argued that an individual could gain salvation from some initiative of his own. If the doctrine of predestination seemed to make God the author of sin, that mattered, too.

When I first contemplated a contribution to this series, I considered what approach would be the most useful for studying the nine colonial colleges together while respecting their critical differences. It became clear to me that each institution had its origin within a particular intellectual milieu, that each, in other words, rather staked out a position within a large corpus of religious and humanistic writings and that its founding gave an institutional expression and location to that position. Such demarcations often defined a religious denomination, and just as often a factional group within one. Harvard, Yale, and Dartmouth were all Congregational colleges, but they were clearly marked off from each other in their intellectual affiliations. The College of New Jersey (now Princeton University) was Presbyterian, but its founding group spoke for a particular segment within American Presbyterianism. So too, within their denomination, did the Dutch Reformed faction that established Rutgers (or Queen's College).

This study offers the first synthetic examination of the nine colonial colleges. It is not a history of the college curriculum in the colonial era, although that subject enters at critical junctures. It deals at various places with student life, but constraints of size have also limited that subject in this book. Rather, I have examined an expansive literature of sermons and pamphlets, public addresses, college texts, and collections of personal papers. These intellectual documents, many of them intensely partisan, brought their authors into the public domain. Their efforts defined and redefined Protestant denominations, they helped create new churches and religious groups, and they influenced the founding of new colleges. Thus Calvinist New Englanders, upset with Harvard's liberalizing trends, founded Yale. New Light partisans of the religious Awakening of the eighteenth century, finding their movement locked out of Harvard and Yale, founded Princeton. New Light Separatists and Baptists, opposed by the Standing

Order of Connecticut and Massachusetts, founded Rhode Island College. Anglicans in New York City, vexed that Dissenter Presbyterians had successfully secured the College of New Jersey, started King's College (Columbia University).

Colleges had a large public visibility. Officials of the state sat on their boards. Commencement exercises were colonywide events, visited by governors and other public officials and attended by large crowds. At Harvard a professor like John Winthrop IV gave Thursday evening lectures to the public, discoursing on earthquakes and storms, emphasizing their natural causes and allaying fears of their providential meanings. Likewise its professor of divinity Edward Wigglesworth gave public addresses, discussing fine points of theology. During the revolution, almost all the colleges felt a direct impact of the war as their buildings served the military operations of American or British forces. In one of the colleges the new state government intervened to change the institution root and branch.

This book brings all the colonial colleges under study but it nonetheless takes an institutional approach, mostly chronological. It begins with Oxford and Cambridge universities and the Puritan movements in England. Two chapters follow on Harvard and Yale to bring the two New England colleges under comparison. William and Mary College, the second oldest of the colonial schools, follows. The College of New Jersey moves the study to the Middle Atlantic colonies, joined there by King's College and the College of Philadelphia (the University of Pennsylvania). Three colleges—Rhode Island College, Queen's College, and Dartmouth College, all products of the Awakening—complete the list. I have added a second chapter on Harvard; having a significantly longer history than any of the schools, it required extended consideration. All of the colleges found themselves immersed in the American Revolution and the events leading up to it. A new political literature emerged in these years and gave drama to the intellectual politics of colonial higher education. Here the colleges performed a particularly significant role in creating an American intellectual culture. That subject constitutes part II of the book.

I have relied on institutional histories to construct the framework for this study, but they have provided me only a point of departure. In the chapter subjects I focus on the extended biographies of the key players and move from there to the textual examination of their literary production. That shift reflects a conviction that biography gives intellectual history its critical axis as well as its adventure. Most of the individuals who became the college leaders that one will meet here brought to their new roles an established record of intellectual activity, polemics, and partisan religious warfare. The personal venue also opens this history to the larger intellectual worlds of Puritanism and Calvinism; to the new departures in rational and liberal Protestantism; to the documents, often passionate and prejudicial, but more often rigorous and scholarly, too, of the religious Awakening; and to the American Enlightenment, nourished by science, the challenge of deism, and religious and philosophical literature from England

and Scotland. Amid their hostilities, their ad hominem disputes, their sectarian assaults, and their learned disputations the colleges opened the American colonies to the intellectual world of the ancients, to the dogmatics of Reformation Christianity, and to the modern thinking that was reshaping Western culture. These resources lay in waiting, as it were, in the tumultuous years of the 1760s and 1770s. College presidents, students, and graduates seized them and, in richly different applications, used them to forge a new intellectual culture for the United States.

I use the expression "Creating the American Mind" as the main title of this book. None knows better than I, who has done studies of poststructuralism and postmodern culture, that since the linguistic turn of the 1970s such reifications as the "American Mind" stand discredited. They speak, putatively, for a logocentric culture that echoes triumphant notions of universal truth that any deconstructive efforts will fragment into multiplicities and contradictions of meaning. Significantly, however, the postmodernist mode has a thematic affinity with the study here. First, "creating" the American Mind was a highly decentered process. It had nothing of a self-conscious dimension to it until the 1760s. To this extent, the chapter arrangements here, looking at the colleges individually, have an additional recommendation. They reflect the ad hoc and piecemeal character of this construction.

Second, readers will see that this study has an overwhelming emphasis on pluralities, and above all in the diverse and specialized readings that the intellectuals in question gave to a larger outline of Western Christianity. To be sure, these thinkers all sought to establish their own truth systems. But by the time of the Revolution, when Americans drew upon religious and classical sources to make their case for independence, they fashioned an American intellect that held diverse and even countervailing components. Part II of this book will clarify that fact.

Also, the use of such terms as the "American Mind" seems not to have gone wholly out of fashion. In 1987 Allan Bloom offered his controversial book *The Closing of the American Mind*, and in 1996 Lawrence Levine answered with his rival volume *The Opening of the American Mind*. Both works dealt with the American university, and both authors measured it by their own partisan assessments of American political, social, and cultural life. Neither author would have said that the "American Mind" to which he refers speaks for all of the United States. Nor by any means do I. The colonial colleges provided one of many cultural and intellectual agencies and outlets in their day, although, as I hope to show, highly significant ones. Appropriation of "American Mind" allows me to take the subject of Bloom and Levine, American higher education, back to its beginnings, the era of its creation.

Note: where deemed helpful, I have modernized spelling and punctuation in citing original texts.

ACKNOWLEDGMENTS

I am indebted to Professor Ted McAllister of Pepperdine University for my involvement in this series and for the valuable series editorship that he and Wilfred McClay of the University of Tennessee-Chattanooga have rendered me. Stephen Wrinn, formerly of Rowman & Littlefield Publishers, encouraged the project, and Mary Carpenter, Jehanne Schweitzer, and Laura Roberts saw it through to publication. To each of these people I express my thanks above all for their help and encouragement.

My interest in the history of American higher education found its inspiration in the very weeks I began my graduate studies in history at the University of Illinois in Urbana, 1965. I had the privilege of working as a research assistant for Professor Winton U. Solberg, then engaged in the first volume of his history of the University of Illinois. Two of my previous books have carried through the excitement I found in this subject. But to speak only of the intellectual rewards that began with this relationship would not fully express my gratitude to the individual who took so great an interest in my early career. It is above all a gratitude for years of valuable friendship since that time. As but a partial expression of my thanks and appreciation, I am pleased to dedicate this book to my Maecenas, Wint Solberg.

Illustration Credits

James Manning, courtesy of Special Collections, The John Hay Library, Brown University

Jacob Rutsen Hardenbergh, courtesy of Special Collections and University Archives, Rutgers, the State University of New Jersey

The Reverend Eleazar Wheelock, oil on canvas by Joseph Steward, 1796, P.793.2, Commissioned by the Trustees of Dartmouth College, Hanover, New Hampshire.

Governor John Wentworth, pastel on paper mounted on canvas, by John Singleton Copley, 1769, D.977.175, Hood Museum of Art, Dartmouth College, Hanover, New Hampshire, gift of Mrs. Esther Lowell Abbott, in memory of her husband, Gordon Abbott.

A *Front View of Dartmouth College, with the Chapel & Hall*, by Josiah Dunham. Boston: C. E. Goodspeed, 1911. Originally from the Massachusetts Magazine, February 1793. Neg. #1305. Courtesy of Dartmouth College.

Edward Wigglesworth, courtesy of the Harvard University Archives.

John Winthrop, IV, courtesy of the Harvard University Archives.

Harvard, by Burgis, 1743, courtesy of the Harvard University Archives.

Ezra Stiles, Manuscripts and Archives, Yale College.

Bishop James Madison, silhouette, P1991.165, University Archives Faculty/ Alumni File, Swem Library, College of William and Mary

John Witherspoon, University Archives, Department of Rare Books and Special Collections, Princeton University Library.

Colonel Frederick Frelinghuysen, courtesy of Special Collections and University Archives, Rutgers, the State University of New Jersey

Nassau Hall, University Archives, Department of Rare Books and Special Collections, Princeton University Library.

Portrait of Myles Cooper (detail) by John Singleton Copley. Columbia University in the City of New York, gift of the New York Historical Society

Part I
INSTITUTIONS

1

⌒

Oxford and Cambridge

Englislı Puritans in the 1620s faced declining fortunes. The king who had variously accommodated, befriended, and often privileged them was turning away from them. The new king who succeeded him in 1625 seemed positively to be their enemy. For decades Puritan teachers and Calvinist ideas had enjoyed an ascendancy at the English universities. Now Oxford and Cambridge came under stricter controls. Ideas heretical to the Puritans gained in influence, supported by the highest offices of the English Church. Demands for strict enforcement compelled dozens of Puritan leaders to abandon their pulpits. Some Separatist Puritans had left England in 1620 and established Plymouth Colony on the other side of the Atlantic. In 1630 another Puritan group also departed. They established Massachusetts Bay Colony. Six years later they established Harvard College.

This study of the American colonial colleges begins with a look at the English background. Harvard formed amid an intellectual milieu greatly shaped by Oxford and Cambridge universities. Much controversy, religious polemic, and politics set this background. They describe a dynamic history, one in which monarchs figured large, but also clergy and teachers, and high church officials. The Puritans who settled Massachusetts Bay Colony left a scene of contest, for the English Church was entering a new era. The provocations of the 1620s, in fact, anticipate much of the intellectual history of American higher education in the colonial era.

The town of Oxford had long been a location of scholars and lecturers. As early as the twelfth century one could find them in goodly numbers. Students now settled there, living in inns and with townsfolk. Important groups and individuals took an interest in these activities, and over the years they formed new colleges—Balliol, Exeter, Queen's, Lincoln, Magdalene, and All Souls. Corpus Christi College appeared in 1517, with the bold announcement that it was to be no "monkish" retreat but a place of liberal education. Cambridge began to form in the early thirteenth century, and new colleges formed near the end of the century. Peterhouse College dated from 1284. There followed Michaelhouse, Clare, King's, Trinity, Pembroke, and Corpus Christi colleges.[1]

A roughly common curriculum prevailed at Oxford and Cambridge. Students (all males) studied the seven liberal arts—grammar, logic and rhetoric, arithmetic, geometry, music, and astronomy. The B.A. degree program took seven years; those who aspired to the doctorate had several more to go. Despite some challenges later, the arts curriculum would have an ascendancy throughout the Puritan era. One could judge the program solid, but hardly conducive to independent thinking or imagination. The ancient Greeks might seem to an English student to enjoy even yet a monopoly of the world's wisdom.

The opening to humanism in the sixteenth century brought Oxford and Cambridge into a new intellectual era. Reformers had long faulted the reigning Scholasticism, especially as scholars who had traveled in Italy sought to stimulate the English universities with the new learning there. The Dutch humanist Erasmus arrived at Cambridge in 1511 and for three years there inspired the new thinking. In fact, he effected a transition. An emerging new generation of ministers took his translated New Testament, which looked to the textual foundations of the faith, and made Scripture the heart of a new spiritual experience. These stirrings of Protestantism awaited only an institutional transformation to give them life in England. In the 1570s new texts shifted the curricular focus. More new colleges arose to accommodate modern thought—Cardinal, Trinity, and St. John's at Oxford; Christ's and St. John's at Cambridge. At St. John's, Cambridge founder John Fischer prescribed the teaching of philosophy, Greek, Hebrew, and cosmography. Natural and moral philosophy, metaphysics, and history also entered the curriculum. Fischer had in mind a more learned ministry, and all graduates were required to pursue that career.[2]

---

1. For general histories of Oxford and Cambridge in the era of this study, see Charles Edward Mallet, A History of the University of Oxford, 3 vols., Vol. I, The Mediaeval University and the Colleges Founded in the Middle Ages, Vol. II, The Sixteenth and Seventeenth Centuries (New York: Barnes and Noble, 1968); V. H. H. Green, A History of the University of Oxford (London: Batsford, 1974); Damian Riehl Leader, A History of the University of Cambridge, 4 vols., Vol. 1, The University to 1546 (Cambridge: Cambridge University Press, 1988).

2. H. C. Porter, Reformation and Reaction in Tudor Cambridge (1958; Hamden, Conn.: Archon Books, 1972), 22–39; Mark H. Curtis, Oxford and Cambridge in Transition, 1558–1642: An Essay on Changing Relations between the English Universities and English Society (Oxford: Oxford University Press, 1959), 5; John Morgan, Godly Learning: Puritan Attitudes towards Reason, Learning, and Education, 1560–1640 (Cambridge: Cambridge University Press, 1986), 226–27. At the universities, then, students had likely read from a list that included Aristotle's Ethics and Politics; a Greek grammar and lexicon; Cicero's letters, orations, and the De Officiis; Ovid's Metamorphoses; Erasmus; Valla's Elegentiae; the Greek New Testament; Terrence; Virgil; Horace; Quintilian; Plato; Plutarch; Caesar's commentaries; Aesop; Livy; and Sallust. See Lisa Jardine, "Humanism and the Sixteenth-Century Arts Course," History of Education Quarterly 4 (1975), 16–31.

After the English Reformation Henry VIII had gained a new measure of royal control in the universities with the act of 1544. It empowered him to dissolve any college at either of them. Some feared that the colleges would have the same fate as the monasteries. Henry did in fact gain new revenue from the monasteries that he put out of business; however, in 1546 these monies gave birth to Trinity College at Cambridge. It had a clear purpose: "the amplification and establishment of the Christian religion, [and] the extirpation of heresy and false opinion." Decades later, this college of loyal Anglicans would evolve into a factory of Puritans.[3]

The unsettled years of Edward VI's reign (1547–1553) saw violent expressions of radical Protestantism that anticipated later Puritan protest. Calvinist ideas from Europe now sparked a greater reformation zeal among some Englanders. The universities especially felt the impact. At Jesus College, Cambridge extremists destroyed six altars then did the same to three others at Queen's. Here also they whitewashed the walls, so wrathfully did they resent decorative elements as papal dressing.[4] Radicals tried to introduce new prayer books and homilies and raised the issue of ecclesiastical vestments that would so rend the Church later. The reign of the Catholic Queen Mary (1553–1558) meant death and exile to English Protestants. But under Elizabeth, Calvinism made clear gains. It held ascendancy at Oxford and Cambridge probably for most of her reign.[5] In 1559 Elizabeth proclaimed the Act of Uniformity. It called for compulsory attendance at church on Sundays and reinstated Thomas Cranmer's Book of Common Prayer, the standard for worship in the English Church. At the same time the queen called for an investigation of Oxford and Cambridge. She made her purposes clear: "to put in order, both for augmentation of good learning and for establishing of such uniformity in the cause of religion, touching common prayer and divine learning, as by the laws of our realm is ordained." But these words deceive a bit. Through the rest of Elisabeth's reign, and despite recurring investigations, the universities usually stayed removed from state control.[6]

Elizabeth's ascension brought the return of the Marian exiles, who gave the Puritan movement an inspired renewal. These Puritans saw themselves as a select brotherhood. They aspired to spread a preaching ministry throughout the realm. From it would come new voluntary religious organizations and new congregations. For some Puritans, the more uncompromising ones, these commitments would lead to the path of separatism, to a break from the English Church.

---

3. Porter, *Tudor Cambridge*, 15.
4. V. H. H. Green, *Religion at Oxford and Cambridge* (London: SCM Press, 1964), 94.
5. To be sure, Calvinism might be said to have a clear acknowledgment in the Thirty-Nine Articles, imposed by Elizabeth on the Church of England in 1563. The articles confirmed original sin, salvation by faith, and good works as flowing only from faith. The articles are clear on two points more: "The Bible contains all things necessary for salvation; nothing can be acquired that is not in the Bible"; "Predestination to life is the everlasting purpose of God." See Stuart E. Prall, *Church and State in Tudor and Stuart England* (Arlington Heights, Ill.: Harlan Davidson, 1993), 76–77.
6. Curtis, *Oxford and Cambridge in Transition*, 167.

But mostly the new Puritanism would generate what Patrick Collinson has called "the puritan church within the [English] Church."[7] The religious history of Elizabeth's reign describes a path of accommodation, even of "symbiosis" in the Anglican/Puritan connection.[8] Anglicanism assumed a dominant Calvinist strain. The universities became Calvinist strongholds. But accommodation did not signify agreement. On matters of worship and polity contending sides could fight bitterly. Those tensions and the state politics they produced set the background of American Puritanism.

While some of the returning Protestants took on itinerant preaching and acquired private patronage, most gained preferments within the Church of England; two from this group even became heads of Oxford colleges. Deprivation of the high Marian clergy now created new openings for former exiles. These Puritans accepted the English polity to the extent of acknowledging the national church as a valid part of the body of Christ. They approved the public nature of religion and its significance for English nationality, but they decried the remaining forms of Catholicism, and, moving against these corruptions, they made their own stamp on the Church. These Puritans wished to extend the reformation of the individual, by which they meant the Calvinist doctrine of justification,[9] to the forms of church worship itself. They would erase all residuals of the old self and of the old institution. The conforming Puritans used the Book of Common Prayer, but in a simplified form. In so doing, the conforming Puritan clergy distinguished between the essential and nonessential forms of worship. They thus allowed a place for history, tradition, and reason. On some matters, though, many rejected compliance. A hallmark of Puritan dissent was the refusal to don the surplice (the clerical white gown). Royal edicts specifically mandated wearing of the surplice and also specified other items of clerical dress. At Oxford Laurence Humphrey and Thomas Sampson refused to comply and denounced these "vestiges of popery."[10]

Nonetheless, the prevailing accommodation made a division in the Puritan ranks. In fact, the conservative, or what Peter Lake calls the "moderate" Puritans, looked fretfully as much to their left as to their right. These conforming Pu-

---

7. Patrick Collinson, *The Elizabethan Puritan Movement* (Berkeley: University of California Press, 1967), 333, 26. Collinson writes, "Puritanism was to take root within the established Church and within its beneficed ministry, not to any significant extent outside it" (59).

8. Peter Lake, *Moderate Puritans and the Elizabethan Church* (Cambridge: Cambridge University Press, 1982), 86.

9. The idea that God has "elected" some persons to win salvation. The term has a contractual meaning by which those "elect" are assured eternal life. Protestants differed in their understanding of how justification related to "sanctification," living a life of moral purity.

10. Collinson, *Elizabethan Puritan Movement*, 59, 49–54, 63, 27–28, 34; Lake, *Moderate Puritans*, 25. I use the term *Anglican* here to refer to those clergy and others who conformed to the prescribed standards of worship for the English Church, essentially the Book of Common Prayer (BCP). The number included many Calvinists who nonetheless "conformed" in this matter. "Puritans" were those, both inside and outside the Church, who modified the BCP or refused altogether to acknowledge it. The dichotomous Anglican/Puritan does not have real meaning until the era of Charles I.

ritans saw enemies both in the papists and in the Puritan radicals.[11] These more extreme Puritans, the "Precisians," insisted on strict and exclusive biblical standards for all things. Thus they held the Book of Common Prayer in general contempt. They faulted the conforming Puritans for insufficient reforming zeal. They also rejected the hierarchy of the English Church. John Field saw the persistence of Catholicism more in the English polity, its elaborate hierarchy, than in the English ceremony and labeled the order of bishops the bearer of "Antichrist." John Stubbs saw the English polity as a threat to church discipline, both among the congregation and the clergy. The Puritan campaign against bishops acquired some of its fuel from exposure to the Continental Calvinists; Theodore Beza[12] denounced episcopacy with particular force. Gradually a presbyterian movement emerged and in fact attained a de facto existence in places of Puritan strength, such as Northamptonshire. Radical Puritan wrath gained a vigorous expression in the famous Admonition to Parliament in 1572. The offices of bishops and archbishops, it proclaimed, came from the "pope's shop." This ecclesiastic apparatus, it urged, was "Antichristian and devilish and contrary to the scriptures."[13]

The English universities under Elizabeth became fertile grounds for the Puritan movement. Here a new generation of leadership took root, armed with a high ambition and purpose. Collinson writes: "These young graduates carried into the wider world of the parishes a sense of belonging to a fellowship and a cause, begun in the university and continued in the ministry." Great teachers inspired them—Edward Dering, William Perkins, Laurence Chaderton, Thomas Cartwright. Chaderton, the "pope of Cambridge puritanism," made Christ's College a virtual Puritan seminary. Trinity and Emmanuel colleges at Cambridge would become the most famous Puritan strongholds, but Oxford, as in the case of Humphrey's Magdalene College, also contributed. From Trinity College would come a group of Puritans that included two future leaders of Harvard—Nathaniel Eaton and Charles Chauncy. Also from Trinity came John Winthrop, who stayed but briefly, and Hugh Peter. Emmanuel contributed John Cotton, Thomas Shepard, and Thomas Hooker.[14]

Just one year after Henry founded Trinity a student named Thomas Cartwright enrolled in the college. He later became Lady Margaret Professor. Upon taking that appointment Cartwright began in 1570 a series of lectures

---

11. Lake, *Moderate Puritans*, 7.

12. Beza, born in France, underwent a conversion in 1548, then traveled to Geneva to join Calvin, becoming a professor of Greek at Lausanne the next year. He produced Greek and Latin translations of the New Testament that became foundations of the Geneva Bible. His other scholarship also helped make Beza a formidable theoretician of Calvinism. In 1581 he gifted to the Cambridge library his acclaimed *Codex Bezae*, with his commentary.

13. Collinson, *Elizabethan Puritan Movement*, 27, 101, 109, 141, 119.

14. Collinson, *Elizabethan Puritan Movement*, 122 (the quotation), 125–27, 129, 334; Samuel Eliot Morison, *The Founding of Harvard College* (Cambridge, Mass.: Harvard University Press, 1935), 87. See also Porter, *Tudor Cambridge*, 243–57.

on the first two chapters of Acts. Here he addressed matters of ecclesiastical polity and a frontal assault on the Anglican hierarchy resulted. Application of his interpretation would have meant abolition of archbishops, bishops, deans, and archdeacons and would have reduced the Church to the apostolic offices of pastor and deacon. Cartwright's arguments prepared a defense of presbyterianism as the original and legitimate structure of the Church. Revolutionary notions, these were, for Cartwright could not but point out the contrast between the existing polity of the Church of England and that of the ancient Church. As his biographer notes: "If Cartwright was right the organization of the Church of England must be radically altered and the existing hierarchy must go."[15]

Quite a sensation followed in the wake of Cartwright's lectures. All at Trinity College, allegedly at Cartwright's urging, abandoned wearing of ecclesiastical garments. Upon order to clarify his views, Cartwright compounded his situation with the authorities. He argued that the Church should abolish the titles and offices of archbishops and bishops. Cartwright wanted to dismantle the top-to-bottom hierarchy of the Church and give basic authority to ministers and presbyteries. These views quickly won Cartwright an emphatic dismissal from his office. But he helped give Puritanism a new inspiration and a more radical basis for ideas and action. Puritans first petitioned Parliament for reform of the Church in 1571 and the second admonition, attributed to Cartwright, followed the next year. The Book of Common Prayer received Puritan invective in unrestrained prose: "an imperfect book, culled and picked out of that popish dunghill, the Mass book full of all abominations." But Cartwright, it should be noted, had faith that needed reforms could occur within the Church, and he disavowed separatism for that reason.[16]

Over at Emmanuel College the Puritan pace quickened even more. Out of Emmanuel would come another retinue of Massachusetts Puritans—no less than thirty-five. Years later, in and around New England's Boston in the 1640s, their parishes could be counted one by one. Emmanuel founder Walter Mildmay, chancellor of the exchequer for Elizabeth, knew his intentions. He wanted a college that would advance Reformation ideals with more zeal than other Cambridge colleges had been doing. Emmanuel would train the next generation of ministers for the Church. To lead the new college Mildmay selected Laurence Chaderton, former fellow-student at Christ's College. Chaderton had already

---

15. A. F. Scott Pearson, *Thomas Cartwright and Elizabethan Puritanism, 1535–1603* (Gloucester, Mass.: Peter Smith, 1966), 26.

16. Pearson, *Cartwright*, 27–29; Curtis, *Oxford and Cambridge in Transition*, 197; Collinson, *Elizabethan Puritan Movement*, 112–13. William Clarke at Cambridge also contributed to the Puritan abuse, saying that the "orders of bishops, archbishops, metropolitans, patriarchs and popes had been introduced into the Church by Satan." See Green, *Religion at Oxford and Cambridge*, 116; Horton Davies, *Worship and Theology in England: From Cranmer to Hooker, 1534–1603* (Princeton, N.J.: Princeton University Press, 1970), 49; Lake, *Moderate Puritans*, 83–86.

made his contribution to Puritanism by training William Perkins, bright theological light of the movement. And from its beginning at Cambridge, Emmanuel exuded Puritanism. Ministers there shunned the surplice and the prayer book ritual. Attendants at communion received the hosts seated around a table. Puritan ideas flourished. Emmanuel continued to grow in the Stuart years and became the second largest of Cambridge's colleges, after Trinity.[17]

Increasingly the Puritan movement created problems for Elizabeth and for the established Church. Independent clergy offended the royal demand for order and uniformity. In 1565 Elizabeth reprimanded her bishops for their inattention to the new Protestant forms and prescribed harsh measures against nonconformity. That policy applied to the universities, too. Further response in 1573 called for imprisoning anyone who defamed the Book of Common Prayer. A "witch-hunt" then moved against the more extreme Puritans. Many lost their pulpits. Persecution, however, only inspired a more resolute separatism, led by Robert Browne, who would take his congregation to the Netherlands in 1581. Then in 1584 Archbishop of Canterbury John Whitgift pronounced new mandates for the Church. The second of these most offended Puritans. It insisted that the Book of Common Prayer and the hierarchy of the English Church "containeth nothing in it contrary to the word of God" and that it "and none other" has legitimate use in the Church. The reference "and none other" notes the fact that this year had seen the first English printing of the Geneva Bible, with all its Calvinist notations. Whitgift now pressed for total subscription. Despite a spate of petitions against the rigid conformity, many ministers agreed to subscribe, if only to keep the peace, and, to be sure, to continue to use the Prayer Book and none other, but to use only parts of it. By these means, though, conservative Puritanism stayed within the Church. By 1595 the Puritan accommodation had become virtually complete. Puritanism as a political force was spent. Radicals, under the aggression of Whitgift, had gone underground.[18]

All the more, however, did moderate Puritanism enjoy a dominant position in the English Church. Two matters have significance here—the theological ascendancy of Calvinism in the established church and the new reign of King James I that began in 1603. Consider the first. Under a Star Chamber decree of 1586, all religious publications in London must have the prior approval of the archbishop of Canterbury or of the bishop of London. Under these controls, Puritan ideas flourished. The year 1590 saw the publication of William Perkins's *A Golden Chaine*, with its strong pronunciation for predestination. The next year Whitgift licensed a sermon with an equally forceful endorsement of the Calvinist notion of the elect. In 1597 there appeared, with the sanction of Richard Bancroft, bishop of London, a four hundred-page Calvinist treatise by Jacobus Kimedoncius

---

17. Morison, *Founding of Harvard*, 92–96; Morgan, *Godly Learning*, 248.
18. Collinson, *Elizabethan Puritan Movement*, 60, 69–70, 150, 165, 204, 244–45, 252–53, 263–66.

of Heidelberg. Equally noteworthy, anti-Calvinist opinion suffered an opposite fate, as in the case of Peter Baro. Finally, at the universities, the vice-chancellors controlled religious publishing and assured an exclusively Calvinist literature. At the Oxford Act and the Cambridge Commencement, "Calvinist orthodoxy invariably prevailed, the conclusions having been approved in advance by the university authorities."[19]

Intellectual discourse in the English Church often appeared to be an exchange between Calvinists. Calvinists themselves in the later seventeenth century had a greater concern with predestination than had Calvin himself. Beza and other Reformed thinkers on the Continent influenced a "second generation" of Calvinists. Beza proffered the notion of double predestination that Calvin had addressed only in his last edition of The Institutes of the Christian Religion.[20] William Perkins subscribed to that notion. Whitgift, seeing very radical ideas thus in circulation, presbyterianism also among them, refuted them by way of recourse to Calvin himself. "If Mr. Calvin were alive and understood the state of our church and controversy," he said, "I very believe he would utterly condemn your doings." Whitgift thereby presented himself as a more authentic Calvinist than his Puritan rivals.[21] And in the Lambeth Articles of 1595, Whitgift moved against an emergent English anti-Calvinism, in the person of Peter Baro especially, an adherent to conditional predestination.[22]

For the intellectual gains of Puritanism, we can also look to the universities. Curiously enough, the battle was first joined in the subject of logic. Peter Ramus (Pierre de la Ramée) lived from 1515 to 1572, dying a victim of the notorious St. Bartholomew's Day massacre of French Protestants. He taught at the University of Paris but soured on the prevailing Scholasticism there. He sought to undo the Aristotelian grip that he complained had rendered learning dry and useless. Logic at his time signified a method of argumentation designed for use in the disputations that formed so vital a part of the university programs. The Ramist system is no easy matter, but it joined to the Puritan program in England and the colonies so formidably that we owe it some attention. Ramus wanted to shift the priority of syllogistic reasoning, which he held valid only for doubtful propositions, to a base of axiomatic truth that would properly form the grounds of discourse. Teaching, too, would be recon-

---

19. Nicholas Tyacke, "The Rise of Arminianism Reconsidered," Past and Present 115 (1987): 201–16.

20. Augustine had maintained that humans require the help of God in winning salvation and this grace is the free gift of God. But Augustine and Aquinas left the rest to their own fate. The Council of Orange in 529 rejected the idea that some are predestined to condemnation. Calvin, however, also faulting Luther, said that "those whom God passes over, he condemns." Hence "double predestination." See Jaroslav Pelikan, The Christian Tradition: A History of the Development of Doctrine, 5 vols., Reformation of Church and Dogma (1300–1700) (Chicago: University of Chicago Press, 1984), 4:222.

21. Lake, Moderate Puritans, 218–20.

22. Tyacke, "Rise of Arminianism," 205; Lake, Moderate Puritans, 220–26. Tyacke even agues that the Lambeth Articles embraced double and absolute predestination.

stituted. "The method of teaching, therefore," wrote Ramus, "is the arrangement of various things brought down from universal and general principles to the underlying singular parts, by which arrangement the whole matter can be more easily taught and apprehended."[23]

The Reformed movement in theology seized on Ramus. His ideas reached England about 1550 and spread quickly. By the 1570s he had supporters at St. Andrews in Scotland and at Cambridge, which became a center of Ramism. His system also gained in New England under the more familiar name of "technologia." Puritans took from Ramus the notion that the purpose of discourse is didactic. Therefore teaching must mainly communicate the content of discourse. Ornamentation and eloquence mattered less and could distract from that content. Here Puritans found inspiration for their "plain style" of sermonizing. But Ramism led also, in education and preaching, to a concern with particulars and their location within a holistic scheme of things, with a concern for the orderly arrangement of God's system. Although Ramism began in a return to axiomatic truths, it ended with a preoccupation with practicality. Chaderton introduced Ramism to Christ's College, Cambridge. His student, the remarkable William Perkins, would count among the followers.[24]

Born in Warwickshire Village in 1558, Perkins came the short distance to Christ's College, Cambridge in 1577. His parents probably had Puritan leanings, for they placed William with Chaderton as his tutor. Perkins fell in with the Puritan spirit of Christ's. In the years after his arrival violations at the college brought the investigation of 1586. The next year Perkins went before the vice-chancellor to answer charges that he had described kneeling for communion as a superstitious practice. Perkins successfully defended himself, and he became a major Puritan influence, especially through his preaching at St. Andrews Church in Cambridge. His earliest biographer wrote, "He would pronounce the word *damn* with such an emphasis, as left a doleful echo in his auditors' ear a good while after; and when catechist of Christ's College, in expounding the commandments, applied them so home, able almost to make his hearers' hearts fall down, and hairs to stand upright."[25] Perkins died in 1602.

Perkins liked to say that he stood for "the Calvinist doctrine," though he owed a debt especially to Beza in securing it. With remarkable skill, he reduced the complexities of Calvinism to a clear formulation that he effectively popularized. His writing—often in little books like *A Case of Conscience* and *A Grain of Mustard Seed, or A Salve for Sick Man*—became best-sellers. He conveyed in his

---

23. Elizabeth Flower and Murray G. Murphey, *A History of Philosophy in America*, 2 vols. (New York: Putnam, 1977), 1:14–17.

24. Flower and Murphey, *Philosophy in America*, 1:19–20; Porter, *Tudor Cambridge*, 225. One should be cautious not to overstate the gains of Ramist logic, though they would be significant even if they made a debut at Cambridge and influenced key personalities there. W. S. Howell, *Logic and Rhetoric in England, 1500–1700* (New York: Russell and Russell, 1961), 179.

25. Green, *Oxford and Cambridge in Transition*, 118.

writings an acute sense of the all-pervasiveness of God. The smallest events became in his depiction the intentions of the deity, the God who "has ordained all
things, either past, present, or to come, for his own glory." Perkins made clear at
the same time the primacy of the Fall. Fallen man remained alienated in body
and mind from God, he said. Ignorance and error remained the human lot.[26]

These principles underscored the centrality of grace in Perkins' Calvinism.
God in his mercy, he urged, had ordained that some should be lifted from their
fallen state. Christ made this redemption possible and his saving grace came from
the revealed knowledge of Scripture, which corrected the errors of the natural
mind. Furthermore, Perkins insisted, faith made possible that new knowledge because it preceded it. The Puritan emphasized as well that fear preceded regeneration. "None can be a lively member of Christ," Perkins wrote, "till his conscience condemn him, and make him quite out of heart with respect to himself."
But most individuals, he warned, remain content with a merely outward and
wholly natural reformation exhibited through ordinary religious activities.
Perkins warned against such ease. He equated this natural state with the Roman
norms of Christianity.[27]

Possibly Perkins influenced so many American Puritans because he gave much
attention to the phenomenon of grace. For him it required acute self-examination.
The believer who looks inward will find a self divided, he said. But that war of flesh
and spirit signified the workings of grace, of God's redemption. "He is the sound
Christ," Perkins wrote, "that feeling himself laden with the corruptions of his vile
and rebellious nature, bewails them from his heart, and with might and main fights
against them by the grace of God's Spirit." Perkins, though, did not make religiosity only an inner reform. Conduct, too, should concern the true Christian, he said.
Perkins spoke for sobriety in dress, honesty in business, moderation in all worldly
pleasures but by no means an ascetic life (he anticipates the favored Puritan expression, "one should love the world with weaned affection"). Redemption did not
mean retreat from the world. It meant a new empowerment, a liberation from the
chains of Satan.[28]

As Puritan and university man, Perkins did not share others' prejudices
against learning. Reliance on the Spirit alone he dismissed as Anabaptist fancy.
Perkins, now a disciple of Ramus, insisted that study of Scripture also required
knowledge of the arts. Perkins expressed the faith of a generation of English and
American Puritans that natural reason may deceive, but regenerate reason took
us back to God, and all knowledge of nature and the world, fortified in Scripture,
assisted in that return. All the while, however, Perkins insisted that the true light
of the Word can emerge only by deduction. Theology, like other sciences, built

---

26. Ian Breward, "Introduction," *The Work of William Perkins*, ed. Ian Breward (Appleford, England: The Sutton Courtenay Press, 1970), 30.

27. Breward, "Introduction," 30–31.

28. Breward, "Introduction," 31–32. For another discussion of Perkins at Cambridge, see Chapter
12 of Porter, *Tudor Cambridge*, 288–313.

on axioms. Logic was essential for the distinction between true and false reading of Scripture. In this precaution Perkins proved vigilant. In this spirit he greatly shaped New England Puritanism, which would always respect reason but mistrust its corruptions.[29]

Even before Perkins won notoriety, Richard Hooker had concluded that Puritan saturation of the English universities had become dangerous. His counteraction, *The Laws of Ecclesiastic Polity* in 1593, though of slow impact, became a landmark of Anglican thought. It represented the beginnings of an Anglican resurgence that would carry through Charles I's reign. Hooker was former fellow of Corpus Christi, Oxford. On some matters, to be sure, Hooker's quarrel with the Puritans seemed like fine differences within a common viewpoint. But the differences had great implications. Thus Hooker, too, could speak of the all-sufficiency of Scripture. It contained, he said, "a full instruction in all things unto salvation necessary, the knowledge whereof man could not by nature otherwise in this lifetime attain." Hooker insisted, though, that scripture could not stand without reason to enlarge its meaning. For reason, Hooker wrote, "is an infallible knowledge imprinted in the minds of all the children of men." It constituted, he said, a sure guide to right and wrong. Reason also played the critical role in discerning the truth hidden in the "saving knowledge" of Scripture. Here Hooker made his major points by showing how central tenets of the Christian faith—the Trinity, infant baptism—do not appear in the Bible, but had to be "deduced" out of Scripture by principles to which we were "already persuaded." Hooker's reference to *all* the children of men reflected a far greater confidence in natural reason than did the Puritans, however much each party may agree that reason and scripture illuminate each other.[30]

The access to scripture through "spirit" as opposed to reason troubled Hooker. His concern led him to see the Puritans as part of a dangerous and schismatic wing in the Reformation. So Hooker sought to rejoin the Reformation to the Catholic Church and thereby to recover a basis of church authority in Protestantism. He chastened the Puritans for an excessive and irrational anti-Catholicism, for he believed that the popish church, despite manifest abuses, had not lost all spiritual authority. So arguing, Hooker surpassed previous Churchmen in saying that the English Reformation should not be considered an emphatic break from an unambiguously evil past. So too, all the controversy surrounding vestments and ritual might now be obviated; it mattered not whether the English Church had "come in" under popery or not, Hooker believed.[31]

---

29. Breward, "Introduction," 36–39; Perry Miller, *The New England Mind: The Seventeenth Century* (Boston: Beacon, 1939), 311. Perkins made another lasting impression on Puritanism through his treatise on preaching, *The Art of Prophesying*, which employed Ramist concerns and influenced the "plain style" of the Puritan pulpit.

30. Peter Lake, *Anglicans and Puritans? Presbyterian and Conformist Thought from Whitgift to Hooker* (London: Unwin Hyman, 1988), 151–52.

31. Lake, *Anglicans and Puritans?* 155–58. Hooker died in 1592. Five of the eight books of *The Laws* were published in his lifetime.

Calvinism continued its supremacy in the English Church and universities under the reign of James I, who as James VI of Scotland assumed the throne in
1603. Here, too, however, the matter is complicated. Moderate Puritans would
have with James a relation that was amicable most of the time, often uneasy,
and eventually conflicting. Precisians would know only the strong arm of royal
rebuke.

In James, England had a king genuinely interested in religious questions, including even the recondite matters of Calvinism. Both parties would soon learn,
however, that James never detached religious considerations from political
ones.[32] English Puritans had great expectations of the Scottish king now on the
English throne. He had grown up in a dominantly Calvinist country and within
the presbyterian polity of the Scottish Church. James was sensitive to the contentious religious situation in England, and responding to Puritan urging, took
action shortly after his ascendancy to deal with it. He convened the famous
Hampton Court Conference in January 1604. The conference revealed the king's
intention to forge a break, permanently, between moderate and radical Puritans.
One could have anticipated his moves by attention to his *Basilikon Doron*,
printed almost immediately on his new reign. James associated extremist Puritans with Anabaptists, Sectaries, and others who would pursue presbyterian
polity or any that subverted royal authority and a strong national church. His
words could give Puritans scant comfort. James denounced those who "are persuaded that their bishops smell of a papal supremacy, that the surplice, the cor-
nered cap and such like are the outward badges of popish error." At the conference, James's thoroughgoing hostility to presbyterianism issued in his formulaic
assertion, "no bishop, no king." This king said he would enforce conformity, and
at the universities, too. James also avowed to produce a new translation of the
Bible, the famous version in his name appearing in 1611.[33]

On the other hand, James mentioned reforms in the Church favorable to
Puritans and said he would not insist on the strictest conformity everywhere. The
king wanted to unite as large a group as possible behind his new administration
and in support of his foreign policy. Some concessions to the Puritans were thus
in order. James assured them of his commitment to a preaching ministry throughout the realm. He promised a review of the Prayer Book. Generally, he meant to
be flexible. With only Precisians and Catholics would he have no tolerance: "either let them conform themselves, & that shortly, or they shall hear of it." And

---

32. James Doelman, *King James I and the Religious Culture of England* (Cambridge: D. S. Brewer,
2000), 12. This book shows James's impressive record and interest in British religious culture.

33. Kenneth Fincham and Peter Lake, "The Ecclesiastical Policy of King James I," *Journal of British
Studies* 24 (April 1985): 171–72. The conference also produced James's oft-quoted threat to the Puritans: "I shall make them conform themselves, or I will harry them out of this land" (Frederick
Shriver, "Hampton Court Revisited: James I and the Puritans," *Journal of Ecclesiastical History* 33
[1982]: 60–61). Shriver argues that the conference did nothing to help the Puritans and nothing to
dissuade James of his contempt for them (p. 65).

hear of it many did. By the end of the next year some ninety beneficed clergy had lost their positions. James led the campaign and carried it through 1609.[34]

Most of the English clergy chose the path of subscription. James thus acquired the high degree of outward conformity he demanded and the semblance of a unified English Church. Thus also Calvinism continued its strength. Archbishop of Canterbury Richard Bancroft (1604–1610) was a Calvinist and likewise, and even more so, his successor George Abbot (1611–1633). As under Elizabeth, many subscribing ministers made their own modifications in the worship. Some English towns, like Ipswich, exuded Calvinist paternalism and practiced a strict Sabbatarianism. The universities showed an independency that evoked a reminder in 1616 that they too must adhere to the 1604 ecclesiastical canons. Collinson summarizes the situation under James: "Calvinism was anything but a declining cause in England for as long as James I lived, and these were lean years for the English 'Arminians.'"[35]

Nonetheless, reaction was under way. It soon became apparent that Hooker's work signaled a growing division in Anglican ranks. One branch remained close to its Calvinist background while another was moving toward Arminianism—a fearful heresy to the Puritans. Jacob Arminius, a teacher at Leyden after 1603, had attacked key principles of Calvinism. He denied an incompatibility of divine sovereignty with human freedom. Arminians rejected the ideas of irresistible grace and thus moved away from a strict predestination as they sought to make a place for some measure of free will. They also wanted a more effective role for good works in salvation, or at least the means of encouraging such works when the doctrine of arbitrary grace would seem not to do so. Those in the Church of England who were inclined to reject Calvinism on these terms won the label "Arminian," although the Dutch thinker himself seems not to have been a very direct influence on them.[36]

Arminian ideas acquired a more precise formulation in the *Remonstrance* of 1610. It faulted Calvinist determinism, its "fatalistic necessity," as hostile to religion. It stressed "the wisdom, justice, and equity" of God. It furthermore removed itself from Calvin and his severer partisans in denying the "irresistible" character of grace and restoring primacy to God's rewards for Christian virtue. Other notions reinforced the anti-Calvinism of the Remonstrants. The 1610 document asserted that Christ "died for all men and for every man" and not

34. Mark. H. Curtis, "Hampton Court Conference and Its Aftermath," *History* 46 (1961): 4–7; Fincham and Lake, "Ecclesiastical Policy," 174–75. Curtis believes that the conference brought significant gains to the Puritans.

35. Kenneth Fincham, *Prelate as Pastor: The Episcopate of James I* (Oxford: Oxford University Press, 1990), 222–23; Tyacke, "Rise of Arminianism," 207; Patrick Collinson, *The Religion of Protestants: The Church in English Society, 1559–1625* (Oxford: Oxford University Press, 1982), 170–71; Collinson, *Elizabethan Puritan Movement*, 461 (the quotation). Collinson tells us that when James asked his council why so many of his bishops favored Puritanism Lionel Cranfield replied that it was because he appointed so many Puritan bishops.

36. Pelikan, *Reformation of Church and Dogma*, 232–35.

only the elect. All who believed could share in the salvation that Christ had made possible.[37]

Hooker and the anti-Calvinists at the Hampton Conference were Arminians before the fact. Likewise Lancelot Andrewes. As early as the 1580s at Pembroke College, Cambridge, Andrewes urged the efficacy of prayer as a saving exercise, citing the scriptural prescription that "whoever shall call on the name of the Lord shall be saved." He saw this spiritual power forsaken by the Puritans in their preoccupation with a preaching ministry. At Oxford in 1607 Humphrey Leech, a Christ's Church chaplain, denounced Calvinism. Silenced by the vice-chancellor, Leech took his case on appeal to Archbishop Richard Bancroft. He had no success. Nonetheless, Calvinism was confronting new opposition. In 1612 John Howson, also at Christ's Church, faulted the Geneva Bible, which had become "the most potent single tool for disseminating Calvinism in England." By 1613 Arminian ideas from the Continent were having a direct influence in England. Under William Laud St. John's College, Oxford became a center for a growing Arminianism. Laud's anti-Calvinism, displayed in a 1615 sermon at the university church of St. Mary's, led one of Oxford's Calvinists to say that "the Papists from beyond the seas can say that [Laud and his like] are theirs." Indeed, the English universities seethed with "political" Arminians, young Turks interested in taking power from senior officers. Laud would always be more concerned with right worship than with right thought and denied an Arminian loyalty for himself. He recognized its political advantages clearly, however.[38]

Arminianism also raised questions about worship. As anticipated in Hooker and Andrewes, the Arminians wanted to restore a more meaningful service, and they moved clearly toward high church forms. They faulted Puritans for neglect of the Eucharist. Andrewes would give it centrality, describing the sacrament as a vehicle of divine grace. Andrewes and others like Bishop John Buckeridge also prescribed bowing and kneeling as appropriate reverences for worshipers. English Arminians generally saw these rites and mannerisms squandered by the Calvinists' fixation on preaching the Word and sermonizing. The Arminian redirection of worship gained more adherents in the early 1620s. Puritans perceived in it a resurgence of popish practices and did not hesitate to decry the Arminian turn on these grounds.[39]

Not until the last years of James I's reign, however, did the Arminians have any hope of changing the English Church. The king embraced a moderate Calvinism

37. Pelikan, *Reformation of Church and Dogma*, 235–36.

38. Nicholas Tyacke, *Anti-Calvinists: The Rise of English Arminianism, c. 1590–1640* (Oxford: Clarendon Press, 1987), 29, 62–63, 69–71; idem., "Rise of Arminianism," 207; Fincham, *Prelate as Pastor*, 232–33; Charles Carlton, *Archbishop William Laud* (London: Routledge and Kegan Paul, 1987), 12–14.

39. Fincham, *Prelate as Pastor*, 234–35; Hillel Schwartz, "Arminianism and the English Parliament, 1624–1629," *Journal of British Studies* 12, No. 2 (1973): 56–57; P. G. Lake, "Calvinism and the English Church, 1570–1635," *Past and Present* 114 (1987): 42.

while eschewing an inflexible position on theological questions. But he did react against Arminianism. In 1617 an Arminian sermon at Cambridge led James to summon all the university heads to a meeting. Here he alerted them on the matter of Arminianism and commanded that "no such seed grow in the university." In an event known as the Vorstius case, James took another direct action. In learning that a suspected Arminian might win appointment to a prestigious chair at the University of Leyden, he wrote to The Hague stating, on theological grounds, his opposition to the appointment. But politics figured in James's calculations, too. Arminianism, he believed, affronted the divine-right basis of kingship.[40] Finally, when the Synod of Dort met in 1619 to confront the Arminian heresy, James sent an English delegation to reinforce the effort. It consisted wholly of moderate Calvinists.[41]

But matters were soon to change. James had always had his mind on foreign policy, a delicate and complicated situation going into the Thirty Years' War in 1618 and afterward. Many Calvinists, including Archbishop Abbot, saw the war in providential terms and wanted an English alliance with Protestant states, in particular the palatinate of Frederick V, who also claimed the crown of Bohemia. James instead pursued a marriage connection to Catholic Spain that he hoped would influence a peaceful settlement. He solicited the help of the pope in that effort. Now strong-minded Protestants turned against him. As the war broke out James found himself the object of virulent Puritan attacks. The antipapal zeal that had helped ally him with the Puritans had become a foreign policy liability for the king. And now Puritanism emerged as a political enemy in his eyes. James thus came to question also the validity of his own guiding principle in earlier politics—the distinction between moderate and radical Puritans. The Arminian bishops consequently formed a closer political company with the king and gained in influence in the last years of his reign.[42]

James's son Prince Charles, the object of the Spanish marital connection, became King Charles I of England in December 1625. From here on, the situation became increasingly worse for all Puritans. They had dominant strength in Parliament and maintained a vigilance against the growing Arminian movement and in the first year of Charles's reign acted to repress Arminian publications. But the new king intervened to prevent such action. Charles formed a very clear alliance with Arminians, whose cause now also became associated with royalism.[43] Charles, furthermore, had none of his father's affinity for Calvinist thinking. He came to see in the doctrine of the elect the grounds of hostility against external authority, in both church and state, reaching a conclusion opposite to

40. Fincham and Lake, "Ecclesiastical Policy," 190; Hill el Schwartz, "Arminianism and the English Parliament, 1624–1629," *Journal of British Studies* 12, no.2 (1973), 42–43.

41. Lake, "Calvinism and the English Church," 53. James used the occasion of the synod to specify the errors of Arminianism (Tyacke, *Anti-Calvinists*, 102).

42. Fincham and Lake, "Ecclesiastical Policy," 198–201; Tyacke, "Rise of Arminianism," 211.

43. Christopher Hill, "Parliament and People in Seventeenth-Century England," *Past and Present* 92 (August 1981): 121–24. Hill discusses and references literature that has explored social and economic issues in English Puritanism.

that of his father. Charles's sympathies became clear with his appointment of new Arminian bishops, and one could speak of an "Arminian party" now prominent in the Church. Under Charles the Arminian worship program, crystallizing under James in his last years, now flourished. Under Charles, too, a crackdown against Puritanism now took root.[44]

The situation thus continued to worsen for the Puritans. The next year, when the new king learned that the Cambridge officials intended to make the commencement addresses an affirmation of Calvinist doctrine, he instructed Bishop Richard Neile to prevent the occurrence. The king also had intended to silence what he considered overzealous anti-Catholic rhetoric. Additional royal action amounted to a virtual proscribing of Cambridge Calvinism and thus a further opening to ascending Arminianism. Charles found his right-hand-man for these directions in William Laud, chancellor of Oxford in 1630 and then archbishop of Canterbury in 1633. Within three years Laud had drawn up new statutes for the universities. For on them, Laud believed, the future of the Church of England depended. His specifications, directed at Cambridge, made clear that none was to act or think independently regarding any article of established worship. No more public disputations would hold these matters up for review and discussion. The Laudian policy of uniformity would now apply fully to the universities. Cambridge people questioned Laud's authority in these matters and dallied in their enforcement. So Laud restated his intentions: "If you think to make me forget or forego the business [this in a letter to the vice-chancellor at Cambridge], you will find yourselves much deceived." When Cambridge officials made their case to the king, they met royal rebuke. Charles opted not for local autonomy of any kind but for "the preservation of the great blessing of discipline."[45]

This chapter concludes with some accounts of individuals whose careers demonstrate the transition from the English universities to the American. William Ames was one of them. He never saw New England, but his writings thrived there as instruction to the first generations of Harvard students and later at Yale as well. Ames came from Ipswich, born in an area of Puritan activity in 1576 to parents whose families had succeeded in mercantile businesses. Ames entered Christ's College, Cambridge, probably in 1593, matriculating as a pensioner and circulating with sons of prosperous clergy and merchants. He became a fellow in

---

44. Schwartz, "Arminianism and the English Parliament," 50–52, 57; Tyacke, "Rise of Arminianism," 213.

45. Tyacke, *Anti-Calvinists*, 49–50; Green, *Religion at Oxford and Cambridge*, 130–31 (the quotation). The March 1629 dissolution of Parliament by Charles also weakened the position of Cambridge Calvinists for a majority of the House of Commons had declared for Calvinism (Tyacke, *Anti-Calvinists*, 51). Writes Professor Tyacke, "Thus from June 1626 Cambridge University came more directly under royal control than probably at any time since the ascension of Elizabeth." Puritans complained vehemently of Laud's "promoting of Arminians [and] persons addicted to Popish ceremonies" (p. 49).

1601. Ames entered Christ's a Puritan partisan but his encounter with William Perkins brought about his full conversion. Ames found Perkins's preaching profoundly vitalizing. Ever after he would locate in inner renewal the key to religious life, and he would never rest in mere obedience to moral law. Years later Ames would say of "worthy Master Perkins" and his work with the students that he "instructed them soundly in the Truth, stirred them up effectually to seek after Godliness, [and] made them fit for the kingdom of God."[46]

Ames's education at Cambridge concurred with outbursts of Puritan rage against the Church. In 1596 John Rudd injudiciously issued his opinion that "not the tenth part of the ministers for the Church of England were able ministers or teachers, but dumb dogs."[47] If Ames refrained from such aspersions, he nonetheless pursued the intellectual training that standardized his name later at Harvard. From Perkins and others he acquired a solid grounding in Ramist logic. He later published his own edition of Ramus's *Dialecticae*. In the heady days of the early 1600s Ames came under official censure. In 1610 he opted for exile in the Netherlands, there to accomplish his work of lasting influence for New England.

In Hugh Peter, Harvard would find a genuine mover and shaker. He came from the town of Foy in Cornwall. Flemish Protestants had earlier fled to this area, an outlaw region already from its pirating activities against trading vessels. Hugh matriculated at Trinity College, Cambridge in 1613. He received his master's degree in 1622 and was ordained bishop the next year. Sometime thereafter, though, he became a Puritan. The conversion clearly began under the Trinity College Puritan atmosphere. There Calvinism dominated the theological instruction and logic had absorbed the stamp of Ramus. Peter embraced this methodology and incorporated it into his sermons. Almost certainly Peter knew many in that remarkable, emerging generation of Cambridge Puritans—John Cotton and Thomas Hooker most importantly. Later, after exile from England, Peter went to Holland and sought out Ames. He came to New England in 1635.[48]

Finally, Thomas Shepard, friend and spiritual patron of Harvard, provides another story of the transition from Old England to New. Born in 1605 in Towcester, Northamptonshire, Shepard grew up the youngest of nine children. Thomas lost his mother when he was four and his father when he was ten. His brother assumed his care. Thomas entered Emmanuel College in 1619. Here he listened to the preaching of Laurence Chaderton and other ministers. Their portraits of hell had their terrifying effects, but they did not easily overcome the intractable worldliness of the young Shepard. The pleasure principle proved for the time the stronger of his leanings.[49]

---

46. Keith L. Sprunger, *The Learned Doctor William Ames: Dutch Backgrounds of English and American Puritanism* (Urbana: University of Illinois Press, 1972), 3, 6, 11–13 (the quotation).

47. Sprunger, *Learned Doctor Ames*, 16.

48. Raymond Phineas Stearns, *The Strenuous Puritan: Hugh Peter, 1598–1660* (Urbana: University of Illinois Press, 1954), 3, 7, 15, 17–19.

49. Thomas Werge, *Thomas Shepard* (Boston: Twayne Publishers, 1987), 4.

The Cambridge experience, then, became for Shepard a spiritual tug-of-war. He attended the church services and became "much affected" by the powerful sermons. "But I shook this off," Shepard wrote in his *Autobiography*, "and fell from God to loose and lewd company, to lust and pride and gaming and bowling and drinking." Shepard endured more such trials. Finally, under the influence of John Preston, new master of the college, Shepard got rerouted on the better path. He took up a ministerial position at Earles-Colne in Essex, but the vigilant Laud silenced him. In 1634 he sailed for Massachusetts. In only a short time he became one of the most influential ministers of the new colony.[50]

We have observed so far some divisions among the English Puritans—essentially radical and moderate. These divisions had important implications for Harvard College's early history. Its founding, in 1636, occurred amid intellectual and political warfare in New England. That turmoil derived from roots planted years before the migration and intensifying in the open environs of the new location. In his history of the Puritans, William Haller described a "Spiritual Brotherhood," Puritan preachers at Cambridge, who gave Puritanism its dominant characteristics in England. This group, with Richard Sibbes and John Preston its foremost figures, emphasized human sin and frailty, but also highlighted the transforming love of God as manifested in Jesus and his compassion. These Puritans also described regeneration as a dramatic experience, complete and powerful and effectively bridging the separation of God and individual. A loving oneness with God marks the transformation, they believed. These convictions coexisted more or less easily with the Anglican establishment. As noted, they became well established in sixteenth-century Anglicanism.[51]

All along, another Puritan party was forming. It expressed a radical, committed Puritanism; it yielded to no authority and thus made for itself a record of censure, legal retaliation, and exile. These Puritans had a deeper sense of man's depravity and a harsher notion of God, whom they described in terms of power, knowledge, and will, all subsumed under the overriding idea of divine sovereignty. The radical Puritans made the covenant essential to regeneration. It came wholly from God's initiative and it rendered regeneration a protracted process, a struggle, and at best an uncertain victory over sin. Regeneration, did, however, produce signs of sanctification—a moral life denoted by adherence to the law. This more strictly Calvinist faction among the English Puritans confronted many problems. Its partisans did not gain pulpits and therefore their movement grew amid a print culture, in contrast to the pulpit medium of the Spiritual Brethren, for whom attendance on the spoken word had special significance. Hardened by their English experiences this group, "ecclesiastical radi-

---

50. *God's Plot: Puritan Spirituality in Thomas Shepard's Cambridge*, ed. Michael McGiffert, rev. and exp. (Amherst: University of Massachusetts Press, 1994), 43.

51. William Haller, *The Rise of Puritanism* (New York: Harper & Brothers, 1938), 49–82; Janice Knight, *Orthodoxies in Massachusetts: Rereading American Puritanism* (Cambridge, Mass.: Harvard University Press, 1994), 3–4, 81, 84, 118.

cals" as Janice Knight labels them, solidified their movement in exile and established their interconnections by an active press. They supplied important leaders for New England—Thomas Shepard, Peter Bulkeley, Thomas Hooker, Hugh Peter, and John Winthrop. They had one paramount intellectual leader—William Ames.[52]

These events, and these personalities, lay a foundation for much of what follows. The Anglican–Puritan rivalry, sometimes as ecclesiastical politics, sometimes as intellectual warfare, shaped much of the history that is our subject in this study. These rivalries persisted. They remained alive in the era of the American Revolution.

---

52. Knight, *Orthodoxies*, 2–3, 36, 38, 52–53, 58, 75–76.

2

⌒

Harvard I:
School of the Puritans

Harvard College expressed essential Puritan aspirations for its new world community. Many have marveled that the Massachusetts Bay leaders committed themselves so early to creating an institution of higher learning. Governor John Winthrop had brought his fellow Puritans to New England in 1630, and within only a few years a college had emerged to high status in the public agenda. The idea lay in the mind of John Eliot, later famed for his missionary work among the Indians. Writing to an English Puritan friend in 1633, Eliot implored him and other Puritans there to take an interest in a collegiate project for New England. Eliot appealed above all for "learning's sake, which I know you love, & will be ready to further." The Puritan wanted education "both church and common," and these goals would always prevail at colonial Harvard.[1] A learned ministry may have been the Puritans' first concern regarding Harvard, but this frontier society had a remarkable respect for learning in its own right.

New England's First Fruits, a promotional piece written by Hugh Peter and other college fund-raisers sent to England in the early 1640s, provides another statement of the Puritans' work in founding Harvard. The oft-quoted passage reads:

> After God had carried us safely to New England, and we had built our homes, provided necessaries for our livelihood, reared convenient places for God's worship, and selected the civil government, one of the next things we longed for, and looked after, was to advance learning and perpetuate it to posterity, dreading to leave an illiterate ministry to the churches when our present ministers shall lie in the dust.[2]

---

1. "A College First Proposed for Massachusetts Bay, 1633," in Richard Hofstadter and Wilson Smith, eds., *American Higher Education: A Documentary History*, 2 vols. (Chicago: University of Chicago Press, 1961), 1:5–6.
2. "New England's First Fruits, 1643," in Hofstadter and Smith, *American Higher Education*, 1:6.

Two generations later the formidable Puritan Cotton Mather confirmed these concerns: "Without a nursery for such men [of learning] among ourselves *darkness must soon have covered the land, and gross darkness the people.*" Mather, though, added another point. Harvard, he said, showed Protestantism's better record in education and public enlightenment, contrasted to the Catholic history. Mather wanted from the Puritans a wise emulation of the learned Jews.[3]

The Bay Puritans had no John D. Rockefeller to whom they might turn for a helping financial hand in this work—no Cornelius Vanderbilt, no James Duke, no Leland Stanford, no Paul Tulane. In contrast to the colleges of Oxford and Cambridge, too, Harvard did not have the money and interest of the frequent college founders from the private sector. They had for now only the General Court. The court acted on October 28, 1636, by agreeing to give £400 "toward a school or college" and it asked the next session to decide on a location.[4] American higher education thus began as a public enterprise. In this regard, too, it confirmed the Puritan social ethic. John Winthrop's important statement "A Model of Christian Charity," penned aboard the good ship *Arbella*, outlined broad communitarian values for the Puritan enterprise.[5]

In 1637, the colonial legislature arranged for a committee "to take order for the college." It entrusted responsibility for the institution to the governor, deputy governor, and treasurer, plus three magistrates and six ministers. In 1639, Harvard became a quasi-corporation as its board, the Overseers, became a self-perpetuating body for legislative and administrative privileges. Then in 1650 the General Court granted Harvard its own charter of incorporation, a remarkably bold act on the surface, for English practice had left sole authority for such purposes to the monarch. Harvard, however, was now receiving important assistance from private sources, and incorporation facilitated fund-raising. Indeed, Puritan Harvard set a general pattern for the colonial colleges—formal public oversight of the colleges with the enhanced financial support of friends in the private sector. Harvard remains the oldest corporation in continued existence in the United States.[6]

The General Court chose Newton for the site of the college and quickly renamed it Cambridge, in justifiable deference to the many graduates of that English university that partook in the founding. Newton seems to have had one spe-

3. "Cotton Mather's History of Harvard, 1702," in Hofstadter and Smith, *American Higher Education*, 1:13–15.

4. Samuel Eliot Morison, *The Founding of Harvard College* (Cambridge, Mass.: Harvard University Press, 1935), 168.

5. See *The American Puritans: Their Prose and Poetry*, ed. Perry Miller (Garden City, N.Y.: Doubleday Anchor Books, 1956), 78–84.

6. Jurgen Herbst, *From Crisis to Crisis: American College Government, 1636–1819* (Cambridge, Mass.: Harvard University Press, 1982), 5–8, 11, 17. For more on the significance of the 1650 incorporation, see pages 14–16. Hugh Peter had a critical role in the fund-raising (Raymond Phineas Stearns, *The Strenuous Puritan: Hugh Peter, 1598–1660* [Urbana: University of Illinois Press, 1954], 138–43).

cial recommendation. Here lived Thomas Shepard, the young graduate of Emmanuel College, and already one of the leading ministers in New England. Shepard, furthermore, had kept the place free of Antinomian inroads and Newton thus seemed like a "safe" location for the college. In his autobiography, Shepard noted that God had preserved Newton "spotless from the contagion" of Anne Hutchinson's dangerous delusions.[7]

In fact, the very month in which the General Court acted to establish a college, ministers in the colony organized to confront an emerging crisis. Massachusetts had just endured the challenge of radical separatism posed by Roger Williams, exiled from the colony the previous year. Now religious leaders were learning of the charges brought by a woman recently arrived from England. Anne Hutchinson had been holding weekly meetings to discuss the sermons of Boston ministers. Commentary was moving into criticism, and Hutchinson charged that a doctrine of works, the notion that one could win salvation by good and proper living, prevailed among the generality of the ministry. Hutchinson soon had a following and something of a movement. Much was at stake. Indeed, Hutchinson herself appeared to key clerical leaders as the radical extension of a set of ideas and practices that were spreading from the Boston church, to which she belonged. Not she, but the minister there, was the greater concern. Attention then focused on her minister, John Cotton.

Cotton was born in Derby, England, in 1584, the son of a struggling lawyer. He would enroll at Christ's College, Cambridge and there encounter the two formative influences of his life. Like other innocents who entered there, Cotton found William Perkins's Calvinism troubling. How to confront the fact that all mankind stood condemned under Adam's sin? How to work toward salvation when God had elected, irrevocably, those to be saved and had damned the rest? Cotton wanted to pursue these questions and at age eighteen took a fellowship at Emmanuel College. Six years later he lapsed into depression, but he then encountered the second influence—Richard Sibbes. Sibbes, a "physician of the soul," as his colleagues called him, taught Cotton how to address his doubts and to see signs of his election. When Cotton took up his ministry in Lincolnshire that approach prevailed in his preaching. His message was one of assurance, but only to the extent that God gave his grace, and gave it absolutely, to his elect. Neither good works nor proclamation of faith sufficed to earn it.[8]

Cotton had a successful ministry in his "first" Boston, in Lincolnshire. He became one of England's most respected Puritans, and many wonder how for so long he evaded the conformist dictates of William Laud. Cotton heard talk of the Puritan party organizing to go to America, but resisted that idea for himself.

---

7. *God's Plot: Puritan Spirituality in Thomas Shepard's Cambridge*, ed. Michael McGiffert, rev. and exp. (Amherst: University of Massachusetts Press, 1994), 70.
8. Larzer Ziff, *The Career of John Cotton: Puritanism and the American Experience* (Princeton, N.J.: Princeton University Press, 1962), 3–4, 21, 23.

Nonetheless, in spring 1630 he traveled to Southampton and delivered the farewell sermon to those Puritans who now set out across the Atlantic, aboard the *Arbella*, on their way to the new world. His own fortune, however, could not last. Laud summoned Cotton before the High Court in 1632 to answer questions about his nonconformity. Cotton opted to go into hiding, finding his way eventually to London. In June 1633 he boarded the *Griffin*, with wife and daughter, and sailed for America.[9]

Cotton became a teacher at the Boston church. But it soon became apparent that he was not of one mind with the other Bay ministers. In fact, he stood at the heart of an intellectual schism that began to crystallize with his preaching. Within the general Calvin–Perkins framework, as Larzer Ziff observed, differing interpretations contested for influence.[10] Cotton continued to stress the utter inability of the individual to win salvation, and he wholly detached good works from any indication, for there was none, of the elect. He thus returned to the centrality of inward spiritual transformation as the singular mark and the singular experience of the elect. That accentuation had severe implications for the New England enterprise. For Cotton, the church covenant, as contrived by the ministry, signified a church of congregants annealed by their moral and spiritual purposes. But, as Darren Staloff describes it, Cotton was trying "to transform the church of Boston from a covenanted assemblage of cultural initiates into a charismatic community." In other words, he was effecting a significant shift. Heretofore, membership in the churches had derived from an individual's religious understanding and from virtuous social behavior. Cotton judged these standards too easy; he considered them a covenant of works and demanded a test of saving grace, offered as a personal confession thereof, as the standard for church membership. None should be admitted, he wrote, "till we be convinced in our consciences of the certain and infallible signs of their regeneration." Only then, he avowed, can we preserve "the purity of the church." Other Massachusetts churches now followed him in this procedure.[11]

Cotton represented that "Spiritual Brotherhood" that had formed under Sibbes and others in England as the mainstream voice of Puritanism.[12] In its orb

---

9. Ziff, *John Cotton*, 42, 47, 53, 60, 65–66, 70.

10. Ziff, *John Cotton*, 108–9.

11. Ziff, *John Cotton*, 109; Darren Staloff, *The Making of an American Thinking Class: Intellectuals and Intelligentsia in Puritan Massachusetts* (New York: Oxford University Press, 1998), 29; Janice Knight, *Orthodoxies in Massachusetts: Rereading American Puritanism* (Cambridge, Mass.: Harvard University Press, 1994), 124; Norman Pettit, *The Heart Prepared: Grace and Conversion in Puritan Spiritual Life* (New Haven, Conn.: Yale University Press, 1966), 134 (the quotations). One must conclude that no clear pattern prevailed in these issues. Thus, as Stephen Foster notices, Thomas Shepard himself imposed the new criterion at his own church in 1635. *The Long Argument: English Puritanism and the Shaping of New England Culture, 1570–1700* (Chapel Hill: University of North Carolina Press, 1991), 162.

12. Cotton seems to have gone beyond Sibbes in stressing the utter passivity of the believer in being brought into the covenant and even in having "assurance" of salvation. See Mark E. Dever, *Richard Sibbes: Puritanism and Calvinism in Late Elizabethan and Early Stuart England* (Macon, Ga.: Mercer University Press, 2000), 162–87.

one found other American preachers like John Wheelwright and John Davenport. But in Massachusetts the founding lead had been taken by another group. Knight calls them the "Intellectual Founders." They had all arrived before Harvard's creation in 1636. John Winthrop came in 1630; Thomas Hooker in 1633; and Thomas Shepard, Hugh Peter, and Peter Bulkeley in 1635. This religious set represented a fringe element in England come to power in America. In the absence of external opposition they became more visible and dominant. And they gave New England its governing orthodoxy.

Harvard College assumes a new significance within this context. Indeed the case offers an early illustration of this study's focus, the American colleges within their intellectual milieu. For in October of 1636 when the General Court established the college, concerned Bay ministers assembled in Boston to confer with John Cotton, Anne Hutchinson, and John Wheelwright to discuss their views about grace and election. Two months later the ministers again met with Cotton and Hutchinson and now reached an impasse. Then in November the clerics submitted sixteen questions to Cotton and asked for written answers from him. Leading the case against Cotton and soon against Hutchinson was Thomas Shepard. Question thirteen went to the heart of the matter: "Whether evidencing justification by sanctification be a building my justification on my sanctification, a going on in a covenant of works?"[13]

What lay behind this question? Shepard and the Intellectual Founders greatly mistrusted Cotton's notion of grace as a spiritual conversion in which the individual had no initiative in winning and disclosed no moral course of behavior that evidenced justification in the aftermath. Shepard warned against too great a passivity in seeking grace and affirmed the importance of individual effort and adherence to the commandments of God as conditions of that covenant. In summer 1636 Shepard had begun to preach a series of sermons to this effect. Following the influence of Hooker, he urged that "the gate is strait, and therefore a man must sweat and strive to enter. . . . it is a tough work, a wonderful hard matter, to be saved." Shepard and Hooker saw the path to grace as incremental and orderly, not passive or spontaneous. Hooker indeed became a major contributor to the New England orthodoxy by his abundant outline of a "preparation" theology. Nor for the Intellectual Founders did grace bestow that absolute certainty that Cotton guaranteed. They insisted that grace was conditional. Doubt still plagued the justified and all in that condition must strive to demonstrate a sanctification (that is, a purity of conduct and behavior) that reflected it. Otherwise, as Hugh Peter averred, we prepare the way for "enthusiasm," for a religion concerned only with inward spirituality and indifferent to social behavior.[14]

---

13. David D. Hall, "Introduction," in *The Antinomian Controversy, 1636–1638: A Documentary History* (Middletown, Conn.: Wesleyan University Press, 1968), 6; Ziff, *John Cotton*, 118–19.
14. Knight, *Orthodoxies in Massachusetts*, 17, 38, 99; Hall, "Introduction," 18–19; Staloff, *Thinking Class*, 35, 69; Michael P. Winship, "'The Most Glorious Church in the World': The Unity of the Godly in Boston, Massachusetts, in the 1630s," *Journal of British Studies* 39 (January 2000): 71–98. For more on preparationist theology, see Pettit, *Heart Prepared*, ch. 4.

Hutchinson, taking up Cotton's warning against confidence in "works," pronounced against those "legalist" preachers who she believed were adhering to it. She had become an ardent follower of Cotton in his English parish and sailed for Boston in 1634 to join his church there. Particularly troubling in her views were claims of a personal sense of communion with the Holy Spirit, a direct revelation. Puritans acknowledged no such revelation since the time of Jesus. Furthermore, she, and any who had received the Spirit, never had to doubt their condition. That view rendered the matter of behavior moot. Cotton uneasily dissociated himself from Hutchinson's wild charges against the ministers, but his opponents readily associated the two. Some clearly used Hutchinson to get at Cotton. The General Court ordered her into exile in March 1638.[15]

Shepard's role in the matter has given rise to the story about the location of Harvard at Newton, now rechristened Cambridge. The court made the decision for Newton at the same time Hutchinson's trial began. Cotton Mather remembered Shepard as the vigilant watchdog against "the rot" of Antinomian sentiments.[16] Indeed, in a series of sermons he was just then beginning at the Newton church, Shepard prescribed for the regenerate and unregenerate alike a regime of constant moral striving after grace. He considered Antinomianism but a rationale for the slothful.[17] Shepard had been instrumental in launching the college and became an overseer of the institution. He would address Harvard students by sermons for years, importune Englanders for gifts of books to the school, and defend it against critics of the "heathen" authors read there. Harvard clearly had a place in Shepard's larger program and his defense of orthodoxy. As opposed to the charismatic authority and the preaching ministry so favored by the Spiritual Brethren as the essence of God's ministry, Shepard and the Intellectual Founders favored learning and wisdom via the medium of the printed word. Antinomianism signified anti-intellectualism, in their judgments. They sought to establish authority in institutions—of church, school, state. Harvard would serve, among other purposes, to prevent any recurrence of the challenges that the colony now was facing.[18]

---

15. Shepard had taken the matter before the General Court in May and preached a sermon denouncing his opponents as enemies of the colony. At his behest the court passed immigrant controls and applied them against friends of Wheelwright the following month (Winship, "'The Most Glorious Church,'" 91). The matter had other important reverberations in the larger colony politics. Henry Vane, a friend of the Hutchinsons, won election to governor in 1637, only to be removed from office with the reelection of Winthrop, Hutchinson's main persecutor, the next year.

16. Morison, Founding of Harvard, 179–83.

17. Hall, "Introduction," 18–20.

18. God's Plot, 6–7n; Staloff, Thinking Class, 35, 45, 91, 93. The Antinomian crisis has received much historical attention. Recently Darren Staloff has interpreted the issues in terms of social classes: "In social terms the Antinomian controversy is a classic example of class conflict. In this case, the conflict was between the urban bourgeoisie and the thinking class, particularly the strata of ministerial intellectuals. The issues at stake were nothing less than the control of the colonial government and the continued existence of the system of cultural domination" (Thinking Class, 40). Janice Knight sees it differently: "What divided these preachers most profoundly were ideas—they were a generation animated by religious and philosophical problems. Having limned their careers, one must go beyond and beneath biographical fact to the ideas that inspired allegiances and actions" (Orthodoxies in Massachusetts, 71). This study leans more to this view, but with attention to how ideas become institutionally situated.

In establishing Harvard, the Intellectual Founders secured an institutional base for orthodoxy. But not until 1638 did instruction begin at the new college. Even then things got off to a bad start. Nathaniel Eaton, who arrived with high Puritan credentials from Emmanuel College, became first master of the college. He had no recommendation, it seemed, other than his previous study with William Ames.[19] Eaton had left England because he could not accept the Prayer Book or the church government that mandated its use. He settled in Cambridge and became next-door neighbor to the Shepards.[20] But Eaton, as Jurgen Herbst puts it, "made his mark more on the backs than on the minds of the students." Cotton Mather reported that Eaton once beat a student while two others held him. The court, upon hearing a complaint, intervened against Eaton and fined him. Then they got rid of him altogether.[21] The incident informs significantly of the colony's vigilance toward the college, its public trust. The ideal of institutional autonomy for colleges awaited a later era of American history.

Better days soon came to the school at Cambridge. John Harvard had arrived in Massachusetts after achieving much commercial success in London. He came from parents of moderate loyalty to Puritanism and received baptism at the church that later became Southwark Cathedral in that city. He entered Emmanuel College in 1627 and clearly took from it an earnest Puritan loyalty, for his migration to New England came from no financial necessities. He entered into farming and served as an assistant minister in Charleston. We know little more about him than that. Harvard died an untimely death in 1638, barely thirty-one years old. He gave half his estate and all of his library to the college. With this loving gesture Harvard bought his legacy at the new school. The General Court honored the gift with the ultimate recognition: "Ordered, that the college agreed upon formerly to be built at Cambridge shall be called Harvard College."[22]

Henry Dunster rose next to leadership of Harvard, becoming its first president in 1640. Born in 1609 in England he graduated from Magdalene College at Cambridge, earning an M.A. degree in 1634. He had already become a committed Puritan and joined his compatriots in Massachusetts, where he was almost immediately offered the Harvard office. He enjoyed a close friendship with Shepard and frequently preached at his church. Under Dunster, the college established a curriculum that emulated the English universities but also showed the influence of the English dissenting academies. Harvard's statues in 1646 spell out the terms of admission to the school. They should be cause for wonder to today's students. First, not only did Harvard impose on its students a four-year program in the ancient languages, but no student could even apply

19. Morison, *Founding of Harvard College*, 143.
20. Susan Drinker Moran, "Thomas Shepard and the Professor: Two Documents from the Early History of Harvard," *Early American Literature* 17 (1982): 24–25.
21. Herbst, *From Crisis to Crisis*, 7; "Cotton Mather's History of Harvard," 15.
22. Morison, *Founding of Harvard College*, 105–6, 214–20.

to the school lest he were "able to read Tully or such like classical Latin author *ex tempore*" and speak Latin in verse and prose. The students must also know how to decline the Greek nouns and verbs, "nor shall any claim admission before such qualifications." The statutes made clear the essential religious purpose of the college. Each student "shall consider the main end of his life to know God and Jesus Christ, which is eternal life." Students should read Scripture twice a day and be ready to show the results of their reading. They were never to speak English, save in the frequent events of public oratory; otherwise they spoke Latin, as did all their instructors in class. Each scholar would be called by his last name, until he acquired the master's degree.[23] Among the undergraduates, logic, grammar, some mathematics, a little history, and moral philosophy rounded out the curriculum. Morison notes that Harvard made two improvements on this standard medieval arts menu by including instruction in Hebrew and other Oriental languages—Dunster's specialty. Students did not face the semester quandary of deciding which courses to take. They faced instead a required four-year curriculum.[24]

We glimpse the undergraduate experience at midcentury Harvard if we follow young Increase Mather and his older brother Eleazer into the college in 1651. Their father, Richard Mather, had become one of the colony's formidable ministers. Born in 1596 near Liverpool to a yeoman family, Richard came under the suasion of a minister who stressed the Pauline doctrine of salvation. It terrified him, but he gained some comfort by reading a book by William Perkins. Mather now understood that one may go far in sin but yet the hand of God may reach out and save the lost soul. Richard Mather attended Brasenose College at Oxford but found it a hellish place. He left to take orders in the Anglican Church, but his plain style of preaching reflected his Puritan ways. Indeed, when William Laud became archbishop of Canterbury in 1633, he had Mather investigated and dismissed from the Church. In 1635, Mather, his wife Katherine, and their children set out for Massachusetts. He took up his ministry in Dorchester.[25]

Richard Mather's son Eleazer Mather was fourteen and his brother Increase twelve when they departed for Harvard. The ten-mile route to the school would have taken them on a dirt road past the home of John Eliot in Roxbury by way of the north bank of the Charles River into Cambridge. There, next to President Dunster's home, the boys would see Thomas Shepard's meetinghouse and behind it the angular college building "Old Harvard." Within a few days, most likely, Dunster conducted the boys' entrance examination. He asked them to translate on sight Virgil, Tully, and some other Ro-

---

23. "Statutes of Harvard, ca. 1646," in Hofstadter and Smith, *American Higher Education*, 1:8–9.
24. Morison, *Founding of Harvard College*, 205–7.
25. Robert Middlekauff, *The Mathers: Three Generations of Puritan Intellectuals, 1596–1728* (New York: Oxford University Press, 1971), 10–19.

Increase Mather

man writers. They fielded questions posed in Latin by the president and re-sponded in kind. They would further demonstrate their skills by writing some Latin verse. And so it would go with the other forty undergraduates that en-rolled in 1651. Eleazer and Increase were placed at the head of their class not by virtue of their entrance performances but in recognition of their father's high social standing.[26]

The academic routine followed. Rising at dawn, the boys descended from the second-floor dormitory to attend morning prayers and then to replenish hun-gry stomachs at the "buttery hatch," where they had a breakfast of beer and bread. Money counted at Harvard, so for a little extra cost some butter and cheese could supplement the standard fare. Lessons followed through the morn-ing until eleven o'clock. Lunch offered the same beer and bread, but also beef,

26. Michael G. Hall, *The Last American Puritan: The Life of Increase Mather, 1639–1723* (Middle-town, Conn.: Wesleyan University Press, 1988), 31–34.

and once in a while some pudding, served in the great hall. A late meal followed evening prayers and offered pies or oatmeal and eggs to be taken with, what else, beer.

Harvard was the first college of the Puritans. It existed to educate leaders of church and state and to equip all others who entered its doors with the intellectual foundations of Puritanism. For those intentions Harvard could draw upon a vast accumulation of Reformed learning. Many of the Harvard founders had experienced it in England, but the next generations would find the repertoire expanded and refined. In William Ames, Harvard had an intellectual authority who eminently suited its needs and who consolidated the theological orthodoxy of the Intellectual Founders who controlled the college.[27] For all of them followed him devotedly. Since his departure from England Ames had gone to Holland, undertaken ministerial work, and then begun an academic career at the University of Franeker. Under his powerful influence there, Franeker became the Dutch center of Ramism. Ames's own contribution to that stable of Puritan erudition came with the posthumous publication of his *Technometry* in 1638. It made Ames an intellectual force in Calvinist learning in Europe and profoundly so in New England. At Harvard, students honed their disputing skills in their "theses technolgiae," and college commencement ceremonies featured these presentations into the eighteenth century.[28] Thomas Shepard once said that one could be essentially informed in divine matters had he read nothing but Ames's works. And Increase Mather, as late as 1717, referenced only Ames in describing works to be read by ministers.[29] Ames himself followed the New England Puritans with great interest and hoped to join them. He had former students in Massachusetts, and his two sons later attended Harvard. He wrote to his friend Governor Winthrop saying "I long to be with you" and had he made the trip to New England he certainly would have been made president of Harvard. Ames's unexpected death in 1633 prevented that happening.[30]

Today's readers might find Ames's *Technometry* dense and prolix. If we appreciate what he wanted to do, however, we learn much about Puritan habits of thought and a good deal about its contents. Ames believed that all knowledge is one because God creates and governs all things. The arts, the several categories of learning, individually inform us of the divine mind insofar as they derive from it and reflect it. No art can be an end or entity unto itself, Ames believed, even

---

27. Ames represented the lengthened shadow of Peter Ramus at Harvard. Ramus also had an important place in the preparationist theologies advanced by Hooker and Shepard. See David L. Parker, "Petrus Ramus and the Puritans: The 'Logic' of Preparationist Conversion Doctrine," *Early American Literature* 8 (Fall 1973): 140–62.

28. Perry Miller, *The New England Mind: The Seventeenth Century* (Boston: Beacon, 1939), 161.

29. John D. Eusden, "Introduction" to William Ames, *The Marrow of Theology*, ed. John D. Eusden (Boston: Pilgrim Press, 1968), 1.

30. Lee W. Gibbs, "Introduction" to William Ames, *Technometry* (Philadelphia: University of Pennsylvania Press, 1979), 41; Eusden, "Introduction," 9.

though he sought to establish the boundaries of each. Ames, we will observe, confirmed what Calvin taught about the fall of man and humanity's alienation from God. But the arts help us restore a connection with God. God embodies perfect reason, but he has left a witness, in human reason itself. Ames liked to say that what is Archetype in God is Ectype in man. Ames thus allowed that "sense, observing, and experience" all might be conveyors of God the artist's intelligence.[31]

How then did the arts differ? They differed in what Ames called "eupraxia." Ames believed all of the technometria to be practical, and even theology ultimately signified to him simply right living. Ames wrote, "Art is the idea of eupraxia methodically delineated by universal rules." Each art works by universal laws—the laws of truth, justice, wisdom, and prudence (as stated by Ramus). Each works according to a habit or direction of the mind. Ames, with his liking for charts and diagrams, could eventually move to a specific location of these intellectual habits in the curricular subjects of the seventeenth-century college, to wit, logic, grammar, rhetoric, mathematics, physics, and theology. Ames's construction anticipates the precisely calculated "faculty psychology" that reigned as the pedagogical norm of America's early nineteenth-century colleges. He rested supremely confident in his technometria. "These six arts," he wrote, "perfect the whole man."[32]

And they perfect the "whole man" in right living. No art, for Ames, has purely contemplative use. Ames's thought conveyed an activist bias readily seized by his Puritan readers. He rejected the Aristotelian division of the arts into the theoretical and the practical. Ames saw the perversion of this categorization in the medieval universities. The Scholastic tradition had made metaphysics the ontological foundation of the arts, and Ames wanted none of it. Metaphysics had placed divine knowledge in a remote and abstract state, he complained. So Ames excluded metaphysics from the arts (calling the Devil "the greatest metaphysician" of them all) and made theology one of them. So doing, Ames brought theology into the realm of the practical, or more precisely, the practical/theoretical. Thesis 89 of Technometria states, "For there is no contemplation that should not be practice and have its own work; nor is there any action in general such as to exclude all contemplation."[33]

Ames had the opportunity to elucidate this principle in his major work, *The Marrow of Theology* (*Medulla Theologica*). A brief edition appeared in 1623 and the full-text edition in 1627, in Latin. The first English version came in 1642. A major contribution to Calvinist literature, *The Marrow* would have student readers at Harvard and Yale for many decades. It owed much to the inspiration of Ames's teacher, William Perkins, though Ames moved from the evangelical to

---

31. Keith L. Sprunger, *The Learned Doctor William Ames: Dutch Backgrounds of English and American Puritanism* (Urbana: University of Illinois Press, 1972), 116–17.

32. Sprunger, *Learned Doctor Ames*, 117.

33. Sprunger, *Learned Doctor Ames*, 119; Ames, *Technometry*, 108.

the scholarly in extending the teacher's ideas. Intellectual though it was, Ames wrote *The Marrow* as a book for teaching purposes and in this end it succeeded well. It is an indispensable asset for studying New England Puritanism, for students and ministers and other readers learned from it.

In making theology one of the arts, Ames also carefully made a distinction. Theology, he said, differed from the other arts because it had its roots in Scripture. Ames enshrined in *The Marrow* the key supporting references to the Old and New Testaments. In his differentiation, Ames insisted that empirical knowledge, effective and legitimate for the other arts, did not apply in theology. Neither did logic or a priori principles apply. "The basic principles of theology," Ames wrote, "though they may be advanced by study and industry, are not in us by nature." The Puritan Ames understood this fact to be a consequence of the Fall, for thence man lost the ability to see the highest good. That effort now required special revelation. Ames thus left no room for a natural theology or a natural ethics.[34]

Some particular points in Ames's *Marrow* instruct us in its Calvinistic emphasis. For one thing, Ames accentuated conversion as decisive in the epistemology of the believer. His own conversion under Perkins had made the experience central to Ames in his understanding of religion. Ames described conversion in terms of the covenants by which God dealt with a faltering humanity. Thus, the first covenant, the one with Adam, underscored a doctrine of works that humans soon demonstrated they could not uphold. ("Do this and you will live; if you do it not you shall die.") The third chapter of Genesis describes how God made the second covenant with man, a covenant of grace. Unlike the first covenant, the second incorporated no bargaining prescriptions. It placed no restrictions on the complete autonomy of God, leaving all to his reason. The covenant of grace, in short, pertained to the elect only by reasons known to God alone. It also showed how divine and human reason varied to this extent. The covenant, wrote Ames, "from the human point of view is often offered indiscriminately." Puritans thus confronted a sovereign God who worked by his own will and whose ways struck fallen man as capricious.[35]

This Calvinist doctrine of predestination fascinates and confounds the modern student. What should one make of a theology that says that winning salvation "depends upon no cause, reason, or outward condition, but proceeds purely from the will of him who predestines"? This calling, Ames said, making the idea as explicit as could be, "does not depend on the dignity, honesty, industry, or any endeavor of the ones called, but only on the election and predestination of

---

34. Ames, *The Marrow of Theology*, I, 1, 3; Norman Fiering, *Moral Philosophy at Seventeenth-Century Harvard: A Discipline in Transition* (Chapel Hill: University of North Carolina, 1981), 48.

35. Sprunger, *Learned Doctor Ames*, 150–51. Sprunger details nine ways in which the new covenant differed from the old. Ames described the sacraments as signs by which Christ seals the covenant.

God."[36] Not goods or church-going, not social prestige or civic prominence assured anyone of salvation. How then might one know of one's condition? By certain signs, the Puritans answered. From this assurance came the famous Puritan introspection, that vigilance for the signs of inner renewal that marked the Puritan consciousness, the self-reflection and self-examination, the journal-keeping that recorded one's spiritual sojourn.

The Marrow of Theology has sixty-one chapters in book one and twenty-two more in book two. Here Harvard students read about such subjects as "Creation," "Man's Apostasy or Fall," "Original Sin," "Actual Sin," "Glorification," "Holy Scripture," "The Sacraments," "Good Works," "The Manner of Divine Worship," and "Justice and Charity Toward Our Neighbor." Two of these subjects, in particular, clarified key points of Amesian Calvinism. Thus, in "Justification," Harvard students read what it means to be an individual whom God has brought into the covenant of grace. Ames wrote: "Justification is the gracious judgment of God by which he absolves the believer from sin and death." It brings about no physical change in condition, for it is a legal matter, a contractual promise of salvation. Ames therefore faulted Aquinas for describing justification as an increase in righteousness, with remission of sin. For Ames, though, justification removes only the guilt, "the guilty obligation to undergo eternal death." Justification also brings a release of anxiety from the experience of our sin, though that sin persists. These views, of course, inform us why the Intellectual Founders embraced Ames and rejected the ideas of Anne Hutchinson and the rival Calvinism of the Spiritual Brethren. She made regeneration a new condition of holiness, so that she could claim to live under guidance of the Holy Spirit in that state. Ames absolved the elect from the punishment of sin, but not from the fact of it. Hence the necessity of moral striving remained. "Not only are past sins of justified persons remitted but also those to come." [37]

When he discussed "Sanctification," Ames became less clear-cut, but he nonetheless made critical Puritan points. "Sanctification," he wrote, "is the real change in man from the sordidness of sin to the purity of God's image." We mean by the term, he added, a change in the believer, such that he has righteousness or indwelling holiness imparted to him. Sanctification involves a real change of qualities and disposition. The change, Ames maintained, is progressive, not immediate; it begins first in the soul and moves to the body. Sanctification comes from the calling, to be sure, and thus derives from nothing natural in us. But Ames does insist that "sanctification is imperfect while we are here" on Earth; "for perfect sanctification is not found in this life" (to which Ames adds "except in the dreams of some fanatics"). Even the best works of the saints are corrupted by the flesh (read "inordinate desire," the hard residue of fallen man). And even

---

36. Ames, Marrow of Theology, I, 1, 25, 9; I, 26, 9.
37. Ames, Marrow of Theology, I, 6–8, 20–23, 27.

the elect, under Ames's Calvinist regime, could lapse into no easy or comfortable state of mind.[38] Clearly, here, Ames spoke to the concerns of the Founders, his views of the covenant distinct from such interpreters as Cotton and Hutchinson.

Thus Ames entered the Harvard curriculum. Of all the curricular subjects in the colonial colleges, one in particular became the bellwether of intellectual change. By the time of the American Revolution, and in a continuing tradition well into the nineteenth century, moral philosophy stood as the capstone of the undergraduate program. Eventually, in literally hundreds of American colleges, the president of the institution would instruct the seniors in this subject. The moral philosophy textbook became an academic cottage industry. Both theoretical and practical ethics carried the instruction, as this course sent exiting students into the world to become virtuous citizens thereof. The subject generally evolved from a religious to a mostly humanistic one. Colonial colleges, however, had to answer the questions whether moral philosophy was a human science or a supernatural one and what supplied its intellectual foundations.[39]

Because Ames wanted to make theology one of the arts and therefore rooted in practice, one might have thought that moral philosophy would claim his attention. In fact, though, Ames distrusted the subject, and so did many other Puritans. "Ethics" smacked too much of good works, a doctrine of salvation by means other than divine grace. Some Puritans also associated the subject with "casuistry" and the intellectual twists of the wily Jesuits. Significantly, therefore, Ames himself would not permit ethics an independence from theology. From Aristotle's golden mean through the treatises of the Schoolmen, he condemned any notion "that the judgment of prudent men is the rule of virtue." He also resisted another notion, that theology deals with the inner state of the individual and ethics with his outward behavior. "They say that the subject of ethics is a good, honest, honorable man," wrote Ames, "and the subject of theology is a godly and religious man." Not at all, he retorted. Inner spirituality determines the character of all works, and thus the two domains cannot have separate considerations. Finally, though Ames did allow for the efficacy of conscience and right reason in moral action, he insisted that Scripture was "the sole rule in all manners that have to do with the direction of life."[40]

Ames's strictures on moral philosophy addressed a long-standing and contentious issue in Western thought. As Norman Fiering explains in his important study of seventeenth-century Harvard moral philosophy, Christian writers very early confronted the question: What use should they make of the ancient thinkers' great achievements in philosophical ethics? St. Augustine had supplied

---

38. Ames, *Marrow of Theology*, I, 29, 6–7, 10, 15, 29, 32–36.

39. For an extended study of this subject, see D. H. Meyer, *The Instructed Conscience: The Shaping of the National Ethic* (Philadelphia: University of Pennsylvania Press, 1972).

40. Sprunger, *Learned Doctor Ames*, 155–57, 161, 169 (the quotations). Ames did write a popular moral philosophy book, *De Conscientia* (often known as *Cases of Conscience*), which he described as a kind of "Book Three" of *The Marrow*. It appeared in 1630 while he was at Franeker. While read in New England it does not seem to have been incorporated into the Harvard curriculum.

one answer by urging their complete incorporation into Christian teaching, confidant of its enhancement by the amalgamation. Others wanted to validate common grace, or the ordinary moral life, as outlined in pagan ethics, acknowledging that God gave it to humanity to assist its progress in worldly business. Both Catholic scholars and Calvin made that endorsement, though Luther did not. Often this allowance underscored more liberal forms of theological Protestantism, as in Anglicanism. Its literature maintained that the Fall only partially corrupted human nature and left some of the original capacities damaged but not destroyed, including humans' natural or moral understanding. That condition suggested the validity of a natural or human ethics.

A third alternative would show that the early learning of the Greeks and Romans merely anticipated later Christian truths and thus no great breach divided pagan and Christian. The fourth possibility—the one Ames, as noted, rejected—was to divide inner and outer realms, applying moral thought to one and Christian to the other. Ames and some Protestant sectarians saw the long hand of Aristotle here and detected a priority of civic-republican ethics over an inner-spiritual one.[41]

In moral philosophy, despite Ames's views, Harvard arrived early to a liberal position that anticipated its future intellectual history and in a manner that would make key distinctions from its sister Puritan college, Yale. President Charles Chauncy illustrates the point. Chauncy, born in 1592 in Hertfordshire, England, graduated from Trinity College, Cambridge with two degrees. As a young minister he showed a strong Puritan persuasion. He defiantly refused to read the Athanasian Creed or follow the required litany. He rejected the surplice. He decried Sabbath day abuses in the realm. Twice brought before the king's authorities, he faced charges, among several, that he had labeled as "dumb divines" those church leaders who had spoken favorably of popery or Arminianism. When appearing before Laud, Chauncy recanted a bit and promised moderation. But he reverted to old habits and alienated many in his own town. He left for Massachusetts where he had parishes at Plymouth and Scituate. He could irritate people with his doctrinal inflexibility, but he won great respect for his scholarship.[42]

Chauncy used the occasion of the 1655 commencement to address the question of moral philosophy. Two years previously a William Dell had issued his *Trial of Spirits.* . . . and called for an exclusively scriptural education for ministers. The Harvard president noted that Dell spoke for sectarian Antinomian partisans in England. Chauncy judged the matter an urgent one. He meant to offer the case for the essential compatibility of the ancient classics and Christianity. He defended humane learning, which embraced all the arts except theology, all those

---

41. Fiering, *Moral Philosophy at Harvard*, 12–19.

42. Allen French, *Charles I and the Puritan Upheaval: A Study of the Causes of the Great Migration* (Boston: Houghton Mifflin, 1955), 287–95. On the subject of the surplice, Chauncy remarked that the cloth that produced it could just as easily make "a whore's frock" (p. 297).

writings that have been written "even in corrupt nature." "Many excellent divine moral truths," he said, were to be found in Plato, Aristotle, Plutarch, and Seneca. And "they have treated of the works of God most excellently in many places." He challenged the religious purists. "Should all these [good writings] be thrown away as anti-Christian or lies?" Chauncy referenced grammar, logic, and rhetoric, but also mentioned physics, ethics, and politics. "These in the true sense and right meaning thereof," he urged, "are theological and Scripture learning, and are not to be accorded as [merely] humane learning." In short, Chauncy made the commencement sermon of 1655 a defense of the Harvard curriculum as it had always existed.[43]

Fiering summarizes this significance:

> By the time Harvard was founded some form of study of Aristotle's ethics was a deeply ingrained, if always precarious, component of university education. To have ignored this tradition would have exposed Harvard graduates to the risk of exclusion from the republic of learned men. For a newly founded, provincial institution such a risk was all the greater. The Puritan clergy who dominated the college were men who hoped to have the best of both worlds: the freedom to exercise discrimination in what they accepted of the old ways, and, at the same time, the satisfaction of being full-fledged participants in a culture grander than their own.[44]

Thus from Theophilus Golius Harvard students read an endorsement of the Nichomachean ethics, albeit a qualified one. Golius, professor at the newly founded Protestant University of Strassbourg, was the author of *Epitome Doctrinae Moralis. . . .* (1592), an early moral philosophy work used at Harvard. Golius saw the ethical life as a triumph of a "rational principle" that successfully resists the appeal of the lower appetites. He did acknowledge ultimate dependency on God's assistance in this effort, however.[45]

Beyond Ames, Harvard teachers had other sources of moral philosophy quite within a Puritan tradition. Adrian Heereboord, who succeeded Franco Burgersdyck at the University of Lyden, shared with him a common location in ethics. Heerebord published *Melematic Philosophica*, in 1662, a massive tome. He posited an original moral state in Adam, the basis of an innate, natural ethic, which the application of reason could generate into full visibility. Heereboord believed that this natural ethics had a more explicit expression in the Mosaic code. Heereboord, like Burgersdyck, wanted ethics to embrace more than the mere public and civic definition of morality supplied by a natural ethics. Heereboord surpassed Aristotle in insisting that ethics in human life transcends virtue and happiness. It embraces the religious life, and with it the individual's glorification of God. Thus,

---

43. Charles Chauncy, *God's Mercy, Shewed to His People in Giving Them a Taste for the Ministry and Schooles of Learning for the Continual Supplies Thereof* (Boston: n.p., 1655), 35–37.
44. Fiering, *Moral Philosophy at Harvard*, 63.
45. Fiering, *Moral Philosophy at Harvard*, 67–76.

Harvard texts that did not go so far as Ames in rejecting a natural ethics nonetheless stopped short of a pagan ethics that rested in good works and right living. Ultimately, though, one could conclude that "the beauties of Classical moral thought in general were received and appreciated at seventeenth-century Harvard."[46]

Along the way of these intellectual developments, Harvard faced recurring serious problems. One of them took the college quite by surprise. The recovery under Henry Dunster had endeared him to the college officials and the Cambridge community. But controversy arose in 1654. When the Dunsters, members in good standing in the local church, had a son, the president announced that he would not present the newborn for baptism. Dunster had, it turned out, been reading seriously on the subject of baptism and had concluded that child baptism had no foundation in Scripture. Local religious authorities spoke with him at length and on several occasions to persuade him toward the orthodox Puritan view on the matter.

Historian Samuel Morison in 1930 wrote that Dunster's announcement might be compared to a contemporary American president saying that he had become a communist.[47] The news was that shocking. Baptists had few adherents in New England, and despite locating some churches in Rhode Island and New Hampshire, had none at this time in Massachusetts Bay colony. But the young denomination had seen its first church established in England in 1612, and here and there in New England individual adherents surfaced. This form of Baptism came directly from Puritanism. It accepted a Calvinist dogma and congregationalist piety. In the 1630s Roger Williams, however, had severely challenged the Puritans on infant baptism. Antipaedobaptism suggested to New England Puritans an extreme, dangerous Protestantism.[48]

Dunster openly defended his views at a baptismal service of the Cambridge church in July 1654 and submitted to public admonishment by one of the magistrates. Meanwhile, the General Court, perceiving the dangers for Harvard, made a statuary requirement that all teachers at the college (and in the public schools), should they be "unsound in faith," must yield their offices. Dunster resigned the presidency. He made no proclamations for academic freedom or the rights of private conscience. He did not seek rebaptism and was not excommunicated. The issue raised no great or universal principles concerning rights of conscience or academic freedom in seventeenth-century Massachusetts.[49] Nevertheless, in choosing Dunster's successor, the college was vigilant for orthodoxy.

---

46. Fiering, *Moral Philosophy at Harvard*, 97–103 (the quotation).
47. Samuel Eliot Morison, *Builders of the Bay Colony* (Boston: Houghton Mifflin Company, 1930), 214.
48. William G. McLoughlin, *Soul Liberty: The Baptists' Struggle in New England, 1630–1833* (Hanover, N.H.: University Press of New England, 1991), 15–19.
49. McLoughlin, *Soul Liberty*, 32–34; Morison, *Builders*, 215–16.

Charles Chauncy was so literal-minded in these matters that he would celebrate the Lord's Supper only in the evening!

The Dunster affair alarmed the community, but the next issue divided it badly. Chauncy's openness to a mixed curriculum did nothing to compromise his religious orthodoxy. His stance on the confusing issue of the Half-Way Covenant in 1662 so illustrates. This matter also concerned baptism. For some time the New England churches had been experiencing a decline in the number of persons offering themselves for church membership by way of relating their experience of grace. These individuals had been baptized because their parents had been admitted to church membership under this procedure. Now they wanted their children, their own unredemption notwithstanding, to receive baptism. The early New England Puritans had assumed that baptized children would later enter into the covenant and become church members. What now to do when this assumption proved erroneous? The question came forth in the later 1640s when a proposal then would allow the children to have these, the grandchildren in essence, have baptism. One who helped defeat the proposal at that time was Charles Chauncy. But now in 1662 the General Court called a synod to take up the issue again. It won approval. One who wanted to defeat the proposal again was Chauncy.

It is not easy to find solid patterns in this Half-Way Covenant dispute.[50] John Davenport, an old supporter of Cotton, opposed it, vehemently. John Norton, an old supporter of Cotton, supported it, cautiously. Richard Mather endorsed it; sons Increase and Eleazer Mather opposed it. Later, after his father's death, Increase changed his views. Generally, though, the older established ministry supported the change. It would augment church membership.[51] Both sides, however, posed themselves as traditionalists in discussing the new covenant. Defenders did not proclaim a bold innovation. Their majority insisted that the half-way arrangement would assure the purity of the Lord's Supper; none would feel compelled to invent a conversion experience so that their children might be baptized. And they said of the dissenters that they were condemning the parents for failing to achieve what they could not do of their own. Saving faith came only from God's initiative.[52] And when Increase Mather reversed his opinion and defended the Half-Way Covenant he did so (convincingly, according to Sacvan Bercovitch) by mustering a preponderance of evidence from the earlier Puritans themselves. Mather published his *The First Principles of New England* in 1675, referencing Hooker, Norton, Cotton, and others.[53]

---

50. Staloff sees a power struggle between the lay brethren and the ministerial intellectuals. *Making of an American Thinking Class*, 139. Knight sees the conflict as something of a reenactment of the Antinomian factionalism (*Orthodoxies in Massachusetts*, N.J., 184–87).

51. Robert G. Pope, *The Half-Way Covenant: Church Membership in Puritan New England* (Princeton, N.J.: Princeton University Press, 1969), 23, 43, 51–52; David D. Hall, *The Faithful Shepherd: A History of the New England Ministry in the Seventeenth Century* (1972; New York: Norton, 1974), 200–201.

52. Pope, *Half-Way Covenant*, 58, 71.

53. Sacvan Bercovitch, *The American Jeremiad* (Madison: University of Wisconsin Press, 1978), 63.

Harvard's president made himself a leading dissenter in the Half-Way Covenant debate. He insisted that he stood emphatically for orthodoxy on the matter. He believed that the new policy, a dangerous concession to pragmatism, signaled declining times in New England. Chauncy defended the purity, as he saw it, of the New England churches. He had invited controversy on the subject of baptism earlier. At his Plymouth pulpit he had said that only baptism by full immersion represented the biblical way. He was bold enough to reiterate those views when he moved to the church at Scituate. Suspicions that Chauncy was a crypto-Baptist make us wonder why Harvard, following the Dunster debacle, invited him to the presidency. But Chauncy promised to keep his views on baptism to himself and then won the appointment. So when he went all-out against the Half-Way Covenant in 1662 he at first published his lengthy appeal, *Antisynodalia Scripta Americana*, anonymously. Chauncy said that the petitioning parents, whom he considered blameworthy, could not demand the privilege of bringing their children to baptism. He would himself simply have preferred removal of all unregenerate members from the church and would have restricted the sacrament to those capable of consent, therefore to adults. Harvard had in fact hired another Baptist.[54]

This issue convinced some Puritans that New England had lost its way, was falling out of the original covenant, and out of God's grace as well. In 1675 King Philip's War raged and the Wampanaog chief burned towns and villages, leaving thousands homeless. A dreadful fire followed shortly after the war, and it destroyed forty-five buildings in the North End of Boston. Then in September 1678 a smallpox epidemic struck the colony, killing as many as thirty people a day and several hundred individuals in all. Barely a year later, fire raged through Boston, destroying 150 homes and businesses in the city center. Winter of 1680–1681 brought bitter cold and the summer following brought drought. Then in August of 1682 that most providential of events occurred. A comet lit the sky. Increase Mather wrote of the occurrence and called it "Heaven's Alarm to the World." Did God have a quarrel with New England? Many so feared. The prolific literature of the jeremiad conveyed anguished fears that the people had forsaken the promise of their forebears and had turned from God. The literature brought calls for renewal as many of the ministerial leadership guarded against any further deviations from the old ways. Increase Mather, as always, took up voice and pen to warn the citizenry of New England. In 1674, Mather had preached "The Day of Trouble is Near." In 1679, he offered his "Discourse Concerning the Danger of Apostasy." In 1685, he became president pro tem of Harvard.[55]

In 1685 Increase Mather presided over a college in decline. Eleven years previously, his son Cotton had enrolled at Harvard. Less then two dozen students

---

54. Such is the conclusion of E. Brooks Holifield in his study *The Covenant Sealed: The Development of Puritan Sacramental Theology in Old and New England, 1570–1720* (New Haven, Conn.: Yale University Press, 1974), 179–82.

55. Middlekauff, *The Mathers*, 114.

constituted his classmates. President Leonard Hoar and two tutors made up the faculty. The campus had one building that served as dormitory, library, and lecture hall. As Increase Mather traversed the Dunster Street Bridge and introduced Cotton to the president for his examination, cattle and sheep grazed on the Common and around the local residences. "Captain Gookin's turkeys moved freely about a fenced section of his property."[56]

Increase Mather was one of New England's most prominent individuals. Although Mather stood for Puritan orthodoxy in its Calvinism and polity, and his judgmental habits alienated many people, he did not always hold to a rigid stance. He surely was the most politically active of the Massachusetts ministers. Mather also presided at Boston's North (Second) Church, one of the city's three, where pastoral obligations kept his hands full. For all his vigilance for Harvard, however, the ubiquitous Mather could not bring himself to relocate to residency at Cambridge. The seven or eight miles in transit to or from Boston would have wreaked havoc on so time-conscious a Puritan as he. But in his nonresidency there lurked future troubles for him.

In England, the Stuart Restoration of 1660 found the returning monarch desirous of bringing the colonies under greater control. Parliament passed new navigation acts in 1660 and 1663. New England especially commanded attention, and in 1676 Charles II sent Edward Randolph to Boston to impose new royal policy. Governor William Leverett cooperated little in rewriting colonial laws to square with England's, but successor Joseph Dudley headed a new party given to reconciliation. Increase Mather spoke for those who wanted no accommodation. He held the colony charter sacred and believed that submission to the Crown meant betrayal of God. The matter takes on special significance when one understands that the royal initiative had forced a greater religious tolerance in New England—for Quakers and others, and of course, for Anglicans. In 1686 Anglicans organized their first church in Boston. In 1684 England had ruled the Massachusetts charter invalid. James II formed the Dominion of New England and made Dudley president of the council. In 1685 a troubled Mather went off to England for three years to help shape the new charter of 1691.[57]

That situation left Mather mostly out of the picture at Harvard, a decisive turn of events. Instruction therefore fell to the three tutors, and they made a difference. Mather himself had appointed them. Two, John Leverett and William Brattle, shared common beginnings and upbringings. They were born in Boston in 1662 to affluent mercantile families, new products of New England's third generation. They went through Boston's Latin School together and did the same at Harvard, graduating in 1680. They became tutors, Leverett in 1685 and

---

56. David Levin, *Cotton Mather: The Young Life of the Lord's Remembrancer, 1663–1703* (Cambridge, Mass.: Harvard University Press, 1978), 23–24.
57. On these matters, see Hall, *Increase Mather*, chs. 6, 7.

Brattle in 1686; both were married in the same month. "A more talented, sympathetic, and devoted pair of tutors Harvard College has never had," wrote Morison. When Mather went off to fight for New England they became the authorities in charge.[58]

These changes may have looked like ordinary adjustments to the college's operations. In fact, they helped prepare Harvard for the liberalizing course that carried into the next century. Much of the new direction came from English influence, but with Leverett and Brattle that influence received considerable favor. England after the Restoration, as noted, entered a spirit of greater tolerance. Despite the Test Acts of 1673 and 1678 and measures by the returning monarchs to reassert conformity, the Stuarts did back off from religious persecution, of Quakers particularly. Anglicanism in turn entered a new era of religious rationalism and flourished with a contagious liberal religious theology. The new "catholic" spirit acquired the label "Latitudinarianism." The new Anglican literature steadily found its ways to the American colonies, appearing in private libraries and at Harvard itself. The American response to these new influences partly defines the beginnings of the American Enlightenment. Harvard's place proved critical in the transition to a new era of American intellectual history.[59]

A significant sign of intellectual change at Harvard itself was the influence of the Cambridge Platonists. They constituted a component of the latitudinarian movement that began in England in the 1650s and flourished after the Restoration. They had influence in England and the colonies by fostering a rational and tolerant Christianity. The latitude-men drew upon classical sources most importantly, but also upon the Scholastic tradition of natural law, and the Dutch Remonstrants. They hoped to fortify religion by rooting it not in scriptural authority or supernatural faith alone, but in an affinity with human nature and the innate authority of the human mind. All these weapons, the latitude-men hoped, would fortify a mild and rational Protestantism against atheism, dangerously ascendant in their judgment; against Calvinism, an antiquated and burdensome impediment to Christian suasion in the modern world, they believed; and against Catholicism. Reason would find an alliance with the revealed word of God in Scripture. If the latitude-men had a maxim, surely Simon Patrick provided it: "Nothing is true in divinity which is false in Philosophy, or the contrary."[60]

---

58. Samuel Eliot Morison, *Harvard College in the Seventeenth Century*, 2 vols. (Cambridge, Mass.: Harvard University Press, 1936), 2: 504–5.

59. On these larger trends, see G. R. Cragg, *From Puritanism to the Age of Reason: A Study of Religious Thought within the Church of England, 1660–1700* (Cambridge: Cambridge University Press, 1950) and Roland N. Stromberg, *Religious Liberalism in Eighteenth-Century England* (London: Oxford University Press, 1954).

60. Isabel Rivers, *Reason, Grace, and Sentiment: A Study of the Language of Religion and Ethics in England, 1660–1780, Volume I: Whichcote to Wesley* (Cambridge: Cambridge University Press, 1991), 25, 35, 44–45, 47, 63, 67–68 (the quotation, from Patrick's *A Brief Account of the New Sect of Latitude Men*, published in 1662).

Significantly, almost all of the Platonists, who became especially influential at Harvard, came from the Puritans' former basis of power, Emmanuel College at Cambridge. Benjamin Whichcote had entered there in 1626. Ralph Cudworth was fellow and tutor at Emmanuel and later a master at Christ's College. Henry More had a long career at Christ's, the exception to the Emmanuel affiliation of the group. Furthermore, the Platonists, almost all of them, came from Puritan backgrounds. They retained from that experience the moral earnestness of the Puritans. But they did reject Calvinism. More said that he could not "swallow down that hard doctrine concerning fate." Cudworth attributed to the doctrine of predestination a malevolent influence on religion in general. The Platonists wanted to define a new religiosity and a new moral philosophy. Harvard would welcome them.[61]

More, who had the greatest influence at Harvard, wished, with the other Platonists, to show the affinity of natural and revealed religion. Most importantly in this effort the group tried to demonstrate that individuals may receive the light of God directly, by an inner reason that illustrates the near relation of divine and human nature. Faith does not come to us as an imposition against our natural instincts, Platonists said, and neither does religion ask of belief anything that reason cannot immediately justify as right. The Cambridge thinkers constructed a kind of Christian humanism. They built on a Puritan faith that reason, when reinforced by grace, has a large authority. The later group rather naturalized the divine–human relationship. "They are greatly mistaken who in religion oppose points of reason and matters of faith," wrote Whichcote, "as if nature went one way and the author of nature the other."[62]

A closer look at the Platonists' understanding of reason helps us appreciate what a significant step their appearance at Harvard signified. In fact, they distinguished two kinds of reason. Reason first of all embraced a discipline of the mind that encouraged exact thinking. This reason put all dogma under scrutiny and demanded intellectual precision. In the spirit of the "latitude men" the Platonists hoped such a scrutiny would cut through the bitter and fruitless doctrinal warfare of their times. This kind of reason interacted with the world of experience and the evidence of the senses. But it therefore also had its limitations. It did not embrace all of knowledge. The Platonists thus upheld a reason properly labeled "the organ of the supersensuous." As a replica, albeit a less than perfect one, of the divine reason, this human faculty had access to spiritual truths. Later the American transcendentalists, building on Immanuel Kant and Thomas Carlyle, would distinguish the two mental faculties by the terms "Understanding" and a capital-R "Reason." For the Cambridge thinkers, then, reason provided an access to a higher truth and to a source by which the soul is inwardly enlightened. Henry More would call this reason "the very eye of the

61. Gerald R. Cragg, "Introduction," *The Cambridge Platonists*, ed. Gerald. R. Cragg (New York: Oxford University Press, 1968), 3, 8–10.
62. Cragg, "Introduction," 17–18.

soul."[63] Reading More's *Enchiridion Ethicum* at Harvard in the 1690s, a Ralph Waldo Emerson might have felt a quickening enthusiasm.

The Platonists did not mean to deliver religion into a vague, speculative passivity. More's famous work, the *Enchiridion Ethicum*, defined ethics as "the art of living both well and happily." Any Amesian would have found the words familiar. The religious life does not come automatically. The access to the divine comes through great moral striving, by an individual's efforts ("diligent application" in More's words) to gain holiness. More wrote that "the only safe entrance into divine knowledge" is "true holiness"; he added that "the oracle of God is not to be heard but in his Holy Temple, that is to say, in a good and holy man, thoroughly sanctified in spirit, soul and body." John Smith defined theology not as a divine science but a divine life. And Whichcote wrote, "*The state of religion*, lies, in short, in this; *a good mind, and a good life.* All else is *about* religion."[64] For a good mind and a good life the individual had the invaluable assistance of Scripture, where God's revealed word nurtures the inner reason and its access to divine truth. Hence also More's revealing statement: Men may preach Christ "though they do not name Christ in every sentence."[65]

Some Calvinists might have perceived how More's Platonic intervention at Harvard had a connection back to Ramus.[66] But other Calvinists did not welcome the idealistic tendencies of the Platonists. One complained to Whichcote that reason took the place of grace in their accounts of religion.[67] Perhaps, too, More's arrival at Harvard lay behind Increase Mather's complaint about a seeming classical takeover of Harvard ethics, though he did not make a big deal of it.[68] Mather, or any serious Christian, could appreciate what the Cambridge Platonists were trying to do. They wished to make as strong a case as they could against some serious intellectual challenges. Besides the religious ones cited, they had in mind above all the aggressive materialism of Thomas Hobbes, as promulgated in his monumental work of 1662, *The Leviathan*. Hobbes meant by morals nothing more or less than what suits our base appetites, so that ethics simply signifies the judgments of diverse individuals as they experience the world in their own ways.

---

63. Cragg, "Introduction," 18–19; Henry More, *Enchiridiom Ethicum*, in Cragg, *The Cambridge Platonists*, 265.

64. More, Smith, and Whichcote quoted by C. A. Patrides, "Introduction," *The Cambridge Platonists*, ed. C. A. Patrides (Cambridge, Mass.: Harvard University Press, 1970), 14; More, *Enchiridion Ethicum*, 265. More ranged widely through Greek philosophy in this work. He and the Cambridge thinkers owed much not only to Plato but to Plotinus and others. The *Enchiridion Ethicum* also references Aristotle on many occasions.

65. Fiering, *Moral Philosophy at Harvard*, 277n. In Theophilus Gale Harvard moral philosophy had another Platonic input. Gale authored his massive *The Court of the Gentiles* beginning in 1669, and this and others of his works had use at Harvard from 1690 to 1730, according to Fiering. Gale wrote that "there is no virtue natural, or truly moral, but what is supernatural." As predecessors to his own efforts to form a theory of ethics, Gale cited Wycliffe, Hus, Savanarola, Melancthon, and Ramus. He also showed considerable debt to Augustine (pp. 279–94).

66. Fiering, *Moral Philosophy at Harvard*, 250.

67. Patrides, "Introduction," 20–21.

68. Hall, *Increase Mather*, 284–85.

It is merely reactions to our ordinary lives, he believed. Hobbes sought no ante-
rior or transcendent source of authority for moral fact. His naturalism related
ethics to the affections and made moral science a species of behaviorism. Against
him More directed much of his writing. He postulated a "Boniform faculty" to
further secure moral truth in the human constitution itself.[69] In doing so, however, the Platonists in England helped wean intellectual New England from its
Calvinist origins. There resulted a milder and somewhat muted Christianity, one
with greater confidence in the human soul and one that bridged the great Reformation divide between God and humanity.

These developments shed light on the critical decade of the 1690s at Harvard. More's adoption by Harvard teachers signaled the college's opening to
the new liberal intellect emanating from England. Leverett and Brattle welcomed the spirit of the new Anglicanism, and it became the catalyst for Harvard's embrace of a liberal Congregationalism. Henry Newman, a graduate in
the class of 1687, recalled years later how the tutors "recommended to their
pupils the reading of Episcopal [i.e., Anglican] authors as the best books to
form our minds in religious matters and preserve us from those narrow principles that kept us at a distance from the Church of England." Newman also remembered Brattle expressing affection for the "order and beauty" of that
church. Newman, incidentally, went over to the Anglican Church, and he
testified that Brattle and Leverett influenced others at Harvard eventually to
do the same.[70]

The most popular voice of liberal Anglicanism was John Tillotson. That
colonists throughout America read his sermons indicates that Harvard both
reflected and advanced in the rational directions of the Enlightenment.
Tillotson, who died in 1694, gave religious writing an eloquent and appealing
flavor. The former archbishop of Canterbury wonderfully conveyed the latitudinarian spirit. He was thoroughly antidoctrinal when it came to religious
thought. For the laws of God, he said, require nothing "but what is recommended to us by our own reason, and from the benefit and advantage of doing it." None could do more disservice to religion, he believed, than to take
it off "the rational and solid basis upon which it stands." He said repeatedly
that revealed religion is underscored by natural. "Natural religion," he wrote,
"is the foundation of instituted and revealed religion; and all revealed religion
does suppose, and take for granted, the clear and undoubted principles and
precepts of natural religion, and builds upon them." Leverett and Brattle also
introduced Tillotson to Harvard, and even Increase Mather could not resist
Tillotson's appeal. He called Tillotson a "man of a clear head, and a sweet
temper" and "the best preacher of his age." Furthermore, Mather found in

---

69. Fiering, *Moral Philosophy at Harvard*, 256–57.

70. Morison, *Harvard in the Seventeenth Century*, 2: 505–6; Fiering, *Moral Philosophy at Harvard*,
236, 243; Norman Fiering, "The First American Enlightenment: Tillotson, Leverett, and Philosophical Anglicanism," *New England Quarterly* 54 (September 1981): 326.

Tillotson a sympathetic mind who assisted him in his diplomatic efforts for the colony.[71]

Finally, we take up some political matters that affected Harvard. In 1691 Mather had devised and secured from the colony a new charter for Harvard. It placed all authority in the hands of a corporation of ten individuals. It was to be self-perpetuating and subject to no intervention by visitors or overseers. Selected for the new corporation were leading ministers of Boston, Cambridge, and Charlestown. Brattle and Leverett also joined. Interestingly enough, this effort to seal the college from unsafe outside influence had not the liberals but the conservatives in mind. (The new charter gave the corporation the right to confer higher degrees, and they promptly approved them for Brattle and Leverett). To illustrate, major opposition to Mather came from Elisha Cooke, a Boston physician powerful in the political structure. He had opposed Mather's efforts on the colonial charter, saying that Mather conceded too much to royal authority. He would also accuse Mather of urging too much restraint in the matter of the witch trials at Salem two years later. The charter, however, made no provision for royal visitation, and in 1695 King William III rejected it.[72]

By the later years of the decade, Mather had come to worry about the direction of the college—the liberal direction. Following years of personal vexation and trial, Mather looked to Harvard as the last best hope for New England and its Puritan heritage. In 1697, he delivered an urgent "epistle" to the church and scholars at Cambridge. He spoke for the traditional worship practices of the colony's churches, with an eye to the Cambridge church where William Brattle, having left Harvard, had been ordained the previous year, and where he quickly introduced changes in the traditional service. Then Mather looked at Harvard, "that nursery for religion and learning, which for a long time has been the glory, not of Cambridge only, but of New England." The churches of the region, he said, could not subsist but with the ministers supplied by the college. But if the fountain became corrupt, what then of the streams that flow from it? What if Harvard, he asked, should become a "degenerate plant"? Speaking to Brattle and Leverett, Mather minced no words. "It was my recommendation," he reminded them, "that brought you into [your] station." He urged faithfulness to the charge.[73]

Two years later Mather really did have reason for concern. A group of individuals who had welcomed the new "catholic" religious spirit from England met and planned the establishment of a new church at Brattle Street. They had the backing of some prominent Boston merchants. This group had definite intentions

71. The first two quotations from Tillotson are supplied by Fiering in "The First American Enlightenment," 340, 344; on Mather and Tillotson, see Kenneth Ballard Murdock, *Increase Mather: The Foremost American Puritan* (Cambridge, Mass.: Harvard University Press, 1925), 236, 239; Rivers, *Reason, Grace, and Sentiment*, 67 (the longer Tillotson quotation).
72. Murdock, *Increase Mather*, 339–40, 346.
73. Morison, *Harvard in the Seventeenth Century*, 2:542–43.

to modernize. In November 1699 it issued its famous "Manifesto" outlining the innovations in the church and making explicit the new directions it intended to pursue. Thomas Brattle, brother of William, gave the land for the church. William Brattle and Leverett (who had recently left Harvard and become speaker of the House of Representatives in the General Court) were prime movers in the group, as was Ebenezer Pemberton, one of the new liberal tutors at Harvard. The leaders announced also their intention to appoint Benjamin Colman, Harvard M.A. in 1695, as the new minister. Harvard people were indeed fully involved in this new symbol of liberal Puritanism.[74]

The construction of this, Boston's fourth church, signified a changing city. It was the work of the city merchants, now come into an economic ascendancy and indeed a social acceptance. This group had earlier sided with the Antinomians. In these later years they embraced a different religious style—more moderate, more decorous, less demonstrative. As they emulated England in style and fashion, they also welcomed Anglican attributes in worship. They shunned the embarrassing personal testimonies of spiritual conversion. As Larzer Ziff has written of the merchants, "The church order they sought was one that, cleansed of the crudities of primitive Puritanism, would reflect the dignity of their stations and the politeness of their times."[75]

The Manifesto stated that the Brattle Street Church would accept any child for baptism. "Visible sanctity" would qualify an individual to partake of the Lord's Supper. This church, therefore, would no longer require one's testimony of regeneration as a condition of church membership. Instead, "sanctity" and "contribution" to the church (read financial support) would suffice for full standing in it. All members, including women, could elect the minister. The Manifesto also allowed the minister to read from Scripture without comment, an Anglican practice the Puritans considered "popish." Modernization, or liberalization, however, really went no further than these practices. The church intended to subscribe to the Westminster Confession and thus made no theological challenge to Calvinism as such. In Colman, however, Brattle Street located a man who had spent years in England, had admired English poets and the pulpit eloquence of church leaders there, and later acknowledged "the catholic air I had there breathed in." Colman, a Harvard graduate who had studied with Brattle, also had a great fondness for Tillotson, who rationalized and softened his Calvinism. Colman also preached a Puritanism wherein the social ethic and a moral life constituted not only the essence of the religious life, but also an ingredient in "the pleasure of life." Such an ethos also spoke meaningfully to the prominent merchant class of Boston. But none at the Brattle Church embraced Arminianism, and none had intentions of going over to Anglicanism. Nonetheless, the Brattle

---

74. Perry Miller, *The New England Mind: From Colony to Province* (Cambridge, Mass.: Harvard University Press, 1953), 241.
75. Larzer Ziff, *Puritanism in America: New Culture in a New World* (New York: Viking, 1973), 268–69.

Street people took no chances. They had Colman receive Presbyterian ordination in London before his return to the colony.[76]

Increase Mather had gotten wind of the Brattle Street designs before the November appearance of the Manifesto. In July he tried to have a religious test inserted in the new charter bill for Harvard; it passed both houses of the colonial legislature. The president also dropped the names of Brattle and Leverett from the proposed corporation planned for in that charter.[77] Cotton Mather saw in the Manifesto principles that "would utterly subvert our churches."[78] He and Increase, joined by other area ministers, protested the document. Although Samuel Willard of Boston's Third Church facilitated a temporary peace between the parties (both Mathers preached with Colman in January 1700), Cotton Mather went into print again. He issued his "Order of the Gospel," an effort to recall to all New Englanders the great charge that history had given to them. Mather's words showed that he understood, correctly, that the disputes of the day were very much a generational matter. Some of the new generation, he lamented, lacked the "principles, spirit, and grace of their fathers and grandfathers." Harvard College had much at stake in the disputes, he urged. It needed tutors who will "not hanker after new and loose ways." Although Mather cautioned against "a rigid severity" in the traditional examination for church membership, he considered it a "pernicious error" to abandon the old procedure.[79]

Mather's protest occurred amid a complex series of events by which Harvard tripped fitfully toward a new era in its history. Or so the politics made the situation appear. Intellectually, however, the process moved more certainly. Mather's scheme for a religious test met the royal governor's veto, as well it might, for its enactment would have prevented any Anglican from holding a college office. Then, when the king rejected the charter of 1691, Mather contemplated Harvard's having no charter at all and becoming a non-degree-granting institution immune from public control and protecting its own doctrines. Harvard would then become something like a theological seminary. Mather did not press this alternative publicly, though. He soon had yet another threat with which to contend.[80]

Several people wanted Mather out of the Harvard presidency. They included not just the former liberal tutors, Brattle and Leverett, but old enemies like Cooke. Now they saw their opportunity. The residency issue remained unsettled, and now Cooke pressed it. When the legislature did come up with a new charter

76. Everett Emerson, *Puritanism in America, 1620–1750* (Boston: Twayne Publishers, 1977), 143–44; Miller, *The New England Mind: From Colony to Province*, 241–42; Morison, *Harvard College in the Seventeenth Century*, 2:545; Hall, *Increase Mather*, 292–98; Fiering, "First American Enlightenment," 324–25.

77. Morison, *Harvard in the Seventeenth Century*, 2:544.

78. Levin, *Cotton Mather*, 290.

79. Murdock, *Increase Mather*, 359–62. Mather's "Order of the Gospel" brought a biting, ad hominem retort from the Brattle Street partisans.

80. Hall, *Increase Mather*, 302–3.

in 1699 it in effect required Harvard's president to reside at the college. Mather had occasionally expressed a desire to be relieved of the presidency, but he hung on. With greatest reluctance he removed to Cambridge, his congregation consenting, also with reluctance. But it did not work. Mather languished at Cambridge (he did, after all, long to be in London in preference even to Boston), and did not even see why he needed to be there. In June of 1701 Mather delivered a farewell sermon to the students and the next month returned to Boston for good. Then, by a count of eleven to ten, the council voted to replace Mather as president. The House followed suit.[81]

Fine and good Mather might have said. The council, however, acted in a manner that he found galling. It chose his friend Samuel Willard to succeed him. Willard, however, said that he too had no desire to relocate from Boston to Cambridge. So the council appointed no president and made Willard vice president, thus circumventing the residency requirement of the new charter. Mather was indignant. The next year he delivered what his biographer described as "the most pessimistic sermon Mather had preached since the days of King Philip's War."[82]

But Mather's personal reaction should not distract us from the larger picture. When the council selected Willard, they chose a man who very much reflected the changed Puritanism of his time. Willard endorsed a wholly cognitive faith. Revelation did not constitute for him a special kind of knowledge outside the domain of human reason. As he wrote: "Though God be to be seen by an eye of faith, yet he must be seen by an eye of reason too; for though faith sees things above reason, yet it sees nothing but in a way of reason."[83] More significantly, Willard preached a thoroughgoing legalism, as more of the New England ministry had begun to do. As David Hall describes: "For Willard the way to Christ was open to all men upon performance of conditions. His God was no secret, distant figure, but a God who was 'pleased to reveal himself to us' and tell men what their duties were." Willard thus lies in the tradition of Thomas Shepard. He stayed within the bounds of Calvinism (indeed he was to write A Compleat Set of Divinity, the only systematic treatise by an American Puritan), and though he said that "duties cannot work the saving change," he assured that the performance of duties brought the believer closer "to the blessing."[84]

Willard's term at Harvard constituted a holding pattern. He died in early fall of 1707, and the corporation acted within weeks to name his successor— John Leverett. The move confirmed Harvard's transition to its liberal era. The council would have to give its consent, and the interim allowed for a nasty exchange among the factions. Significantly, though, Leverett's cause gained support among thirty-nine area ministers who signed petitions for him. Half of

81. Murdock, Increase Mather, 348–52; Hall, Increase Mather, 303–5.

82. Michael G. Hall, The Last American Puritan: The Life of Increase Mather, 1639–1723 (Middletown, Conn.: Wesleyan University Press, 1988), 305–6.

83. Ernest Benson Lowrie, The Shape of the Puritan Mind: The Thought of Samuel Willard (New Haven, Conn.: Yale University Press, 1974), 42.

84. Hall, Faithful Shepherd, 258–59.

them had been educated at Harvard under Leverett's tutelage. His selection thus signified not merely a political shift; it summarized an era of intellectual evolution. The Mather forces, though, were not out of the picture, and Cotton especially spoke out against Leverett. The resourceful Governor Joseph Dudley, however, devised a clever means to pacify each faction. If the General Court (the council and the House) would grant Leverett a decent salary the governor would undo the royal charter and restore that of 1650. The House, which had rejected Leverett, could not resist its nostalgia for the old days and went along. It seemed like the old New England order had returned. In fact, though, a new one had arrived.[85]

This chapter, building on the first, has studied the dynamics of Puritanism. It has focused on those aspects of this remarkable movement that best help us understand the early history of the first college in what became the United States. Puritanism was never an intellectual monolith. The foundations laid by John Calvin produced a large and diverse religious literature. English Calvinists, in and outside the Church of England, contributed. New Englanders in the 1630s thus had carried to their new location different forms of Puritanism that became points of contention and partisan politics. No precise pattern explains this early history. Harvard College, though, seems to have a particular place within these dynamics.

We have seen that those who took the early lead in Harvard's beginnings and first years generally represented a group of Puritans that established their identities outside the religious establishment in England. They could not locate themselves within the Puritan Spiritual Brotherhood that had coexisted with the English Church for a good half-century. Nor could their covenant theology give them the confidence and assurance, even as the elect of God, that justification assured them full sanctification. This group continued to live with anxiety about the state of their souls and the fact that they had to conquer sin through righteous living. Their sanctification might have then provided some measure of assurance. They learned to view suspiciously others who celebrated their justification, their inward experiences that marked God's spiritual renewal, and who seemed to rest assured in it. They feared in them a dangerous subordination of the moral life and an opening to mystification, Anabaptism, Antinomianism.

Granted that this group, the Intellectual Founders, took the early lead in establishing Massachusetts, it nonetheless seems also natural that they should be the party that established Harvard and had the closest connections to it. Responsible as these Puritans were for establishing community, they looked beyond the churches for institutions of authority and public discipline. Its understanding

---

85. Samuel Elliot Morison, *Three Centuries of Harvard, 1636–1936* (Cambridge, Mass.: Harvard University, 1942), 53; Hall, *Increase Mather*, 321. Also, the charter change reduced the number of fellows on the corporation from fifteen to five, eliminating members who opposed Leverett.

of the covenant, with its focus on sanctification, certainly inclined this group toward a role in establishing a college for the Bay colony. What the colony needed, clearly, was public order and Christian benevolence. It needed a social ethic, not an individualist one. Furthermore, as they now occupied the positions of power (a significant reversal from its English history), the Founders became the more vigilant against such movements of individualism as they perceived in Anne Hutchinson and her spiritual father John Cotton. The theological debates that surrounded this conflict had clear social implications. The ultimate fate of Anne Hutchinson is a familiar part of New England history.

The early Puritan leaders of Massachusetts had already established an intellectual identity in England under the influence of William Ames. We are not surprised then to have observed how significant to Harvard in the seventeenth century were the writings of this important Puritan thinker. He gave the Calvinist–Ramist–Perkins continuum a lasting place in that college's curriculum. But we have observed also how other influences entered the school—those from the classical world and from contemporary England. One may understandably see in this influx a challenge to the Calvinist hegemony. Indeed, to some extent it was, and not a few Puritans themselves greatly worried about the consequences. But it might be wrong to emphasize a cultural clash here. Instead, against the background of Puritanism in England and America, we can better conclude that the classical program entered as a supplement and reinforcement of the Founders' program. For ethics and moral philosophy lent a humanistic and natural authority to the moral life. Ames might sustain the Founders' preoccupation with righteous conduct and obedience to the divine law, and he might seek to do so by rooting moral authority *sola scriptura*. But the later Puritans enlisted the aid of the Cambridge Platonists and Tillotson for the same moral ends. The alliance of the Christian and the pagan would not by any means constitute a staple compound. The later Harvard Puritans clearly laid the foundation for the more rational and humanistic Enlightenment now visible in the era of Leverett. Notwithstanding, we have in this very phenomenon a theme we may anticipate in later chapters—the tendency in the American colleges to blend and reconcile. From it will come an American product that we shall trace to our concluding look at the colleges in the era of the American Revolution.

3

Yale: Precarious Orthodoxy

Hopes for a college in Connecticut go back to as early as the 1640s. Thus, they arose in the beginning years of the colony's history. In 1638, the towns of Hartford, Windsor, and Wethersfield had adopted the Fundamental Orders of Connecticut. They established terms for election of a governor and the role of the freeholders, who must be "Trinitarian male householders," in choosing that officer. Also, two settlers had founded New Haven colony, annexed later by Connecticut in 1662. That same year, John Winthrop, Jr., son of Massachusetts Bay's first governor, secured a royal charter for the colony. In the decades following collegiate hopes remained indefinite. With the turn of events at Harvard, however, they took on a new urgency.

No sooner had Increase Mather left his presidency at Harvard than he was writing to ministers in Connecticut about establishing a new college. "We should be very glad to hear of flourishing schools and a college at Connecticut," he said, "and it would be some relief to us against the sorrow we have conceived for the decay of them in this province."[1] The Connecticut clergymen who met in 1701 to discuss the matter knew whereof Mather spoke. Nine of these ten were Harvard graduates. The group gained an additional cohesiveness by an extensive interconnection of marriage and blood. Collectively, they represented a powerful consortium of influence and prestige in the colony. James Pierpont, James Noyes, Abraham Pierson, Israel Chauncy, and Thomas Buckingham formed the active avant-garde of the group.[2]

---

1. Richard Warch, *School of the Prophets: Yale College, 1701–1740* (New Haven, Conn.: Yale University Press, 1973), 18–19.
2. Warch, *School of the Prophets*, 19; Brooks Mather Kelley, *Yale: A History* (New Haven, Conn.: Yale University Press, 1974), 8.

In a sense, these new Yale men were carrying on the earliest Harvard tradition, born of the Intellectual Founders and now carried over to Connecticut. Here, under the lengthened shadow of Thomas Hooker, Puritan orthodoxy, in ideas and polity, had remained well intact. It helped give Connecticut its conservative character.[3] What would become Yale University had its modest beginnings in the town of Saybrook as the Collegiate School of Connecticut. The legislative act of 1701, passed by the General Assembly, revealed the school's connection to the state. The act granted the founders £120 "country pay" per annum for the college. Both the General Assembly and the ministers agreed that the college would be a place where youth would be trained for service to both church and state. Nonetheless, the colonial government had no jurisdiction over the college, as it made no provision for overseers, as in Harvard's example. Yale would thus have closer ties with the churches than with the state, an arrangement reflective of traditional Reformation ideals respecting universities. Left to formulation by the Connecticut ministers, the school's charter expressed their "sincere regard and zeal for upholding and propagating of the Christian Protestant religion by a succession of learned and orthodox men." The word *orthodox* demonstrated how clearly Yale's beginnings sprang from ministerial aspirations, and fears.[4]

The school at Saybrook quickly established an academic pattern. In 1710 Samuel Johnson and eight other new students arrived there to begin their course of study. They arose at about five-thirty and walked to the college building to recite morning prayers, in Latin. After an hour of recitations the students had breakfast, to be followed by more classroom time throughout the morning. Lunch provided the major meal of the day. An hour and a half for recreation preceded an afternoon of recitations. A light meal at sundown and evening prayers completed the formal activities of the day. The young men then retired to their rooms for study until eleven o'clock.[5]

The ministers' resolve for orthodoxy at Yale had yielded a requirement in the curriculum that students study William Ames. Nothing more clearly illustrated Yale's identification with the Calvinism of Harvard's early Intellectual Founders. Johnson would later remark that Saybrook students were not allowed "to vary an ace in their thoughts from Dr. Ames' *Medulla Theolgiae* and some writings of [Johann] Wollebius."[6] In science, the curriculum remained locked in Aristotelian astronomy and its heliocentric view of the universe. But even Aristotle was not above reproach. Johnson's class notes state that "heathen Aristotle" might be faulted for not including an account of heavenly spirits in his physics.[7]

---

3. See David M. Roth, *Connecticut: A Bicentennial History* (New York: Norton, 1979), 1, 37–40.

4. Kelley, *Yale*, 5–7; Warch, *School of the Prophets*, 27, 30–31.

5. Joseph J. Ellis, *The New England Mind in Transition: Samuel Johnson of Connecticut, 1696–1772* (New Haven, Conn.: Yale University Press, 1973), 18.

6. Johann Wollebius (1586–1629), teacher, publisher, follower of Johann Heinrich Bullinger in the Reformed tradition, helped formulate the Covenant theology.

7. Warch, *School of the Prophets*, 38–39; Ellis, *Samuel Johnson*, 25, 26.

After much infighting, and a prolonged struggle that carried into the legislature, the Collegiate School relocated to New Haven, in 1718. The dispute over
this move produced a resisting faction that set up its own academic operation at
Wethersfield. Just at this time, the good offices, and careful arm-twisting, of Cotton Mather secured for the school a substantial gift of money. It came from Elihu
Yale, a wealthy Londoner who had acquired his fortune as governor of the
Madras colony in the East Indies. Mather, in a none too subtle way, suggested
that a bequest to Yale might secure a "perpetuation of your valuable name, as
would indeed be much better than an Egyptian pyramid." The governor's dona-
tion arrived in summer 1718, and in haste the trustees threw away the printed
program for commencement and produced another one. Gone was the "Collegiate School"; the new program read "Yale College."[8]

The Saybrook years of Yale's history might seem to record only intellectual
stagnation. However, an event of great moment occurred there. In 1714, a collection of books arrived at Saybrook, the gift of Jeremiah Dummer. The nine
boxes constituted only the first shipment of some eight hundred volumes that
Dummer had collected in London for the college. Dummer, a Harvard graduate
in the class of 1699, had served Connecticut and Massachusetts as an agent. He
worked actively for the Collegiate School in securing donations of books from
private sources, and he had been the first to suggest an approach to Elihu Yale.[9]

Virtually overnight, Yale entered the modern intellectual world. The Dummer collection contained writings of Robert Boyle, John Locke, Isaac Newton,
and Edmund Halley in science and of Walter Raleigh, Richard Steele, Chaucer,
and Milton in literature. It included the important works in medicine and philosophy, Francis Bacon among them, and major works in history. The collection
also included writings of the Cambridge Platonists—More, Cudworth, and Still-
ingfleet. As Richard Warch writes, "The collection was a rich one and contained
the best in English thought on every subject from theology and medicine to literature and travel."[10] The books moved over to New Haven when the school relocated. Soon all New England would see the startling upshot of the intellectual
ferment they created.

The careers of two individuals register the impact. Jonathan Edwards was a
Connecticut product. Born in East Windsor in 1703, he was the eleventh child
and only son of minister Timothy Edwards and Esther Stoddard Edwards. Timothy Edwards graduated from Harvard in 1694. Jonathan matriculated at the
Wethersfield campus, transferred to New Haven, and returned to Wethersfield
with other disgruntled students. He had his one full year at New Haven as a senior, but then stayed on as graduate student, finishing in 1722. He made good use
of the library for his early studies in philosophy and natural science.[11]

---

8. Warch, *School of the Prophets*, 84–85.
9. Kelley, *Yale*, 17; Warch, *School of the Prophets*, 60–69.
10. Kelley, *Yale*, 16–17; Warch, *School of the Prophets*, 66 (the quotation).
11. Wallace E. Anderson, "Biographical Background," in *Jonathan Edwards: Scientific and Philosophical Writings*, ed. Wallace E. Anderson, *Works of Jonathan Edwards*, John E. Smith, general editor
(New Haven, Conn.: Yale University Press, 1980), 6:3–11.

It remains a matter of uncertainty in Edwards scholarship as to when and to what extent he came under the influence of the Dummer collection. Biographer Perry Miller described in breathtaking manner the great illumination Edwards received from reading Locke and Newton. Instantly, Miller said, Edwards was delivered from an outmoded technologiae into the realm of modernity. Now his Calvinism could be fortified by the new science. Edwards would break into bold, new theological directions by incorporating Locke into a new account of religion as experiential, and all-transforming. Newton would supply Edwards with a God on whom all being depended, the all-inclusive principle of reality itself.[12] Edwards's intellectual genealogy has proved to be more complex and diverse than Miller allowed, but the Yale contribution certainly weighs heavily in shaping the foremost religious thinker of colonial America.[13]

Samuel Johnson also reflects the Dummer impact, and dramatically so for Yale's early history. He had come to Saybrook from Guilford. Grandfather William Johnson had moved there in 1653 and became a successful farmer and prominent citizen. His youngest son, William, married Mary Sage in 1694 and welcomed their son Samuel two years later. Samuel's intellectual bent emerged early; he had "an impatient curiosity to know everything that could be known." His grandfather read passages of Scripture to him and he mastered them by heart. He could read and write by age four and began to study Hebrew at five. Public school education and private tutoring prepared Samuel for Yale.[14]

After leaving Yale in 1713, Johnson taught in the grammar school at Guilford—an unexciting assignment for so heady a thinker as he. Johnson nonetheless supplemented his teaching with his own studies. He prepared a philosophical treatise—*Technologia Ceu Technometica*. It shows Johnson still in the "orthodox" mold of his undergraduate training. Opportunity came for Johnson with the arrival of the Dummer books. Johnson could now travel back and forth between Guilford and Saybrook, "his saddle bags filled with copies of Bacon's *Advancement of Learning*, Locke's *Essay on Human Understanding*, and Newton's *Principia*, and his mind filled with the profound speculations of Europe's most renowned thinkers."[15]

Johnson could not contain his enthusiasm. Soon he had enlisted area ministers in meetings to discuss the books. Daniel Brown journeyed from New Haven. Jared Eliot, Johnson's former grammar school teacher, came over from Killingworth. Samuel Whittelsey, from Wallingford, joined the group. So did

---

12. Perry Miller, *Jonathan Edwards* (n.p.: William Sloane Associates, 1949).
13. For a more technical discussion of Edwards and the Yale collection, see Anderson, "Biographical Background," 15–27. See also, Norman Fiering, *Jonathan Edwards's Moral Thought and Its British Context* (Chapel Hill: University of North Carolina Press, 1981), 28–33; an illustration of Edwards's merging of Newtonianism and Calvinism is Christopher Lukasik, "Feeling the Force of Certainty: The Divine Science, Newtonianism, and Jonathan Edwards's 'Sinners in the Hands of an Angry God,'" *New England Quarterly* 73 (2000): 222–45.
14. Ellis, *Samuel Johnson*, 1–6.
15. Ellis, *Samuel Johnson*, 30–34 (the quotation).

John Hart of East Guilford and James Wetmore of North Haven. More significantly, Timothy Cutler of Stratford heard of the meetings and joined in. Johnson's biographer, Joseph J. Ellis, writes of these events:

> Johnson and his scholarly allies were involved in an intellectual adventure. It was as
> if they had been placed in a time machine that carried them from the Middle Ages
> into modernity. All of the old authorities were in disrepute; the scholastic reference
> points learned at the Collegiate School were useless as guides. The methodological
> chart of Ramus now appeared to Johnson as "a curious cobweb of distributions and
> definitions."

Bacon now replaced Ramus and Ames. Newton replaced Aristotle. Lockean
epistemology supplanted the deductive method with the inductive. Johnson
would write later that the more he studied the New Learning the more he "found
himself . . . emerging out of the glimmer of twilight into the full sunshine of open
day."[16]

Something else occurred. The Yale books also contained important works
of Anglican divines: Isaac Barrows, William Chillingworth, Richard Hooker,
the Cambridge Platonists—More, Cudworth, and Stillkingfleet—and John
Tillotson among them. All but Hooker were confirmed Arminians. Furthermore, the Anglican literature contained arguments for episcopal government
and with it the convictions that the Anglican Church stood in closest proximity to the ancient church. This matter dogged the Connecticut readers. More
and more, as the argument for an apostolic succession in the Church of England
became persuasive to them, these ministers questioned their own ordination.
Johnson had become a tutor at Yale in 1716, joined in New Haven by Brown in
1718. Cutler became the college rector the next year.[17] Yale, unknown to any
but this inner circle, was harboring sedition.

Johnson and Cutler helped introduce the New Learning to Yale classrooms.
It took place on the campus without fanfare as Locke and Newton and others became integrated with the older Puritan curriculum, without immediately replac-
ing it. To be sure, rumors circulated outside the college about the presence of
"Arminian" books in the library. But the trustees saw no reason to take alarm. In
fact, when the Wethersfield students who had come down to New Haven
protested against Samuel Johnson's teaching and then left, the matter of the New
Learning did not enter the controversy. Just after Cutler arrived, Johnson resigned his position at Yale.[18]

The ordination issue smoldered, however. Cutler had privately decided for
Anglicanism. Born in Charlestown, Massachusetts, in 1684, he graduated from

---

16. Ellis, *Samuel Johnson*, 35–36.

17. John Frederick Woolverton, *Colonial Anglicanism in North America* (Detroit, Mich.: Wayne
State University Press, 1984), 175–76; Warch, *School of the Prophets*, 103–8.

18. Warch, *School of the Prophets*, 99; Ellis, *Samuel Johnson*, 47–49, 50–51.

Yale College

Harvard in the year of the Collegiate School's founding. In his early Stratford ministry he had led a group in defending the Puritan faith against Anglicanism. But the Yale books had changed his thinking.[19] Meanwhile, Johnson's sermons were becoming distinctly less Calvinist as he acquired a new admiration for the Cambridge Platonists whom he discovered in the Dummer collection. Also, his preoccupation with the ordination question led him into extensive reading in early church history and church government. In 1722, he believed God had settled the matter for him. He met one George Pigot, an envoy of the Society for the Propagation of the Gospel (the SPG), the Church of England's missionary outreach to the colonies, and he took up the subject with him in earnest. Throughout the summer Pigot met with the discussion group. Finally, Johnson and his six friends had decided that they must convert to Anglicanism, no matter the public wrath they would incur for their apostasy.[20]

The shocker came at the Yale commencement exercises on September 12, 1722. When Cutler concluded prayers, he pronounced the Anglican refrain, "and let all the people say amen." There followed the next day his and his associates' announcement that they had decided for Anglican ordination and would go to England to secure it. Yale historian Brooks Mather Kelley wrote in 1974:

> This was an earth-shaking pronouncement. No exact parallel can suggest the shock this statement must have given its auditors, but it was something like what might be expected if the current president and faculty of Yale . . . were all to announce suddenly that some had decided and others were close to deciding that Russian communism was superior to the American economic and political system.[21]

The apostates had brought Congregational and Presbyterian ordination into question. What did that say of the standing order of the New England Puritan ministry? And what did this turn of events say of Yale, hope of New England Orthodoxy? "How is the gold become dim!" exclaimed one of the trustees, "and the silk become dross, and the wine mixed with water!" And in only two decades since Yale had emerged to countervail the liberal trends at Harvard.[22]

Governor Gurdon Saltonstall did not try to dismiss the converts. He wanted a debate held on the matter before the colony legislature. Complaints registered everywhere, however. A pamphleteer implicated the Yale library, stocked with "Episcopal things," in influencing the sedition. And with good reason. Even Benjamin Colman in Boston admonished Dummer for sending so many Anglican books to Yale. At a Fast Day sermon, Increase Mather "much bewailed the Connecticut apostasy." Some Yale people turned to Cotton Mather and even offered him the rectorship of the college. Now it is time, they said, "that we must put on our armor and fight, or else let the good old cause, for which our fathers

19. Kelley, *Yale*, 29.
20. Ellis, *Samuel Johnson*, 55–77.
21. Kelley, *Yale*, 32.
22. Kelley, *Yale*, 32.

came into this land, sink and be deserted." The Mathers prepared to circularize all the Congregational clergymen of New England to awaken their vigilance. Ever ready with pen, Cotton denounced Cutler and the other "degenerate offspring" of the New England founders and bewailed their willingness to "assist the common enemy."[23] Withal, however, it should be noted, the Yale trustees took no action to remove the controversial books, although they did impose a mild loyalty oath on all college officers.[24]

The events of 1722 took place within a larger and more important context of colonial Connecticut. Indeed, they acquire a different meaning when understood against some significant changes in Connecticut society. Connecticut, of course, had emphatic Puritan beginnings. It envisioned an orderly and peaceful community in which both church and state would play contributing roles. That partnership gave Connecticut a hierarchy of authority extending down to the individual towns themselves and into their member families. "The total impact," writes historian Richard Bushman, "was immense, because each institution was an integral part of a monolithic whole." The system of reinforcing structures promised to preserve Connecticut in public order and moral law.[25] By the time of the events at Yale, however, this arrangement was clearly weakening. Social and economic changes fueled the disintegration, but so also did new attitudes on the part of the ministry. Yale could not exempt itself from the consequences.

Sheer growth explains part of the change. Connecticut towns had controlled their expansion by allocating land lots to new citizens, but by the end of the seventeenth century a speculative spirit had taken over in the sale of lands. New owners were less inclined to settle down as farmers and join in the civic life of the towns. Also, nonresident proprietors grew in number, so now the towns, which had often insisted on resident ownership, lost control as new purchasers bought cheap wilderness land, remote from the towns themselves. Some of the new inhabitants were tenants without the social standing brought by land ownership while new owners had economic power but no political rights in the town. Distance, too, now prohibited frequent and broadly representative town meetings. The Connecticut Assembly, to be sure, tried to resist the loosening effects of this transition, but clearly the social power of eighteenth-century communities had eroded. The cohesive interconnection of government, economics, and geography now less described Connecticut realities than once had been the case.[26]

Connecticut ministers often felt that the colony was losing its religious character and cohesiveness. Some feared the emerging of a commercial economy and the speculative spirit that seemed to accompany it. Troublesome signs of rising

---

23. Kenneth Silverman, *The Life and Times of Cotton Mather* (New York: Harper & Row, 1984), 368; Warch, *School of the Prophets*, 109–15; Kelley, *Yale*, 33.
24. Warch, *School of the Prophets*, 114.
25. Richard C. Bushman, *From Puritan to Yankee: Character and the Social Order in Connecticut, 1690–1765* (New York: Norton, 1967), 3–17. The quotation is on page 16.
26. Bushman, *From Puritan to Yankee*, 76–77, 82.

personal debt suggested a loosening of older habits of restraint. One minister, in 1721, wrote, "The [people's] concern is not as heretofore to accommodate themselves as to the worship of God and get an edifying minister; but where they can have most land, and be under best advantages to get money."[27]

Clearly, also, ministers saw a decline in their own authority and control, and found the source of it among a more leveling, or democratic spirit in the land. Rev. Eleazar Williams, in 1723, complained of men who "will endure no yoke of government and restraint, who are saying, *All men are of the same flesh and blood, and why should any exercise government over others?*"[28] These feelings also expressed an increasing alienation of the ministers from their own congregations. Puritan polity gave congregations primacy in church authority, and ministers came and served at the congregations' pleasure. In fact, the ministers had already taken some action in this concern. Seeking more independence and wider control, and with the support of Governor Saltonstall, they had established the Saybrook Platform in 1708. It organized the churches of each county into new consociations of ministers and lay delegates. These bodies could hear appeals in matters of discipline from the local churches. The ministers hereby acquired an enlarged authority. Connecticut had taken on a presbyterian-like polity. Not surprisingly, some congregations, and some ministers, too, perceived a break from orthodoxy and resisted the change.[29]

By the early eighteenth century, suspicions had deepened between clergy and people. The more sensitive among the latter watched for any sign of clerical consolidation and their vigilance led to accusations of an emerging church establishment—not a small matter in Connecticut. An election sermon in 1721 lamented that even suggestions of presbyterian polity induced protest. Complainers, said the sermonizer, accused the ministers of seeking "sole power of church government" and of desiring to "cut off the privilege of the brotherhood." Significantly, Cutler was one of the defensive clergy. He expressed his resentments in 1717: "We know the vile words that are cast about, of *priest-craft*, and priest-ridden, and an *ambitious* and *designing clergy*, and the like effusions of men's corrupt minds, and the jealousies the world has of us."[30]

These contentions directly affected the matter of ordination and thus led to the events of 1722 as well. Those ministers now trying to secure their independence and

---

27. Bushman, *From Puritan to Yankee*, 137.

28. T. H. Breen, *The Character of the Good Ruler: Puritan Political Ideas in New England, 1630–1730* (New York: Norton, 1970), 211.

29. Bushman, *From Puritan to Yankee*, 150–51; Ellis, *Samuel Johnson*, 12–13.

30. Bushman, *From Puritan to Yankee*, 155–56. The complaints did not register from Connecticut alone. In Massachusetts, Benjamin Colman spoke in 1708 of *The Piety and Duty of Rulers*. He insisted that "the ministerial work is not to be leveled with *mechanic* labors," nor any other activity that sought parity with its authority (Breen, *Character of the Good Ruler*, 210). The issues of lay and clerical authority had been fought to a stalemate earlier in the 1648 Cambridge Platform, which indicates a long-standing, sensitive issue respecting the New England Way. See Stephen Foster, *The Long Argument: English Puritanism and the Shaping of New England Culture, 1570–1700* (Chapel Hill: University of North Carolina Press, 1991), 170–72.

authority recognized that congregational policy still made them beholden to their flocks. Many found that subordination humbling or embarrassing. Few, to be sure, wanted to resort to the Anglican model—location of clerical authority through an apostolic succession. For Johnson, Cutler, and the other Yale defectors, however, just such a model had great appeal. At the least, it provided a way around the problem of clerical dependency on the congregation. Other ministers would struggle to find alternatives to both episcopacy and radical congregationalism.[31] At any rate, we should note that the problems that descended on Yale in 1722 did not come simply from an Anglican challenge to the Puritan heritage in Connecticut. They derived from an historical evolution and an internal dynamics within Puritanism itself.[32]

With the firing of the rector and tutors, Yale set its sights on an orthodox recovery. It selected Elisha Williams as the new rector. He had grown up in his father's parish in Hatfield, Massachusetts, and graduated from Harvard in 1711. He had practiced law and then teaching and had served in the General Assembly. Williams entered the ministry by becoming the first pastor of a new church in Wethersfield. There he secured a reputation for strict Calvinism, and at Yale he reinforced it. In Williams, Yale received a defender of the new ecclesiastical order in Connecticut (he would in fact have surpassed the new controls it established) and a polemicist for orthodoxy. He denounced all notions of works as means to salvation, saying "the best we can do in the matter of salvation should be accounted by us as menstruous rags." Speaking before the colonial legislature in 1728, he insisted that grace came from God as a free gift to the sinner, unearned.[33]

Yale stabilized under Williams's leadership. It gained in students, producing graduating classes of twenty-four in the mid-1730s. It received gifts of scientific equipment, and students could expand their intellectual horizons while they continued to hear sermons in the Calvinist vein. They also continued to deal with William Ames in the required curriculum. Entering students still faced the initial hurdle of the Latin and Greek examinations and the laws still required students to converse, in class and chambers, in the Roman tongue.[34]

The gains for Yale's intellectual life once again came from the outside. In 1733, philosopher and Anglican dean George Berkeley gave to Yale a magnificent collection of books. Berkeley had left Ireland on an intended trip to Bermuda where he hoped to begin a college. He met frustrations, however, and meantime had settled on a farm in Rhode Island. Johnson sought out Berkeley, and his new acquaintance with him and Jared Eliot aroused Berkeley's interest in

31. Bushman, *From Puritan to Yankee*, 173.
32. Ellis, *Samuel Johnson*, 80.
33. Elisha Williams, *Divine Grace Illustrious* (New London: n.p., 1728); Christopher Grasso, *A Speaking Aristocracy: Transforming Public Discourse in Eighteenth-Century Connecticut* (Chapel Hill: University of North Carolina Press, 1999), 165 (the quotation); Warch, *School of the Prophets*, 133, 165; see also the portrait of Williams in Francis Parson, *Six Men of Yale* (1939; Freeport, New York: Books for Libraries Press, 1971), 1–31, 41–42, 45.
34. Kelley, *Yale*, 37–45; Warch, *School of the Prophets*, 186–235.

Yale. Although Johnson had left Yale, he persuaded Berkeley to consider a gift to it. When Berkeley did so, he remarked that Yale had been producing an out-standing ministry, as noted by the fact that so many recent Yale graduates had "left the Presbyterian Church and come over to ours."[35] Johnson, in turn, even intimated to Berkeley that Yale had received Berkeley's immaterialist philosophy and "would soon become Episcopal."[36]

The Berkeley gift arrived at Yale in 1733. The trustees welcomed it en-thusiastically, the benefactors' hopes notwithstanding. The bequest, with its 880 volumes, instantly increased the library's holdings by half. Now Yale housed new Anglican theological books and an abundance of English litera-ture—works by Edmund Spenser, Shakespeare, Ben Jonson, Milton, Samuel Butler, John Dryden, and others. Yale had suddenly and greatly enriched its cultural environment and now possessed one of the finest collections of books in colonial America.[37]

The Berkeley collection signified something else. Yale had now made itself the repository not only of extensive collections in Anglican religious thought, but in English belles lettres, too. The accumulation represented a contribution not only to intellect but to taste. In provincial Connecticut, growing in com-merce and trade and making transatlantic connections, English ways, from reli-gion to culture and fashion, gained in appeal among a certain group in the colony. The phenomenon occurred elsewhere in America and would have its af-fects on higher education. In Connecticut, new Anglican churches appeared. Samuel Johnson, upon his return from England in 1723, had become the colony's only Anglican minister. Twenty years later Connecticut had twenty Anglican ministers and the Church of England could claim over two thousand communi-cants. And all of its ministers had graduated from Yale![38]

By the early eighteenth century one could see the walking emblems of what T. H. Breen describes as a New England "Court Party." Its members were the devotees of high culture and taste, and that preference almost always meant a fondness for things English. They saw themselves as a genteel presence in a rough, democratic society, cosmopolitans in provincial America. One could find the Court Party among the later Winthrops, the Dudleys, and the pompous Governor Saltonstall. They were less self-consciously Puritan than their parents had been and less inclined to see events in Connecticut in terms of an inherited Puritan history. Some moved toward a rational Christianity. Others idealized an

---

35. Kelley, *Yale*, 39.
36. Warch, *School of the Prophets*, 172–73. For more on Berkeley's immaterialism see the discussion in chapter 6.
37. Kelley, *Yale*, 38–40.
38. Warch, *School of the Prophets*, 124. Anglicans often displayed a contempt for New England Congregationalism. Caleb Heathcote, an Anglican layman, accused Connecticut of the "sin of schism." George Pigot used the term "inveterate schismatics" and said they lived in a "deluded coun-try." These Anglicans generally had a missionary resolve to transform a backward province by insti-tuting Anglican liberality (Woolverton, *Colonial Anglicanism*, 126–27).

education in enlightenment, broad and worldly, and conducive to gentlemanly habits. Thus Timothy Cutler could look to the liberal arts because they "civilize men and cultivate *good manners*." The lack of them, he said, induces "bestiality and rudeness, barbarity and fierceness, and all those ill and crooked dispositions that make society less pleasant and delightful."[39]

The Berkeley books' arrival at Yale raised more fears about Arminianism.[40] President Williams sought to neutralize that influence by acquiring some "Presbyterian books" from Isaac Watts in England.[41] Nonetheless, the Yale trustees made no effort to censure or control the collection. They clearly took pride in the college's intellectual expansion. One actually suspects that they even welcomed the new works for their contribution to the refinement of the colony and its gains in cultural maturity. This conclusion gains persuasion when we now turn to another development. In fact, Yale soon was feeling the challenge of a presence more threatening than the Anglican temptation. And again Yale would find itself in the midst of colonial politics.

In 1740, Yale College welcomed a new president. Thomas Clap was born in Scituate, Massachusetts, in 1703 and reared in an orthodox Puritan tradition that he never forsook. Grandfather Thomas Clap had emigrated to the new world in 1633 and settled his family in the small town. Stephen Clap, father of the future college president, served the colony in politics and the military. He and his wife Temperance trained their son early in religion, and Thomas had developed an introspective habit by the age of seven. As a student at Harvard he underwent a fuller conversion. But signs of salvation never gave him assurance. Harvard instructor Henry Flynt impressed on the collegian the human capacity for self-delusion and described a world that tempts even the most godly with all kinds of carnal attractions. Flynt could render his portraits of hell in a most graphic way besides.[42]

Clap launched a ministerial career at Windham, Connecticut, in 1725, a year before his formal ordination. In 1727 he married Mary Whiting. Clap's grim Calvinism was further educated in personal tragedy. The couple had six children, four of which did not survive their first year. Then Mary Clap died in 1736 at the age of twenty-three. A little later, after "lonely and melancholy mourning," Clap poured out his heart: "All the afflictions which I have ever met with in my whole

---

39. Breen, *Character of the Good Ruler*, 220–21, 208, 218 (the quotation).

40. And again from such an unlikely source as Benjamin Colman, who wrote several letters to inquire about them. He and some friends feared that conditions might attach to the reception of the books and compromise "the known and true intent of the honorable founders of your college" (Warch, *School of the Prophets*, 175).

41. Williams wrote to Watts, saying that "writers of the Arminian camp" had been filling up the Yale library, and adding that he "feared some unhappy influence on the minds of our youth" (Warch, *School of the Prophets*, 179).

42. Louis Leonard Tucker, *Puritan Protagonist: President Thomas Clap of Yale College* (Chapel Hill: University of North Carolina Press, 1962), 1–4, 16, 22.

life put together are small in comparison to this [loss]. My spirits have been sunk and my body emaciated by it."[43]

Personal sorrow, though, seems only to have committed Clap all the more to his work. His ministerial labors, as described in Tucker's excellent biography, anticipated in key ways the habits that would make Clap's Yale presidency so memorable. For instance, he gave unyielding attention to every detail of his work. He overlooked nothing in his daily administration of the job and nothing in the lives of his parishioners. He made pastoral visits systematically. He recorded points to be remembered from each visit, and after one tour had inscribed more than seven hundred names in his notebook. This zeal for scrutiny also signified a passion for discipline and order. Shortly after his arrival in Windham, Clap instituted a committee of deacons and laymen to find out and report to him any activity suggesting "public sin" or "scandalous evil." So involved did Clap become in the transactions of the cases that he became known as a "terror to evil doers."[44]

In another anticipatory event, Clap fought against the local Anglicans. When he learned of one couple in his parish who seemed sympathetic to the Church of England, Clap ordered the pair to appear before the parish. When they refused, he censured them. When the couple further enraged Clap by inviting two missionaries of the SPG into their home, he intervened to stop the meetings and eventually drove the dissenters out of town. Clap showed in this affair his overriding fear of disunity. Whatever his religious animosity toward the Anglican Church, he could not abide it as a refuge for malcontents seeking asylum from his authority. As we shall observe, Clap never tolerated a situation he could not control.[45]

This maxim certainly explains Clap's reaction to the first crisis of his new presidency. By the time he had arrived in New Haven to take leadership of the college, all hell had broken out in Connecticut. The events that describe what we have come to call the Great Awakening go back to about 1721 in this colony. We have reports of some demonstrable conversions in central and eastern Connecticut at that time. Clergy in general, however, continued to complain about the decline of piety here and throughout New England. Then there arrived the remarkable George Whitefield. He showed up in Newport, Rhode Island, in late summer 1740, a preacher but twenty-five years old. He had just completed an electrifying tour of the Southern and Middle Colonies. For the next six weeks his evangelizing held audiences spellbound and mesmerized. His travels took him to Boston, to Northampton, down the Connecticut Valley, and along the Long Island shore.

---

43. Tucker, *Clap*, 29–30, 35–38.
44. Tucker, *Clap*, 39–41.
45. Tucker, *Clap*, 42–43. Clap's rage for order also found him warring against any gains for Arminianism in his region. See Tucker's account of the Beck incident in *Clap*, 47–49. Clap upheld the Saybrook Platform and in the earlier controversies had lashed out against parishioners who bridled at ministerial authority, petulants who "take a pride in discovering some error and imperfection in their minister, because that seems to imply as if they were wiser and could see further than their teachers" (Bushman, *From Puritan to Yankee*, 156).

The Awakening had dramatic and unsettling effects that would persist for years to come. Jonathan Edwards remarked how all social classes seemed to be affected by the revival: "all orders and degrees, or all ages and characters; some that are wealthy, and of a fashionable, gay education; some great beaus and fine ladies." They cast off their worldly vanities, Edwards reported, and avowed a new humility.[46] One eyewitness gives this account of a mass of people flocking to attend Whitefield's visit to Middleton, Connecticut, on October 23.

> I saw before me a cloud of fog rising; I first thought it came from the great river, but as I came nearer the road, I heard a noise something like a low rumbling thunder and presently found it was the noise of horses' feet coming down the road and this cloud was a cloud of dust made by the horses' feet; it arose some rods into the air over the tops of hills and trees and when I came within twenty rods of the road, I could see men and horses slipping along in the cloud like shadows and as I drew nearer it seemed like a steady stream of horses and their riders, scarcely a horse more than his length behind another, all of a lather and foam with sweat, their breath rolling out of their nostrils every jump.

When some four thousand people have gathered, the slim and youthful Whitefield mounts the scaffold. With voice ringing clear to the perimeter of the crowd, he tells them of their frightful spiritual condition. He warns of the damnation that awaits them, unworthy as they are of any redemption. Their only hope is Jesus Christ.[47]

Much trouble lay ahead, however. Whitefield often spoke indiscreetly. He let it be known that he judged the generality of New England ministers unregenerate and not able to preach a truly spiritual religion. Facing such a situation, he inferred, church members should seek out other leaders or institute private religious meetings. In fact, separate churches now sprang up in Massachusetts and Connecticut. This urging received an even more emphatic call when Gilbert Tennent arrived in Connecticut. One of the most vitriolic of the Awakening's adherents, large and boorish in manner, Tennent urged unfulfilled churchgoers to crash parish boundaries to find new inspiration. Thus the line was being drawn between the "Old Light" ministers and the "New Light" revivalists.

The extreme New Lights had their own ideas for church polity. They wanted a return to strict congregationalism with authority returned to the visible saints, those church members who demonstrated their true regeneration. They attacked the religious consociations and all forms of presbyterian arrangements. Most New Lights wanted to undo the Saybrook Platform and replace it with the Cambridge Platform. In New Haven the issue of polity raged especially strong.[48]

To make the festering tensions yet more pressing, James Davenport, the "wild man" of the Awakening, entered the picture. Davenport, great-grandson of

---

46. Bushman, *From Puritan to Yankee*, 185.
47. Edmund S. Morgan, *The Gentle Puritan: A Life of Ezra Stiles, 1725–1795* (New York: Norton, 1962), 20–21.
48. Bushman, *From Puritan to Yankee*, 193–94, 206.

a New Haven resident himself and a graduate in Yale's class of 1732, took up preaching in Southold, Long Island. He became one of the many Whitefield aspirants. Thus inspired, Davenport set out on his own in 1741 to preach where it pleased him. He claimed the ability to detect who was in a state of grace and who was not. Those he judged unconverted he forbade to partake of the Lord's Supper. He lashed out at other ministers, calling them pharisees and wolves in sheep's clothing. They were leading their people into hell, he said. Davenport seemed intemperance itself, unrestrained in his invective. At one gathering, he and his followers collected wigs, cloaks, hoods, and jewelry—symbols of worldliness and fashion—and threw them into a heap to set them on fire. He reached his limits when he arrived at New Haven and denounced the Reverend Joseph Noyes, urging that his parishioners abandon their minister. Some of them did so and forced a division of the church's property.[49]

Neither Old Lights, nor Arminians, nor Anglicans could ignore the earth-shattering effects of the Awakening. In Connecticut, though, Old Light Congregationalists had the political power, at least for now, and they resolved to move against the insurgents. Isaac Stiles, father of the future Yale president, opposed the revival from the beginning. In fact, he made the first public attack on it in Connecticut. In his own parish in North Haven more than a dozen families had caught the spirit of the movement and constantly flocked to the Stiles home to urge his support of it. Stiles advocated moderation and warned against "extravagance." He himself, however, did not speak moderately. In 1743, he would warn that the late enthusiasm "loudly threatens a subversion to all peaceable order in a government" and inspires contempt against "authority both civil and ecclesiastical." He bade his fellow ministers stay their course, ignoring those New Lights "whose throat is an open sepulcher and their tongue an unruly evil, full of deadly poison, and set on fire of hell." He accused the New Lights of ignoring the institutional means of grace and "awhoring after their own lusts."[50] Thus did Old Light opinion rage against the rival party.

The Old Light/New Light dispute assumed the form of classic religious debate. Old Lights, of course, insisted on the imperative of grace, from God's initiative, in the winning of salvation. They also insisted, however, that the Spirit entered through the reason. Thus, study of Scripture opened the soul for God's outreach. Old Lights, too, it must be said, now favored moral conduct and personal order, as signs of a holy individual. They preached no covenant of works, but, at this point in the eighteenth century, stood clearly for social decorum and public order. They saw their own clerical role more in terms of edification than reproof. Emotional preaching now appeared to them unfashionable if not unsavory.[51] Many of these

---

49. Edwin Scott Gaustad, *The Great Awakening in New England* (New York: Harper and Brothers, 1957), 37-41; Bushman, *From Puritan to Yankee*, 192–93; Kelley, *Yale*, 53; Morgan, *Stiles*, 31–33.

50. Grasso, *Speaking Aristocracy*, 1; Morgan, *Stiles*, 40.

51. Bushman, *From Puritan to Yankee*, 201–2.

Old Lights, however, faced audiences impatient with learned sermons and yearn-
ing for excitements.

Old Lights led the counteraction to the Awakening. Leadership came first
from Stiles and then from Clap himself. The Yale president had at first welcomed
the revival. He granted the use of Yale Hall to the itinerants and entertained
Tennent when he first came to town. But Clap got a clearer picture of things
when the combustible Davenport unleashed his attack on Noyes. Clap organized
a meeting that yielded the "Guilford Resolves." They described a situation in
which emotionalism had won the day. The New Light ranters, Clap believed,
threatened religious learning. They would replace the current ministry with a
generation of mystics, and they would render Yale College of no account.[52] Clap
could point to Davenport and others as well. Ebenezer Pemberton, a New York
minister and Whitefield follower, also came to Yale to preach. Clap gave him use
of the college hall only to hear Pemberton quote I Corinthians 2:2 and go on to
denounce the value of learning to a man of true piety. Learning "puffs up the
mind," Pemberton said, and "raises the natural vanity."[53]

The next year the Connecticut Assembly joined in the raging controversy.
Dominated by Old Light sympathizers, it passed in 1742 "An Act for Regulating Abuses and Correcting Disorders in Ecclesiastical Affairs." Clap had his
hands in this business, too. The new law forbade a licensed preacher to enter
any parish not immediately under his charge. The penalty specified loss of all
clerical privileges, including salary.[54] Next the assembly decided it had seen
quite enough of Mr. Davenport and invoked the law against him. It placed Davenport under arrest, but even as his trial proceeded he preached to a crowd outside. Davenport would be deported from the colony, but the assembly expressed
more of pity than of anger. It wrote in its judgment: "Yet it further appears to
this assembly, that the said Davenport is under the influences of enthusiastical
impressions and impulses, and therefore disturbed in the rational faculties of his
mind, and therefore to be pitied and compassionated, and not to be treated as
otherwise he might be."[55]

If Clap gained some satisfaction from the expulsion of Davenport, he gained
little ease. Matters at Yale got progressively worse. Many of the Yale students
caught the revival fever. In the spirit of the New Lights they denounced any tutor they suspected of being unregenerate. Clap thought he could control the matter by barring all itinerants from the campus. He took this action after Gilbert
Tennent spoke there. But the students, having heard Tennent once, went ten
miles away to hear him again. They also raised money to secure publication of

---

52. Tucker, *Clap*, 124, 126–32.
53. Morgan, *Stiles*, 30. The biblical passage reads: "For I determined not to know anything among
you, save Jesus Christ, and him crucified."
54. *The Great Awakening: Documents on the Revival of Religion, 1740–1745*, ed. Richard L. Bushman (New York: Atheneum, 1970), 58–60.
55. *Great Awakening: Documents*, 46.

the sermon they heard from Pemberton in College Hall. These students now had less tolerance for their teachers than before. The board of trustees intervened. They passed a new regulation, and we get a good notion of the Yale situation by observing the language they used. The resolution forbade students from referring to the tutors as "hypocrites, carnal or unconverted men." Students defied the restrictions, however, and for a while Clap closed the campus, sending the students home.[56] Nor did the matter end there. In another instance of college and colonial connections, the Connecticut General Assembly investigated the campus. It decried the "rash judging" of teachers by the students and blamed outside agitators for provoking their indiscipline.[57]

Perhaps Clap was thinking he could calm the situation at Yale in 1741. He invited Jonathan Edwards to deliver the commencement address that year. Edwards, stationed in Northampton, Massachusetts, had witnessed the beginnings of the Awakening in New England and had emerged as its most respected champion. Edwards used the occasion of the Yale visit to make an important statement about the Awakening. He knew what criticisms he had to answer. Opponents of the revival derided it for generating more heat than light among its stricken participants. They questioned the authenticity of the many conversions and decried the rampant "enthusiasm" that now substituted for genuine spirituality. Edwards was prepared to concede some points to the critics. Yes, he said, revivals do often produce counterfeit conversions. The devil could mimic "both the ordinary and extraordinary influences of the Spirit," he warned. He hoped that the churches could find a means to distinguish between the true and the false. Edwards then catalogued the Awakening's dreadful excesses—tears, trembling, groans, uncivil behavior, outrageous accusations. Yet all these indiscretions, Edwards told the Yale audience, did not prove that the Awakening was *not* the work of God. Revivals were opportunities for Satan as well as for God, he said. Enthusiasts could be under the influence of both simultaneously. At the end of his talk, Edwards chastised the New Lights, warning against their spiritual pride. But by then he had gone virtually the full route to make the case for them.[58]

Thereafter, relations between Clap and Edwards worsened, coming to a severe breach in 1745. By then, it seems, Clap resolved to discredit the Awakening as much as he could and with it its main protagonist Whitefield. So Clap let it be known that Edwards had disclosed to him something Whitefield had told Edwards, to wit, that he intended to replace unconverted New England ministers, indeed "the generality" of all New England ministers, with ones from England, Scotland, and Ireland. Edwards went into a rage upon learning of Clap's announcement, and he went into print to refute it. He challenged Clap to produce witnesses. He accused

---

56. Norman Pettit, "Prelude to Mission: Brainerd's Expulsion from Yale," *New England Quarterly* 59 (1986): 33; Tucker, *Clap*, 122–24, 132–34.

57. *The Great Awakening and American Education: A Documentary History*, ed. Douglas Sloan (New York: Teachers College Press, 1973), 134–35.

58. Morgan, *Stiles*, 33–35.

him of rearranging and distorting the words in the letters Edwards had written him in a deliberate attempt at deception. Edwards also threatened to produce the original letters if Clap did not do so himself. He charged that Clap could have but one purpose in this evil-doing: "to render Mr. Whitefield the object of a general detestation and abhorrence through[out] the country."[59]

One other incident here deserves our attention. It concerns David Brainerd. Brainerd was born outside of Haddam, Connecticut, in 1718. A sensitive young man, he fretted considerably about his spiritual state, but finally satisfied himself of his rebirth in 1739. Later that year he entered Yale only to find himself lonely and weakened by study. He went home to Haddam. On his return to Yale the next year he heard George Whitefield preach, and he would not be the same person again. He then listened to the other itinerants—Tennent, Pemberton, Davenport. He recovered from his social isolation with a new enthusiasm and by the close company of like-minded New Light students at Yale.[60]

Jonathan Edwards, Brainerd's great admirer, provided the first account of the incident that made Brainerd notorious at Yale, but he did so selectively. The New Light students at Yale had found a common cause in their dislike for Rev. Noyes. Some continued also to denounce the tutors. With other students in the great hall one day, Brainerd was discussing the unmoving prayers of tutor Chauncey Whittelsey. Brainerd remarked that Whittelsey had "no more grace than a chair." The comment was spread beyond the campus and then reported to the president. Coming right after the trustees' new policy, the event gave Clap the opportunity to make a big point. He interrogated Brainerd and the students and then expelled Brainerd from the college. Clap was sending a message to all the New Lights.[61]

Clap did nothing halfway and more was to follow. He heard in 1744 of an impending second visit to New England by Whitefield. So he secured from the Yale faculty a resolution against him. This time he specifically accused Whitefield of undermining the standing churches and of attempting "to vilify and subvert our colleges." Yale people knew that Harvard had already denounced Whitefield, and they specifically endorsed that action. Anti-Awakening forces in New England were now beginning to regain the field. At Yale, New Light students felt discouraged and defeated.[62]

Clap secured another personal triumph at Yale with the creation of a new charter for the college in 1745. It gave the institution an unprecedented degree

---

59. *Jonathan Edwards: Letters and Personal Writings*, ed. George S. Claghorn, *Works of Jonathan Edwards*, John E. Smith, general editor (New Haven, Conn.: Yale University Press, 1998), 16: 153–71.

60. Norman Pettit, "Editor's Introduction," in *Jonathan Edwards, The Life of David Brainerd*, ed. Norman Pettit, *Works of Jonathan Edwards*, 7: 37–38; Pettit, "Brainerd's Expulsion," 34–36.

61. See Edwards, *Life of Brainerd*, 154–55, for a full account of the incident. Brainerd remained for Edwards a personal inspiration. He completed his short life as a missionary to the Indians. Above all, he demonstrated for Edwards a model of the New Light personality, by no means flawless, but a superb empirical example of a spiritual life. For all of Edwards's writings on Brainerd, see the volume of Edwards's works cited above.

62. *Great Awakening: Documentary History*, 142–49; Morgan, *Stiles*, 47.

of autonomy from the colonial legislature. The rector now became president, with genuine authority. Yale itself became an "incorporate society" with attending legal privileges. Also, Clap gave Yale a new set of laws. He had begun to work on this reconstruction immediately on his arrival at Yale. The new laws specified codes of conduct for the students, defined the powers of president and tutors (including the right to enter students' rooms after nine o'clock to ascertain that they were studying), and specified penalties for legal infractions.[63]

The new Yale laws reflected the zeal for organization and institutional control that describe Clap's administrative leadership. He was what we would call today a "hands on" leader. As Tucker noted, all the functions of the vast bureaucratic rivulets of the modern university were exercised by Clap—up close and personal. He was dean of students, dean of faculty, director of development, superintendent of buildings and grounds, and public relations officer. Above all, he was head librarian. He and a tutor systematically reorganized Yale's 2,500 books, numbering each one and placing them in order on the shelves. He then produced three catalogue guides for the library—one describing their order of arrangement, another an alphabetical listing by author, and the other a subject guide. He furthermore worked energetically to enhance the collections and the library grew significantly after 1743.[64]

And so did the college. In 1747 it had some 120 students. After 1753 it graduated more students than Harvard. In 1753 Clap dedicated Connecticut Hall, so named in recognition of the colony's continuing financial support. Clap designed the new building and watched its construction. The proud new edifice conveyed a happy picture of Yale's progress.[65] But things were not all right at Yale. They never were.

At Yale, the Anglican menace persisted. Anglican students attended the college, but Clap did not allow them to worship off campus at Anglican denominational services. In 1753 he announced yet another bold policy—that all students, including Anglican, would receive religious instruction, and worship, within the college itself. Clap's containment policy did not sit well with certain influential parents, and they demanded that Yale acknowledge a policy of religious freedom. Clap did not intend to. He had watched Anglicanism grow in Connecticut and in New Haven, much of that growth resulting from Congregationalists and others who recoiled from the Awakening. These transfers found a more reasonable and stable religiosity in the Church of England. Anglicans had now become the largest religious minority in the colony.[66]

---

63. *American Higher Education: A Documentary History*, ed. Richard Hofstadter and Wilson Smith, 2 Vols. (Chicago: University of Chicago Press, 1961): 149–61; Tucker, *Clap*, 73–74.
64. Tucker, *Clap*, 72–73, 70–71.
65. Tucker, *Clap*, 74–77; Kelley, *Yale*, 59–60.
66. Tucker, *Clap*, 176–77, 166–67.

The matter forced Clap into further retrenchment. He now defined Yale not as a college but as a "religious society." As such, it existed mainly to train young men for the ministry. In making a reply to his Anglican critics, Clap cited institutional histories of Oxford, Cambridge, and the Scottish universities. He showed how, in their location within the religious and political structures of authority in England and Scotland, they were essentially religious societies themselves. Clap's account amounted to a detailed legal brief, but it signified above all that Yale had no obligation to practice religious toleration.[67] Clap's rebuke left Anglicans furious. Samuel Johnson said he would pursue the case even to the point of challenging Yale's charter, of dubious legality, he said, because Yale's incorporation had not received the imprimatur of the Crown. With that threat pending, Clap backed down.[68]

In the meantime, Clap pulled off a surprise. Around 1750 he switched his allegiance from the Old Lights to the New Lights. Much could be said about the change. Some thought it blatant opportunism. The New Lights were gaining politically among the Connecticut populace. They now controlled the lower house of the legislature, although voters' deference kept the Old Lights in control of the upper house. Nonetheless, charges abounded of convenient "conversions" to the New Lights among the politicians.[69] Also, Clap seemed to fear that growing New Light popularity in the American colonies might hurt Yale. A new college had appeared in Princeton, New Jersey, in 1746, the first to give a welcome to the Awakening. Clap dared not allow the new school to raid the pool of New Light students in New England.[70]

Other explanations make Clap's switch appear more reasonable. For one, the Old Lights did seem to be moving toward theological liberalism. The incessant and intemperate charges against them by the New Lights seemed to make them welcome a more rational and moderate religion. Isaac Stiles was going that way. So also, apparently, was Joseph Noyes in New Haven. That shift troubled Clap. On one matter about Noyes all seemed to agree—he gave terribly boring sermons. One person called him the "dullest preacher of the generation." Yale students attending Noyes's sermons gained nothing, Clap believed. Noyes waffled on the central doctrines of Calvinism, and Clap suspected Arminianism. Noyes thus supplied Clap another reason to bring the students into the campus for church worship. Simultaneously, Clap established a new professorship of divinity for religious instruction on the campus and appointed Solomon Williams, a New Light, to the chair in 1752. (The arrangements did not work out and Naphtali Daggett occupied it in 1755. He later succeeded Clap in the presidency.)[71]

---

67. Thomas Clap, *The Religious Constitution of Colleges*. . . . (New London, Conn.: Green, 1754), 4; idem, *The Answer of the Friend in the West* (New Haven, Conn.: Parker, 1755), 8–11.
68. Tucker, *Clap*, 180–81.
69. Bushman, *From Puritan to Yankee*, 254–55.
70. Morgan, *Stiles*, 104.
71. Morgan, *Stiles*, 103; Bushman, *From Puritan to Yankee*, 241–42.

Ultimately, Clap's switch to the New Lights had logic and sense. The New Lights had been from the beginning the bearers and invigorators of New England Calvinism. That tradition was eroding, challenged by Anglicans and atrophying among many Old Lights. What Clap had earlier seen in the New Lights was disorder and institutional subversion. Clap could abide neither and increasingly sealed off Yale from the incursions of the Awakening. Now in the 1750s, however, the wild days of the revival had mostly passed. Davenport and Tennent had both repented their excesses. Furthermore, New Light thinking was expressing an intellectual maturity, soon to be summarized in the "New Divinity" movement as the leavening effects of Jonathan Edwards's theology gave a new theological vigor to Calvinism. Clap now had every reason to feel at home with the New Light party.[72]

Under this new allegiance, Clap again sought to consolidate his control. In 1753, he imposed a religious test on all Yale College officials—from trustees to tutors. It coincided with his bringing the Yale students onto the campus for religious services. All must now subscribe to the Westminster Assembly Catechism and the Saybrook Confession of Faith. This "orthodoxy act," as he called it, or the "Test Act," as his opponents called it, gave Clap powerful controls. He became a watchdog president more than ever. We should note, however, what he had achieved. He had turned the institutional rebellion of the New Light Calvinism back into the ecclesiastical order of Connecticut.[73]

By all appearances, Yale had succumbed to the order that Clap craved. But nothing could have been more deceiving. From 1756 on, student rebelliousness rattled the college. One could recite a dreary chronicle here; indeed the record would repeat throughout the colonial colleges and afterwards. Students showed no respect for the laws and displayed their contempt for their instructors, including the college president, with defamatory libels posted around the campus.[74] Now the Old Lights seized on Yale's plight to criticize Clap. Mocking his pretension to make Yale a religious society, they showed that less than half of Yale graduates became ministers, and 10 percent of them became Anglicans. More revealing, they raised their case against Clap to high political standards. In the emerging era of the American Revolution they employed Whiggish rhetoric against him. They likened him to a king or pope. They associated him with the hellish dark ages long gone. Clap might suit such an age, they said, "but as to us in this country, we are free-born, and have the keenest sense of liberty."[75]

The most vicious attack against Clap came from one Benjamin Gale. Gale identified with the Old Lights but expressed Enlightenment ideas about separation

72. Tucker, *Clap*, 211. For more on the theological impact of the Awakening, see Gaustad, *Great Awakening in New England*, chapter 8.
73. Kelley, *Yale*, 61; Tucker, *Clap*, 165–66.
74. Tucker, *Clap*, 232–62.
75. Tucker, *Clap*, 196, 199. Quoted here is Thomas Darling, who also happened to be Joseph Noyes's son-in-law.

of church and state. Described as a man of "volatile temperament and bulldog tenacity," Gale hated religious bigotry and any ecclesiastical extensions into the state. Clap signified to him the worst of these abuses. Gale and other Old Lights had begun their assault on Clap in 1755 by urging the colonial legislature to withdraw its annual payment to the college. In 1759, Gale called for a legislative investigation of the college, and after a setback that year, came back in 1761 to try again. This time the matter of student unrest spurred the petition. Finally, two years later, the assembly yielded to the urging, as it now became clear that opinion from all over the colony, much of it expressed by Yale graduates, wanted such a review. A dramatic scene presented itself at Hartford as two prestigious attorneys, brought on to press the case hard, laid forth the accusations against Clap. They were also two former students—Jared Ingersoll and William Samuel Johnson.[76]

Clap made his own defense and showed himself every bit the lawyer as his opponents. Now he himself employed the argument for separation of church and state, rehearsed Yale's history as an institution begun by the Connecticut ministry, and went on to plead eloquently for the autonomy of the college. However dubious the historical argumentation, Clap persuaded his audience. His plea anticipated Daniel Webster's later powerful brief for Dartmouth College in the famous case heard by John Marshall's Supreme Court in 1819. For now, Clap won the day. The assembly voted to reject the petition and spared Yale an investigation.[77]

Clap had won, but he had little to celebrate. By 1765, in a colonial America festering with revolutionary fever, students pressed more and more against him. In 1766, they signed a petition stating their "grievances" and presented it to the corporation. They also boycotted classes and stayed home in numbers after leaving the campus for vacation. Clap at last recognized his hopeless situation and offered to resign. He presided over his last commencement in September 1766.[78]

Finally, intellectual life at Yale took the form that Thomas Clap gave it. Clap wanted to preserve Yale's Calvinist identity. Under him, Yale would still shine as the school of the prophets. His code of allegiance had inscribed orthodoxy on Yale when he saw that orthodoxy was threatened from within and without. At the college Clap opposed religious liberalism. He warned that "Arminianism, Arianism,[79] and other errors approaching heresy have greatly prevailed in our nation and land and are likely more and more to prevail unless a proper stand be made

---

76. Tucker, *Clap*, 222–24. William Samuel Johnson was Samuel Johnson's son. For an informative discussion of this issue see Grasso, *Speaking Aristocracy*, chapter 3, "Legalism and Orthodoxy: Thomas Clap and the Transformation of Legal Culture." Ingersoll was a member of Noyes's church in New Haven.

77. Kelley, *Yale*, 68; Tucker, *Clap*, 226–29.

78. Kelley, *Yale*, 69–70.

79. A Christian heresy of the fourth century. Arius, a priest in Alexandria, taught that before he created the world God created a Son, the first creature. He was neither equal to nor coeternal with the Father.

against them."[80] Clap remained alert to any doctrines that proffered "an easy path to salvation." His own sermons to the Yale students reinforced Calvinism. A favorite one had the title "The Importance of Realizing Death and the Grave." Moral excellence was not enough for the Christian life, he urged. And against liberal fashion, he asserted that we should not construct too human a portrait of God. Clap effectively preserved old Puritan distinctions between divine and human nature.[81]

Clap's own efforts in moral philosophy instruction helped define Yale orthodoxy. In a pattern that would long prevail in the American colleges, Clap taught the senior classes in this subject. The year of his retirement he published a moral philosophy textbook. He wrote it for future use of Yale students, but we may assume that it incorporated his own teaching of the subject in previous years. At the very outset, Clap showed himself to be more orthodox than the orthodox. Liberal New England moralists had begun to separate ethics and theology, confident that God and reason would not be in conflict. Reason, then, could supplement Scripture. But in an age of ascending deism, Clap dared not permit reason this kind of independence. So he described his book, which had the title *An Essay on the Nature and Foundation of Moral Virtue*, as an effort to discern the roots of ethics, apart from a consideration of what constituted specific moral laws. Clap meant to fault any ethical systems that separated the subject from religion. Such systems that rely on man to find moral law "by his own powers" without any intermediate authority, Clap said, "have very much paved the way to deism."[82]

Clap then proceeded to define moral virtue as conformity to the moral perfection of God. He argued that God bestows on his creatures some part of his moral nature, the more so as we advance up the chain of being. Man, then, is blessed with powers of moral discernment. But Clap did not allow that conformity to moral behavior constituted a true ethical life. One could practice virtue merely out of self-interest or in quest of social honor, he said. In short, a "moral" life may derive from our most base instincts. In contrast to "external" conformity to good, Clap emphasized "internal" conformity. True morality can derive only from what lifts us from our fallen state, he urged. We have that source in Scripture, which discloses the great moral attributes of God—holiness, justice, goodness, truth. "Divine revelation," Clap wrote, "fully informs us that our highest duty and obligation is to be like God, and conformed to his moral perfection."[83]

Clap threw himself into prevailing discussions of moral philosophy. He took on Archibald Campbell, a Scottish professor of ecclesiastical history at St. Andrews,

---

80. Tucker, *Clap*, 151.
81. Tucker, *Clap*, 23, 151–54.
82. Thomas Clap, *An Essay on the Nature and Foundation of Moral Virtue; Being a Short Introduction to the Study of Ethics* (New Haven, Conn.: n.p., 1765), 1–2.
83. Clap, *Moral Virtue*, 2–4, 41–55; the quotation is on p. 53.

who in 1733 had published *An Inquiry into the Original of Moral Virtue*. Clap disliked Campbell's efforts to locate virtue "in the nature of things."[84] He also faulted the more important Scottish philosopher Francis Hutcheson (as indeed had Campbell) and his linking of morality with taste and sense.[85] In another section Clap criticized Samuel Clarke's theory of "the moral fitness of things," thus moving in against the British rational moralists.[86] Also, he examined William Wollaston's *Religion of Nature Delineated* and its notion of ethics as "conformity to truth," and showed its shortcomings.[87] Altogether, Clap, in a volley of rapid fire, made his case against various Enlightenment expressions of ethical theory and held to a religious foundation of ethics that even most of his predecessor Calvinists thought unnecessary. Yale, it seemed, meant to stand athwart the intellectual currents of the eighteenth century.

And yet, Yale College made remarkable intellectual gains under and because of Clap. The Yale president, for example, was far more tolerant and open-minded than he often appeared to be. In moral philosophy, for example, Clap himself introduced Wollaston to the Yale curriculum. However much he might fault it, he found in *The Religion of Nature Delineated* an excellent account of external virtue. Yale library collections grew in the Clap years, and the college accumulated more works of an Arminian persuasion. Clap, to be sure, had but a mixed record in Yale's eclecticism. At one point he prevented a gift to the college that contained works of Samuel Clarke. Clap held out despite pleas for greater academic freedom from Ezra Stiles.[88]

Clap did his best service for Yale in promoting science. He had a genuine interest in the subject and for its own sake. He did not look at science for illustrations of God's wondrous creation and in his own writings relied on naturalistic explanations without recourse to supernatural agency. Clap himself dabbled in various investigations—temperature charts, silk raising, and astronomical observations. In the very year before his death, Clap traveled to southwestern Connecticut, equipment in hand, to observe a meteor. His interests found him in correspondence with Benjamin Franklin on many different matters. He acquired new scientific instruments for the college whenever possible. Perhaps the connection to Franklin also explains Clap's interest in practical science. Yale students could also learn surveying and navigation.[89]

Clap, however selectively, opened Yale to new ideas because he believed he could contain them within the old intellectual structures. But he could not. Yale students took the corn, ate the kernels, and left the husks. Student Ezra Stiles supplies a case in point. He loved Yale just for the intellectual excitement of new

---

84. Clap, *Moral Virtue*, 13–14.
85. Clap, *Moral Virtue*, 22–25; James McCosh, *The Scottish Philosophy, Biographical, Expository, Critical, from Hutcheson to Hamilton* (New York: Robert Carter and Brothers, 1875), 89–90.
86. Clap, *Moral Virtue*, 29–33.
87. Clap, *Moral Virtue*, 33.
88. Tucker, *Clap*, 156–58.
89. Raymond Phineas Stearns, *Science in the British Colonies of North America* (Urbana: University of Illinois Press, 1970), 652–53; Tucker, *Clap*, 94–97, 109.

learning. He pursued all aspects of it eagerly but made no systematic arrangement of it. He became greatly influenced by the religious interpreters of Newton, so that his introduction to the new learning took him out of Calvinism but not into deism. He emerged a moderate Puritan, but above all a man at home in a world exploding with knowledge and inviting him to enjoy it for its intellectual delights. Through all his education into the new, Stiles had, and remembered, the friendship of President Clap. Later, when all Connecticut seemed to be ganging up on Clap, Stiles could not turn against his former teacher. When Clap died in 1767, Stiles wrote to Chauncey Whittelsey, "You and I knew him perfectly—he was a good friend to us. From 1742 to 1752 I found him my best friend though upon his political conversion his love waxed cool, yet I still honor the memory of my once Maecenas."[90]

More than any colonial college, Yale stood at the crossroads of intellectual contention in the eighteenth century. Established to secure Puritan orthodoxy it confronted Anglicanism on one side and the Awakening on the other. Both challenged the college from within and from without. Much bitterness marred the college's early history as Yale took up the challenges. These preoccupations may seem to have impeded Yale's intellectual progress; they did recurringly intervene to disrupt, distort, and politicize its academic life. On the other hand, one might be impressed by the gains that it made. Orthodox trustees accepted new books that brought new ideas. Thus, Berkeley's theistic immaterialism found its way into Yale as a Christian Platonism had done at Harvard late in the previous century. Some of the books changed students' lives, and not always in the manner these authorities would have wished. President Clap, an authoritarian president if ever there was one, saw to it that Yale students learned modern science and appreciated it for its own sake. For even as Yale sought to thwart the voices of opposition it stayed on a course that also sought to make it a place of intellectual reputation. Yale never welcomed the Enlightenment whole; but neither did Harvard. In its piecemeal accommodation to it, however, Yale assured that any student attending in the years we have studied could have experienced an exciting cross-fertilization of ideas.

---

90. Morgan, *Stiles*, 54–57, 108 (the quotation).

4

William and Mary: Beleaguered Anglicanism

Virginia was a land of great expectations, well before the English adventurers settled it. Virginia was a land of great disappointments, long after the English colonized it. The people who arrived at the James River in 1607, naming it for their king, represented other people's expectations for profit and glory. Before this date, and for decades after, an expansive descriptive literature about this part of the world fueled the great hopes of the investors and migrators who hoped this colony would pay off. Richard Hakluyt in 1582 offered his *Divers Voyages Touching the Discovery of America* and followed two years later with *A Discourse on Western Planting*. All the while Humphrey Gilbert, Sir Walter Raleigh, and John Hawkins excited English minds and enriched royal treasuries with their expeditions to the new world. Hakluyt made the case for English expansion persuasively. He presented to Queen Elizabeth the prospects of English bases in America, from which the royal navy could raid Spanish outposts in the Caribbean. He described new possibilities for lucrative trade with the Indians and of plantations growing tropical foods that would loosen England from its dependency on Asian trade. The Roanoke adventure failed in 1587, but before the arrival at Jamestown Thomas Hariot and John White had produced reports on the region. They studied the natives and outlined the commercial potential in English colonization.[1]

The early promotional literature suggests a commercial purpose in the founding of that colony and has served to mark off Virginia from the more intensely religious motivations of the later New Englanders. But religion also figured in the Virginia enterprise. King James used the occasion of the Virginia

---

1. Richard Beale Davis, *Intellectual Life in the Colonial South, 1585–1763*, 3 vols. (Knoxville: University of Tennessee Press, 1978), 1:4–7.

Company's charter in 1606 to celebrate England's new role in the "propagating of Christian religion to such people as yet live in darkness and miserable ignorance of the true knowledge and worship of God." Nor did Virginians lack a sense of providential significance about their new work. John Rolfe described the Virginians as "a peculiar people, marked and chosen by the finger of God, to possess [the land], for undoubtedly he is with us." In 1619 the House of Burgesses proclaimed that "men's affairs do little prosper where God's service is neglected." "For the men of 1600 to 1625," wrote Perry Miller, "the new land was redemption as well as it was also riches."[2]

The years ahead, however, signified only promises unfulfilled. Economic hard times bore so heavily on the colonists that when salvation seemed to arrive in the form of tobacco, they seized on it. They grew it relentlessly, exhausting the soil in the process. Every reformer tried to woo Virginians from their one-sided pursuit but planters acquired more and more land and acquired more and more slaves to sustain their commitment. As an abundant literature suggested, even into the next century, Virginia had not begun to realize the great commercial potential of her other natural riches. In 1705, Robert Beverley offered his account, *History and Present State of Virginia*, describing a land of lush beauty and material promise. His account ends, however, with a censure of his fellow Virginians, who had utterly failed, in his judgment, to reap its rewards. "The many fruits and grains are not cultivated for market. Nor are the many varieties of woods. There's no use made of them, either for profit or for refreshment," he wrote. Also, Beverley, like so many others from John Smith on down, spoke to the character of the Virginians. He found them to be a lazy and indulgent people. "I should be ashamed to publish the slothful indolence of my countrymen," he wrote, "but that I hope it will rouse them out of their lethargy and excite them to make the most of all those happy advantages which nature has given them."[3]

Nor did the religious promise of Virginia bear good fruit. The Church of England never thrived in the colony. Its clergy seemed to be men of dubious ability and even questionable moral character, but it could attract none better. Most served at the behest of powerful vestries dominated by the men of local wealth. The Anglican Church also lacked any effective organization. It had no bishop in the colonies so ordination required a voyage to England. Parishes spread widely over the expansive rural areas and deprived the churches of that organic closeness that prevailed in New England towns and villages. Virginia, in addition, had an unruly population. The "desperate young men"—indentured servants without family, small planters in debt, ex-convicts who had made their way from England, refugees from other colonies escaped to the southern frontier—did not fall easily under church discipline, or any other. Virginia had far more men than

---

2. Perry Miller, *Errand into the Wilderness* (1956; New York: Harper and Row, 1964), 98–101.
3. Robert Beverley, *History and Present State of Virginia* (1705; Indianapolis: Bobbs-Merrill, 1971), 170–71.

women in the seventeenth century, a prescription for illicit sex and births out of wedlock. All men in Virginia habitually carried guns.[4] We should not be surprised then at a ministerial report of 1662 that detailed the low estate of religion in Virginia and appealed to the bishop of London for remedy. Economically and spiritually, Virginia so failed its champions that they produced their own literature of lament, worthy even of the Puritan jeremiads of second-generation New England. Furthermore, as the colony approached the last decade of the seventeenth century, it did not even have a college.[5]

Dealing with so unruly a population made great demands on both church and state, which tried to impose on Virginia strong moral and legal restraints— a Puritanism without Calvinism and without the immense religious learning that flourished in New England. Moral offenses kept the local courts busy; they dealt constantly with couples who appeared with children born too soon after marriage, for example. They dealt with men habituated to drink, making one of them stand before a church door with a pot tied around his neck. Laws required attendance at church on Sundays, even for Saturday night's attendees of the tavern.[6] Furthermore, the Virginia assembly looked to general Sabbath observance as a boost to social discipline in the colony. Original laws on the matter proscribed any form of gaming on Sunday. The record indicates many years' enforcement of these codes. In 1679 one John Edwards and some friends faced a grand jury because they opted for a game of checkers on the Sabbath. The laws evolved to the point that by this time Sabbath violations included not only fishing, killing deer, and selling liquor, but also shucking corn, trimming shrubs, and fetching shoes from a cobbler.[7]

Such preoccupations did not mean that the prospect of a collegiate institution languished only as an afterthought in the minds of Virginians. The first notion came from England, however, and from no less than King James I. He outlined the possibilities of a college in a letter of 1617, written to his archbishops. He pursued the idea further in instructions to George Yeardley, who was returning to Virginia as governor. Here the king mentions "the building and planting of a college" for the training of Indian children and "the planting of a university"

4. Edmund S. Morgan, *American Slavery/American Freedom: The Ordeal of Colonial Virginia* (New York: Norton, 1975), 235–40.

5. Davis, *Intellectual Life in the Colonial South*, II:779. The Virginia clergy may have gotten unfair press. Distance imposed on them burdens of time greater than those faced by New England ministers; they did not show deference to the Virginia gentry, who may in turn have born anti-Scottish prejudices against the many clergy who came from Scotland; and they made even have described their own moral plight in such acute terms that it would encourage appointment of an Anglican bishop to the colonies to impose order upon the Church there. See James P. Walsh, "'Black-Coated Raskolls': Anti-Anglican Criticism in Colonial Virginia," *Virginia Magazine of History and Biography* 88 (1980): 22–33.

6. Morgan, *American Slavery/American Freedom*, 150–51.

7. Winton U. Solberg, *Redeem the Time: The Puritan Sabbath in Early America* (Cambridge, Mass.: Harvard University Press, 1977), 88, 101; Jon Butler, *Awash in a Sea of Faith: Christianizing the American People* (Cambridge, Mass.: Harvard University Press, 1990), 45–51.

at Henrico (fifty miles up river from Jamestown), to be supported by a ten thousand-acre grant as endowment. The next year fund-raising efforts began in England. Thereafter, we hear little of the idea. Through the years of the Commonwealth legislative records keep alive the hopes for a university, but clearly a stronger commitment and perhaps the dedication of a particular individual were now necessary.[8]

That next step brings us to the remarkable career of James Blair. Bombastic, confrontational, ruthless, shrewd, wily, and withal a devoted public servant, Blair would dominate the early history of Virginia's first college. He was Scottish by origin, born in the parish of Alva in Banffshire, "on the bleak northeast coast facing the sea," probably in 1655. His father, Robert Blair, ministered to the parish over a course of forty-three years. Young James learned the local ways, digging peat for fires and shearing sheep. He went off to Marischal College in Aberdeen University in 1667 and then attended the University of Edinburgh, earning an arts degree in 1673. He received ordination in the Church of Scotland and took up a ministry in the Presbytery of Dalkeith near the capital city. Blair had Episcopalian sympathies, but not Roman Catholic ones. Reacting against the efforts of James II to reinstate Catholicism, Blair refused to sign a test oath that would have effectively placed the Catholic king at the head of the Scottish church. The defiance cost Blair his parish post.[9]

Blair found his way to London, where he became an under clerk of the master of the rolls in the Fleet Street area. He found his life invigorated by the cosmopolitan city. He thrilled to its intellectual activities and its theater. The severe Puritanism of his Scottish upbringing melted as he found the milder Anglicanism more suited to his new tastes. He associated with major leaders in the English Church, including John Tillotson, who would be archbishop of Canterbury in 1691. More decisive were his connections with Henry Compton, bishop of London. Compton at the time was looking for clergy to serve the Church as missionaries to North America and the West Indies. Men were not exactly waiting in line to answer the call. Compton looked for a new supply among Protestant refugees who had fled Scotland and other parts and had come to England. In 1685 Blair responded to the call and enlisted for service in Virginia.[10]

Blair took on a ministry at Henrico Parish, now thriving with large tobacco plantations and imposing Georgian homes of powerful families in the colony. He made connections quickly and effectively and in less than two years purchased a hundred acres of farmland in the area. Also, he married well. He met the seventeen-year-old Sarah Harrison, daughter of Benjamin Harrison II of Wakefield in Surry County. Despite her present engagement to another

8. Davis, *Intellectual Life in the Colonial South*, 1:331–33.
9. Parke Rouse, Jr., *James Blair of Virginia* (Chapel Hill: University of North Carolina Press, 1971), 5–17.
10. Rouse, *James Blair*, 19–21.

James Blair

man, and despite the opposition of the father, the thirty-year-old Blair pursued her relentlessly and persuaded her to marry him. The union brought Blair into the social and political elite that ruled Virginia. This clergyman would thereupon use that connection to every advantage in the political domain of the colony.[11]

One other circumstance set the stage for Blair's role in founding a new college. In 1690, a young bachelor and military man, Francis Nicholson, arrived in Virginia as its new lieutenant governor. His instructions for the office are revealing. He was to punish "drunkenness and debauchery, swearing and blasphemy" and generally clean up the moral rot in the colony. He also brought with him a commission from the bishop of London naming James Blair as commissary of Virginia. As such, Blair was to represent the bishop in the colony, over which he had an informal jurisdiction. Colonial America never did have

---

11. Rouse, *James Blair*, 29–33.

an Anglican bishop, so the appointment made Blair the leading Anglican official in Virginia. And it gave Blair yet more power. He immediately put it to use
with a proclamation of his intention to impose a new moral regime on the
colony. His own list of moral offenses greatly extended Nicholson's and specified "all cursers, swearers and blasphemers, all whoremongers, fornicators and
adulterers, all drunkards, ranters, and profaners of the Lord's Day and condem-
ners of the sacraments, and . . . all other scandalous persons, whether of the
clergy or laity within this dominion and colony of Virginia." The mandate was
not well received, despite the fact that Blair tried mightily to get improved
salaries for the ministers. In any case, Blair's direct encounters with the religious
plight of the colony now helped clarify for him the need for a college to train
an American Anglican ministry.[12]

Nicholson called the colonial assembly to meet in April 1691, and among
other items it drafted an act to establish a college. Since the previous year a committee, appointed by the council, had been in place to secure subscriptions and
money for the college and make more specific proposals to the assembly. Meanwhile, the clergy, under Blair's leadership, composed an appeal for funds to the
merchants of London. Next the assembly appointed a joint committee to draw
up a petition to the king and queen, the recently seated William and Mary of Orange, for a college that would bear their names. Blair played a role in this effort
also and was chosen to make the appeal directly in England to the monarchs.
Nicholson gave full support to the project.[13]

So soon Blair found himself in England, supplicant for an unborn college.
He made many contacts, but when he confronted the attorney general for the
king and queen, and pleaded how the new school would help save the souls of
Virginians, he met the defiant reply, "Souls! damn your souls! make tobacco."[14]
It was not in Blair's nature to be deterred by such disdain of his efforts. Finally,
he found himself kneeling before the monarchs, humble petition in hand, and
receiving the full endorsement for the project by King William. The search for
benefactors then proceeded, and Blair proved himself resourceful beyond expectations. One case illustrates his skill. In 1688, Virginia officials had apprehended
three pirates in the James River and sent them to England for prosecution. Blair
seized on the occasion to extract a gift of £300, a quarter of their loot, to the college. With that agreement made, the pirates gained amnesty for themselves.[15]
Later it was a liquor tax that supported the college.

---

12. Samuel Clyde McCulloch, "James Blair's Plan to Reform the Clergy in Virginia," *William and
Mary Quarterly* 3rd Series, 4 (1947): 70–73; Rouse, *James Blair*, 37–42. The quotation is on p. 40.
13. Richard L. Morton, *Colonial Virginia, Volume 1: The Tidewater Period, 1607–1710* (Chapel
Hill: University of North Carolina Press, 1960), 337–39. For Blair's own interesting account of these
efforts, see *Historical Collections Relating to the American Colonial Church*, 5 vols., *Volume 1: Virginia*,
ed. William Stevens Perry, 3–29.
14. The Editor, "Early Presidents of William and Mary," *William and Mary College Quarterly Historical Papers* 1, no. 2 (October 1892): 64.
15. Rouse, *James Blair*, 68.

Blair's opportunism did not end with this novel event. It occurred to him that the new college would need a president. Where to find one? He conveyed his thoughts to Nicholson about so daunting a search for the office. The effort, he said, would require writing many letters and paying expenses for visitations. Blair hastened to add that having seen the project off to so good a start he felt more anxious than ever about seeing it through. Then he added:

> Though I never sought a place in my whole life time, I could find it in my heart to seek this, being well assured that though (if we could persuade them to go to Virginia) there are many men in England much fitter for it upon the account of learning, prudence, and authority, yet perhaps there is none to be found that has a greater zeal for the country, or is more concerned in point of honor to see this work prosper than I am.

Enough said. Blair not only received appointment as first president of the College of William and Many, he was named to serve "during his natural life." As such, he became America's first tenured professor.[16]

The charter for the college described the several purposes and uses by which the institution would benefit the colony: it would provide it with a seminary to supply ministers for its churches, educate youth in good letters and manners, educate Indians of North America and train them in the Christian gospel. The charter envisioned a "perpetual college of Divinity, Philosophy, Languages, and other good Arts and Sciences." It would have a president and six professors and about a hundred students.[17] In fact, it would take years before the colleges had these things, but it quickly had one item worthy of its boasting. On August 8, 1695, the governor, council, and trustees gathered at Middle Plantation and witnessed the laying of the cornerstone for the college building. The imposing structure, usually attributed to England's famed architect Christopher Wren, reached completion four years later. It dominated the sleepy town and could claim to be the largest structure in the colony.[18]

This arresting edifice figured in a remarkable event that occurred a few years later. Often in the history of American higher education we find efforts to locate a college in a major urban center or in a state capital. More often, though, we see deliberate efforts to avoid such locations. (Consider the sites of the "Big Ten" colleges of the Midwest; only one was placed in its state's most populous center.) In 1698, the capital town of Jamestown suffered a horrible fire that consumed the state house. Nicholson, now governor, seized on longstanding sentiments for relocating the capital away from its marshy locale, where a dearth of well-drained areas prevented more building. Blair again saw opportunity. He urged relocation

---

16. Rouse, *James Blair*, 75–76.
17. Henry Hartwell, James Blair, and Edward Chilton, *The Present State of Virginia, and the college*, ed. Hunter Dickinson Farish (1727; Charlottesville: University Press of Virginia, 1940), 72–73. This account, first written in 1697, contains an appended copy of the charter, pp. 72–94.
18. Rouse, *James Blair*, 91–93.

to Middle Plantation because, with the college, it was now "the chief of the towns." The dual location would thus give Virginia "one good town at once," said Blair. He threw into his plea a good measure of Virginia boosterism, too:

> There is one thing perhaps worthy of our consideration, that is, that by this method we have an opportunity not only of making a town, but such a town as may equal if not outdo Boston, New York, Philadelphia, Charleston, and Annapolis; and consequently such a town as may retrieve the reputation of our country, which has suffered by nothing so much as by neglecting a seat of trade, wealth, and learning, and running altogether into dispersed country plantations. If ever we would equal these our rivals, we must contrive to join our heads and purses together, and by companies and societies to improve our shipping and navigation, our trade and commerce, our minds and manners.

Hence the real value of such a "friendly cohabitation" as the joint location of college and capital.[19]

On a May Day program in 1699, councilors and burgesses gathered to hear orations by the students. Nicholson and Blair had planned well, for they meant to have the occasion demonstrate the college's suitableness as a neighbor for the capital. The speeches themselves had Blair's marks all over them. By the time the notables had heard them all, they could have given a dozen reasons why the relocation made sense. They even learned, if they had not already, how Middle Plantation might soon rival the big cities to the north. The burgesses probably did not need such urging and readily approved the renaming of Middle Plantation, now and forever to be "called and known by the name of the city of Williamsburg, in honor of our most gracious and glorious King William." The elaborate planning and reconstruction that followed produced a splendid showpiece of colonial America.[20]

When Blair pleaded for the capital relocation he spoke as college president, to be sure, but as a troubled Virginian, too. Two years before he and two others—Henry Hartwell and Edward Chilton—had contributed a significant piece to the colonial literature of Virginia, a work they titled *The Present State of Virginia, and the college.* It was not published until 1727, but it spoke to the realities of the day, and in a poignant way. This document reinforces the theme of promise unfulfilled in the several chronicles of the colony's history. Blair was primary author, and his writing reflected the views of the man just arrived as first president of the College of William and Mary.[21]

Blair and his coauthors began in familiar style with a chapter called "Of the Natural Advantages of the Country." They also followed in familiar judgment:

---

19. Glenn Patton, "The College of William and Mary, Williamsburg, and the Enlightenment," *Journal of the Society of Architectural Historians* 29, no. 1 (March 1970): 26–27.

20. Rouse, *Blair,* 118–23; Morton, *Colonial Virginia,* 2:356–60.

21. For more material on this document, see Robert A. Bain, "The Composition and Publication of *The Present State of Virginia, and the college,"* *Early American Literature* 6 (Spring 1971): 31–54.

"For the most general true character of Virginia is this, that as to all the natural advantages of a country, it is one of the best, but as to the improved ones, one of the worst of all the English plantations in America." Details followed—discussion of minerals, silks, potash, grain, fruits, flax, hemp, and cotton. The authors spoke of tobacco, and offered the standard lament: "Tobacco swallows up all other things, everything else is neglected, and all markets are often so glutted with bad tobacco, that it becomes a mere drug." The authors went on to portray a listless and unambitious population and then addressed their major recommendation for the economic woes of the colony. Virginia must have merchants and towns, they believed. Blair and company spoke as voices of Whig modernization. They looked for a moneyed economy fueled by the entrepreneurial skills of a commercial class driven by pecuniary ambition. New England supplied a good model, they believed.[22]

As college president now Blair might have been looking at New England for further modeling. In Harvard College he might have seen an institution neatly allied with a healthy ministry, learned and committed to education as the necessary support of its religious activities. When he looked at Anglican Virginia, however, he saw only further cause for regret. Blair felt genuine sympathy for his ministerial colleagues. *The Present State* fully addresses their plight—the poor incomes, the uncertainty of their tenure in office, their subordination to powerful vestries.[23] As commissary, though, Blair had to deal with immediate realities. He meant to be tough. He called for new penalties for "whatsoever minister shall be found guilty of fornication, adultery, blasphemy" and other offenses. One wonders, even with Blair's propensity for hyperbole, with what kind of people he had to deal. He wanted a test to see if a minister was drunk. He wanted sanctions for "staggering, reeling, vomiting, incoherent, impertinent, obscene or rude talking" or anything else that was "scandalous, indecent, and unbecoming the gravity of a minister."[24]

If Blair found it easy to lord it over the Virginia clergy, he showed no less shyness in handling its political leadership. Governor Edmund Andros was his first victim. Andros had earlier served the king in New York and the English army in the war against the Dutch. He became Virginia's governor in 1692 and established a record of efficiency and honesty. He clearly lacked democratic sympathies, however, and found himself often at odds with the colonial legislature. Soon he was seriously at odds with Blair. The commissary often allowed the most trivial of occasions to ruffle his feathers. Once aggrieved, he did not hesitate to petition the king for redress, as he did in 1694. Then he worked to secure the support of the clergy, who perceived an indifferent friend in the governor, and now moved against Andros with vengeance. Blair made the issue appear to be

---

22. Hartwell, Blair, Chilton, *Present State*, 3–4, 7 (the quotation), 9–16.
23. Hartwell, Blair, Chilton, *Present State*, 66–67.
24. Rouse, *James Blair*, 145–46.

one involving the friends of the college, on the one hand, and Andros and its enemies on the other. In *The Present State* Blair and his colleagues charged Andros
with financial ineptitude in providing for the college, which now "is in danger of
being ruined by the backwardness of the government."[25] He charged that the
governor gave appointments to enemies of the college and conspired against its
acquiring lands promised to it.

The case found its way to England, and when it all unraveled, with a rep-
rimand to Andros, the governor resigned, to be succeeded by Nicholson.
While other factors entered into this outcome, Blair's unrelenting assaults on
Andros certainly were decisive. He left nothing unsaid. The governor, Blair
urged, could not serve effectively because he was too old even to keep a tidy
house.[26]

One had every reason to think that Blair and Nicholson would get along
handsomely. They had cooperated in the difficult efforts to get the college established and Blair welcomed Nicholson as successor to Andros. But that relation, too, quickly turned sour. It would make a better story if we could hang the
estrangement of Blair and Nicholson on their differing political ideologies and
integrate William and Mary's history into it. To be sure, Blair had strong Whig
sympathies in his politics. He had endorsed John Locke's two *Treatises on Government*, published in 1685, and saw in Locke a British voice sympathetic to
colonial Virginia. The two had a nice epistolary friendship, and Locke provided
Blair a supportive voice on the Board of Trade.[27] Nicholson, however, had Tory
leanings, supported the extension of royal authority in the colony, and often
spoke contemptuously of the burgesses. For Blair, however, personalities usually
mattered more than ideologies. It took much less than a quarrel over ideas for
Blair to make an enemy.

As Nicholson's relation with the burgesses soured, Blair seized on the occasion to draw up two affidavits against the governor. Anything he could think of
to malign him he inscribed in the complaints. Blair addressed some serious issues
pertaining to Nicholson's manner of governing, and these complaints did have a
Whiggish edge to them. Nicholson, he also charged, had neglected the college's
well-being and it suffered badly under his governorship. In addition, he held the
governor up to ridicule in the manner of his recent and foolish-looking courtship
of a certain Lucy Burwell. Blair also threw in a charge that Nicholson had conspired to murder him. Blair made Nicholson look very bad indeed, given especially to irresponsible talk. "I have heard him often debase and vilify the gentlemen of the Council," Blair wrote, "using to them the opprobrious names of rogue,
rascal, cheat, dog, villain, and coward." Blair even excoriated the modest-living
bachelor governor for his choice in housing. "He lives in a very sorry house not
worth £10 or 12 a year. . . . [and] his furniture and attendance are miserably

25. Hartwell, Blair, Chilton, *Present State*, 71–72.
26. Morton, *Colonial Virginia*, 1:353–55.
27. Rouse, *Blair*, 110–11, 115–16.

mean."[28] Nicholson was recalled from Virginia in 1705, and Blair scratched another notch in his gun.

Blair soon acquired another connection, as minister of the new Bruton parish church in Williamsburg. The church, designed by Governor Alexander Spotswood and built between 1711 and 1715, became the religious center of the capital. The transept pews housed the councilors and members of the House of Burgesses. The governor's pews stood across from the pulpit. The college students had places reserved for them in the balcony. And now presiding over Bruton parish was James Blair.[29]

For all his powerful connections, however, Blair could do little for his college. It languished, undernourished financially and claiming low priority among the preoccupations of Virginians. Blair's political enemies placed him at fault for the unhappy situation. Rev. Hugh Jones, in his own contribution to Virginia's literature of self-examination, gave some attention to the college. Jones had allied himself with Spotswood who, in the early 1720s, stood increasingly athwart the college president. Jones, also serving as a master in the college, published his piece *The Present State of Virginia* in 1724. He described an institution in poor estate, a victim of political fighting, to be sure, but withal "a college without a chapel" and "a library without books." In fact, he said, William and Mary "scarcely merits the name of a college."[30]

Not until 1727 did Blair have the resources to begin hiring a regular faculty. It is instructive that he went to England to do so. There he worked with Anglican officials in his endeavor and hired three new professors for the school. Most important among them was Rev. William Dawson. He came from Cumberland County and at age fifteen had entered Queen's College of Oxford. Given the clerical reputation in the colony, Blair surely welcomed Dawson for his acknowledged, impeccable character. Dawson now became professor of moral philosophy, arriving in Williamsburg in 1729. He also became curate at Bruton parish, as college faculty usually augmented their salaries in some way. Dawson also attended condemned criminals (for which he would also ask for additional compensation), preached before the General Court, and served as chaplain in the House of Burgesses. Teaching and scholarship made only partial demands on the faculty at William and Mary.[31]

The Virginia college had a curriculum not unlike those of the New England colleges. Students had to acquire proficiency in Greek and Latin before admittance. They studied rhetoric, logic, and ethics, and could learn science in the post-Aristotelian mode. Books by Bacon, Locke, Newton, Harvey, and Boyle

---

28. Rouse, *Blair*, 156–57.
29. Patton, "College of William and Mary," 28.
30. Hugh Jones, *The Present State of Virginia. . .* , ed. Richard L. Morton (1724; Chapel Hill: University of North Carolina Press, 1956), 108–13.
31. Dan M. Hockman, "William Dawson: Master and Second President of the College of William and Mary," *Historical Magazine of the Protestant Episcopal Church* 52 (1983): 200–202.

gave access to modern ideas. The school, however, unlike its New England counterparts, did not support the established churches very effectively. Despite many
empty parishes in the colony, William and Mary did not attract students for the
ministry. Ordination in the Anglican Church still required a voyage to England
for that purpose, as the American colonies lacked a bishop for the rite. As matters stood in 1743, the college enrolled fewer than fifty students.[32]

Other factors also retarded the progress of William and Mary. Ostensibly, the
institution had an advantage that the New England colleges lacked. It spoke to,
and for, an Anglican Church in which a large consensus on intellectual matters
prevailed. It did not emerge from intellectual warfare, in England and America,
as did Harvard and Yale. Inheriting at the outset a mild rationalism that underscored its liberal theological tradition, Anglicanism did not produce those internal quarrels by which Puritans fought each other, and in turn Anglicans, in
defining their biblical religion. In Virginia, the Church, for all its many troubles,
faced no external challenge to its dogma. Nor did it have to resolve schismatic
tendencies that would rend it from within. And yet for those very reasons, perhaps, the College of William and Mary, school of the Anglicans, displayed none
of the intellectual dynamics, the disputations, even the spiritual anguish in
which New England higher education abounded. What it produced, instead, was
a record of personality clashes, bitter polemics, and ad hominem arguments ad
nauseam. The college inherited an identity and did not have to defend it. In Virginia, intellect did not mean politics, and politics meant personalities. Three of
its governors, deposed by William Blair, could so attest.[33] Virginia Anglicanism,
however, was soon to meet a formidable challenge.

Blair died in 1743. He had served a full half-century as William and Mary's first
and only president.[34] William Dawson succeeded him. Like Blair before he also
became commissary for Virginia. Although Dawson would hold a much shorter
term of office, dying in 1752, he quickly inherited a mountain of problems that
affected the Church of England directly and the college by implication. In the
late 1730s, new religious forces in Virginia were beginning to stir. They belonged
to the same movement of intensity and emotionalism that challenged Harvard
and Yale in New England. In Virginia, too, they would cut deep divisions in the
population and arouse the colonial leadership, in church and state, to staunch resistance.

In the South, the remarkable George Whitefield had won an immediate following. In his first tour, in 1739, he had even preached at Bruton Parish Church
in Williamsburg. His popular appeal fortified an already emerging "New Light"
party in the colony, and it soon produced a new leader of that group—Samuel

---

32. Rouse, *Blair*, 215–16, 224–25.
33. Alexander Spotswood in 1722 was the third.
34. Before we award any prizes for this tenure, we should note that in the nineteenth century
Eliphalet Nott of Union College served as president no less than sixty-two years!

Davies. He came from a Welsh family that moved to America in 1684. Morgan David (original family name) was a Baptist and settled in tolerant Pennsylvania. After their parents died, David and brother Shionn moved to Delaware and assumed the surname Davies. Samuel was born to David and his wife in 1723. Martha Davies became attracted to Presbyterianism, and Samuel followed her into the church. He studied at an academy started by Samuel Blair, a graduate of the much derided "log college" run by Gilbert and William Tennent.[35]

The New Light movement grew particularly strong in Hanover County. The established church had little appeal here and poor institutional representation. Itinerant preachers therefore attended to the believers. But their activities made them outlaws and here, as elsewhere, the government complained and interfered against them. The evangelical ministers, in turn, often used harsh language against the Anglican church personnel, "speaking pretty freely of the degeneracy of the ministry." One of their following even suggested that the bishop of London might be an "unconverted man."[36] Many of the New Lights now called themselves Presbyterians. Although Davies, when he arrived in Hanover County in 1747, observed and described a condition of spiritual neglect among the populace, he did not specifically attack the Church of England. He even made a favorable impression on the governor and preached in the county without further interference.[37]

Davies exemplified New Light preaching. Many commented on his beautiful voice, though he was often stern and judgmental. Although plagued by ill health, he knew his mission and pursued it with zeal. He consciously addressed the situation of his listeners, most of them frontier people, caught in the precariousness of that uncertain and always dangerous existence. He often spoke of death, knowing its imminence and his listeners' awareness of it. "I preach," he said, "as if I should ne'er preach again, and as a dying man to dying men." Davies wanted to save his people from spiritual death, "to save my country . . . to save souls," and in New Light fashion he looked to the inner spiritual state of his listeners.[38]

Anglicans would find a formidable opponent in Davies. He was not a ranter and he warned against mere "enthusiasm"; one could not be merely a "fiery, superficial" preacher, he said. Davies titled one of his major sermons "On the Danger of Lukewarmness in Religion." He described his ideal: "a popular preacher, of ready utterance, good delivery, solid judgment, free from enthusiastic freaks, and of ardent zeal." Davies did not encourage uninhibited bodily reactions to

---

35. George William Pilcher, *Samuel Davies: Apostle of Dissent in Colonial Virginia* (Knoxville: University of Tennessee Press, 1971), 1–4, 8–9. A greater background on American Presbyterianism follows in the next chapter.
36. Rhys Isaac, *The Transformation of Virginia, 1740–1790* (Chapel Hill: University of North Carolina Press, 1982), 148.
37. Pilcher, *Samuel Davies*, 63.
38. Pilcher, *Samuel Davies*, 65.

the experiencing of the holy spirit and under his leadership the Awakening in Virginia seems to have given less cause for complaint on that ground than in the New England of James Davenport. In a sermon Davies gave before his presbytery in 1752, he urged that the New Light ministry strike a balance between "the wild reveries of *enthusiasm*," which some in that party did display, and the "droning heaviness and serene stupidity" of some Old Light Presbyterians and Anglicans.[39]

In general, the established church party feared the awakeners and sought to control them. Rev. Patrick Henry, uncle of the famous revolutionary and the Anglican rector at St. Paul's Parish in Hanover County, appealed to the authorities at the capital. He expressed his outrage at the arrogance of the itinerants, especially at their claim that they could discern the conversion status of any minister simply by judging appearances. Dawson, as commissary, shared the concerns of the many Anglicans. He considered the Anglican Church as Christianity's sane middle way, "equally distant from superstition [often a word for Catholicism in Anglican parlance] on the one hand, and enthusiasm on the other."[40] Dawson also related the religious revival to old problems in Virginia. Writing to the bishop of London in 1750, he noted how Davies seemed to appeal mostly to poor people. The preacher held forth on working days, Blair said, and did much violence to the "religion of labor," whereby these individuals are obliged to be at work in support of themselves and their families. Were these trends not "seasonably prevented," wrote the commissary, the government would soon have a big problem on its hands.[41]

Politics and power may seem to have been ascendant in these disputes, but doctrinal issues mattered also. All supporters and detractors of the Awakening entered into one of the great intellectual issues of the eighteenth century. To the Anglicans, the new insurgents were usurpers, violators of colonial law, and, in the judgment of some, social radicals, too. But they were also wrong-headed. Rev. Henry, therefore, carefully outlined an ample list of theological errors in New Light preaching. Among them: that a sense of sinfulness so deep as to put one in despair is required for conversion; that one must be able to testify precisely as to the moment of his or her conversion; that by aid of the Holy Spirit within the convert, that person can tell who is a sincere Christian and who is merely a "formal" one, and hence a hypocrite; that a formal ordination is a call to service not by men but by God.[42]

In the 1750s, the College of William and Mary, too, entered into these disputations. William Stith had long wanted the presidency of the institution and

39. Pilcher, *Samuel Davies*, 59–62.

40. Joan R. Gunderson, *The Anglican Ministry in Virginia, 1723–1766: A Study of a Social Class* (New York: Garland Publishing, 1989), 187.

41. Leonard W. Labaree, "The Conservative Attitude toward the Great Awakening," *William and Mary Quarterly* 3rd Series, 1 (1944): 341.

42. Morton, *Colonial Virginia*, 2:588.

had fought brother-in-law Dawson for it on Blair's death in 1743. He could certainly claim to be one of the colony's leading intellectuals. He had attended the grammar school at William and Mary and studied at Oxford, receiving his master's degree in 1728. He then became master of the grammar school. Already he was known for his liberal religious views and his Whig political sentiments. The school assignment gave Stith little inspiration, however, and he resigned to take on the rectorship of Henrico Parish, serving there for sixteen years. Such was his prestige that he also served in the House of Burgesses. He made a significant contribution with the publication of his book of 1747, *The History of the First Discovery and Settlement of Virginia*. This narrative betrays the antiroyalist prejudices of its author, but it surpasses all previous histories of the colony, Richard Beale Davis says, by drawing on careful study of the primary sources. In 1752, Stith became president of the college.[43]

Through Stith, the College of William and Mary entered into the controversies of the day. Stith's own Anglican liberalism placed him clearly at odds with the New Light movement. He had held office but a year when he decided to make his own strong statement against the evangelicals. Furthermore, he used the occasion of an address before the Colonial Assembly of Virginia to do it. Stith titled his presentation "The Nature and Extent of Christ's Redemption." He clearly wanted to expose the distortions of the Christian faith in the hands of the New Lights, and it was their neo-Calvinism especially that became his object of attack. He would wipe from the gospel "the strain of cruelty and injustice, cast upon it by the rashness and violence" of the New Light preachers.[44] In making his case, Stith produced a remarkably liberal document. He spoke as president of the college (Stith, to his disappointment did not get the commissary assignment), and he placed the college emphatically on the side of rational Christianity.

In some interesting introductory remarks, Stith commented that while he was finishing preparing his thoughts for the colonial assembly he had consulted John Locke's book of 1695, *The Reasonableness of Christianity*. Locke put Christianity to the test of reason and found it not wanting. Even the ostensibly irrational elements of the Bible and the tenets of Christianity—the Fall, Christ's atonement, the divine inspiration of the Scriptures—Locke found acceptable. Stith noted how much Locke's ideas coincided with his own and took pleasure in finding so authoritative an endorsement. He added that although he had studied Locke considerably, he had not previously consulted this particular work. He did allow the possibility that years ago as a student at William and Mary he may have consulted Locke's apologetic; perhaps, he said, it had seared itself indelibly on his thinking.[45]

43. Davis, *Intellectual Life in the Colonial South*, 1:96–101.
44. William Stith, *The Nature and Extent of Christ's Redemption* (Williamsburg, Va.: n. p. 1753), A3.
45. Stith, *Christ's Redemption*, vii–viii.

Stith wanted to make his own contribution to rational Christianity. The condemning God of the New Lights and their impossible standards of salvation did not square with his own notion of the Christian faith and its essentially benevolent aspects. Stith made the centerpiece of his discussion the familiar passage of Mark 7:13–14: "Enter ye in at the strait gate: for wide *is* the gate, and broad *is* the way, that leadeth to destruction, and many there be which go in thereat: because strait *is* the gate, and narrow *is* the way, which leadeth into life, and few there be that find it." Such passages, said Stith, were seized upon by "fiery zealots," who, he said, "without mercy, or the least hesitation, condemn the bulk of their fellow-Christians to eternal perdition." Stith conceded that this passage would seem to confirm the severer of the Calvinist New Lights. He then went to great pains, however, to show that this message actually spoke to the Jews and reflected the prophetic perspective of the Old Testament, that is, that only a few would accept the Messiah upon his arrival and that most men would go the way of the world and not the path of true spirituality. Here, he said, Christ is actually urging his fellow Jews not to enter at the wider gate. Stith took up other passages, including the parable of the wedding in Matthew, which he described as another reference to the Jews' rejection of the Messiah.[46]

More important, though, Stith considered the question of salvation under a more rational standard. God would not condemn the mass of humanity to eternal death, he said, and certainly not those who had not been able to receive the gospel message. Will Socrates and Confucius live forever in hell? he asked. Christian understanding of this matter, Stith believed, must be a "dictate of natural equity" that a loving God would not allow himself to violate. Therein lay the larger intellectual significance of Stith's address. For he virtually equated Christianity with an ethical humanism. One could win salvation outside the parameters of the Christian gospel, he said, for all will be judged "according as they have acted up to the laws of Nature." In contrast to the restrictive terms of the Calvinists, Stith's standards anticipated the salvation of most of humanity.[47]

Even some of Stith's Anglican colleagues faulted him for a dangerously expansive reading of the gospels. But Stith did not embrace universalism, and he made Christ's mission central to the redemption of all the world. Furthermore, he precisely kept his reading within the boundaries of traditional Anglican thought. He insisted that those who received and accepted the gospel assumed a special burden. Much more will be expected of them (Luke 12:16), and this principle, too, he believed, falls under "right reason" and "the principles of common sense." Stith insisted that the matter of salvation is "no trifling affair." It requires a steady course of holy living, piety, and obedience to God. It must embrace deeds of "justice and charity to mankind, and a regular discharge of duty to our-

---

46. Stith, *Christ's Redemption*, 16.
47. Stith, *Christ's Redemption*, 25–26. For support of his views, Stith cited John 1:29: "Behold the lamb of God which taketh away the sin of the world."

selves and our families." In short, Stith upheld the moral life as the near sufficient grounds of salvation. And all may aspire to fulfill them. Stith wanted nothing of the uncertain standards of the Calvinists and the "despair" that results
from their elusive path to salvation. Neither did Stith look for the drama of internal renewal and spiritual rebirth, in the manner of the New Lights. Altogether, his message fell quite within the historic Arminian standards of Anglicanism.[48]

William and Mary produced a record of slow progress through the middle of the
eighteenth century. It could not support a full-time faculty committed to academic achievement, though some respectable scholars served it. Resources were
meager. The colony seemed but little inclined to nurture it or make it an institution symbolic of its aspirations and success. If its collective record seemed modest, however, its place in the life of at least one individual made it momentous.

Thomas Jefferson arrived in Williamsburg in 1760, a tall and lanky, even a
bit awkward sixteen-year-old. He came from the Virginia frontier where his father, recently deceased, had pioneered. Jefferson, though, was certainly a young
man of the aristocracy. He brought two horses with him to the college and rode
them daily. He bore the marks of the frontier also. He brought his fiddle, too.

Jefferson's education to date conformed to a prevailing pattern in the careers
of the Virginia gentry. They often made their first contacts with books in the expansive private libraries accumulated by their families. Peter Jefferson possessed
a modest library of his own. As Virginia and the South lacked the public schools
early established in New England, Jefferson, like others of his social standing, attended private academies, many of them run by the local Anglican ministers.
Such was the case with Jefferson's first teacher, the remarkable James Maury.[49]

Born in Dublin, Maury had moved to America with his father in 1719. He
spent some time at William and Mary before a return to London and then a second endeavor in America. He became rector of King William Parish and, about
ten miles from Jefferson's home, established a school that soon became the most
highly regarded in the colony. Jefferson's guardians selected it for him and paid
£120 annually for him to board there. Jefferson typically lived during the week
with the Maury family and then returned home to Shadwell to stay with his
mother.[50]

At Maury's school Jefferson immersed himself in Greek and Latin, for Maury
was an accomplished classicist, whose writing and speech reflected learning and

---

48. Stith, *Christ's Redemption*, 25, 30–31. On behalf of the New Lights, Samuel Davies prepared a
reply to Stith and drafted a brief titled *Charity and Truth United; Or, The Way of the Multitude Exposed: In Six Letters to the Rev. William Stith.* Whereas Stith died in 1755 as Davies prepared his reply,
he did not publish it.

49. Willard Sterne Randall, *Thomas Jefferson: A Life* (New York: HarperPerennial, 1993), 4–7.

50. Silvio A. Bedini, *Thomas Jefferson: Statesman of Science* (New York: Macmillan, 1990), 15–16,
21; Randall, *Jefferson*, 23.

force. Jefferson also had access to Maury's splendid personal library. Maury, how-ever, set himself apart from other schoolmasters and their programs in classical studies. For versed as he was, he did not want American education to remain locked in by so traditional an emphasis. Maury became an early and major theo-rist of American education. He urged that a restless new society would not have the patience to acquire mastery in ancient literature, nor would that realm of knowledge serve this society very well. The aristocratic youth of Virginia, Maury believed, would need a more practical education. For their future roles in politi-cal leadership, he specified study in English grammar and rhetoric, in geography and history. Even for their leisure hours, he argued, the new generation would have its greatest enjoyment in the literature of its own tongue. Jefferson all his life took an interest in education. As founder of the University of Virginia, in the years after his presidency, he drafted the most modern and practical curriculum of any American college. Maury early inspired Jefferson's reforming role.[51]

Secondly, Maury spoke out strongly on issues in religion. Here, too, he quite possibly became an early influence on Jefferson. Maury strongly defended a ra-tional Anglicanism and he became a major critic of the new revivalism. We have two of his sermons to this effect. In "The Flesh and the Spirit," Maury reflects the spirit of Tillotson and makes a sharp contrast between reason and passion, a standard contrast by which the Anglicans sought to check the excesses of "en-thusiasm" so marked, he believed, among the New Lights. Maury, though, could make the contrast with as much zeal and emotional fervor as his rivals. Also, in "The Character and Divinity of Christ," Maury takes major steps to render Christianity a natural religion, a move that shows him much in accord with the most liberal English rationalists of his time.[52]

At William and Mary Jefferson found a more formidable influence yet. For the rest of his life he would remember and acknowledge his professor, William Small. Small came from Scotland, born there in 1734, the son of a noted math-ematician. He attended Marischal College, studied medicine with John Gre-gory, then came to William and Mary in 1758. He took on his appointment to teach mathematics, but when another professor, too given to the bottle, had to quit his post, Small took on the teaching of moral philosophy. This subject em-braced ethics, rhetoric, and belles lettres. Small, but nine years Jefferson's sen-ior, became virtually Jefferson's sole teacher—his tutor, in essence. They be-came personally close, sharing many thoughts, visits together, and strolls in the vicinity of the college. The relationship lastingly benefited Jefferson, "fixed the destinies of my life," he would later write. He described Small as "a man pro-found in most of the useful branches of science, with a happy talent of commu-nication, correct and gentlemanly manners, and an enlarged and liberal mind." Furthermore, Small introduced the lecture system to William and Mary, indeed

51. Davis, *Intellectual Life in the Colonial South*, 1:382–83.
52. Davis, *Intellectual Life in the Colonial South*, 2:741–42.

William and Mary College

into American higher education. Breaking from classroom drills that honored only rote memorization of the subject, Small's methodology, carried from his training in Scotland, allowed for a large transmission of learning to the students. Jefferson could not have been more fortunate than to have found Small during his brief American stay.[53]

Beyond Jefferson's personal testimonies about Small, an interesting speculation points to his larger significance in Jefferson's intellectual career. Historian Garry Wills offered a bold thesis in his 1978 book *Inventing America: Jefferson's Declaration of Independence.* Against the traditional view that presents Jefferson as an American disciple of John Locke, Wills argued that Jefferson's thinking derived decisively from the Scottish Enlightenment. (This subject will receive more attention in the next chapter.) Francis Hutcheson and Thomas Reid among the Scottish savants earn most of the credit in Wills's interpretation. In the transmission of the Scottish philosophy to America, Small, in Wills's judgment, deserves much recognition. He believes that Small introduced Jefferson to the "moral sense" theory of the Scots. Jefferson, he maintains, seized on this notion, and it became central to his views on race. The Scottish philosophy also provided another intellectual framework for Jefferson's core arguments in the Declaration, described by Wills as, in essence, a "moral document." Wills explains that Small became the conduit of Hutcheson's moral sense philosophy, which posits a critical moral faculty in all human beings. Also John Gregory, Small's teacher, was the key figure of a "philosophical" circle in Aberdeen that helped establish this idea in Scottish thought. Through Small at William and Mary, Wills believed, that thinking influenced Jefferson.[54]

Small left William and Mary in 1764, returning to England, putatively for a rest. Probably, though, he had grown unhappy with the college. It lacked academic seriousness. Thomas Dawson, brother of William and president of the college from 1755 to 1761, drank to ineffectiveness and had to leave. Small's service to the college, however, had one more step to go, for in 1768 he sent to it some advanced and highly useful scientific equipment.

As for Jefferson, Small did him one other favor. He introduced him to his close friend George Wythe. With Wythe, Jefferson would remain in Williamsburg to study law. And through Wythe, Jefferson entered the social world of Virginia politics. He became well known among the political elite in the capital,

---

53. Bedini, *Thomas Jefferson: Statesman of Science*, 25–27.

54. Garry Wills, *Inventing America: Jefferson's Declaration of Independence* (Garden City, N.Y.: Doubleday, 1978), 177–80. Wills's book has not persuaded many scholars, but this is not the place to adjudicate its fine points. Jefferson clearly admired Small, but it is not easy to make Small an emphatic voice of the Scottish Enlightenment. There is no evidence that he partook of the Aberdeen philosophical circle (actually a literary society) so it is not clear how he absorbed the main tenets of the Scottish thinking. Gregory published his *Comparative View of the State and Faculties of Man with Those of the Animal World* in 1764, six years after Small left for America. See Ronald Hamowy, "Jefferson and the Scottish Enlightenment: A Critique of Garry Wills's *Inventing America: Jefferson's Declaration of Independence*," *William and Mary Quarterly* 3rd Series, 36 (1970): 337–68.

even before completion of his collegiate studies. He impressed people both with his intellect and his fiddle. Lieutenant Governor Francis Fauquier provided Jefferson his most valuable connection, and not just by virtue of his political office. Fauquier, a devotee of the high life, also loved science and literature. Versed in Addison, Swift, Bolingbroke, and Pope, he acquainted Jefferson with the modern literary world. At his table the younger man learned of news from England and the goings on in Europe. Fauquier's scientific interests had a special focus on weather patterns. He kept a daily record of temperatures, winds, and rainfall, as would Jefferson thereafter.[55]

What William and Mary gave to Jefferson, or at least confirmed in him, was a lasting love of knowledge and a relish for the pursuit of it. His curiosity knew no limits, as the vast record of his writings, even his private letters, attest. This kind of love marked the personality of a lifetime. One of Jefferson's college friends, John Page, recollected the ways of Jefferson and himself at the college: "I never thought . . . that I had made any great proficiency in any study, for I was too sociable, and fond of the conversation of my friends, to study as Mr. Jefferson did, who could tear himself away from his dearest friends, and fly to his studies."[56]

Nor did Jefferson's later political career deter him from these quiet and more endearing pursuits. "Science is my passion, politics my duty," he said.[57] So also, literature and languages. The inspiration instilled by Maury led Jefferson in later years to learn French and Italian, even Anglo-Saxon, source of much legal terminology so prominent in his profession.[58]

For Jefferson the reluctant politician, the life of the mind had its therapeutic effects. That he pursued it long after his William and Mary years tells us that it had an intrinsic value for him as well. Among the intimacies that Jefferson cherished, family, friends, and books ranked high. In 1788, he wrote to a friend: "I had rather be shut up in a very modest cottage, with my books, my family and a few old friends, dining on simple bacon, and letting the world roll on as it liked, than to occupy the most splendid post which any human power can give."[59]

Thomas Jefferson finished his undergraduate studies at William and Mary in 1762. The American colonies were about to take their first steps toward rebellion and independence. At the college, the years since Blair's death had compelled it to define its Anglican identity amid the challenges of the religious revival and its many sectarian voices. Its doing so did not produce a great literature. We have little more than Stith's contribution to see how the college upheld Anglican tradition against

---

55. Bedini, *Thomas Jefferson: Statesman of Science*, 28–29.
56. Bedini, *Thomas Jefferson: Statesman of Science*, 33. For a general discussion of Jefferson at William and Mary, see Dumas Malone, "Jefferson Goes to School in Williamsburg," *Virginia Quarterly Review* 33, no. 4 (Autumn 1957): 481–96.
57. Bedini, *Thomas Jefferson: Statesman of Science*, 1.
58. Bedini, *Thomas Jefferson: Statesman of Science*, 47–48.
59. Fawn Brodie, *Thomas Jefferson: An Intimate History* (New York: Bantam, 1974), 307.

the tide of radical Protestantism. That piece, however, usefully clarified for Virginia the colonywide kulturkampf that raged between partisans of the Awakening and of liberal religion. To that extent the college made its own contribution to the American Enlightenment. And it often did more. In a student such as Jefferson it prepared the way for secular rationalism and deism. But William and Mary remained the first American college of the Church of England. The American Revolution would put that identity to the test.

5

The College of New Jersey: The Dangerous Middle

The College of New Jersey, known since 1896 as Princeton University, began its life in 1746. Behind its debut lay years of controversy, intense and often bitter. Theological disputation flourished amid institutional schism and factionalism. Before this college could exist, American Presbyterians had to settle quarrels among themselves. They did not do so completely (and they never would), but the realization of an American Presbyterian identity laid the foundations for the colonies' fourth college. Princeton would find its first leaders among those who over two previous decades had helped to shape the denomination. It had many polemic encounters along the way and into the college's early future—encounters with doctrinal Calvinists, liturgical Anglicans, and champions of rational religion. Already on record were volumes of religious treatises and pamphlets, marks of an intellectual renaissance that ranged far and wide as it addressed the most important questions of theology and polity in the eighteenth century. In Princeton's early history, intellect was politics.

Scottish Presbyterianism bore the marks of religious warfare in the 1500s. It grew in opposition to Catholic parties in the land and would forge its own identity in later resistance to English imperialism. John Knox had sharpened his Calvinist mind during his exile years in Geneva and returned to Scotland to secure the nation for Protestantism. In the Scottish Kirk's *Book of Discipline* and in Knox's *Book of Common Order*, the Church gained its presbyterian arrangements. The Scottish Parliament also adopted Knox's Calvinist confession of faith, and that theological tradition received its ultimate confessional formulation in the Westminster Parliament of 1647. In England it would not outlive the English civil wars, but it remained the standard in Scotland and traveled with those Scots who migrated to Ulster province in Ireland. If any principle of unity defined the Scotch-Irish who moved to America in the eighteenth century, the Westminster Confession did so.[1]

Presbyterianism made its first organizational effort in the colonies with the establishment of a presbytery in Philadelphia in 1706. Churches in the area so multiplied thereafter that they could form the Synod of Philadelphia ten years later. Its ministerial leadership reflected various roots—New England, Wales, Scotland, and Ireland. While these churches formed a kind of urban cluster, the new American denomination would gain even more on the expanding colonial frontier. Here there flourished a simple Christianity, services sometimes held in barns and often without a pastor. In places there existed no institutional religion at all. On the frontier, many settlers fell into a hard-bitten, competitive life marked by concentration on narrow economic gain and even mere survival. Many drank heavily. Educational activities and formal social life took root very slowly. An imposing challenge lay in these conditions and it demanded more than ordinary church work. Arising to meet it came a new kind of ministry.[2]

William Tennent arrived in America in 1718. Born probably in northern Ireland in 1673, he graduated from the University of Edinburgh in 1693 and took Anglican orders in 1704, perhaps because the Irish Parliament had imposed severe penalties the previous year against Presbyterians and Catholics. Now, however, he renounced Anglicanism and Arminian theology. Tennent served churches in the Philadelphia area and began to introduce a revivalist style of preaching, which gained in appeal. More significantly, Tennent organized a small school to prepare a ministry for this kind of evangelicalism. Located near Philadelphia at Neshaminy, after 1735 it received all of Tennent's attention. Its critics labeled it "the log college." The historian of the American denomination calls its founding "the most important event in colonial Presbyterianism."[3]

Tennent's school embodied an academic tradition he brought from Scotland and Ireland, that of the dissenting academies. These schools existed outside the religious establishment and anticipated a commitment to popular education that would identify the Scottish effort later. In the American colonies, and in the Middle Atlantic especially, these schools appeared in fair number, and Tennent's was not the first.[4] But here at Neshaminy, he educated his three sons, and after a decade or so had produced some twenty-one new ministers. By this time, however, controversy had broken out among Presbyterians and the Log College now added to it. For Tennent was graduating ministers of a certain style and commitment, and they were changing the face of the denomination.

---

1. W. Sanford Reid, *Trumpeter of God: A Biography of John Knox* (New York: Scribner, 1974), 7–9.

2. Leonard Trinterud, *The Forming of an American Tradition: A Re-Examination of Colonial Presbyterianism* (Philadelphia: Westminster Press, 1949), 30, 34, 36.

3. Trinterud, *American Tradition*, 63.

4. For an extended discussion, see Douglas Sloan, *The Scottish Enlightenment and the American College Ideal* (New York: Teachers College Press, 1971), 36–72.

We earlier witnessed the emerging of presbyterian sympathies in New England, symbolized in Connecticut's Saybrook Platform of 1708. A New England group was now emerging among American Presbyterians. Although it adhered to Calvinist theology, it placed less faith in its formulation into creeds and confessions; that is, it mistrusted such formulations as forged by human reason. Among the Scotch-Irish leaders in the larger colonial denomination, however, sentiment grew for a tighter discipline in the synod. It seemed that the best route to that end was precisely a requirement of firm loyalty to the Westminster Confession among the ministers. Such a proposal came to the meeting in 1721. Records of that event do not exist, but a formal oath of sorts did become a requisite for the licensing of new ministers in the denomination. More significant, the issue provoked an important intellectual debate and set the stage for the factions that prepared the way for the College of New Jersey.

Reaction against the new procedure came at the very synod meeting that adopted it. Jonathan Dickinson emerged then as the major voice of that Presbyterian group that had roots in New England. Its activities in the denomination over the next two and a half decades placed that element in the prime leadership position for launching the school at Princeton. Dickinson came from the Connecticut River Valley, born at Hatfield, Massachusetts, in 1688. Hezekiah Dickinson, a merchant, and Abigail Blackman Dickinson had six children, of whom Jonathan was the second. Young Dickinson enrolled at Yale College the year after its opening, in 1702, and resided with the Reverend Abraham Pierson. He studied with Daniel Hooker, grandson of the noted Puritan thinker. Two years after graduating from Yale, Dickinson married Joanna Melyen, and took up his pastorate in Elizabeth Town (today Elizabethtown), New Jersey. The couple lost their first child a month after birth, but seven who followed all survived infancy.[5]

As the issue of loyalty oaths to the Westminster Confession emerged, Dickinson stood forth as a strong opponent of subscription. It made a dangerous shift, he believed, in the standards for the ministry. These standards should derive from the Scriptures themselves, he said, and not from any secondhand formulation of them. "The only rule and standard of a minister's work," he told the synod, "that by which he may be perfect, fully acquainted with the work of God, and directed into the discharge of his office . . . is the sacred Scriptures."[6] Furthermore, he warned, subscription misdefined the nature of the ministerial calling. It established a protocol by which a human government determines the calling of those who will preach God's word. But Dickinson urged that ministers "have their commission not of man, nor by men, but from Jesus Christ."[7] Nonetheless, the General Assembly imposed subscription in 1729.

---

5. Bryan F. Le Beau, *Jonathan Dickinson and the Formative Years of American Presbyterianism* (Lexington: University Press of Kentucky, 1997), 13–16.

6. Jonathan Dickinson, *A Sermon Preached at the Opening of the Synod. . . .* (Boston: T. Fleet, 1723), 3.

7. Dickinson, *A Sermon*, 4.

Jonathan Dickinson

This situation laid the groundwork for a significant ethnic division among the Middle Atlantic Presbyterians. Dickinson's sermon established his leadership among the New England-rooted Presbyterians, who now perceived in the subscription ruling an effort by the Scotch-Irish Presbyterians to keep the denomination in their control. The Scotch-Irish bore resentments of their own. They had received but a chilly reception among their fellow Calvinists in New England when they had attempted to settle there earlier. Nor did the Scots and Scotch-Irish have to go far back in their history to invoke memories of bad treatment by the English, memories that colored their feelings toward the "new" Englanders. These mutual animosities would continue. In 1738, angry townspeople in Worcester, Massachusetts, burned down the Presbyterian church.[8]

---

8. Trinterud, *American Tradition*, 48. Cotton Mather, on seeing the Scotch-Irish arrivals in New England, had once referred to an invasion of "Satan and his sons" in his domain. See also Leigh Eric Schmidt, "Jonathan Dickinson and the Making of the Moderate Awakening," *Journal of Presbyterian History* 63 (Winter 1985): 341–53.

While the Scotch-Irish party thus pursued an intellectual purity for Presbyterianism, the ground was moving beneath its feet. Now the Log College men, too, were getting active. Areas without ministers provided them an opportunity to deliver their messages. They received invitations from local congregations but did not bother to seek permission from the presbytery within whose bounds they preached. Such was the case with Gilbert Tennent, son of William. He preached at Maidenhead, New Jersey, in 1737, but within the year the Presbytery of Philadelphia reacted by prohibiting any minister from preaching in its jurisdiction without its permission. Tennent reacted by preaching again at Maidenhead, again without permission.[9]

Several ingredients fueled the religious revival that was now under way. Early in the previous decade Theodorus Frelinghuysen had arrived from Holland to stir Dutch congregations in the Raritan Valley. The New England contingent also contributed. Aaron Burr (father of the better-known future vice president of the United States), inspired by Jonathan Edwards in Connecticut, brought the awakening to Newark in August 1739. Then in November that year George Whitefield arrived in Philadelphia. He preached at the Anglican church (to which denomination he formally belonged) and from the city's courthouse steps. Huge crowds gathered to hear him. Whitefield met William Tennent during his protracted stay in the city and then proceeded into the areas where the Log College men and the New England group had gained footholds. Indeed, he called these groups "the burning and shining light of this part of America." Whitefield also dined with Jonathan Dickinson and accepted his invitation to preach at his pulpit in Elizabeth Town. Along the points of his tour, thousands thrilled to the preaching of the twenty-four-year-old phenomenon. Benjamin Franklin was also duly impressed.[10]

In the meantime, the revivalist group had acquired organizations of its own by establishing the Presbyteries of New Brunswick and New York in 1738. They intended to flex their muscle, too. When the Synod of 1738 ruled that any ministerial candidate within its province must have a degree from a New England or European college, the Log College men perceived an affront at least, and, at worst, an effort to wreck the college. The New Brunswick Presbytery declared the act unconstitutional.[11] This conflict prepared the way for two of the most remarkable years in American religious history. An energized evangelical party, the "New Side," now moved against their rivals and critics.[12]

In 1740, at Nottingham, Pennsylvania, Gilbert Tennent delivered a confrontational, intemperate sermon, later called "one of the most severely abusive

---

9. Le Beau, *Dickinson*, 107.
10. Le Beau, *Dickinson*, 110.
11. Le Beau, *Dickinson*, 108–10; Trinterud, *American Tradition*, 86.
12. "New Side" and "Old Side" Presbyterians have the same general categorization as the "New Light" and "Old Light" Congregationalists in New England. The one group sponsored and defended the Awakening; the other had severe reservations about it.

sermons that was ever penned," and he directed it against the generality of the Protestant ministry in America. He called the ministers the "Pharisee-Shepards"— "as crafty as foxes"—who entangle the church in fine points of creeds and doc-trines. They did so, Tennent charged, because they were personally "ignorant of the new birth." Here was the militant Awakeners' line in the sand, and their bat-tle cry. The standing ministry, for the most part, they charged, had not themselves experienced personal regeneration—what the Puritans called the covenant of grace—and could not claim status among God's elect. Thus, they remained "natu-ral men." Worse, lacking grace themselves, they could not discourse on this key subject in their sermons. "The pharisee-teachers," said Tennent, "having no expe-rience of a special work of the Holy Ghost, upon their souls, are therefore neither inclined to, nor fitted for, discoursing frequently, clearly, and pathetically upon such important subjects." This ministry could speak only formally and intellectu-ally, preaching only "duty, duty." They could convey nothing of the "terror" of the troubled soul in its sinful misery. Tennent laid on the "carnal" ministers whom he condemned blame for all the false doctrines of the day. "Is not the carnality of the ministry," he asked, "one great cause of the general spread of Arminianism, Socini-anism, Arianism, and deism, at this day through the world?"[13]

Tennent's scurrilous attack ill served the cause of the Awakeners. In many quarters it confirmed the case against the group—that it had more heat than light in its work, more emotion than reason. It became Jonathan Dickinson's task to disarm the critics by taking a careful look at the nature of religious experience and ascertaining the legitimacy of the revival and its effects. Dickinson con-tributed a major piece in doing so. His sermon of 1740, "The Witness of the Spirit," supplemented the analyses being offered by Jonathan Edwards in his de-fense of the revival events in New England. Through it Dickinson fully secured his reputation as the intellectual leader of the Presbyterians and as its most rea-sonable persuader.

Dickinson saw the America of 1740 much as Edwards did. He found it smug and secure, dangerously indifferent to its spiritual condition though all around the ministers warned against the prevailing easy comfort. To shake the world from its spiritual slumber, Dickinson said, would be no simple task. Neither would the means or the effects be moderate. When God reaches to convince the sinner of his sin, Dickinson warned, he may do so in a sudden manner, "filling the soul with the greatest agony and distress." He may alarm all the powers and passions of the soul. The sinner will tremble and feel distress. Acute feelings of "guilt and misery" will rend the heart.[14] Dickinson's sermon thus reverberated with Calvinist rhetoric and upheld inner conversion as the sole requisite of sal-vation. He wished above all to demonstrate that the revival made sense, that its visible, though much maligned, effects wholly conformed to the ways of spiritual

---

13. Gilbert Tennent, "The Danger of an Unconverted Ministry. . . ." in *The Great Awakening*, ed. Alan Heimert and Perry Miller (Indianapolis: Bobbs-Merrill, 1967), 71–72, 74, 78, 82 (quotations).
    14. Jonathan Dickinson, "The Witness of the Spirit," in *The Great Awakening*, 101–2.

transformation in human beings, the turbulent path from sin to spiritual health. Leonard Trinterud wrote of Dickinson's "Witness of the Spirit": "The die had been cast, and the future character of American Presbyterianism had been determined."[15]

The future history of Princeton was also being determined. Now the fault lines in American Presbyterianism were emerging clearer than ever. The Awakening and the schisms of the denomination concern us here just to this extent. We need to note particularly that a leadership class among the New Side had emerged. Dickinson had acquired the most influence and represented the intellectual wing. But an energetic young ministry was also taking charge. Samuel Blair was one of that group. Born in Ireland in 1712, he came to America and graduated from the Log College. He took up a ministry at Fagg's Manor, Pennsylvania, in 1740 and there started his own school for the education of ministers. He gave both voice and intellect to the cause of the revival. He seemed to thrive on controversy and threw himself into the defense of Whitefield as opposition rose to discredit him.

The formal charges against Whitefield came from members of the New Castle Presbytery, and they registered Old Side skepticism about the revival. Whitefield replied to the "Querists," his accusers, and then a second document answered his reply. The Querists discredited the authenticity of the Awakening by the words they chose to describe its normative effects: "strange fits, convulsions, involuntary raptures, horrid noises, and visions." These behaviors registered "the black marks of impostors in all ages," they charged. In short, they said, the revival was a fake, the work of "devilizing men." The Querists employed that universal condemnation, "enthusiasm," and charged that the revivalists were fomenting disorder and rebellion in the denomination.[16]

Blair answered the Querists in defense of Whitefield, and in invective that now rather typified the language of the feuding factions. The Awakening will make no sense to those who have not experienced the power of God's reforming grace themselves, Blair asserted. "Dead secure formalists," he charged, who know nothing of the soul's horrible confrontation with sin and guilt, can lend nothing to the great cause of arousing a people from their sleepful security. Thus Blair threw the matter back in the faces of the "sapless, careless ministers" who dismissed the good work of Whitefield and the evangelical party.[17] Blair also added to the narrative literature of the Awakening with his description of the events in the early 1740s, *A Short and Faithful Narrative, Of the Late Remarkable Revival of Religion In the Congregation of New-Londonderry, and other parts of Pennsylvania* (1744).

More aggressive even than Blair was Samuel Finley, who best exemplified a populist strain often evident in colonial revivalism. Also born in Ireland, in

---

15. Trinterud, *American Tradition*, 94.
16. "The Querists," "A Short Reply to Mr. Whitefield's Letter," in *The Great Awakening*, 138–39, 145.
17. Samuel Blair, "A Particular Consideration of the 'The Querists,'" in *The Great Awakening*, 131.

Samuel Finley

1715, he too graduated from the Log College and became an itinerant minister. When he tried to assume a pastorship in Connecticut, the legislature forcibly prevented him from doing so. He attained a permanent post at Nottingham and there set up a school from which Benjamin Rush later graduated. Finley worked closely with Gilbert Tennent to promote the revival and he was quick to defend it against detractors. He believed the revival made sense, for Christ moves to advance his cause when the Church becomes lax, or, as he said, falls into "empty form." Thus it was at the time of Athanasius in the fourth century and at the advent of the Reformation. So also was it now. "And what had we lately," he asked, "but a dry formality?" People and ministers were alike at ease in Zion, he asserted. Finley also explained that Christ, in his work of redemption, will pass by the "established, but proud, bigoted, gainsaying clergy." He chooses, instead, Finley said, to work among the people, "unpolished men," like the fishermen around Galilee. Disowned by the clergy in his time, Christ gained his following from "what we call the mob, the rabble, the common and meaner sort."

Finley, in this manner, thus wrapped the Awakening in the trappings of a democratic ethos, a vanguard movement against the elite and privileged clergy.[18]

New Side Presbyterians thus struggled to define themselves against the Old Siders in their denomination. All the while, however, they waged a two-front war. For as the Old Siders challenged them with a rigid orthodoxy, the Church of England challenged them with an Arminian alternative. Here too as the Presbyterian pulpit sermonized on theological issues and turned its preachings into pamphlets aplenty, New Side Presbyterians took on weighty religious subjects. With its intellect and polemical swords sharpened in the process, the group further staked out an evangelical center in the religious politics of colonial America. By the middle 1740s, it was ready to give an institutional expression to its identity in the founding of Princeton college.

Within the next decade Dickinson and other Presbyterians were laying the plans for creation of the College of New Jersey, and they would quickly see that the major denominational effort made against that design came from the Anglicans. By that time, Dickinson had been long engaged against this group and had emerged as Presbyterianism's most ardent spokesmen against its Protestant rivals. Anglicans represented to the Presbyterians not only a theological challenge, for their Arminian liberalism had always set them off from Protestantism in the Reformed tradition. Ecclesiastical matters also entered the disputes, to say nothing of the struggle for power in colonial American politics.

Dickinson's battles on this front go back a decade earlier. In 1723, John Checkley, "perhaps the most notorious American Anglican polemicist of his time," published *A Modest Proof* of apostolic succession and the legitimacy of the Church of England on this ground. Checkley, a lay Anglican from Boston and a homegrown Jacobite, took a prominent role in launching the Society for the Propagation of the Gospel (SPG) in the colonies. He bristled at the sight of almost every Dissenter in the city and recoiled from their "wicked" books that stocked local bookstores. But Checkley was as thoroughly anti-Romanist as they, a prejudice that enabled him to place the Church of England between iniquitous Calvinism, on the one hand, and carnal Catholicism, on the other. Furthermore, he allied prelacy with royalty, supporting both. Checkley became the first to pen an anti-Calvinist tract in New England and he did so right in the aftermath of the apostasy at Yale.[19]

Checkley maintained that Christ's appointment of the twelve apostles carried an intention for a succession, a "permanent" apostolic mission and not merely an "extraordinary and temporary one." Checkley argued that the apostolic offices—teaching, administering, governing, and exercising the sacraments—

---

18. Samuel Finley, "Christ Triumphing and Satan Raging," in *The Great Awakening*, 156–57.

19. John Frederick Woolverton, *Colonial Anglicanism in North America* (Detroit, Mich.: Wayne State University Press, 1984), 95, 118–20.

constituted "an unalterable constitution" of the Church. "The apostles were actually bishops," Checkley wrote, "and their Apostleship is a proper episcopacy."
Checkley could find no other way to legitimize the Christian churches after
Christ and he thus defended episcopacy, "the primitive model," as the only reasonable polity to be drawn from Scripture.[20]

Dickinson, replying for the Presbyterians, would have none of this argument. He called Checkley's account of ecclesiastical authority "a daring usurpation," and labeled it an act of hubris "for any to assume the character of Christ's
ambassadors, that have not their mission from them." Dickinson could find no
mission in Scripture, and neither, he said, could Checkley ("He cannot find one
word in the Bible to support this prelacy").[21] In a forty-four-page reply to Checkley, Dickinson attacked the details of his argument, but also expressed his revul-
sion at what he saw as a species of Anglican tyranny. He described a warfare between the Presbyterians, "a small upstart sect," against "the High Church party."
The Anglicans' contentions, he said, would "unchurch all the Protestant world
but themselves." None of the early Christians, Dickinson wrote, knew the doctrine of the divine right of episcopacy, nor did the Reformation, and nor did even
the original Anglicans themselves.[22]

In ensuing years, Dickinson grew more perturbed at the Anglicans. He gave
increasing emphasis to historical issues, as when in 1733 he reminded New Englanders that the Church of England had been the source of their ancestors' persecutions. Three years later Dickinson had reason to renew the quarrel with Anglicans in his area. At that time the Reverend Edward Vaughn, who had begun
Anglican services in Elizabeth Town the same year that Dickinson had begun Presbyterianism, invited one Reverend John Beach of New Town, Connecticut, to
preach in his pulpit. Beach had graduated from Yale and under the influence of
Samuel Johnson had taken Anglican orders in England. Also, in 1736, Anglicans
started a church in nearby Newark. Beach's large audiences and the appeal of Anglican theology brought some Presbyterians into the Newark church and raised
new fears about Anglican designs.[23] Dickinson renewed his pamphlet attack on the
Anglicans with his issuing of *The Vanity of Human Institutions in the Worship of God*,
originally a sermon to the Presbyterian congregation in Newark. Dickinson faulted
specific Anglican forms of worship and voiced opposition to liturgies as such; "they
deprive the Spirit of free entry into our prayers." He further labeled the Book of
Common Prayer as mostly an extract of the "Popish Liturgy." He also recalled a

---

20. John Checkley, *A Modest Proof of the Order and Government Selected by Christ and His Apostles
in the Church* (Boston: Thomas Fleet, 1723), 1, 9–11, 16–17, 32–35, 43–44.

21. Jonathan Dickinson, *A Defense of Presbyterian Ordination* (Boston: Henchman, 1724), ii, 2.
Checkley did cite Acts I, 20 in defense of his thesis.

22. Dickinson, *Defense*, ii, 7–8, 43–44. Checkley gave an angry reply to Dickinson, saying that he
would quarrel with him no more, not caring to "have my reputation arraigned for contending with
an adversary of your size." He told Dickinson "to mind your own business" (John Checkley, *A Letter
From the Author of a Postscript of the Defence of a Book. . . .* [Boston: n.p., 1725], 12).

23. Le Beau, *Jonathan Dickinson*, 67–81.

record of abuse by the Church of England in its resolve to enforce its inventions against the consciences of those who wished no part of the "commandments of men." Here Dickinson invoked Lockean language in citing the "natural right" of all to chose for themselves in matters of religion. Dickinson thus anticipated a theme of Anglican tyranny that would emerge in louder strains in the years of the American Revolution.[24]

Even when in his most furious and emotional mood, at the time of his attack on the ministry, Gilbert Tennent called for a new effort in education for his party. He labeled the American colleges "corrupted and abused," and demanded new schools or seminaries of learning "which are under the care of skillful and experienced Christians; in which those only are admitted, who upon strict examination, have . . . the plain evidence of experimental religion."[25] Tennent's own polemics, however, kept Presbyterians divided in a way that would prevent agreements on the nature and purpose of any college they might have in mind. Certainly others in the denomination would want none of the restrictions intimated in Tennent's reference. A number of circumstances, however, soon changed the picture and by the middle of the 1740s was producing a unity among the Presbyterians that prepared the way for Princeton's founding.

Tennent, in the next year after his infamous sermon, retracted his expressions. In a letter to Dickinson, Tennent confessed that he could no longer justify the "excessive heat of temper" he had earlier shown. Tennent had just toured New England and encountered there the crazed ranting of James Davenport and it gave Tennent a second look at himself. He did not like what he saw. He also perceived how Davenport's denunciations of the clergy had provoked dangerous schismatic effects. He now doubted any person's ability to detect unconverted ministers and warned against the practice. Tennent also called it injudicious to send out "unlearned men," on the assumption of their superior piety, to spread the gospel. In a remarkable shift, Tennent now warned against "enthusiasm."[26]

Other Presbyterians also saw the need to detach themselves from the excesses of the Awakening. Dickinson, in his second meeting with Whitefield in 1740, felt uneasy with the young evangelist and his glib assaults on the clergy. Having solidified against the Anglicans, Presbyterians now coalesced against the extremists in the revivalists' ranks. The Moravians in the Middle Colonies exemplified the worst habits there, taking New Light tendencies, some believed, into outright Antinomianism. (Count Nicholaus von Zinzendorf, Moravian founder, had arrived in Pennsylvania in 1741, preparing to enhance the ranks of his followers.) Dickinson and Tennent feared the Moravians and believed they had designs against the Presbyterians.

24. Jonathan Dickinson, *The Vanity of Human Institutions in the Worship of God* (New York: John Peter Zenger, 1736), 11, 17–28.
25. Tennent, "Danger," 85.
26. Le Beau, *Dickinson*, 131–32.

Dickinson himself now came under assault by the radical New Lights. One Andrew Croswell led the charge. A Harvard graduate, he served as pastor of the Second Church of Groton, Connecticut, and in 1746 moved to Boston, there to lead a constant assault on the liberal clergy. Croswell took exception to a piece that Dickinson wrote in 1742, in which he detected deviation from strict Calvinism in the matter of one's preparation for grace. Dickinson had allowed for some preparationist activity on the part of the believer, but Croswell said that he allowed too much. Many, he said, will take that activity to be a sign of God's election, a dangerous self-deception. He accused Dickinson of a lapse into Arminianism and legalism. Nor could the point have been lost on Dickinson when Thomas Clap at Yale wrote to tell him that Croswell and others had joined with Davenport to have a book-burning bonfire at a New London Church. Clap regretted to tell Dickinson that the proscribed books included Dickinson's own.[27]

Yale was rejecting the worst aspects of the Awakening, but it was rejecting the best of them, too. So did Dickinson and other moderate Presbyterians believe. The David Brainerd case at Yale forced that conclusion upon them. Dickinson, Aaron Burr, and Jonathan Edwards had all interceded on behalf of Brainerd. Dickinson, Burr, and Ebenezer Pemberton hired him as a missionary in 1744 and the Presbytery of New York, a New Side stronghold, ordained him. By this time, too, Harvard had made clear its opposition to the Awakening. To Dickinson a new college seemed all the more imperative.[28]

The formal effort began in 1739. The Synod of Philadelphia, where the Old Side faction, too, saw the need for a college, appointed a committee to pursue the plan. Dickinson, who worked well with both the Old Side and New Side Presbyterians, joined that group. For the most part, the New England leaders in the denomination led in the founding efforts. Most remarkably, six of the seven founders of the new college had graduated from Yale, a measure of that institution's complete routing of the Awakening there. The College of New Jersey thus stood boldly as a departure from New England's colleges—the liberal Congregationalism at Harvard and the orthodox Congregationalism at Yale. New Side Presbyterianism made Princeton the first college of the Awakening. As if to secure that fact, and as a reflection of the mellowing of difference in the Presbyterian ranks, affiliates of the "Log College" now joined the Princeton board of trustees. The death of William Tennent awakened the interest of his successors in the college and Gilbert Tennent, William Tennent, Jr., Samuel Blair, and Samuel Finley counted among the school founders. Bearing the name of the College of New Jersey, the Presbyterians' new college opened at Jonathan Dickinson's home at Elizabeth Town in May 1747.[29]

---

27. Leigh Eric Schmidt, "'A Second and Glorious Reformation': The New Light Extremism of Andrew Croswell," *William and Mary Quarterly* 3rd Series, 43 (1986): 212–44; Le Beau, *Dickinson*, 96, 117, 158–60.

28. Le Beau, *Dickinson*, 170–72.

29. Thomas Wertenbaker, *Princeton, 1746–1896* (Princeton, N.J.: Princeton University Press, 1946), 124; Le Beau, *Dickinson*, 166–67.

The passage to this event, however, did not go smoothly. Princeton grew from the commitments of Dissenters, an underprivileged group in England and in many of the colonies. New Jersey, in Lewis Morris, had an Anglican governor, one "none too friendly to Dissenters."[30] So wisely referencing New Jersey's own statement of religious freedom, the Presbyterians made it policy at the college. The school would not deny admission to anyone on the basis of that person's "speculative principles of religion." The College of New Jersey probably purchased itself a measure of independence with this statement. The charter had no provision requiring a governmental voice in the running of the college. On the other hand, the principle here surely reflected Dickinson's mature thinking on personal liberty in religion. He defended the school's open policy, writing, "This is a natural right that cannot be justly denied to any."[31]

The college did get one important break. Governor Morris died on May 21, 1746, and John Hamilton, another Anglican, succeeded him. But Hamilton, very weak in health, could not function in his office and active governing fell to a group of advisors. All were friends of the college and they prevailed upon Hamilton, against his initial reluctance, to grant a charter. Furthermore, the hard work of other New Jersey Dissenters secured the appointment of Jonathan Belcher, a Massachusetts Congregationalist, as the next governor. He received a warm welcome upon his arrival to New Jersey in August 1747 as Dickinson entertained him in his home. Belcher knew and lamented the conditions of the New England colleges as he cited Arminianism and Arianism and their corrosive effects on the honored doctrines of free grace. "How horribly and how wickedly," he said, "are these poisonous notions rooting out those noble pious principles on which our excellent ancestors founded those seminaries." Here indeed was a friend to the Princetonians.[32] And with matters thus in place, the trustees chose Jonathan Dickinson to be the college's first president.

Some young men already studying for the ministry with Dickinson effectively became the college's first students. Dickinson would have the further task of organizing the college and preparing it for its ambitious educational endeavors. Even as he and his colleagues were taking the final steps in founding Princeton college, however, their struggle with the Anglicans became more intense. In New Jersey, Anglicans fought against the very notion of a Presbyterian college in the colony. Early in 1747, they took their case to the bishop of London, who had jurisdiction of New Jersey, and urged that he reject the new charter. James Wetmore of Rye, New York, a longstanding combatant with Dickinson, led the effort. He described the Presbyterians as "the most bitter enemies of the Church." He implicated the Princeton group in the falsehoods of George Whitefield and his outlandish methods. Wetmore cited Dickinson particularly and called him one of the most abusive of the American Dissenters in his strenuous

---

30. Wertenbaker, *Princeton*, 19.
31. Le Beau, *Dickinson*, 177, 184.
32. Wertenbaker, *Princeton*, 25–26.

anti-Anglican pronunciations. Establishment of the new college, he believed, could only spread these vicious attitudes in the region.[33]

Dickinson died in 1747, having served only a year as the college's president. Along with this loss, Princeton confronted all the problems that a new institution inherits. In May less than a dozen students reported for work at Elizabeth Town where the Reverend Caleb Smith assisted Dickinson in the teaching. With Dickinson's death, Aaron Burr agreed to take over the college, so students packed up their belongings and moved six miles over to his home residence. Here an ordinary and probably quite uninspiring collegiate routine set in. Every morning the young men arose for chapel service, a simple service of Scripture reading and prayers, and on Sundays they attended the nearby Presbyterian meeting house. The college as yet had no dormitories for the students, so some lived with the president and others boarded in the town. Money, too, remained a problem. The college received no funds from the colonial legislature and had to find its benefactors among sympathetic New Siders. In 1751, the trustees asked Samuel Davies to undertake a fund-raising effort for the school in England and Scotland. Gilbert Tennent joined him.[34]

Academic politics, the two Princeton envoys found, prevailed in England as in the colonies. Davies and Tennent soon discovered that Anglican and Old Side Presbyterian interests in England had set up obstacles to their effort to raise money. Opponents dragged up Tennent's infamous Nottingham sermon and distributed it in an effort to embarrass him. Opponents also portrayed the College of New Jersey as a factional school born of the excesses of the colonial Awakening. Tennent again disavowed his earlier views and the Princetonians tried to present the college in terms of its nonsectarian admissions policy. Finally, however, success came. Davies made a strong appeal before the Presbyterian General Assembly of Scotland. It responded in a resolution that echoed Davies's plea: "The young daughter of the Church of Scotland, helpless and exposed in this foreign land, cries to her tender and powerful mother for relief." The assembly ordered a collection at every church door for the New Jersey college and urged generosity for the school from all Scottish Presbyterians. Davies departed with warm good feelings about the Christian spirit and the good will he found in Edinburgh.[35]

The good news from Great Britain emboldened the Princeton trustees to look for a permanent site for the college. Newark, Elizabeth Town, and New Brunswick sought the prize. So too did some people at Princeton, a preference of Governor Belcher also, as he looked for a location midway between Philadelphia and New York. The trustees decided to settle the matter by asking for contributions of land and money from the competing towns. In early 1753 Princeton of-

33. Le Beau, *Dickinson*, 181–82. Dickinson's major opponent among the American Anglicans was Samuel Johnson. See below, chapter 6.

34. Wertenbaker, *Princeton*, 25, 28, 34–35.

35. George William Pilcher, *Samuel Davies: Apostle of Dissent in Colonial Virginia* (Knoxville: University of Tennessee Press, 1971), 137–49.

Samuel Davies

ficials announced that they had secured plentiful subscriptions, and the town that would later give the college its modern name received the College of New Jersey. The trustees, furthermore, believed that nothing would better secure the permanent standing of their college than a grand stately building on the new location. In September 1754, a gathering of dignitaries witnessed the laying of the cornerstone for Nassau Hall, a landmark of colonial academic architecture. It also had the distinction of housing the first church organ used in Presbyterian services in America, a modern turn that drew frowns from conservative Yale. The trustees wanted to name the new building for Governor Belcher, but he requested instead that it honor "the immortal memory of the glorious King William III," of the house of Nassau.[36]

Princeton had grown to a college of some seventy students when Burr died in 1757. The trustees turned to his father-in-law Jonathan Edwards and made him

---

36. Wertenbaker, *Princeton*, 39.

president. They made a bold statement in doing so, for no one in colonial America surpassed Edwards as the formidable intellectual defender of Reformed Protestantism. They were placing in the leadership of the college the brilliant defender of that tradition against the many incursions of liberal Christianity. Edwards arrived at Princeton in early 1758, welcomed by a throng of cheering students. Tragedy lay ahead, however, for upon taking a smallpox inoculation, Edwards developed an intense fever and succumbed. The trustees then turned to Davies and after a failed first appeal prevailed on him to accept. At Princeton, however, Davies imposed on himself a rigorous routine of scholarship and administration, too much for his long-weakly constitution to sustain. He died in February 1761. Another New Side loyalist, Samuel Finley, succeeded him. His five years of service until his death in July 1766 must have been a welcomed longevity to the college, but it yet again faced another presidential search.[37]

At this point, the early life of Benjamin Rush offers a glimpse at how many of the factors we have discussed converged in Princeton's early history. Rush was one of eight children born to John and Sarah Rush in a house near Philadelphia that sat on ninety acres of farmland. He received baptism in the Church of England the year of his birth, 1745, and he attended services as a boy in Christ's First Church in the city. His mother's sister, however, had married Samuel Finley, and that connection sent Benjamin and his brother to Finley's school, the Presbyterian academy at Nottingham. By this time Nottingham had become a feeder school for the College of New Jersey and Rush's great admiration for Finley had placed him firmly in the Presbyterian denomination. As an upperclassman Rush took courses in mathematics, logic, Latin, and Greek. Davies became president just after Rush's arrival. He served long enough to make a difference, though. The new president acquired, per his request, more books in mathematics and "Newtonian philosophy" and added a new course in math and one in English composition. The latter departure reflected Davies's own fondness for writing hymns and patriotic poems.[38] In fact, Rush would remember Davies especially for invoking a public spirit and citizenship from his students. At the commencement ceremony in 1760 Davies told the Princetonians that without a public spirit their lives would lack real meaning. Rush said of the sermon that "it deserves to be printed in letters of gold in every young candidate's heart." Davies's joining of college and country anticipated the later Princeton careers of John Witherspoon and Woodrow Wilson: "Princeton in the nation's service."[39] Soon Rush would

---

37. Wertenbaker, *Princeton*, 41–46
38. Ned C. Landsman suggests that Davies represents a new concern among American evangelicals, a concern for the sentiments and affections that underscored the moral life. Poetry, novels, and even the theater might enliven the sensibility. A pious woman like Esther Burr read novels, and under the presidency of her husband Princeton students put on their own plays (*From Colonials to Provincials: American Thought and Culture, 1680–1760* [New York: Twayne Publishers, 1997], 132–33).
39. David Freeman Hawke, *Benjamin Rush: Revolutionary Gadfly* (Indianapolis: Bobbs-Merrill, 1971), 8–10, 12–14, 18–21.

play a decisive role in Princeton's history. But first we must review again the political situation at the college in the 1760s.

The unity of sorts that enabled the establishment of the college at Princeton was by no means solidified. Finley's death encouraged some Old Side Presbyterians to attempt a takeover of the college. Their group had tied to operate a rival Presbyterian school at Newark, but it was going nowhere. Samuel Purviance, Jr., a Philadelphia merchant and member of the committed Old Side First Church collaborated with minister Francis Alison and others in the scheme. In 1766 Purviance wrote to Ezra Stiles and explained their intentions. They would use the next meeting of the trustees, he said, to spring a surprise—the offer of funds to establish three new professorships. Purviance said he had secured the financial support of some New York lawyers to back the proposal and he had specific individuals in mind for the appointments. The letter was remarkably frank, and uncharitable. "So sensible are we," wrote Purviance, "of the narrow bigotry of our brethren the New Lights, that we dare not disclose these our benevolent and generous views for fear of defeating our intentions." He added that we "hope to take our friends off their guard," and then, "if this looks like cunning I'm sure it's such as you'll approve." [40]

The New Siders got wind of the scheme to highjack the college and acted fast when the meeting took place. They voted that day to offer the Princeton presidency to John Witherspoon, a Scotsman. This extraordinary turn of events had more of good logic and sound politics about it than the quickness of the move would suggest. Witherspoon could claim the goodwill and support of both factions in the Presbyterian struggles. (The groups had taken some additional steps in the healing process in 1758.) Purviance, for example, ultimately welcomed the prospects and hoped that it would lead the Presbyterians fully to close ranks.[41]

The trustees had a huge task before them, however. Witherspoon from the beginning seemed interested, but his wife did not. Letters and visitations would occur in a feverish effort over several months, but Witherspoon had to tell his persuaders that he was making no headway on the home front. Benjamin Rush, now located in Edinburgh for medical studies, took up the cause of persuasion with zeal. He besieged Witherspoon and would not let up in his importuning. "O, sir, does not your heart expand with unutterable sentiments of love and benevolence when you think that you are to be the means of rescuing so important a seminary from ruin?" When Witherspoon sadly sent his regrets, the chastened parties joined to make the three appointments to the college, but without the sectarian purposes of the original plan. Then Princetonians heard good news. Witherspoon had prevailed on his family at last and

---

40. L. H. Butterfield, *John Witherspoon Comes to America: A Documentary Account Based Largely on New Materials* (Princeton, N.J.: Princeton University Press, 1953), 4–5.

41. See his letter to Stiles in Butterfield, *Witherspoon Comes to America*, 35–36.

he now announced his intention to come to America. When he arrived at last in August 1768 many of Philadelphia's most prominent people turned out to welcome the family, as did a mass of Princeton students when the Witherspoons appeared at the college.[42]

Who was John Witherspoon and why all the fuss over him? Answering these questions requires a look at the religious and intellectual developments in Scotland, events that describe the remarkable Scottish Enlightenment, its evangelical religion, and its great significance for America. Francis Hutcheson made himself a key early figure in the Scottish Enlightenment with his treatise of 1725, *Inquiry into the Original of Our Ideas of Beauty and Virtue*, and his *Essay on the Nature and Conduct of the Passions, with Illustrations of the Moral Sense*, in 1728. Hutcheson had studied at Glasgow University, taught at a private academy in Dublin, and then returned to Glasgow in 1729 to assume the chair in philosophy. Both his father and grandfather were Presbyterian ministers, but Hutcheson's philosophical writings looked toward the transformation of the Scottish Church. In a letter, Hutcheson once wrote that he hoped to "put a new face upon theology in Scotland." In earlier works, he had written that Scotland's harsh Calvinism had deprived religion of its good influence in his country. Of religion and philosophy, he said, we have made "so austere and ungainly a form that a gentleman cannot bring himself to [them] . . . so much have they changed from what was once the delight of the finest gentlemen among the ancients." For Hutcheson, the concerns of religion lay within the domain of beauty, reason, morality, and utility. Following the Earl of Shaftesbury in England, he set out to establish a morality based on the constitution of human nature and independent of religion. He would, however, show also that examination of the conscience, the will, and the reason fortify our knowledge of God.[43]

Hutcheson revealed much here. He spoke for a rising generation, in the universities and the ministry, who wanted religion to speak more meaningfully to the middle and upper classes of Scotland. The nation was being visibly transformed in its beginning industrial era, and the city of Glasgow symbolized Scotland's role in the new commercial and transatlantic economy of Great Britain. Hutcheson helped inspire a rationalist culture, more befitting the prosperous and educated classes in the nation. He moved moral philosophy out of the doctrinal confinements of Calvinism or any biblical foundations and into the realm of human nature itself. The cardinal principles of virtue and disinterested benevolence in Hutcheson better suited Scotland's more comfortable and prosperous

---

42. Butterfield, *Witherspoon*, 35, 40–41, 57–58 (the quotation).

43. Francis Hutcheson, *An Inquiry Concerning Beauty, Order, Harmony, Design* (1725; The Hague: Martinus Nijhoff, 1973), 25n (vol. 1 of the two-volume *Inquiry into the Original of Our Ideas of Beauty and Virtue*); idem, *A System of Moral Philosophy* (1755; New York: A. M. Kelley, 1968), 1; James McCosh, *The Scottish Philosophy, Biographical, Expository, Critical, from Hutcheson to Hamilton* (New York: Robert Carter and Bros., 1875), 64 (the quotation).

classes, the new social elites so prominently visible in the streets of Aberdeen, Glasgow, and Edinburgh.[44]

Hutcheson, however, had his major impact in the Scottish Church. A new generation of students, from Scotland and Ireland, came to study with him at Glasgow. Alexander Carlyle, for example, left Glasgow and moved over to Edinburgh, enjoying the fresh intellectual atmosphere there. Soon he would be a leading voice of what became known as the Moderate party in the Church of Scotland.[45] Like all the academics in the Scottish Enlightenment, Hutcheson had close connections to the Church. At the university, he gave Sunday lectures and used the occasions to illustrate the "truth and excellency of Christianity" and to draw the New Testament into his own moral system. He urged the divinity students to de-emphasize speculative sermons and to inspire moral activity, "which is the main thing the sacred orator should be concerned about." Hutcheson spoke frankly about his intentions. "I hope," he said, "I am contributing to promote the more moderate and charitable sentiments in religious matters in this country."[46] The Moderate ministry advanced Hutcheson's general outline. The Church of Scotland remained officially Calvinist, but its Moderate leadership avoided doctrinal issues and looked for an alliance of religion and culture. They wanted a new literary eloquence in the pulpit, and they wrote and talked about esthetics. Dugald Stewart, later the most widely adopted of the Scottish philosophers in American classrooms, credited Hutcheson with spreading "a liberality of sentiment, and a refinement of taste, unknown before in this part of the land."[47]

The Moderates did not take all of the Church of Scotland with them. Already there were voices who dissented from the rationalist inroads in the Church. This group spoke to countrymen who cared little for matters of refinement and taste or rhetorical elegance in the pulpit. Here the old Calvinist concerns of sin and redemption remained the personal obsession of old believers. Fiery preachers like Ralph and Ebenezer Erskine among the Calvinist Seceders, Thomas Boston, and others kept alive the old spirit of the Covenanters who had

---

44. Sloan, *Scottish Enlightenment*, 7–9. As Sloan notes, Scotland's intellectual leadership was tied to the political and economic, took an interest in programs of improvement in a modernizing Scotland, and wished to present the nation to the world in that character. See also, Richard B. Sher, *Church and University in the Scottish Enlightenment: The Moderate Literati of Edinburgh*, ed. Richard B. Sher and Jeffrey R. Smitten (Princeton, N.J.: Princeton University Press, 1985), especially chapter 2, "The Moderate Revolution."

45. Andrew L. Drummond and James Bulloch, *The Scottish Church, 1688–1843: The Age of the Moderates* (Edinburgh: The Saint Andrew Press, 1973), 47.

46. Hutcheson, *System*, 67.

47. Dugald Stewart, "Account of the Life and Writings of William Robertson. . . ," in *The Collected Works of Dugald Stewart*, 11 vols. (Edinburgh, 1858), 10:105. In his *A System of Moral Philosophy*, published, by his intention, posthumously in 1755, Hutcheson grounded his system more emphatically in the workings of divine providence. He had begun this shift in intervening writings and it may have registered his troubling reactions to Berkeley and David Hume. See James Moore, "Hutcheson's Theodicy: The Argument and the Contexts of *A System of Moral Philosophy*," in *The Scottish Enlightenment: Essays in Reinterpretation*, ed. Paul Wood (Rochester, N.Y.: University of Rochester Press, 2000), 237–60.

fought Catholicism and episcopacy a century before. The Erskines, it was said, had no time for "the dry sapless harangues of a heathenish morality." Boston looked to Scripture for a saving knowledge, which no ethical account of human nature could supply. Now a rival party, the Evangelicals, emerged to challenge the Moderates. In the political realm, this group angrily attacked the 1712 Patronage Act that assured local gentry power of ministerial appointments, which were now going overwhelmingly to Moderates. The more radical individuals in the Evangelical ranks led secessionist movements from the Church of Scotland in 1733 and 1752, establishing separate religious bodies.[48] Others stayed in the Church to challenge the Moderates. The resisting Evangelical party soon had a leader to be reckoned with, the minister from Paisley, John Witherspoon.

Witherspoon came from a long line of ministers and public officials in Scotland. One ancestor had signed the Solemn League and Covenant in 1643. James Witherspoon, the father, served as pastor in Gifford, and John was born there in 1723. He attended the grammar school at Haddington, where young John Knox had studied. He then continued his education at the University of Edinburgh and earned a master's degree. Witherspoon was serving the Presbyterian congregation at Beith in 1745 when Bonnie Prince Charlie, the Young Pretender, attempted to seize the English throne. Presbyteries across Scotland denounced the Jacobites and some resolved on taking up the resistance. Witherspoon threw himself into that cause and not only organized a Beith militia, but personally led it. He and his men reached Glasgow, but did not see battle. For his efforts, though, he was seized by the rebels and placed in Castle Dunne, there to serve a short term of imprisonment. In 1748, Witherspoon married Elizabeth Montgomery.[49]

The militia event shows Witherspoon's combative way, for he could project himself eagerly into causes he cared about. Now the Church of Scotland would give him another. Witherspoon had watched the growing ecclesiastical power of the Moderates and it vexed him considerably. He did not share their easy, rational faith and their correlation of religion with virtue and taste. Witherspoon adhered to the older Calvinism both in its theology and its moral severity. His opposition to the Moderates was known locally, but in 1752 Witherspoon gained a national notoriety with the publication of his acutely satirical broadside, *Ecclesiastical Characteristics*. It immediately raised the emotional content in the disputes between the Moderate Party and the popular Evangelical party. This piece first brought notice of Witherspoon to American Presbyterians, so it bears looking at. Witherspoon listed cardinal tenets of the Moderate clergy, intending to hold them up to ridicule. He formulated this "Moderates' Code":

---

48. McCosh, *Scottish Philosophy*, 86; Sloan, *Scottish Enlightenment*, 11–12.
49. Varnum Lansing Collins, *President Witherspoon*, 2 vols. (1925; New York: Arno Press, 1969), 1:12, 22–24.

A minister must endeavor to acquire as great a degree of politeness in his carriage and behavior, and to catch as much of the air and manner of a fine gentleman as possibly he can.

Good manners is undoubtedly the most excellent of all accomplishments.

A moderate man is quite at liberty to indulge in what his forefathers regarded as sin, but which have now been called by a hopeful youth *good-humored vices*.

You must be very gentle in dealing with heretics, and speak of them as men of exalted genius.

As to preaching, you should not dwell much on sin and repentance: these topics may be liked by the vulgar, for whose favor we do not care, but they are obnoxious to the upper classes, with whom the patronage of the kirks lies and with whom we wish to associate.

You must, above all things, use refined and polite language, and not talk of grace, but of virtue—not of conviction of sin, but a sense of honor and beauty.

You must speak with Francis Hutcheson on morality . . . order, and proportion, taste, and the nice balance of the affections.

It is thus we do all we can to make religion respectable, especially to the better classes. We never mention hell or damnation in the ears polite of my lords and ladies.[50]

Ecclesiastical Characteristics caught the attention of Samuel Davies as he toured Scotland with Gilbert Tennent. Making the rounds of his fund-raising efforts, Davies noted in his journal that "there is a piece published under the title of Ecclesiastical Characteristics ascribed to one Mr. Witherspoon, a young minister." Davies added that he thought its satirical power "nothing inferior to Dean Swift." As the prospects of Witherspoon's coming to Princeton emerged, a Philadelphia firm issued an American edition of the publication. It served to enhance public interest in the prospect that, for the first time, a foreigner might come to America to head one of its colleges.[51] It was thus that Princeton's leaders hired a leading voice of Scottish evangelicalism, a man equipped in every way, it seemed, to assist in their struggles against Anglicans and liberal Congregationalists, America's partisans of moderate and rational Christianity. Once thus introduced to Witherspoon, New Side Presbyterians learned more about him. They learned that in 1756 he had written *Essay on Justification* and more recently, in 1764, *Treatise on Regeneration*. Both showed Witherspoon to be a learned Calvinist.[52] Then in 1759 a published sermon of his made clear that true morality derived only from piety, a point stressed by John Erskine and other Seceders.[53] All the more rose the hopes that he would assume the Princeton presidency. In fact,

50. Extracted from John Witherspoon, *Ecclesiastical Characteristics*, in *The Selected Works of John Witherspoon*, ed. Thomas Miller (Carbondale: Southern Illinois University Press, 1990), 57–102.

51. Butterfield, *Witherspoon Comes to America*, 12, 36.

52. Sloan, *Scottish Enlightenment*, 107–8.

53. Ned C. Landsman, "Witherspoon and the Problem of Provincial Identity in Scottish Evangelical Culture," in *Scotland and America in the Age of Enlightenment*, ed. Richard B. Sher and Jeffrey R. Smitten (Edinburgh: University of Edinburgh Press, 1990), 36.

however, Witherspoon carried with him more than just these credentials. Witherspoon, the Princeton officials might have noticed, was a product of the University of Edinburgh; had studied with John Stevenson, classics professor; and had not joined the radical evangelicals in secession from the established church. Princeton under Witherspoon was in store for some surprises.

When Witherspoon arrived at Princeton he hit the ground running. He had already expressed from Scotland his concern about the state of the college library and the low number of students at the college. Even before his departure for America, Witherspoon visited London and Holland and arranged for purchase of new books and scientific apparatus. Soon new volumes arrived at the library, many of them from the repertoire of the Scottish philosophers. There followed establishment of Princeton's first professorship in mathematics and natural philosophy. In the classrooms, Princeton followed the lead of the English dissenting academies and the Scottish universities in employing English as the language of instruction. Furthermore, the energetic Scot became known outside the Middle Atlantic colonies. He toured far and wide for the college and his effort to attract money, as well as new students, extended Princeton's name. Under Witherspoon it probably had the most national student body of the colonial colleges.[54]

Princeton was now also set for intellectual change. Things took a particularly interesting turn in the subject of philosophy. Witherspoon discovered upon arrival to Princeton that a form of philosophical idealism had won endorsement by the three Princeton tutors and found its way into the classrooms. Idealism in Western philosophy had secured a new triumph in the recent systemization of Bishop George Berkeley, whom we met earlier. As generally understood, it postulated the divine intelligence as the underlying principle and sustaining support of all reality. Berkeley built on Locke and his analysis of primary and secondary qualities of objects. He overcame the distinction by making primary qualities also matters of perception, to which the sum of our knowledge is limited. Objects have only an ideal existence, and not a material one. All objects, furthermore, depend for their existence on a universal mind. Berkeley intended these truths to enhance theology. Critics of idealism often used the term *immaterialism* to describe his system.[55] The tutors who advanced a form of this idealism at the college included Jonathan Edwards, Jr., son of the brief early president.[56]

---

54. Butterfield, *Witherspoon Comes to America*, 71–72; Sloan, *Scottish Enlightenment*, 110–11, 113.

55. Berkeley maintained that we know objects directly but that these objects were themselves ideal. He did not follow Locke's representational theory of knowledge, but held, like Witherspoon, to a presentational theory. The latter, though, insisted that the objects of knowledge were real things. See Bruce Kuklick, *Churchmen and Philosophers: From Jonathan Edwards to John Dewey* (New Haven, Conn.: Yale University Press, 1985), 69–70.

56. It is not clear exactly how philosophical idealism found its way to Princeton. The idealistic part of the senior Edwards, father, was not generally known until the 1820s. See Elizabeth Flower and Murray G. Murphey, *A History of Philosophy in America*, 2 vols. (New York: Putnam, 1977), 1:236–37.

Witherspoon set out immediately to drum philosophical idealism out of Princeton. This system of thought set squarely against Witherspoon's intellectual training, and in his preoccupation with setting philosophy right at Princeton he brought to the college that other part of his past, the Scottish Enlightenment. Witherspoon himself took on the instruction in philosophy, and in teaching the senior students reinforced the emerging academic tradition in America that would endure well into the nineteenth century—the college president instructing the seniors in moral and mental philosophy. Here Witherspoon drew upon academic traditions in his native country. Francis Hutcheson, Adam Smith, and Thomas Reid had occupied the moral philosophy chair at Glasgow University, as did James Beattie at Aberdeen and Adam Ferguson at Edinburgh. Witherspoon himself, apparently, used to frequent an Edinburgh tavern where "the deistical controversy and moral philosophy" dominated the conversation.[57]

Finally, we have in Witherspoon's "Lectures on Moral Philosophy" the outlines of his classroom instruction in this subject. The "Lectures," in fact, are barely that and we may assume that they merely suggest matters that the president discussed and analyzed in greater depth in his classes. They do not constitute a formal treatise of moral philosophy, and Witherspoon did not intend them for publication. They do have the advantage, however, of providing us rare documentation of what students actually had presented to them in the classrooms of an American colonial college. Witherspoon's instruction begins the long ascendancy of the Scottish philosophy in the American academic curriculum.[58]

Witherspoon knew that the topic of moral philosophy had been controversial in America and he knew Cotton Mather's disparagement of it. So he began his lectures by legitimating the subject. Moral philosophy, he said, is an inquiry into the nature and grounds of moral obligation by reason, as distinct from revelation. Witherspoon thus placed the subject within the recent demarcations made by Samuel Clarke and the Earl of Shaftesbury in England,[59] and Hutcheson in Scotland. And Witherspoon asked the question, "Is it lawful, and it is safe or useful, to separate moral philosophy from religion?" He answered by saying that the great gains made in science since Newton had actually enhanced religious knowledge, so why might not new gains in the "science" of morality do similar service? Although "infidels" do seize the standards of reason for their own cause, the religious-minded, he urged, should not shy from the challenge. "The best way is to meet them upon their own ground," Witherspoon wrote, "and to show from reason itself, the fallacy of their principles." He added his conviction that "the whole of Scripture is perfectly agreeable to

57. Jack Scott, "A Biographical Sketch," in John Witherspoon, *Lectures on Moral Philosophy*, ed. Jack Scott (Newark: University of Delaware Press, 1982), 26.

58. Flower and Murphey, *Philosophy in America*, 1:233–34.

59. Among other contributions, Clarke wrote *The Scripture Doctrine of Unity* in 1712. Shaftesbury (Anthony Ashley Cooper) published *Characteristics of Men, Manners, Opinions, Times* in 1711.

sound philosophy," but also said that Scripture was not intended to bear the whole burden of guiding our moral conduct. Moral science had its own value and use, he insisted. Witherspoon was registering a major shift here. To secure the ground against the skeptics he allied with the rational moralists and not the Edwardsean Calvinists, who grounded the moral sentiments in supernatural inspiration.[60]

In his "Lectures" Witherspoon drew upon two aspects of the Scottish Enlightenment. First, he took a lot from Hutcheson without giving him due credit for it.[61] Witherspoon, the legendary critic and satirist of the Moderates, may have been cautious not to open up Princeton so visibly to the rationalist Scottish Enlightenment. However, to secure morality on a secure intellectual foundation, Witherspoon appealed to the moral faculty as an innate principal of the human mind. In the face of the severe, skeptical challenge of fellow Scot David Hume, Witherspoon found Hutcheson, with his case for the autonomy and authority of the moral faculty, indispensable. Witherspoon also borrowed from Hutcheson's aesthetic theories. The mind, Witherspoon asserted, much in the manner of Hutcheson's esthetics, can recognize order, proportion, simplicity, intricacy, variety, and uniformity in such arrangements that it is led to acknowledge these forms as beautiful. By a similar process, said Witherspoon, we can discern the moral qualities, or their lack, in any actions. He also insisted, similarly to Hutcheson, and contradicting Hume, that we do so without attention to any particular self-interest connected to them.[62]

Scottish philosophy had still another use for Witherspoon. In the years before his departure for America, Witherspoon had become acquainted with some thinkers in the northeast sections of Scotland. Aberdeen was the cultural center of the Highlands, and here in 1758 a social group that included Thomas Reid, John Gregory, and George Campbell formed the Aberdeen Philosophical Society, James Beattie joining them in 1760. They met from time to time at area taverns, took turns in buying the port, and toasted David Hume, if only to strengthen their resolve in refuting his ideas. Reid became the most influential of the group. He came from Strachan, near Aberdeen, where his father served fifty years as local pastor. The son followed for a while in the ministry before launching a university career that began at King's College and continued at Glasgow. Reid identified strongly with the Moderates in the Scottish Kirk. He

---

60. Witherspoon, "Lectures," 64–65; Flower and Murphey, *Philosophy in America*, 1:234; Francis L. Broderick, "Pulpit, Physics, and Politics: The Curriculum of the College of New Jersey, 1746–1794," *William and Mary Quarterly* 3rd Series, 6 (1949): 58.

61. Flower and Murphey write, "Throughout the *Lectures* the Hutchesonian tone is evident: indeed he has even adapted Hutcheson's organization of moral philosophy which was his heritage to the whole school of social thinkers from [Adam] Ferguson to Hume and [Adam] Smith" (*Philosophy in America*, 1:235). Landsman believes that Witherspoon took Hutcheson's idea of a moral sense and his Whiggish political ideas and "made those principles into the basis of his own lectures on moral philosophy" ("Witherspoon and Provincial Identity," 37).

62. Scott, "Biographical Sketch," 27–28; Witherspoon, "Lectures," 77–78.

disdained the general tastes of the populace and the "fanatic" character of its evangelical religion. He called it all the more regrettable that the clergy encouraged this kind of religiosity among the masses.[63]

Here again in America Witherspoon had recourse to the Scottish Enlightenment, this time to strike against the idealism of the tutors. He turned to Reid and Beattie. Reid, like Kant later, had awoken from his dogmatic slumber in reading Hume. Reid had once been persuaded by Berkeley, but had seen that philosopher's idealism carried into rank skepticism by Hume. Hume based all knowledge on experience. He confirmed the existence of an external world, but insisted that we cannot demonstrate its existence, for all perceptions existed only in the mind. Mind itself, in Hume's reasoning, could have no demonstrated reality differentiated from the complex of perceptions that compel us to infer its existence. Reid, like Witherspoon, wanted to return philosophy to a more certain foundation. In 1764 he published his book *An Inquiry into the Human Mind, on the Principles of Common Sense*. The book gave rise to the term *Scottish "Common Sense" Realism* and would gain a larger currency later in the writings of Dugald Stewart. The more blunt and confrontational Beattie, in the meantime, had issued *An Essay on the Nature and Immutability of Truth in Opposition to Sophistry and Scepticism*, in 1770.

Witherspoon used the Scottish thinkers to refute idealistic error and materialistic fallacy. He owed most to Reid in this matter for the Glasgow philosopher had stood resolutely for a dualistic reality. The Scottish cosmology posited a radical division of spirit and matter, of soul and body. Probably no other notion better secured the Scottish philosophy's place as the "official" academic norm for the Protestant colleges of the United States in the late eighteenth and early nineteenth centuries, so clearly did it underscore religion. With Witherspoon's intervention one could say that "Princeton was a bulwark of antimaterialism."[64]

One may be disappointed in Witherspoon's lectures, for they do not engage Berkeley or Hume in any analytical way. It was said of Witherspoon, in fact, that he simply chose to ridicule idealism right out of the college. The "Lectures" do hint at his methodology. They charge that "immaterialism" takes away the distinction between truth and falsehood and would lead to the preposterous notion that in perceiving a tree I have only a distinct and lively impression of a tree. Witherspoon replied that one can have a distinct and lively idea of a thing that does not exist, so that notion gets us nowhere. "The truth is," Witherspoon wrote, "the immaterial system is a wild and ridiculous attempt to unsettle the principles of common sense by metaphysical reasoning, which can hardly produce anything

---

63. McCosh, *Scottish Philosophy*, 194–95; Dugald Stewart, "Account of the Life and Writings of Thomas Reid, D.D.," in *The Works of Thomas Reid*, ed. Sir William Hamilton (Edinburgh: Maclachlan and Stewart, 1854), 3–5, 205.

64. Donald Robert Come, "The Influence of Princeton on Higher Education in the South Before 1825," *William and Mary Quarterly* 3rd Series, 2 (1945): 363. See also, D. H. Meyer, "The Uniqueness of the American Enlightenment," *American Quarterly* 28 (1976): 178.

but contempt in the generality of persons who hear it, and which I verily believe, never produced conviction even on the persons who pretend to espouse it."[65]

Witherspoon gave a special notice to Hume, who, he said, had confounded everyone's thinking in such philosophical matters as cause and effect, personal identity, and the idea of power. Against Hume's assault, Witherspoon observed, "some late writers" had taken up an opposition. These "authors of Scotland," as he further identified them, had sought to secure these questions "on certain first principles or dictates of common sense." These certainties come to us as either simple perceptions or are seen "with intuitive evidence," he wrote. In so declaring these late triumphs, the work mostly of Reid and Beattie, Witherspoon also revealed why the Scottish philosophy was now beginning its long primacy in American academic thought. Witherspoon had no doubt that the certainty of first principles underscored the major ideas—spiritual and moral—of theological understanding. Thus Witherspoon could refer to Hume "and other infidel writers" as those whose bad influence the Scottish philosophers now were undoing.[66] Witherspoon thus reoriented Princeton, intellectually, toward the Scottish thinkers—selectively, to be sure. He prepared a legacy carried out by his successor Samuel Stanhope Smith. Smith's biographer Mark Noll summarized this significance:

> Witherspoon's philosophical allegiance . . . was no minor matter. It not only united him with Scottish Moderates and Old Side Presbyterians. It also divided him from the philosophical orientation of the New Side/New Light American Calvinists. . . . In other words, when Witherspoon set in place a pattern of instruction grounded in Scottish moral philosophy, he materially altered Princeton's traditional approach to ethics, epistemology, and the interconnections of knowledge. In particular, his commitment to Scottish common sense meant that there was no longer any room at Princeton for the influence of Jonathan Edwards. Nothing in the college's early history so significantly shaped its destiny.[67]

The legacy extended beyond Princeton. Scottish realism became the academic prop of American higher education, in its Protestant domain, from Witherspoon's introduction of it at Princeton through the middle of the nineteenth century.

---

65. Witherspoon, "Lectures," 74. Compare to Reid on the skeptical philosopher:

he sees human nature in an odd, unamiable, and mortifying light. He considers himself . . . as born under a necessity of believing ten thousand absurdities and contradictions, and endowed with such a pittance of reason as is sufficient to make this unhappy discovery. . . . Such notions of human nature tend to slacken every nerve of the soul, and spread a melancholy gloom over the whole face of things (David Fate Norton, *David Hume: Common-Sense Moralist, Skeptical Metaphysician* [Princeton, N.J.: Princeton University Press, 1982], 197).

66. Witherspoon, "Lectures," 96–97.

67. Mark Noll, *Princeton and the Republic, 1766–1822: The Search for a Christian Enlightenment in the Era of Samuel Stanhope Smith* (Princeton, N.J.: Princeton University Press, 1989), 37, 43.

The College of New Jersey, with its founding in 1746, summarized three decades of intellectual contention. American Presbyterians, from synod meeting to pamphlet publication to Sunday sermon, struggled to define who they were, where they fit in the catalogue of Protestants. Those individuals who established the college had painstakingly set themselves apart from the strict subscriptionists within the denomination, but they had also qualified their identity with the more intemperate voices of the Awakening. At the same time, they clearly perceived and forcefully confronted the danger posed to them by Anglicanism. It had already posted gains at Yale, and it grew as the oppositional party to the Awakening. The Anglican threat had both an institutional and theological dimension. For these reasons, the intellectual background of Princeton is as complex as that of any of the colonial colleges. It has taken us into discussion of the early church, the relation of ethics to revelation, grace as opposed to virtue. And, as we have observed, both the internal and external issues approached clarification, if not complete resolution, only in the years immediately prior to the founding of the college. Indeed, they may be said to have been its prerequisite.

But little proved stable in the Presbyterian environment. By the time of John Witherspoon's arrival, as he so effectively perceived, Presbyterians, to be sure, and all Protestantism generally, faced a greater challenge. The Enlightenment in Great Britain and on the Continent was fostering forms of both idealism and materialism. Witherspoon felt little inclined to invoke either Calvinism or New Light passion to thwart these inroads. Instead, he went to his own Scottish background and imported a native version of the Enlightenment to undo its other forms, for the Scottish version set comfortably with a religious understanding of things. Neither Scotland nor the American colonies, nor the later United States, for that matter, would see a truly formidable Enlightenment challenge to Christianity akin to that which appeared on the Continent. Witherspoon's opening to the Moderate Enlightenment in Scotland, furthermore, took Princeton into the more rational and liberal religious climate of the nineteenth century without any formal concessions to the Arminianism or the rite of the Anglican Church. Witherspoon, like Dickinson before him, steered Princeton through the dangerous middle. It soon became clear that Witherspoon's new country would readily adopt the Scottish philosophy for its own larger purposes.

6

King's College:
Battle for New York

In 1753, William Smith, Jr., took stock of the colony in which he lived and judged it wonderfully blessed. He said of New York, "with respect to what nature has done for us, there is not a happier people in the world, than the inhabitants of this province." The necessities of life, he wrote, "we possess with the richest affluence." He could cite the fertility of the soil, the vital river of the Hudson and its access to the sea, and extensive highways for trade and commerce. He boasted of the colony's superiority to Pennsylvania and the city's superiority to Philadelphia.[1] Smith had joined a party of other champions of New York and they were pooling their literary skills in a new publication called *The Independent Reflector*. On another matter, however, Smith and his group did not boast at all. He believed that New York trailed other colonies in cultural and intellectual achievements. "This province above any other," he wrote, "has felt the miseries of ignorance, and they still remain our sorest affiliations." Smith saw New Yorkers consumed by "a sordid thirst after money" and he judged the upper classes of the colony "wealthy, distinguished, illustrious, and exalted blockheads."[2]

Smith employed a little hyperbole here, but did express a genuine concern. The other members of the *Reflector* group shared that concern and made it a cause. William Livingston and John Morin Scott completed the editorial circle of the magazine and were called "the Triumvirate," or more commonly "the Reflectors." Their campaign for cultural improvement soon had them looking for a

---

1. William Smith, Jr., "A Brief Consideration of New York. . . ," *The Independent Reflector*, January 18, 1753, in *The Independent Reflector or Weekly Essays on Sundry Important Subjects More Particularly Adopted to the Province of New York by William Livingston and Others*, ed. Milton M. Klein (Cambridge, Mass.: Harvard University Press, 1963), 103–7.
2. David C. Humphrey, *From King's College to Columbia, 1746–1800* (New York: Columbia University Press, 1976), 38.

new college in the colony, with its desired location in New York City. They spelled out in a series of essays what kind of college could best serve the state, and they had clear ideas about its curriculum and governance. But the Reflectors confronted a major obstacle to their objectives. Another group in the colony also had collegiate ambitions. They too wanted a college in the city and they wanted it under their control. They were Anglicans. They felt a rising tide of influence for their church in the American colonies and believed they must challenge the Congregationalists and the Presbyterians in higher education. A more dismal and frightening prospect could hardly have occurred to the Reflectors. A pitched battle loomed. Out of it came King's College. Today it is Columbia University.

For its part, too, New York City was poised for greater prominence in America. To be sure, its rural beginnings persisted. When Theodore Roosevelt wrote his biography of Gouverneur Morris he described a city just emerging from its countryside background.

> New York City was a thriving little town, whose people in summer suffered much from the mosquitos that came back with the cows when they were driven home at night-fall for milking; while among the locusts and water-beeches that lined the pleasant, quiet streets, the tree frogs sang so shrilly that a man in speaking could hardly make himself heard.[3]

In 1685 New York City had a population of about three thousand inhabitants, a number that grew to seven thousand in 1720. It had more than doubled to eighteen thousand in 1760. At midcentury, New York City's imports from England had tripled from the level of only two decades before, and its exports to the home country grew apace. The city was acquiring a cosmopolitan tone. Residents followed London fashions as English commodities and fineries arrived weekly into their booming port. No wonder Anglican strength in the northern colonies would consolidate in this city above all. Altogether New York began to make favorable impressions on visitors. An English naval officer said of it in 1756, "The nobleness of the town impressed me more than the fertile appearance of the country. . . . I had no idea of finding a place in America, consisting of near two thousand houses, elegantly built of brick. . . . Such is this city that very few in England can rival it."[4]

The work of interconnected social elites began to give New York some definition in the 1750s. Major families that dated to the Dutch era had consolidated their wealth. They still held vast estates along the Hudson River, but they thrived economically through their connections to the city commerce. The complexities of the modern economic order tied this powerful group to a rising generation of

---

3. Theodore Roosevelt, *Gouverneur Morris* (Boston: Houghton, Mifflin and Company, 1888), 1.

4. Humphrey, *King's College*, 37; Joseph J. Ellis, *The New England Mind in Transition: Samuel Johnson of Connecticut, 1696–1772* (New Haven, Conn.: Yale University Press, 1973), 178; Richard Middleton, *Colonial America: A History, 1585–1776*, 2nd ed. (Cambridge, Mass.: Blackwell, 1996), 411 (the quotation); Michael Kammen, *Colonial New York: A History* (New York: Scribner, 1975), ch. 7.

lawyers. Indeed, many of them saw to it that at least one of their sons studied law. This other group, in fact, would take the lead in New York City's new quest for cultural respectability. Historian Thomas Bender describes their concerns and goals:

> They sought to bring their city more clearly into association with the metropolitan culture of London and Edinburgh. Or, put differently, they sought to reconstitute English culture but under American conditions, and this implied an embrace of Enlightenment rather than traditional ideas, civic rather than traditional institutions. For all of them, the promise of city culture was a new and secular hierarchy of learning, one which would reward and honor their individual talents, while advancing the prestige of the local milieu that gave significance to their lives.[5]

Their concerns, we shall see, had implications for the college issue.

On the day in October 1746 that New Jersey's acting governor chartered the College of New Jersey, the New York assembly took note. The next day it authorized preparation of a bill to raise funds, by means of a public lottery, for that colony's own college. The bill became law in December.[6] The action gave a green light to a partisan group of Anglicans in New York City who wanted a college under their denominational control. They had watched Dissenters in the New England and Middle Colonies seize the lead in founding colleges and they resented those gains. James Murray, Anglican polemicist, regarded Princeton with disdain. In and around New York City and next-door Connecticut, a generation of American-born Anglican leaders had emerged—Samuel Johnson most notably, but also Samuel Seabury, Henry Barclay, Samuel Auchmuty, and others. They viewed the college as means for greater ecclesiastical influence and the extension of the Church into the political and professional life of the colony. Anglicans constituted a minority in the city, only one-seventh of the population in a city of Dutch Reform, Presbyterians, Quakers, Huguenots, Lutherans, Anabaptists, and Jews. But in the four-county area that included the city they had privileged, established status, because taxes supported their ministry. The colony, moreover, had a royally appointed governor, assuring Anglican domination in the executive branch.[7]

The Anglicans also took encouragement from a recent trend. Many who became disillusioned with the religious Awakening, or otherwise recoiled in horror at the excesses of "enthusiasm," were finding their way into the Anglican Church. Samuel Johnson observed that "the madness of the times . . . does remarkably engage people's attention to our preaching and administrations." The shift had important consequences in giving the Anglicans their own identity as

---

5. Thomas Bender, *New York Intellect: A History of Intellectual Life in New York City, from 1750 to the Beginning of Our Own Time* (New York: Knopf, 1987), 11–12.
6. Humphrey, *King's College*, 3.
7. Humphrey, *King's College*, 26–27.

a principle of authority and stability in a faltering world. Henry Craner had seen an Anglican opportunity as early as 1743, as these prejudicial words indicate:

> Where the late spirit of enthusiasm has most abounded, the Church [of England] has received the largest accession. Many of those deluded people, having lost themselves in the midst of error, wearied in the pursuit, and as their passions subsided, sought for rest in the bosom and communion of the Church; and others, reflecting on the weakness of their present disorders, have likewise thought proper to take shelter under the wings of the Church.[8]

The real Anglican advantage in the matter of the new college, however, came in an unexpected way. For some years, as discussion of a college founding continued, opinions as to its location varied. Some, like the influential Cadwallader Colden, preferred a rural location. He thought a rural retreat would lay a safe, moral foundation for the colony's future leaders, indeed the city's as well. Others scoffed at that notion, associating a rural site with cultural backwardness, coarse and unpolished mannerisms. For a while, it seemed like Newburgh, up the Hudson River, would win the prize, but in May 1752 New York City's Trinity Church offered five hundred acres of choice land for a campus in the city. With that offer on the table, New York City's moneyed elite, many of them Trinity Church members, campaigned the more strenuously for the city location. Reverend William Smith (no relation to William Smith, Jr.), in particular, became the most prominent of the Anglican clergy in championing the city site. Smith, later the first provost of the College of Philadelphia, ridiculed the rural option and called for a new college that would "unite the scholar with the gentleman." He looked for graduates who would "know men and the world." Anglicans gained other city allies, most notably the Dutch Reformed. Then, too, city patriots generally gave their assent to a city college. Philadelphians, they knew, were well under way to establishing a college in their city.[9]

One group, however, rose to fight the prospects of an Anglican college and used every devise it could to defeat the plan. The ensuing struggle created a moment of great intellectual significance for colonial America. Those who opposed the college raised the issue to principles of society and politics that transcended the immediate details at hand. As opponents to Anglicanism made and expanded their case against the Church's domination, they sounded ideas that would echo down to the years of the American Revolution. Advancing that case were the editors of the remarkable *Independent Reflector*.[10]

---

8. Ellis, *Samuel Johnson*, 118–19.

9. Humphrey, *King's College*, 6–7, 9–16.

10. Bernard Bailyn says of the *Reflector's* political commentary, it "contains in a few sections propositions altogether modern, far in advance of anything one might expect from the mid-eighteenth century and from a society that venerated the concept of a monarchy" (*The Origins of American Politics* [New York: Knopf, 1968], 114).

Creation of the *Independent Reflector* marked a significant act in colonial New York. The *Reflector* appeared in November 1752, the first periodical publication in the colony; indeed, for a while it would be the only one in all the colonies. Inspired by the single-essay format of Joseph Addison and Richard Steele's *Tatler* and *Spectator* in England, it sought to address New Yorkers on all matters political. Livingston was the magazine's most outspoken member. Only twenty-nine years old when the *Reflector* appeared, Livingston came from the Philip Livingston family, proprietors of the Livingston manor, second in size only to that of the Van Rensselaer family in New York. Livingston grew up in "ease and affluence," by his own description. The Livingston manor constituted a vast complex—ships, warehouses, mills, and farmlands, with locations in Albany, where William grew up, and in New York City. It extended even to the West Indies. Philip Livingston educated his sons for future management of these extensive holdings, and William and three of his brothers attended Yale College. The father chose a legal education for William, who clerked in the firm of the esteemed lawyer James Alexander. The young Livingston did not find the situation likeable, however, vexed by the endless tedium of the legal work. Furthermore, he early showed the brashness that would mark his reputation. In print, he attacked Alexander's wife, whose social pretentiousness he could not abide. For his sport, he was dismissed. Livingston then pursued his greater love of literature. He is best remembered in this activity for his long poem *Philosophic Solitude, or the Choice of a Rural Life*, published in 1747. He impressed all with his vigorous and eloquent writing, a compensation, perhaps, for his own social awkwardness and deficiency as a public speaker.[11]

Livingston soon found a common cause with William Smith, Jr., and John Morin Scott. All were Yale graduates, had worked in Alexander's offices, and were Presbyterians. Smith's grandfather had come to America in 1697, established himself in New York City, and sent his son Thomas to Yale, where he became a tutor, read law, and entered the New York bar. Thomas prospered greatly and allied with the "Presbyterian faction" in colony politics. He became attorney general of New York in 1751 and trained Livingston, Scott, and William, Jr., in the law. The son, born in 1728, also attained fame as the colony's first historian, authoring the weighty chronicle *The History of the Province of New York*. Smith had a reputation for moral severity and fastidiousness. He had once faulted Livingston for excessive drinking at Yale (emphatically denied by Livingston). A dedicated Presbyterian, Smith, in his priggish habits, offended some people; they called him a sycophant and flatterer. Smith married into the Livingston family.[12]

11. Milton M. Klein, *The Politics of Diversity: Essays in the History of Colonial New York* (Port Washington, N.Y.: Kennikat Press, 1974), 58.
12. Michael Kammen, "A Character of William Smith, Jr.," in William Smith, Jr., *The History of the Province of New York:, Volume One: From the Discovery to the Year 1732*, ed. Michael Kammen (Cambridge, Mass.: Harvard University Press, 1972), xviii–xx; L. F. S. Upton, *The Loyal Whig: William Smith of New York & Quebec* (Toronto: University of Toronto Press, 1969), 16–23; Klein, *Politics of Diversity*, 64.

John Morin Scott, by contrast, was "bluff, hearty, and jovial," and flourished in social affairs. At ease himself, he made others the same in his company, winning friends for his humor and generosity and displaying these traits as he held court in the city taverns. Scott had married into the Henry Rutgers family of commercial fame. He worked with Smith to secure the New York courts' judicial independence from the Crown and later became a founder of New York's Sons of Liberty.[13] Their differences notwithstanding, the "Triumvirate" had shared political beliefs in the 1750s. They embraced a simple and rational Christian religion and abhorred the ecclesiastical establishment with all its trappings of power and the pomp and ceremony that advertised that power.[14]

The Reflectors' fear of the powerful church came from a libertarian ideology. In Livingston, especially, liberty was a passion, powerfully expressed, lovingly embraced. Here he writes in the fourth number of the journal:

> Liberty gives an inexpressible charm to all our enjoyments. It imparts a relish to the most indifferent pleasure, and renders the highest gratification the more consummately delightful. It is the refinement of life; it soothes and alleviates our toils; smooths the rugged brow of adversity, and endears and enhances every acquisition. The subjects of a free state have something open and generous in their carriage, something of grandeur and sublimity in their appearance, resulting from their freedom and independence, that is never to be met with in those dreary abodes, where the embittering circumstance of a precarious property, mars the relish of every gratification, and damps [sic] the most magnanimous spirits.

Livingston continued in his essay with an equally graphic depiction of the conditions of life and the state of the human spirit, miserable and unfulfilled, under absolute monarchies.[15]

The *Independent Reflector* took its format from Addison and Steele, but it took its ideology from Trenchard and Gordon. Thomas Gordon and John Trenchard played major roles in fashioning the English Whig school of history. They carried on a tradition that went back to James Harrington, author of *The Commonwealth Oceana* in 1656, to Machiavelli, and to Cato. All these writers had shown concern for defending against abuse and corruption in public life and for assuring the progress of virtue and the public interest against them. They opposed Tory political principles; the divine right theory of monarchy, as associated especially with the Stuart kings; and High Church leaders. Trenchard and Gordon's essays for *The Independent Whig* in 1720 had a special focus on the dangers of a Catholic revival. The *Independent Reflector* borrowed part of that publica-

---

13. Klein, *Politics of Diversity*, 64.

14. Kammen, "A Character," xx–xxii.

15. William Livingston, "The Different Effects of an Absolute and a Limited Monarchy. . . ," *The Independent Reflector*, December 21, 1752, in Klein, ed., *Independent Reflector*, 78–79. The journal essayists published their pieces anonymously.

16. Ned C. Landsman, *From Colonials to Provincials: American Thought and Culture, 1680–1760* (New York: Twayne Publishers, 1997), 155; Klein, "Introduction," 21; Humphrey, *King's College*, 43–44, 45.

tion's name and perpetuated many of its fears. The Reflectors even reinforced their anticlericalism by republishing Gordon's 1720 essay *The Craftsman*.[16]

What the Reflectors saw happening in New York City brought all these principles and the lessons of history into the contemporary scene. They associated Protestantism with personal liberty, especially freedom of belief. They joined virtually all American Protestants in contempt and fear of "popery," and they championed the cause of England and the colonies against the designs of the French in North America. But in New York, and the other colonies, too, they feared the Church of England no less. It is instructive to remember that they supported Yale and the College of New Jersey. But this new college was to be an *Anglican* one. It would represent a national church and a vast ecclesiastical order. Nothing more frightfully illustrated the formula for state corruption. An Anglican college, like an established Anglican Church, threatened individual freedoms and the larger public interest so said the Reflectors.[17]

The Anglicans, in the wake of the Reflectors' assaults, pressed even harder for their dominance in the college. They insisted that its president must always be of their denomination. The Reflectors demanded that New York have a wholly nonsectarian institution. Livingston took his case to the Presbyterians and the Dutch Reformed. He himself had grown up in the Reformed faith of his Dutch family but later embraced Presbyterianism. He looked to both groups for an alliance against the Anglicans and a common resistance to Anglican power. Livingston saw that the Awakening, for whose religious zeal he had little sympathy, was yielding a harvest of recruits for the Church of England in the Middle Colonies.[18] To the Presbyterians he appealed to historical memory. He recalled the "afflictions" and "fiery trials" they had endured at the hands of the English Church, and the infamous Test Acts. He invoked the "pious predecessors" of their denomination and "that ancient yoke of bondage" from which they fled in forsaking land and home in search of their religious freedom. Livingston and Smith also took their case to the rural provinces of the colony, where Anglicans had little support.[19]

How might the Reflectors best make their case to their fellow New Yorkers? They invoked modern political ideology and tried to make the college issue much more than a matter of local or sectional factionalism. When needed, the Reflectors could invoke a large public interest against the special interests of powerful groups. In a splendid rendering of their social philosophy, Scott outlined the principles of the *Reflector* group. With Livingston's libertarianism, compare Scott's communitarian principles:

I would first establish it as a truth, that societies have an indisputable right to direct the education of their youthful members. If we trace the wisdom of Providence in the harmony of the creation, the mutual dependence of human nature renders it demonstrably certain, that man was not designed solely for his own happiness, but also to

17. Landsman, *From Colonials to Provincials*, 160–61.
18. Klein, "Introduction," 23–24; Humphrey, *King's College*, 58–59.
19. Humphrey, *King's College*, 49–51.

promote the felicity of his fellow-creatures. To this bond of nature, civil government has joined an additional obligation. Every person born within the verge of society immediately becomes a subject of that community in which he first breathes the vital element, and is so far a part of the political whole, that the rules of justice inhibit those actions which, though tending to his own advantage, are injurious to the public weal. If therefore, it belongs to any to inspect the education of youth, it is the proper business of the public, with whose happiness their future conduct in life is inseparably connected, and by whose laws their relative actions will be governed.[20]

This persuasion convinced the Reflectors that the city college must be public and nonsectarian.

New York Anglicans could not remain passive in the face of the Reflectors' attacks. They took to the pages of the New York *Mercury* to refute their charges. Henry Barclay, rector of Trinity Church, wrote to Samuel Johnson, citing the "senseless" statements of the *Reflector* and urging Johnson to fight back. William Smith (the Anglican), James Wetmore, and Samuel Seabury went into print for the counterattack. Johnson wrote to the bishop of London telling of "a most virulent and active faction of Presbyterians and Freethinkers" who fought against the college charter.[21]

The Anglicans made their case against the Reflectors by alleging a religious and social radicalism in their views. They rejected any social philosophy rooted in natural rights and dismissed an original state of nature as but the workings of a wild imagination. They wanted a larger principle of authority than a vague public interest. Nor did they accept the Reflectors' notions of religious pluralism for the college. Anglican minister Samuel Seabury asserted that a college so structured would be liable to "all the confusions in the building of Babel."[22] Anglicans warmed neither to the libertarian or the communitarian leanings of the Reflectors. They found a religious sanction in neither of them. Those "whimsical noodles" who blathered about the popular, as opposed to the divine, origins of the state had only their own ends in mind, they said, and kept good company with deists and atheists.[23]

In the contest the Anglicans held the high cards. The Trinity Church land offerings proved decisive in determining the status of the new college. Livingston probably knew the outcome all along, describing Trinity as the "most numerous and richest congregation in this city." Anglicans assumed that the church's gift gave them a clear entitlement to dominant control of the college. They secured the advantage, however, only after a protracted struggle in the colonial legisla-

20. John Morin Scott, "A Further Prosecution of the Same Subject," *Independent Reflector*, April 12, 1753, in Klein, ed., *Independent Reflector*, 191.

21. Samuel Johnson to the Bishop of London, July 6, 1754, in *Samuel Johnson, President of King's College: His Career and Writings*, ed. Herbert and Carol Schneider (New York: Columbia University Press, 1929), 4 vols., 4:20.

22. Jurgen Herbst, *From Crisis to Crisis: American College Government, 1636–1819* (Cambridge, Mass.: Harvard University Press, 1982), 102.

23. Ellis, *Samuel Johnson*, 184–85.

ture and after engineering a deal with the Dutch. That group was promised a professorship to represent its religious interests. So agreeing, the Dutch acquiesced
to Anglican claims to the lottery funds. The Dutch and Anglican social elites
had already formed strong bonds with each other, and some of the Dutch had become Anglicans. The alliance gave the college additional, important connections. It also left, however, another, anti-orthodox, group of Dutch Reformed, led
by Theodore Frelinghuysen, to pursue its own interests in a college.[24]

The Reflectors and their sympathizers had tried valiantly to avoid these out-
comes. But they now saw prominent Anglicans like James Murray, John Cham-
berlain, Benjamin Nicoll, and half the vestry of Trinity Church serving on the
first board of trustees. The Reflectors, however, had not fought in vain. King's
College announced that it would admit students of all religious faiths. Samuel
Johnson, who could cite his efforts to win religious freedom at Thomas Clap's
Yale, assured that King's would be more liberal than either Yale or Princeton. His
advertisement for King's College in 1754 announced a simple principle: "And
that the people may be better satisfied in sending their children for education to
this college, it is to be understood, that as to religion, there is no intention to impose on the scholars, the particular tenets of any particular sect of Christians; but
to inculcate upon their tender minds the great principles of Christianity and
morality in which true Christians of each denomination are generally agreed."[25]
Nor did the Anglicans gain a provision that the college president must forever
be an Anglican, a measure sought by many of them. Dissenters sat on the board
of trustees, Livingston among them. Indeed, on November 22, 1753, Livingston
nominated Johnson for the presidency of the college. He then submitted the
name of Chauncey Whittelsey, Congregationalist, for vice president.[26]

On November 5, 1722 Samuel Johnson and friends had left Yale and sailed for
England, the controversy they had ignited at Yale still smoldering. He, with
Timothy Cutler and Daniel Brown, proceeded to Canterbury and received ordination. The event created the three New England Anglicans. Johnson, who became the most prominent, judged America in need of redemption by England.
In the American colonies, however, a new effort was underway. In the middle of
the eighteenth century more and more colonialists were moving into the Church
of England. And often more than Anglican ritual or liberal theology supplied the
ground for a switch in denominational loyalties. Sometimes it was just a love of
things English. In England, Johnson thrilled to the beauty and antiquity of English architecture. The cathedral at Canterbury dazzled him. So did the theater in
London. At Oxford and Cambridge he walked amid splendid buildings and

---

24. Humphrey, *King's College*, 31, 33, 56, 62–63.
25. "Samuel Johnson Advertises the Opening of King's College (Columbia), 1754," in *American Higher Education: A Documentary History*, ed. Richard Hofstadter and Wilson Smith (Chicago: University of Chicago Press, 1961), 2 vols., 1:207.
26. Humphrey, *King's College*, 31, 47; Ellis, *Samuel Johnson*, 172.

King's College in 1770

basked in the intellectual climate of the universities. How remote and provincial seemed Connecticut to him. How sterile seemed American culture.[27]

So Johnson returned to his own country armed with a cause. He had no doubt that any scheme for the improvement of colonial life required its full absorption into the Church of England. Johnson took up his work at Stratford, Connecticut. Students with whom he had worked at Yale came to study theology with him—Henry Craner, John Beach, and Ebenezer Punderson. Johnson became a recognized recruiter for an American Anglican ministry, getting candidates placed in local schools where a small income could sustain them during their studies. Furthermore, Johnson became the most vociferous champion for appointment of an American Anglican bishop. To Congregationalists, Presbyterians, and others, this activity signaled a direct and aggressive confrontation. Indeed, the bishop issue would agitate increasingly over the years and come to symbolize the perceived ecclesiastic imperialism of the Anglican Church. Johnson wrote letter after letter to the bishop of London. He wanted more than just the several commissaries to hold church power in the colonies. Nothing less than a bishop would do, he insisted. Johnson also extended his own connections to the well-placed in the American Anglican community. In 1725, he married Charity Nicoll, widow of Benjamin Nicoll and daughter of Colonel Richard Floyd, both of prominent New York families. She brought a daughter and two sons into the marriage and Johnson became father to the younger Benjamin, later prominent city attorney and one of the first trustees of the college. William Samuel Johnson and William Johnson were later born to the couple.[28]

Johnson was an early advocate of an Anglican college in the northern colonies. He pressed the need of a native-born clergy, indispensable, he believed, for the Church's future in the colonies. Johnson bristled at Dissenters' domination of higher education in New England and found it galling that the Presbyterians now controlled the only college in the Middle Colonies. Along the way toward King's founding in the 1750s, Johnson took on the Presbyterians on the intellectual front.

In 1745, Johnson published *A Letter from Aristocles to Authades Concerning the Sovereignty and Promise of God*. Johnson used his protagonist to make a sustained attack on Calvinism, particularly its doctrine of determinism. He acknowledged that his commentary would raise the "odious name" of Arminianism against him, but he cared not. Johnson perceived in Calvinism a theology that wholly distorted the true nature of God. He understood Calvinism to mean that all are under an original fate that precludes their acquiring, on their own initiative, a moral control of their lives. That idea, however, removes people from any accountability for their state. Worse, said Johnson, it projects mankind into a condition of everlasting misery and shows us a God who would promote his own glory by casting his creatures

---

27. Ellis, *Samuel Johnson*, 82–85.
28. Ellis, *Samuel Johnson*, 93, 106, 113.

into such woe. So warped an idea, Johnson professed, violates the "holiness, justice, and goodness" of God. In his own understanding of Scripture, Johnson saw a divine scheme by which God intends that all shall come to him and gain repentance. The doctrine of divine sovereignty thus, said Johnson, is "repugnant to the whole general drift of the Word of God."[29]

As might be expected, Johnson's dialogue moved in the direction of a rationalist Christianity. He wanted to show a compatibility of God's divine justice with commonsense human understandings of rewards and punishments. So Johnson insisted that God distributes favors and talents among his creatures, but imposes no permanent condition on them. Only the afterlife implies a determinism, he said, and that condition derives from the use and effects we have made of those favors and talents God has given us. Thus, Johnson maintained, "none shall be miserable at last but for their own fault." Any idea that God might act arbitrarily in the matter of ultimate judgment offended Johnson. God does not treat people as sticks or stones, he said, but "as rational and moral agents."[30]

For Johnson, as for many Anglicans, Christianity meant the personal struggle for moral improvement. He believed that God asks for that effort above all, so that Christian fulfillment means a right life, one lived in accordance with God's scriptural guidance for moral living. The notion that some people inherited a permanent sinfulness and others might be selected for exception from this state made no sense to him. Johnson expressed his concern for the in-betweens, those who knew their sinful state and sought to win a daily victory over it. Aristocles therefore says to Authades, "Tell me, is there no medium between an obstinate, relentless sinner, and one who is thoroughly regenerate, in your [Calvinist] sense of the word, who has gained the mastery of his own lusts, and is universally in heart and life devoted to God in Jesus Christ?" To those individuals, Johnson believed, God gives his special graces.[31]

Johnson made a powerful case against the theology that essentially united all Presbyterians in the 1740s, for Old Side and New Side, and the factions within each, all embraced Calvinist doctrines. Now, as the Presbyterians finally began to coalesce, enough to put the hopes for their new college into place, they found their intellectual foundations under attack. John Beach had joined Johnson in the assault the same year with his contribution, *A Sermon Showing that Eternal Life is God's Free Gift, Bestowed upon Men According to Their Moral Behavior, and that Free Grace and Free Will Concur in the Affair of Men's Salvation.* Never did a title so well state its contents' theme. Dickinson again took up the rebuttal, confronting both Anglicans in his *A Vindication of God's Sovereign Free Grace,* published in 1746, the very year of Princeton's founding. Dickinson asked Johnson to observe some facts about the world. One will see, he said, that God's provi-

---

29. Samuel Johnson, *A Letter from Aristocles to Authades Concerning the Sovereignty and Promise of God* (Boston: T. Fleet, 1745), 1–3.

30. Johnson, *Letter from Aristocles,* 8–9, 12–13, 20–21.

31. Johnson, *Letter from Aristocles,* 25.

dence does not reach the greater part of mankind. Most peoples of the world live in ignorance, impiety, and idolatry. If God can deal with different parts of humanity in this way, why cannot he also deal with individual human beings? Some will never know his special grace and others will receive it.[32]

Then Dickinson reverted to a stricter Calvinism. He asked whether God owed mercy to his fallen creatures. Hardly, he answered, given the horribly sinful state in which they exist. God does, however, over time, grant salvation to some; and how can there be any injustice in his so doing? Shall we forever be complaining, asked Dickinson, that God does not save everyone? He furthermore considered it an aspect of human arrogance to scrutinize divine intentions. God works for his own glory, he urged, "whether our shallow intellects can fathom the unsearchable depths of his dispensations, or not."[33]

Dickinson went on to insist that Calvinism does not deprive man of free will. God offers a general free grace to all, though he knows by foresight that most will not avail themselves of that promise. That foreknowledge, however, said Dickinson, does not mean God's prevention of anyone's effort. "God has put no man under a compelling necessity to be holy or wicked," he affirmed. Misunderstanding in this matter, he said, has led to monstrous confusions about the true moral nature of God, and most evidently among the Anglicans, he suggested. Furthermore, sensing how Anglicans placed so much stress upon the conduct of life and moral virtue, Dickinson urged that the doctrine of divine sovereignty had a direct tendency to make the sinner low and vile in his own eyes and to bring him to a suitable dependence on the mercy of God. "We see," he wrote, "that when this doctrine of God's sovereignty is heartily received, and rightly understood, it has a good influence upon men's *conduct*." Contrary doctrines, he added, had contributed to the false security so dangerously prevalent in modern times.[34]

The debate between Johnson and Dickinson wound into logical sophistry. But the larger issues speak to the opposing intellectual milieus in which the College of New Jersey and King's College began their institutional histories. Johnson published a redirect to Dickinson, in the form of a twenty-eight-page letter, the next year. He asked him, if God knew something would occur, did it mean that he willed it? Thus, did he will Adam's transgression? Did he will Judas's denial of Jesus? Then we should ask, said Johnson, if he willed these things did he take pleasure in them? Such notions, he knew, spoke to Presbyterians' cherished ideas of God's sovereignty and omniscience, and his activity in the interest of his own glory. Johnson pressed his points relentlessly. Does God then take pleasure in the death of every sinner? he asked. He wrote to Dickinson, "It shocks me, I confess, only to mention such horrid thoughts, which are infinitely impossible to

---

32. Jonathan Dickinson, *A Vindication of God's Sovereign Free Grace* (Boston: Rogers & Fowle and Blanchard, 1746), 66–67.
33. Dickinson, *A Vindication of God's Sovereign Free Grace*, 67.
34. Dickinson, *A Vindication of God's Sovereign Free Grace*, 68–72.

be true." He believed, however, that these were the consequences of "your" doctrine. Ultimately, Johnson charged, Presbyterian doctrine made God an agent in
the corruption of the world.[35]

Not alone did Johnson advance the Anglican case against Presbyterianism
and advertise resentment toward the New Jersey school. Other Anglicans also
perceived an affront in the Presbyterians' creation of the College of New Jersey.
Thomas Bradbury Chandler wrote to Johnson in 1753 informing him of its relocation to Princeton. The Presbyterians in control of that college, he said, meant
to stamp out Anglicanism. Anglicans should be wary, he added, because the Presbyterians have "the craft of Jesuits." Johnson believed that the College of New
Jersey "will be a fountain of nonsense" and virtually slurred the school's New
Side personnel when he added that Princeton was "entirely in the hands of the
most virulent Methodists."[36]

More than issues of Protestant doctrine propelled Johnson in his Anglican
commitments and his quarrels with the Dissenters. Johnson idealized an ordered
society, and he made the Church of England a major principle of his pronounced
social conservatism. In the colonies, nothing so disturbed the fragile stability of
American community, he believed, as the emotional distempers wrought by religion itself. In his autobiography, Johnson recalled the "strange, wild enthusiasm"
induced by George Whitefield. He and his followers "broke through all order and
rule," he wrote. Whitefield confirmed to Johnson how erratic was the public
temper, for Whitefield had only to pronounce such horrible doctrines of hell,
damnation, and the devil as to cast hundreds into emotional frenzy. Johnson also
wondered at people's capacity for self-delusion as they gloried in the facile conversions effected by the revivalists.[37] Religious dissent, in general, Johnson believed, fueled an unruly republicanism. Establishment, on the other hand, reinforced social hierarchy, political authority, and personal self-discipline. Johnson
had seen enough public unruliness in Connecticut. There a constitution yielding "a mere democracy and the prevalancy of republican mobbish principles" had
flourished with "enthusiastical principles" in religion, he affirmed. Johnson considered it his role as college president to embrace all efforts to stay these trends.[38]

These matters hardly dominated Johnson's thinking as he assumed the presidency at King's. He had more pressing concerns. The college had land but no
buildings, so it opened to students in the summer of 1754 in a vestry room of Trinity Church. Johnson prepared to remove to New York City from Connecticut,
though he had told the trustees, that, for fear of the smallpox, he would insist on

35. Samuel Johnson, A Letter to Mr. Jonathan Dickinson, In Defense of Aristocles. . . (Boston:
Rogers and Fowle, 1747), 11–13.

36. Thomas B. Chandler to Samuel Johnson, February 26, 1753, Career 1:165; Humphrey, King's
College 23–26; Herbst, From Crisis to Crisis, 97.

37. Samuel Johnson, "Memoirs of the Life of the Rev. Dr. Samuel Johnson. . . ," Career 1:28.

38. Humphrey, King's College, 22; Samuel Johnson to the Archbishop of Canterbury, July 12,
1760, Career 1:295; Samuel Johnson to William Johnson, January 20, 1755, Career 1:209.

the right to vacate the premises at will. He did expect to have a home available for him, but instead the trustees sought funds to erect one large building on the new grounds. It would house students as well as the president and his family. Two years later, on a day marked by much ceremony, the governor laid the cornerstone of the college's new structure. That it would serve the college on its own for three full decades tells something about the continuing problems of King's College.[39]

Students enrolled in the college in small numbers. They first came from families of the original trustees. Never in the colonial era would the school have the large geographical base that Princeton did. Nor would its graduates repay the Anglicans' efforts to establish a college for their denomination. David Humphrey reports that at the time of the American Revolution King's had supplied only twenty graduates for service in the American Anglican ministry. (Princeton had furnished 220 young men for the Presbyterian ministry.) Nor did the generality of the Anglican ministry in the colonies send their sons to King's. Consistently, it seemed, King's students came from the ranks of the New York social elite. One of the Triumvirate said that King's existed "for the education of all who can afford such education." At any given year through the 1750s and 1760s, the New York school was not likely to have more than twenty-five students. In the early 1770s the president could say, with some relief, that enrollments had climbed into the forties. All the while, the school did not lack for money. It charged the highest tuition in America, and in 1762 undertook a successful fund-raising effort. King George III made a personal gift of £400.[40]

The Reflectors had envisioned a broadly secular curriculum for King's College and wanted a college that would supply New York with a cultured and professional class of people. In fact, the Anglicans, and Johnson especially, had similar hopes for the college. At the outset, Johnson proposed for the school the most ambitious academic program yet in the colonies. Indeed, it suggests the characteristics of the modern, expansive university. Johnson specified King's goals:

> to instruct and perfect youth in the learned languages, and in the arts of reasoning exactly, of writing correctly, and speaking eloquently; and the arts of numbering and measuring, of surveying and navigation, of geography and history, of husbandry, commerce and government, and in the knowledge of all nature in the various kinds of meteors, stones, mines, and minerals, plants and animals, and of everything useful for the comfort, the convenience and elegance of life, in the chief manufactures relating to any of these things; and, finally, to lead them from the study of nature to knowledge of themselves, and of the God of nature, and their duty to him, themselves, and one another, and everything that can contribute to their true happiness, both here and hereafter.[41]

---

39. Humphrey, *King's College*, 111–12.
40. Humphrey, *King's College*, 73–74, 81 (quoting Williams Smith, Jr.), 92–97, 122–23, 133, 135–36.
41. "Samuel Johnson Advertises the Opening of King's College (Columbia), 1754," in *American Higher Education* 1:110–11.

Such a vision, of course, far outreached prevailing reality. Early King's College offered a curriculum not much different from the kind Johnson had known at Yale—languages, logic, natural philosophy, mathematics, and metaphysics.[42]

Despite the early trials of King's College, it had one asset—its leader Samuel Johnson. He was a towering intellect of colonial America, a man of great curiosity and philosophical interests. He stood almost unrivaled as the preeminent voice of American Anglicanism, and at King's he had a special opportunity to give it institutional expression. Johnson's intellectual journey illuminates both the religious mind in America and the academic. His church commitment also explains his liberal spirit and its expression at his college. But even in these matters, no simple explanation contains his career. His life took some leads from various sources—from the Puritanism of his native Connecticut to the new philosophical directions of the England he so admired.

Johnson never described himself as an Arminian. He upheld a liberal and rational theology that he believed antedated the ideas of the Dutch Presbyterian, as Johnson called Jacob Arminius. Furthermore, and more confrontational to his Presbyterian rivals, Johnson claimed that his religious thought derived from that of the New England founders themselves. He, too, he said, preached a covenant theology and thought in the Ramist outlines he had learned at Yale.[43] He, too, preached a God all-wise, all-powerful, rational, and just. Johnson's biographer confirms a New England imprint, citing Johnson's personal journal entries and his sermons. We find a man acutely conscious of sin and laboring under the burden of it. Johnson wrote in his journal in 1725, "O Lord I abhor and detest those remainders of my sin which alas, too much cling to me and by which I am too apt to be overcome." By the time Johnson entered the King's College presidency, it has been noticed, his sermons had taken on a pessimistic tone. He never escaped the war within, the battle of the soul against the demons that beset it, and he never doubted that the grace of God alone secured the victory.[44] However, even within the terminology of a Reformed Christianity, Johnson applied clearly Anglican measures of the religious life.

Throughout his intellectual career, Johnson found an important influence in the Anglican philosopher George Berkeley. During the two years that Berkeley stayed at Newport, Rhode Island, 1729–1731, Johnson sought him out. The Anglo-Irish philosopher had done his most important work by that time, most significantly his *Treatise Concerning the Principles of Human Knowledge* in 1710. Answering Locke, Berkeley asserted that both primary qualities (e.g., extension, weight) and secondary qualities (e.g., color, taste) of objects are known only in the mind and therefore there is no existence apart from a perceiving intelligence. But the observing mind of God makes possible the

---

42. Ellis, *Samuel Johnson*, 224.

43. On this matter, see Norman O. Fiering, "President Samuel Johnson and the Circle of Knowledge," *William and Mary Quarterly* 3rd Series, 28 (1971): 199–236.

44. Ellis, *Samuel Johnson*, 127, 136–7, 141 (the quotation)–43.

Samuel Johnson (Detail; oil painting by John Smibert)

continued existence of things, which can have only an ideal and not a material existence. Berkeley intended his radical idealism to be a comprehensive
disproof of atheism.

Johnson perceived in Berkeley's writings a way to underscore theology by extending the insights of John Locke. Johnson's correspondence with Berkeley, however, reveals some hesitations and reflects a New England skepticism. Johnson presented his reservations indirectly, citing doubts that he had seen in others'
approaches to Berkeley. He believed that Berkeley had relocated to the "will of the
Infinite Spirit" too much of the causal factors in all physical and human action. "To
suppose his immediate energy in the production of every effect," Johnson wrote to
Berkeley, "does not seem to impress so lively and great a sense of his power and wisdom upon our minds, as to suppose a subordination of causes and effects among the
archetypes of our ideas." That is, we must think the more highly of a grand designer

who can create a watch that runs on its own, by ingenious coordination of its parts, than of one who must oversee every minute of its operation. Furthermore, such a deterministic understanding of God's role, as Johnson read Berkeley, deprives the individual sinner of his proper culpability and guilt. Johnson referred to the sinful ideas that spur the immorality of the sinner. He insisted that, in Berkeley's rendering, the immediate cause of such ideas is but "the immediate effect of the Almighty on his mind." Johnson did not want to make God the author of our sin. As noted, he faulted Dickinson and all the Calvinists for so doing.[45]

In the intellectual history of the American college, Johnson made his most important contribution through his own collegiate text. In terms of his great hopes and expectations for this work, that contribution was but a modest one. Benjamin Franklin published the text in Philadelphia, but it never realized the anticipated sales. Nevertheless, the work held a central place in the King's College curriculum during Johnson's presidency, as he taught the senior classes in moral philosophy. Johnson reconfigured his earlier writings to accommodate his instruction. In 1746 he had published *A New System of Morality* under his familiar pseudonym Aristocles. The new textbook, *Elementa Philosophica,* appeared in 1754 and included a section on ethics derived from the earlier work.

Few people today would find *Elementa Philosophica* very interesting reading. It deals tediously with narrow philosophical points that did interest some eighteenth-century thinkers—matter and form, real and apparent causes, essence and existence, identity and diversity, and so on. The discerning reader, however, will look closely at this textbook and see what Johnson has accomplished. For one thing, he made a careful and qualified effort to bring the insights of Berkeley into America. For despite his reservations, and despite his initial shock at Berkeley's immaterialism, Johnson saw at this later time overwhelming advantages. As summarized by two historians of American philosophy, Berkeley provided Johnson "not only incontestable proofs of a deity, but moreover the most striking apprehensions of his constant presence with us and inspection over us, and our entire dependence on him and infinite obligations to his most wise and almighty benevolence." We remember how much of his career Johnson had already spent in warfare with Congregationalists and Presbyterians, fighting the institutional power of an entrenched Reformed Protestantism. We know how much he hoped for a wider and more general influence of Anglicanism in the American colonies. Johnson also, however, had perceived a threat from materialist and deistic ideologies. Here he had an opportunity to help in both concerns. By his philosophical work Johnson would underscore the theological principles of Anglicanism. Now with the establishment of King's College he had the institutional base on which to secure those principles. He made the most of it.[46]

---

45. Samuel Johnson to George Berkeley, September 10, 1729, in *Career* 2:264–65.

46. Elizabeth Flower and Murray G. Murphey, *A History of Philosophy in America,* 2 vols. (New York: Putnam, 1977) 1:82–84 (the quotation). For elaboration of Johnson's appropriation of Berkeley in more technical terms, see pp. 82–99.

In the first section of his book, to illustrate his method, Johnson took up the subject of the mind. He made an immediate appropriation of Locke. "Our minds," he wrote, "may be said to be created mere *tabula rasae*"; they have no notice of any objects properly created in them. Johnson did not permit this notion to lead into empiricism, which he would judge a too excessive dependency on experience, or a determinism thus derived. Johnson saw a dependency of a different kind. He perceived a dependency on God for an individual's interior existence as for his physical existence. People, he wrote, "are no more authors to themselves of the objects of their perceptions, or the light by which they perceive them, than of the power of perceiving itself; but they perceive them by a perpetual intercourse with that great Parent Mind, to whose incessant agency they are entirely passive." Jonathan Edwards had used Lockean ideas to reinforce Calvinist notions of human dependency. Johnson could have built in that direction, too, but he quickly established human independence and freedom to choose and act. Johnson thus began by showing a mutuality of human and divine, not a chasm separating them. He also announced that he would proceed to secure this vital distinction between Anglican and Calvinist presuppositions.[47]

Johnson used Locke but also Berkeley, citing his *Theories of Vision, Principles of Human Knowledge*, and *Three Dialogues*. He borrowed also from John Norris's *Theory of the Ideal or Intelligible World*, also a favorite of Thomas Clap. Johnson confirmed the existence of archetypical ideas, external to human minds, existing in the mind of God. Johnson did make a distinction: In the divine mind, archetypical ideas are original and necessary; in us, they exist by way of sense and imagination. In one they are perfect, in the other imperfect. The connection, however, establishes a link of the divine and human and makes possible the communication between God and individual souls. By these means Johnson again established the proximity of the divine and the human, a vital point in Anglicanism. Johnson wrote, "Our ideas, therefore, can no otherwise be said to be images or copies of the archetypes in the eternal mind, than as our souls are said to be images of Him, or as we are said to be made after his image."[48]

In the academic philosophy that Johnson processed through an Anglican understanding, everything conspires to make the individual a role player in his own destiny. God provides all the resources for a successful outcome, so that the Christian life is always a matter of fulfilling an enabling potential. Again, concurrent with Johnson, Jonathan Edwards for the Reformed tradition had made the passions essential signposts of a moving and genuine religiosity. His theological turn thus legitimated the Awakening that so vexed the Christian rationalists, Johnson as much as any of them. Johnson, as much as Edwards, however, rejoiced to locate in the Christian life a great struggle within, one marked by

---

47. Samuel Johnson, *Elementa Philosophica: Containing Chiefly Noetica, Or Things Relating to Mind or Understanding and Ethica, Or Things Relating to Moral Behaviour*, in *Career* 2:374. The editors have used the second edition of the work, edited by William Smith, the Anglican.
48. Johnson, *Elementa Philosophica*, 2:376–77.

tension, anxiety, and emotion. For even the striving to put the passions under discipline registered this struggle. God has equipped us in this combat with the indispensable faculty of reason, Johnson insisted. Also, Johnson always portrayed a benevolent God who wills human good. He wrote, "Since therefore, the Great author of our nature aims at our happiness, and hath given us our passions to be subservient to it, and furnished us with reason, to govern and regulate them in such a manner as to render them useful to that end, it must be his will and law, and the will of our nature, that we should duly exercise our reason in the right government of them." On this article, too, Johnson could base much of his educational system. For what else is education but a critical training in disciplining and moderating the passions under the tutelage of the reason and the conscience?[49]

No Puritan would have denigrated human reason. It still retained a faint connection to the God from which the Fall had alienated the human estate. Also, Johnson's rationalism did not bring him into the more skeptical mode of the radical Enlightenment. He never allowed that humans could rely on reason sufficiently for their moral and spiritual ends. We find consistently in Johnson the language of God-dependence. Unlike in the Puritans, however, dependency always returns us to a loving God who has no score to settle and wishes human happiness. Here is the reasoning:

I say our highest moral perfection consists in freely doing what we know tends to make us entirely happy in the whole of our nature and duration: but then it must be considered, that, as God is our chief good, our great creator, preserver, and governor, on whom we entirely depend for our being, and for all our happiness, and all our hopes; and as he wills our happiness, as his end in giving and continuing our beings, and consequently everything as a means, that is conducive to it; so it must be supposed to be implied in our highest moral perfection, that we are entirely devoted to him, and do every thing conducive to our happiness, in relation to him, and one another, in a designed conformity to him as our great and original pattern, and in compliance with his will, and from a sense of duty to him as our supreme moral governor.[50]

Such a passage as this one, at the least, shows Johnson's own skill in logical reasoning.

Johnson finished the first section of *Elementa Philosophica* with some thoughts on economy and politics, much of which anticipated the appendage on moral philosophy. Here he reinforced the social ethic that he had always espoused. He emphasized the common good and the primacy of community in the moral compass of each individual. Government, he believed, had always the collectivity as a priority, not the individual in separate identification apart from it. For in matters of law and government, both of church and state, he stressed that

---

49. Johnson, *Elementa Philosophica*, 2:420.
50. Johnson, *Elementa Philosophica*, 2:421–22.

"every individual is to resign to the public or prevailing sense (at least as far as his duty to God will permit) as being the safest and most rational method he can take," for in that way does his own best interest lie. Johnson wanted all to be trained in "resignation to the public good" and to be inspired by "public virtue and usefulness."[51]

Johnson appended a small treatise on moral philosophy to his *Elementa Philosophica*. Today's reader may find much of this section rather laborious, but not all of it. It reinforces Johnson's consistent emphasis on happiness. In his third paragraph he states outright, "Ethics is the art of living happily, by the right knowledge of ourselves, and the practice of virtue." Happiness is the end of human living, he assures. Here too, Johnson sought to mark off an Anglican ethics from the sterner talk of the latter-day Puritans.[52] His formidable skill lay in appropriating the liberal language of the Enlightenment and turning it back into the God-centered context of his own religious faith. Again we find that Johnson uses a precise logic. He reasons that God himself is perfect happiness and self-sufficient to that condition; he cannot aim at any further advantage to himself in giving us being; consequently, his great end must be our happiness, which he considers "his interest, his delight, and glory." If God wills our happiness, then we have a duty to pursue it, even to the point that "we forebear what tends to our misery."[53]

One need only glimpse the historical context of Johnson's writing to see his larger intentions. He had made the decision of his life in 1722 in his conversion to the Church of England. He had taken on the presidency of a fledgling Anglican college in New York City, uprooting from the stability of Stratford, Connecticut. He had expressed repeatedly his concern that "Dissenters" had surpassed the Anglicans, here in the colonies of Great Britain, in establishing colleges. Johnson, though, saw a battle of institutions, and with it, a battle of ideas. *Elementa Philosophica*, a pioneering contribution to American academic literature, sought to undermine the Reformed system of his opponents. King's president thus always sought to undermine the intellectual edifice that fortified that institution's rival schools. Any idea that God would contrive to place humanity in constant jeopardy of damnation he rejected wholly. Johnson did not need to name any persons or groups when he asked the question, Why would God place me, through no willful act of my own, into a condition that is worse than not to be at all? Why would he create anyone in a way that compels that person into sin? For sin to Johnson must be an act of free will and not ascribable to God in any way. Ultimately, life made no sense to Johnson if it did not offer a fair fight against evil, if it did not hold out the chance to win moral improvement in a fair fight.[54]

---

51. Johnson, *Elementa Philosophica*, 2:433.
52. Johnson, *Elementa Philosophica*, 2:446–47.
53. Johnson, *Elementa Philosophica*, 2:451–52.
54. Johnson, *Elementa Philosophica*, 2:472.

Never did Johnson's moral philosophy present the course of Christian living in easy terms. As much as the Puritan struggled against the inner demons of his nature and pursued a hard journey toward grace, so for the Anglican Johnson was life a constant trial. He warned his readers that the "long and laborious course of steadfast persisting in the cause of truth and virtue" would always run up against a hostile and indifferent environment. Ours is a world where greed and vice often win prosperity for its practitioners, he conceded. A God who loves virtue as his own essence, however, Johnson said, will surely bring good out of all this evil. That triumph may well await the next life, but for himself, Johnson asserted, he had no doubt, he would have all the happiness he needed.[55]

In his years at King's Johnson needed all the support of such faith to see him through personal tragedy. He lost a beloved grandson, and his own son Billy died when he went to London in 1756 to receive Anglican orders. His wife Charity died two years later. Both succumbed to the dreaded smallpox. In the next two years he lost a daughter-in-law and a stepson. The losses shook his faith in a God of reason and he retreated into a bible-centered faith nurtured by the writings of John Hutchinson.[56] (Johnson, however, did not use Hutchinson's writings at King's.) He recovered from these defeats in 1761, remarried, and regained enough energy to quarrel with the trustees of the college. Their patience with him, however, grew thin, and they sought to secure his retirement. When Johnson lost his second wife, yet another victim of smallpox, he lost the will to continue the presidency. In winter 1763 he hired a sleigh to carry him through a snowstorm back to Connecticut.[57]

The King's College officials had already chosen Johnson's replacement— Myles Cooper. He was of Scottish background, growing up in the Cumberland area in a well-established family. He had gone on to Queen's College at Oxford and earned an M.A. degree and served short terms as schoolmaster, chaplain at Queen's, and curate of a country church near Oxford. Cooper held strong loyalties to the Anglican Church. He traveled widely on its behalf, winning the nickname "Rambling Cooper." Unlike his predecessor, he had no trace of a Puritan background. All knew his fondness for good food and drink and "his high taste for amusement." His bulk and his pudgy face did not suggest a life of worldly denial. He paled before Johnson in learning and would give much more attention at King's to administration than to intellectual matters. At Cooper's death it was said that his books sold for £5 and his wine cellar for £150. If anything, under Cooper, the curriculum at King's regressed, taking on a more emphatic classical content in the model of Oxford.[58]

55. Johnson, *Elementa Philosophica*, 2:480–81, 483–84.
56. Hutchinson (1674–1737) was a High Church Anglican who opposed the science of Newton and charged that Newton and his followers had corrupted the essential truth of Christianity—the doctrine of the Trinity. Hutchinson looked to revelation as the only legitimate foundation of both theology and science.
57. Ellis, *Samuel Johnson*, 231, 241–42.
58. Humphrey, *King's College*, 126–28.

King's College did not fulfill the hopes of its Anglican founders, but in a certain sense it gained its larger mission. The Anglicans, and others who worked for King's, wanted a school that would serve the Church but also the growing city. Many hoped it would be an institution for the city's aspiring young men. They never came in great numbers but there were many who took advantage of what King's offered them.

Among the students who enrolled at King's in the 1760s were John Jay and Gouverneur Morris. They came from the ranks of the city's established families, and King's became their stepping stones to their careers in law and politics. Auguste Jay, grandfather of the first chief justice of the United States Supreme Court, was born in La Rochelle, France, in 1685. His Huguenot ancestors had risen to prominence as merchants and Auguste followed in that line. He had an English education that prepared him for a new career in the colonies. He went first to South Carolina and then Philadelphia. In 1697 he married Anna Maria Bayard and joined a prominent family. They had one son, Pierre, father of John. He joined the family business, and the Jays could be recognized in the city by their large warehouse, piled high with all variety of commodities, many waiting for export. Pierre Jay served on the city council and became an elder of Trinity Church. John Jay was born in the city in 1745.[59]

Gouverneur Morris came from an even more prominent New York family. They had a manor of nearly two thousand acres across the Harlem River from Manhattan and were of Welsh descent. Ancestors of Gouverneur had served in Cromwell's armies. Lewis, a grandfather, served as the first native-born justice of the New York Supreme Court. Lewis, Jr., also won distinction in the New York courts. He married Sarah Gouverneur, of Dutch and Huguenot descent, and the couple had their only son, named for her family, in 1745. He was christened in Trinity Church that year.[60] Gouverneur attended the Philadelphia Academy before entering King's College in 1764.

Jay entered King's in 1760 and studied under Johnson; Morris enrolled in 1763 and studied with Cooper. Jay took an inoculation for smallpox and then underwent the testing for admission. He had to demonstrate skills in reading Tully's *Select Orations* and in translating the first ten chapters of the Gospel of St. John from Greek into Latin. In his examination, Morris translated Sallust, Caesar's *Gallic Wars*, and the Gospel's. Students at King's began their day with morning prayer, performed by the president before breakfast. After a meal of coffee or tea with bread and butter, they went to their classes. The lunch break later offered fare according to the day of the week—roast beef and pudding on Monday, corn beef and mutton chops on Tuesday, pea porridge and beef steak on Wednesday, corned beef and mutton pie on Thursday, leg of mutton and soup on Friday, and fish on Saturday.[61]

---

59. Frank Monaghan, *John Jay: Defender of Liberty* (New York: Bobbs-Merrill, 1935), 16–22.

60. Max M. Mintz, *Gouverneur Morris and the American Revolution* (Norman: University of Oklahoma Press, 1970), 1–6, 9, 16.

61. Monaghan, *Jay*, 26; Mintz, *Morris*, 17–18.

Both Jay and Morris handled the King's curriculum well. Jay, however, confronted a particular problem in the rhetoric course, for he had difficulty in pronouncing the letter "l." The problem made him the object of ridicule among other students so he resolved to address the matter head on. By a regime of practice before a mirror, Jay overcame the frustration and developed a speech pace and pronunciation that became distinct in his public career. Academic success followed, as it did for Morris. Both young men had prominent places at their commencement exercises. Jay presented his oratory, described as "a masterly performance," on the subject of "The Happiness and Advantages Arising from a State of Peace." Morris in his oratory considered the contractual origins of society. He surpassed both Locke and Hobbes in arguing for the principle of beauty as the essential factor in creating the social contract.[62]

These events possibly conveyed a happy picture of academic normalcy at King's. In fact, however, the ground was moving under its feet. Revolutionary events stirred the city and King's College faced a decade of turmoil. President Cooper would pay a heavy price for his loyalty to the mother country, Jay and Morris would throw themselves into political agitation, and King's would soon produce in another student its most famous American patriot.

Samuel Johnson liked to think of the Anglican Church as "the golden mean."[63] The term could serve several purposes. It located the Church of England between Catholicism and radical Protestantism. It situated Anglican rational religion between papal ecclesiastical dogma and Calvinism's strict reading of Scripture. And, Johnson believed, it saved Christianity from the excesses of ecclesiastical authority in Rome and the anarchical tendencies in Protestantdom. That vantage helped secure Johnson's successes, as an intellectual leader for the Anglicans in colonial America, and as chief executive at King's. The identity that King's gained for itself came mostly from Johnson's energetic literary efforts. King's was America's second Anglican college and much more certainly located within an intellectual tradition appropriate to that identity than was William and Mary. But no more than William and Mary could King's effect a link from denomination to college. The non-Anglican colleges that preceded it, and some that would follow, derived from embattled religious parties, or from groups that had historical memories of a struggle to secure their right to exist. Surrounded even though it was in New York City and colony by rival sects, King's rested too much at ease with itself and the world. It had a rich intellectual tradition on which to draw, but the generality of its members felt little anxiety to secure it. It could draw on some institutional loyalty from wealthy merchants who saw fit to send their sons to it, but it did not become a rallying point for its larger clerical adherents. The Church of England gave its parishes a system of hierarchy and in-

---

62. Monaghan, *Jay*, 27–28; Mintz, *Morris*, 24.
63. Samuel Johnson to William Johnson, January 20, 1755, *Career* 2:209.

stitutional integration. Its American churches, lacking a bishop, could not supply this need. And its New York college could not supply the want.

King's College then became an Anglican contributor to American pluralism, even as it responded to that fact of American life. It could not be the solid rock of the English Church transplanted to the colonies even if its founders had wanted it to be, and some surely did. The American Revolution, we shall see, showed how attenuated was that identity. These considerations also apply to Samuel Johnson and highlight his remarkable contribution. The young man who emerged from Yale persuaded to the principles and rites of the English Church remained nonetheless an American product. Johnson's Anglicanism incorporated and thrived with remnants of his New England rearing and Puritan upbringing. He accepted with enthusiasm the new learning that Yale brought to him, but he could not read Newton or Locke with materialist or wholly rationalist understandings. Given too much sanction, Johnson knew, they would undermine Christianity altogether. Berkeleyan immaterialism gave him the way out and the way through. From this vantage, Johnson offered the dominant humane and liberal sentiments that mark his religious and philosophical writings. As he fought mightily against the long legacy of Calvinism, he became one of America's most articulate spokesmen for a reasonable and charitable God. Johnson and King's College thus also made their contributions to an American Enlightenment.

7

The College of Philadelphia: The Perils of Neutrality

The academy in Philadelphia that declared itself a college in 1755 could have been an important historical departure. It would flourish in Pennsylvania, a colony that had established religious toleration. Pennsylvania had no state church. Denominational warfare, ingredients of the other institutions we have seen, might keep its distance here. At any rate, all knew that the College of Philadelphia would have no sectarian identity. The city, in turn, had an established record of achievement in the arts and science. It had the first municipal library system in the colonies; it had scientific and literary societies. Its commercial connections made it the most cosmopolitan of American places and also the largest. Here perhaps a new college might take root and develop, exempt from religious rivalries and provincial politics. It might pioneer in modern subjects. How did it happen, then, that the College of Philadelphia knew political warfare from its very beginnings? How did it have a president so embroiled in colonial politics that he actually spent some time in prison? How did the College of Philadelphia produce some of America's most bitter factional warfare? This chapter looks at the early history of what became the University of Pennsylvania. It illustrates the perils of neutrality.

By 1750 Pennsylvania had become one of the most successful of the British colonies of North America. It led the others in its rate of population growth and in accumulation of wealth. It held a quarter of a million people, and thousands more hastened to the rich, fertile lands in its western areas. The Quaker influence counted for much here. Pennsylvania founders had proclaimed that none, least of all the state, may coerce in religious matters. The policy of toleration attracted a diverse population from different parts of Europe and it enjoyed in Pennsylvania the liberties that the Quakers had secured. Lutheranism and Presbyterianism had their effective American beginnings here. Anglicans had gained in numbers and influence. Even the devotees of radical Protestantism, the Anabaptists so scorned and persecuted by the church/state systems of the Old World, secured new roots in William Penn's colony.

Pennsylvania had historical significance for these reasons. But Penn himself was no democrat when it came to society and politics, and no ascetic when it came to the conduct of life. He reflected none of the political radicalism of the left-wing Protestantism that had invoked strong condemnation from Luther and others. Quaker humanitarianism, which would give that group leadership in antislavery activity, did not translate for Penn into social leveling. "For though [God] has made of one blood all nations," he wrote, "he has not ranged or dignified them upon the level, but in a sort of subordination and dependancy." Penn saw a precise hierarchy in the social make-up, from the scavenger at the bottom to the monarch at the top. Robert Barclay, Quakerism's most important doctrinist, urged that none confuse Quaker benevolence with social reconstruction. "Let not any judge that from our opinion," he said, "any necessity of leveling will follow, or that all men must have things in common. Our principle leaves every man to enjoy that peaceably, which either his own industry, or his parents, have purchased to him."[1] In this regard, one can find no stronger apostle of the proverbial "Protestant ethic" than Penn himself. He excoriated the monastic tradition of Catholicism and committed his followers to the discipline of the shop and workbench. Many Quakers would pursue salvation in a very worldly fashion.

Philadelphia wholly reflected that spirit. Business opportunities assured a growing population. The city had some thirteen thousand inhabitants in 1740 and twenty-two thousand in 1760. It nearly doubled that number by 1776. By that time it outranked Bristol, Britain's second city, as it did Edinburgh and Dublin. The Scotch-Irish were influencing the increase. Although many headed for the frontier to farm, skilled artisans tended to stay in the city. Small businesses spread through Philadelphia. "Retail shops of every description appeared, taverns multiplied, and a host of crafts and small manufacturers came into being." Philadelphia also enjoyed civic amenities. It had extensive street lighting in the 1750s and in the next decade began to pave its streets. It had a number of schools as well. Altogether, it looked very businesslike.[2]

Philadelphia also had a visible commercial elite that set the tone for much of its urban life. The Quakers had taken an early dominance in this group. The humble and outcast English folk who had followed George Fox in the early Quaker movement of the 1640s and afterwards had yielded to a more economically mixed set. London Quakers had established international connections in commerce, many of them through their own Yearly Meetings, and Philadelphia

---

1. Frederick B. Tolles, *Meeting House and Counting House: The Quaker Merchants of Colonial Philadelphia, 1682–1763* (New York: Norton, 1948), 110–11.
2. Carl Bridenbaugh and Jessica Bridenbaugh, *Rebels and Gentlemen: Philadelphia in the Age of Franklin* (New York: Oxford University Press, 1962), 3–4, 9–10 (the quotation), 11, 35–40.

now partook of these connections. By the 1720s one could speak of the "Quaker Grandees," families who by wealth and fashion constituted a city elite. Indeed, Frederick Tolles could write, "The Quaker merchants reared a structure of aristocratic living comparable to that of the Virginia planters, the landed gentry of the Hudson Valley, and the Puritan merchant princes of Boston."[3]

English tastes had a special attraction for this group and the English aristocrat provided a model for its way of living. For many, the temptation proved too great, and conversions to the Church of England became increasingly frequent among the Quaker elite. Even then, however, intermarriage among this elite made its members well-connected. For a long time, a small oligarchy of men held political power in Philadelphia, power they reinforced with their leadership in social and philanthropic organizations around the city. Like Penn himself, the Quaker elite had a partiality for rural life. Philadelphia architecture did not readily show the affluence of the elite, but outside the city one could see the handsome estates of the commercial class. Here its members escaped the summer heat of the city and lived like the English aristocracy they so much emulated.[4]

The political structure of Philadelphia ensured the power of this group, at least for a while. Only one in fifty inhabitants could vote, as most could not meet the property requirements. Philadelphia had no tradition like the New England town meetings that assured some measure of popular democracy. Friends controlled the mayoral office in Philadelphia in almost every year in the first quarter of the century. They came from the ranks of the great Quaker merchants.[5] Quaker toleration, however, would undermine the foundations of Quaker rule. Religiously, Philadelphia became the colonies' most pluralistic city. Baptists, Moravians, Methodists, Catholics, and a small number of Jewish families supplemented the aforementioned Lutherans, Anglicans, Presbyterians, and Quakers. Among the Presbyterians, the Philadelphia group secured an organizational foothold in the colonies with the 1704 establishment of the Synod of Philadelphia. After the arrival of George Whitefield in the city in 1739 an evangelical group of Presbyterians rose to challenge this establishment. Philadelphia would remain the stronghold of Old Side Presbyterianism, however, through the intramural warfare that now ensued. This Old Side group had many men of solid reputation and respect, most notably William Allen, Pennsylvania chief justice.[6]

Also gaining in influence were the Anglicans. Often Quaker conversions to the Church of England signified an honest recognition by the convert that the Quaker credo had lost meaning to him. The converting Quakers had become quite removed from the humble beginnings of the group and the simple ways of the meetinghouse lost appeal. They preferred a more public and elegant

---

3. Tolles, *Meeting House and Counting House*, 109.
4. Bridenbaughs, *Rebels and Gentlemen*, 180–82; Edward Potts Cheyney, *History of the University of Pennsylvania, 1740–1940* (Philadelphia: University of Pennsylvania Press, 1940), 9.
5. Tolles, *Meeting House and Counting House*, 118–19.
6. Bridenbaughs, *Rebels and Gentlemen*, 10, 13, 17–19.

way of worship. They had become commercially connected to the English traders, and the city everyday saw the arrival of English goods and the newest London fashions. Those who aspired to higher social rank joined Christ Church of Philadelphia. Generally, the apostates were wealthy and well placed politically. By 1750 Quakers in Philadelphia numbered only eight hundred families or about 25 percent of the population. Anglicans replaced them in the upper ranks. As the Bridenbaughs wrote, "Anglicans became definitively the congregation of wealth, fashion and position."[7]

These shifts were part and parcel of a political situation in Pennsylvania that shaped the early history of the college. William Penn died in 1718. The family fortune was declining, but Thomas Penn eventually inherited enough shares from his brothers to resume active family management of the proprietary interests in the colony. But he and his brothers did not have the Quaker commitments of their father. Richard Penn had joined the Church of England early in his life. John attended Quaker meetings infrequently. Thomas openly advertised his disaffection from Quakerism and eventually became an Anglican. These departures, however, did not weaken the Pennsylvania Quakers' resolve to maintain their political power in the colony. They concentrated their strength in the colonial assembly, where the narrow electoral base assured their continued domination. Here they claimed exclusive discretion in provincial matters, Indian policy most importantly. They considered themselves the trustees of Pennsylvania's humane tradition and would entrust its preservation to no other group. Until the end of the 1730s, few Quakers saw any reason to challenge the ways of a privileged minority.[8]

At this time, Thomas Penn wished to strengthen his position in Pennsylvania. To do so he had to move against the assembly. He needed allies, and they came from a loose and ill-coordinated group of individuals that would constitute, for lack of a better term, the Proprietary Party. Penn had an effective means for creating this coalition. It lay in his authority to appoint key officeholders in the colony. They included the lieutenant governor, three Supreme Court justices, the proprietary secretary, provincial secretary, clerk of council, receiver-general, and others. Occupants virtually had their positions for life, if they wanted them. Most appointments had more prestige than power, but several provided substantial incomes. Available to fill these offices now was a non-Quaker elite. The group constituted a diverse lot, save for the fact that they had arrived at considerable wealth. Some were Presbyterians; some were Anglicans. A large portion had Scottish backgrounds. They were excluded from the Quaker elite, who now, facing increased minority status in numbers, closed ranks. The non-Quaker elite had no institutions—social, political, educational—they could call their own.

---

7. Bridenbaughs, *Rebels and Gentlemen*, 16–17; William S. Hanna, *Benjamin Franklin and Pennsylvania Politics* (Stanford, Calif.: Stanford University Press, 1964), 12.

8. Hanna, *Pennsylvania Politics*, 8–9, 15–16; Tolles, *Meeting house and Counting house*, 19, 19n.

Penn's new aggressiveness gave them a measure of cohesiveness, though never real party unity. They would seize a new opportunity, however, in gaining control of the new college.[9]

In the years preceding the college founding, Penn and the assembly had locked horns. The issues concerned the taxing of proprietary lands and the authority of the proprietor to amend money bills. Ben Franklin was emerging as an important legislator in the colony, and he allied himself with the Quakers in the assembly in their resistance to Penn's power. Penn sought to enhance his power base by making appointments of non-Quakers to key provincial offices. He made James Hamilton lieutenant governor in 1746. Hamilton, a Philadelphia gentleman, had assembled the colony's first notable art collection for his estate at Bush Hill. His father Andrew had won fame in his defense of John Peter Zenger. James Hamilton was a deist with nominal ties to the Church of England. Penn also named William Allen chief justice. Allen, a leading Presbyterian in the Scotch-Irish Old Side group, had been mayor of Philadelphia and later formed a business partnership with Joseph Turner. He made himself one of the wealthiest of the non-Quaker elite. Penn also made Richard Peters proprietary secretary. Peters, an Anglican, came to have the most direct, personal influence on Penn. The proprietor, in addition, found among the non-Quakers the men he needed to run his estates, surveying and selling his lands and collecting quit rents. Most of the Proprietary Party made their money from land, a situation facilitated by the fact that Peters also ran the land office. He made out the patents that conveyed legal title to the lands. Quakers felt themselves the direct victims of Thomas Penn's policies. In the early 1740s non-Quakers had gained control of the Philadelphia Corporation, and in the next decade they had assumed all the key positions in the executive and judicial branches of the provincial government.[10] They were all in place when the first president of the college arrived to take office.

Factionalism gave a bitter tone to Pennsylvania politics, and more was to come. But the city gained from a good deal of public-spiritedness that brought leading residents into cooperation. It had literary, scientific, musical, and dramatic societies. Philadelphia was a city of books, with many large private holdings, the worldly Quaker James Logan's one of the largest in the colonies. The city also had a good number of book publishers. People might refer to Philadelphia as the Athens of the colonial cities and New York as their Sparta. In one area, however, Philadelphia lagged; it had no college.[11]

Ben Franklin had long hoped to establish an academy in Philadelphia. His ideas reflected the modern intellectual agenda that would establish him as a major

---

9. Stephen Brobeck, "Revolutionary Change in Colonial Philadelphia: The Brief Life of the Proprietary Gentry," *William and Mary Quarterly* 33, 3rd Series (1976): 413–15, 418–19.
10. Brobeck, "Revolutionary Change in Colonial Philadelphia," 418–23; Hanna, *Pennsylvania Politics*, 90–91.
11. Cheyney, *University of Pennsylvania*, 11–13.

voice of the American Enlightenment. Franklin had escaped the confinements of Puritan Boston as a youth and would flourish in the tolerant and freer atmosphere of Philadelphia. He became a man of cosmopolitan interests, and his city *Gazette*, it was noted, conveyed more news of Europe than of Philadelphia, and certainly more than of the rest of Pennsylvania, with which he seemed little concerned. Franklin also represented the mild deism of eighteenth-century America. He supported institutional religion mostly for its social usefulness. He had a strong personal admiration for John Tillotson, the liberal English theologian. Against the intellectual pretensions and obscurities of other religious writers, Franklin admired Tillotson for his clear and moving prose. "If a man would that his writings have an effect on the generality of readers," he wrote, "he had better imitate that gentleman, who would use no word in his works that was not well understood by his cook-maid."[12]

A modern academy signified for Franklin one that did not require training in the classical languages. Philadelphians had been debating this question for some time, and Franklin joined a party that campaigned for reconstruction of the school curriculum away from this emphasis. Some merchants spoke for the change, but so also did mechanics and members of the lower classes. They considered classical education an "ornamental" mark of the privileged classes and obsolescent besides. In Philadelphia some schools emerged that broke from the past, attracting youth from middle classes and the poor as well.[13] Franklin boasted of the new school that students would graduate from it "fitted for learning any business, calling, or profession, except such wherever languages are required." He added that although they will not be acquainted with any foreign tongue "they will be master of their own," and that fact, said Franklin, will be of much greater general use to them. They will have used the unproductive time studying old languages for other studies that will enable their ready entry into "the several offices of civil life." Franklin then outlined a reading list of the best English authors—Tillotson, Milton, Locke, Addison, Pope, Swift—to which he joined "the best translations" of Homer, Virgil, and Horace. He also gave a recommendation of Samuel Johnson's *Elementa Ethica*, which he had published, assured that it would provide for the students "a solid foundation of virtue and piety in their minds."[14]

It was understood from the beginning that the Philadelphia Academy, founded in 1751, would be nonsectarian. Of course, Franklin had worked with other prominent Philadelphians to establish the school. It had supporters from

---

12. Benjamin Franklin, "On Literary Style," in *The Papers of Benjamin Franklin*, ed. Leonard W. Labaree (New Haven, Conn.: Yale University Press, 1959–), 36 vols., 1:329.

13. Bridenbaughs, *Rebels and Gentlemen*, 68. The authors write, "Here was the real revolution of the period, the opening wedge of democracy on the march. The educational accomplishments of these years were to provide the democratic base for the flowering of an indigenous culture, and the intelligent, critical and literate audience for the pamphlet warfare of the Revolutionary era."

14. Benjamin Franklin, "Idea of the English School," *Franklin Papers*, 4:107–8.

the Anglican and Presbyterian churches and from James Logan among the Quakers. They, however, otherwise stayed aloof from the school and as a group gave no priority to higher education. Of the first twenty-seven trustees, about three-quarters were Anglican, several of them from Christ's Church; two were Quakers; and one a Presbyterian. In a midwinter day in 1751 the academy began classes. "On that day with great ceremony [the trustees] walked in procession, the Governor of the province at their head, the six blocks from his house on Market Street to the reconstructed New Building, where before a crowded audience one of their number, Rev. Richard Peters, preached a commemoration ceremony."[15]

Franklin had hoped from the beginning that the academy might become a college. So did the new president when he took office in 1754. This individual was William Smith. He would inaugurate the next phase of the school's history, and he would do much more. He would embroil the school in endless political turmoil. Smith assumed the title of provost as the Philadelphia Academy became the College of Philadelphia and granted degrees. Its "teachers" now became "professors."[16] Nor could anyone fail to observe that Philadelphia proclaimed itself the location of a new institution of higher learning in the colonies the very year after rival New York City established King's College. Few could foresee, however, what unyielding ambition and what flare for controversy Smith would bring to his office. And he was only twenty-seven years old.

Smith came from Scotland, born within a few miles of Aberdeen. His father, "a gentleman of some means," lived on a country estate inherited from his father. William attended the local parish school and had a collegiate education at the University of Aberdeen, from which he earned a degree in 1747. The Smith family had Anglican loyalties, part of the Jacobite tradition of Scotland, strong in the north, that had resisted Presbyterianism. That commitment took Smith to London in 1750 where he did work for the Society for the Propagation of the Gospel, the Church of England's outreach to the colonies. That connection brought Smith to New York City in 1751. His work here won attention in two ways. First, as we have seen, he joined the group that wished to secure Anglican domination of King's College, making himself a prime enemy of the Reflectors in the process. Second, he authored a significant piece called *A General Idea of the College of Mirania*, a vision of educational reform in this mythical province. Here students combined with their education in the classics, mathematics, science and rhetoric, new subjects of agriculture, history, and politics. This college would give no place to the narrow disputations of Calvinists and Arminians. It would teach instead just the simple tenets of Christianity.[17] Smith intended his educational concepts to be a model for King's. He wanted a school that emphasized practical education

15. Cheyney, *University of Pennsylvania*, 37–38.
16. Cheyney, *University of Pennsylvania*, 43.
17. William Smith, *A General Idea of the College of Mirania* (New York, 1753), 9–11.

Provost William Smith (Watercolor by E. C. Marchant, 1871)

and he even cited the published ideas of Franklin, who had long encouraged such reforms. Smith also called for an education stressing virtue and morals. That notion, too, appealed to Franklin.

When Franklin read Smith's tract, he judged that Smith would make an ideal leader for the academy.[18] Smith accepted the offer and on May 22, 1754, wrote in his journal: "Landed in Philadelphia. Put up at Ton Tavern, on Chestnut Street. Kept by John Osborn." Two days later he recorded the beginnings of his career at the college: "Commenced teaching the philosophy class, also ethics and rhetoric to the advanced pupils."[19] Had his new Philadelphia friends noticed what had just recently transpired with Smith they might have hailed his arrival a bit warily. The academy trustees had sent Smith to London in May 1753 with a strong endorsement of him to Thomas Penn and a hope that Penn would support his salary.

---

18. Franklin wrote to Smith, "For my part, I know not when I have read a piece that has more affected me, so noble and just are the sentiments, so warm and animated the language." Franklin did urge, however, that Smith not be so sensitive to his critics or so angry in returning their fire. He would see, to his regret, the wisdom of his cautionary advice (Franklin to Smith, May 3, 1753, *Franklin Papers* 4:475).

19. *Life and Correspondence of the Rev. William Smith, D.D.*, ed. Horace Wemyss Smith, 2 vols. (1879; New York: Arno Press, 1972), 1:45.

Smith and Penn immediately struck a strong friendship. Smith returned with money from Penn, but also with a resolve of his own to do Penn's bidding in the colony. He would write to Penn a few years later, "The good I can do depends upon my doing it silently without being seen. But what I can do shall always be at your service." In fact, Smith did few things silently. He quickly emerged as the proprietor's political agent in Pennsylvania.[20] Also, in December 1753 Smith again returned to England and took orders in the Church of England. The College of Philadelphia trustees, organizing the new nonsectarian school, were appointing to its presidency a committed Anglican.

It did not take long for Smith to be up to his neck in political warfare. In 1756 there appeared in Philadelphia a publication titled A *Brief State of the Province of Pennsylvania*. Published in London, it became immediately controversial, although not until a few months later did Smith's authorship of the scourge become known, and then matters got worse. The manifesto launched an open attack on the Quakers and the assembly. Smith addressed an issue emerging with increasing importance in colony politics—the defense of the western frontiers. On this issue, Smith called Pennsylvania "the most backward." Quaker policies, based on pacifist principles, he said, made the colony powerless to defend itself. Smith, moreover, used this attack to engineer another, now blaming excessive democracy as the root cause. All knew what he meant. In essence, Smith sought to undermine the popularly elected assembly and its longstanding control by the Quakers. Smith then played directly into the interests of Thomas Penn. He called for a more "mixed" government in Pennsylvania in which the proprietor would have a greater share of power. Penn and the assembly had been fighting bitterly over the share of power in the colony for some time, and now Smith, president of the college, cast his lot decidedly for the proprietor.[21]

One must see the complexity of the picture to understand Smith's attack. Smith knew that Quakers dominated Pennsylvania politics by their alliance with the Germans in the colony. Quakers had shorn up their political strength even as they became a numerical minority in the colony. They did so by cultivating the German immigrants, and, with lesser success, the Scotch-Irish. They sought to speak for them against the proprietor on land issues. Furthermore, Mennonites, Dunkers, and Moravians found a cultural kinship in Quaker pietism. The Quakers in turn assured the Germans that their very liberties depended on the perpetuation of Quaker control in the political arena. It worked. Smith and Penn now sought to break up that alliance.[22]

---

20. Ann D. Gordon, *The College of Philadelphia, 1749–1779: Impact of an Institution* (New York: Garland Publishing, 1989), 72–73.

21. Robert Middlekauff, *Franklin and His Enemies* (Berkeley: University of California Press, 1996), 47–48.

22. Allan Tully, *Forming American Politics: Ideas, Interests, and Institutions in Colonial New York and Pennsylvania* (Baltimore, Md.: Johns Hopkins University Press, 1994), 146; Hanna, *Pennsylvania Politics*, 13–14.

A *Brief State* offered some proposals that further challenged the Quakers. Smith wanted them to take an oath of allegiance to the colony, suggesting their treacherousness, and knowing full well that such action violated Quaker tenets. Smith also wanted to suspend the vote of the Germans until they attained mastery in the English language. He would make all legal documents void unless written in English. He would ban all newspapers, almanacs, and periodicals unless they too were English-language, or made available in a dual-language format.[23] In his proposals Smith again did the work of the proprietor. Penn had long sought an alliance with the Germans and believed that he could secure one only if he could break their cultural ties to the Quakers. To do so, he believed, he would have to "anglicize" them. He proposed a new system of charity schools by which to educate the Germans in the colony. Smith joined that cause enthusiastically and successfully. He had spoken in London the year before and warned that the thousands of Germans coming into Pennsylvania were falling dangerously into "barbarian ignorance" and threatened to become an alienated presence in the British colony. Smith called on the archbishop of Canterbury to send missionary teachers to the colony. The preservation of English liberties and the growth of industry and commerce depended, Smith urged, on the virtue and liberty that are the fruits of knowledge and true religion.[24]

College of Philadelphia leaders took the initiative in the charity school movement. Peters and Allen got involved and so did Franklin. He had stood with the Quakers against Penn, whom he detested, but he also championed education and the greater integration of the Pennsylvania Germans. This group opened charity schools in German communities around the colony. They moderated Smith's proposals by publishing a German-language newspaper, directly to challenge the ones that endorsed the Quaker line. They also sought to co-opt the German ministers by paying their salaries in return for political support. Smith in turn used his influence to gain support from Anglican ministers and their congregations. That Smith could also get a majority of the college trustees behind the program showed how much the institution had become, so quickly, identified with the proprietary interest.[25] Pietist leaders among the Germans, such as Christian Saur, saw the scheme for what it was and denounced the charity school program as disingenuous.[26]

Smith joined this issue to another one—the western frontier. In 1751 the French moved into the Ohio area, alarming the Pennsylvania Scotch-Irish, who asked to build a fort for defense. Penn offered to supply the money if the assembly would also take action. But the Quaker-dominated body stalled, further souring relations between it and the proprietor. On this matter, Penn might have forged an alliance with Franklin, but the two had fallen into such acute alienation by 1755

23. *Life and Correspondence of Smith*, 1:122–23.
24. Hanna, *Pennsylvania Politics*, 67; *Life and Correspondence of Smith*, 1:30.
25. Gordon, *College of Philadelphia*, 79–80.
26. Hanna, *Pennsylvania Politics*, 68.

that Franklin turned to a party of "war" Quakers, led by Isaac Norris, for support of an aggressive western policy. This party, however, fought with Penn over who should control the defense expenditures. Franklin wanted defeat of the French and believed that Penn had too many financial scruples to get behind that cause. Franklin threw himself into the assembly's attack on the proprietor and joined the Quakers in their effort to reduce his power. But this alliance could not last.[27]

Smith in turn had sufficient contempt of the Quakers and of the French to inspire his English imperialism. In 1754, he wrote to the secretary of the Society for the Propagation of the Gospel (SPG), warning of French designs in the west. They intended to seduce the Germans by easy promises and they would succeed, he said, because the Germans "place all happiness in a small farm," and would sell out their liberties in return. Hence all the more imperative, urged Smith, was the need to educate them in English ways. Of course, the Quakers again thwarted any effective military actions because of their pacifist principles. In a letter to the archbishop the next year, Smith warned that no solution could emerge so long as the Quakers held political office. By this time, the French had repelled General Braddock and his forces at the Monongahela River and with their Indian allies were spreading terror among the Scotch-Irish western settlers. They petitioned in vain for a response from the government. Smith wrote:

> 'Tis far from my desire to see any set of men hampered by real religious scruples; but surely if these scruples unfit such men for that which is the chief end of all government (the protection of the governed), they ought in conscience to resign to those who are better qualified. The lives and properties of the people are things too sacred to be trifled with. And yet while our government rests in the hands of *Quakers*, they must trifle on the subject of defense. They will suffer no body to share power with them, and as they themselves can take no part of a military power, so they are determined never to suffer it in the province, and some of them say they would sooner see the enemy in the heart of the country.[28]

The next year, when British forces marched west to engage the French, Smith sent them off with a patriotic sermon.[29]

Yet another issue further embroiled Provost Smith in colony politics. This one involved William Moore. Moore, esquire of Moore Hall in Chester County and first judge of the Common Pleas, had long advocated a strong defense policy for Pennsylvania. His opposition to the Quaker party led some in that group to produce evidence of incompetence and corruption against him. The assembly decided to try Moore, and while they were at it, Smith, too. They accused Smith of assisting Moore in publishing a broadside attacking assembly politics and now charged them both with libel. On January 6, 1758, the assembly dispatched its sergeant-at-arms. They found Moore and Smith at a local coffeehouse and arrested

27. Hanna, *Pennsylvania Politics*, 38, 88, 98–99.
28. *Life and Correspondence of Smith*, 1:45–46, 86–87, 118 (the quotation).
29. *Life and Correspondence of Smith*, 1:161–62.

them. The provost of the College of Philadelphia next found himself lodged in
the old jail at the southeast corner of Sixth and Walnut streets. The assembly denied him a writ of habeas corpus.[30]

Seeing the issue for the political matter it was, Smith took to politics to fight
back. He appealed to the Privy Council, which faulted the assembly's action and
used the occasion to cut down other measures it had taken. Smith, presenting
himself as a victim of Quaker tyranny, also rallied the support of the Anglican
clergy. Proprietor Penn also took up his cause, sent more money to the college,
and promised that his English friends would also contribute. The London press
also took an interest, expressing indignation that two Anglican officials had received such treatment from the likes of the Quakers. Smith, defiant to the last,
actually conducted his college classes from his jail cell and pressed the courts until he won release. And finally, Smith married Moore's daughter.[31]

In their actions against Smith, the Quakers had the support of an uneasy
ally, Ben Franklin. Franklin had retired from business in 1748, engaged in
Philadelphia politics, and won election to the assembly in 1751. Pennsylvania
politics then entered another era of turbulence. Franklin supported a large imperial policy for the colonies. Although he cared little for the inland settlers,
considering them mostly boorish and undisciplined, he wanted a stronger defense program. That position stood him athwart Quaker policy, and Franklin
gravitated toward a dissenting Quaker group that supported defensive measures.
What Franklin and the Quakers did share, however, was bitter opposition to the
proprietor and his "party" in the colony. So it would turn out that Franklin and
the young man that he had brought to Philadelphia, with so much hope for the
academy turned college, now fell into an intractable animosity.[32]

Franklin wanted a nonsectarian college in Philadelphia. He now feared that
Smith was contriving to turn the College of Philadelphia into a bastion of Anglicanism and complained that it had become a "narrow bigoted institution."[33]
Worse, it had fallen under the complete control of the proprietor. Philadelphia
newspapers, in which Franklin had a strong voice, took up the matter. One called
Smith "an infamous hireling" with a "pension from the P____s to blacken the
characters of every man who dare oppose the horrid machinations now carrying
on against our Constitution." Critics also charged that Smith did the work of
Penn in the college, too. Another wrote that "he endeavored to get the college
wholly into the hands of the Proprietary faction, that high notions of Proprietary
power may be early inculcated in the minds of the youth of this province."[34]

---

30. *Life and Correspondence of Smith*, 1:167, 172–73.

31. Gordon, *College of Philadelphia*, 93–94; *Life and Correspondence of Smith*, 1:193; Bruce Richard
Lively, "William Smith, the College and Academy of Philadelphia and Pennsylvania Politics,
1753–1758," *Historical Magazine of the Protestant Episcopal Church* 38 (1969): 252–53.

32. Hanna, *Pennsylvania Politics*, 24, 72.

33. Gordon, *College of Philadelphia*, 99.

34. Gordon, *College of Philadelphia*, 85.

Franklin's party moved directly against the college, even while Franklin remained one of the trustees. The academy and then the College of Philadelphia had received funds from a lottery, the first of which had yielded a considerable sum. After 1756, however, the assembly struck at the college by attacking the lottery. A series of newspaper articles held Smith and the college up to public censure. Pamphlet warfare undertaken by one "Pennsylvanicus" tried to make it a moral question. Should a college live off of money gained by "irreligious, uncharitable, and immoral means?" he asked. And should the college trustees "ruin one part of the community and plunge them into poverty and vice in order to rear and educate another?" This campaign came from Franklin ally Joseph Galloway. There followed in 1759 a "Bill for the more Effectual Suppressing and Preventing of Lotteries and Plays." The assembly bill might have become law, save for the intervention of the Privy Council, which acted on behalf of William Smith and his petition against his imprisonment.[35]

These matters only added salt to Franklin's wounds, for he had already lost out in the college. Smith had grown increasingly annoyed at Franklin's attacks, including his charges that the college had been taken over by narrow sectarians. Franklin saw Smith as an agent of the proprietor and of the Church of England as well. The domination of the Board of Trustees by Anglicans in Philadelphia supplied his evidence. Franklin wrote at one point that Smith had become "universally odious" and would "no longer do here." He wanted Smith to "mind party-writing and party-politics less and his proper business more."[36] In fact, however, the trustees were finding Franklin himself odious and decided to turn the tables on him. In May 1756 they took advantage of Franklin's departure for England and held elections for officers. The results put Peters in and Franklin out. Franklin recoiled in bitterness and smarted from the feeling that he had been used. He wrote in a letter: "The trustees had reaped the full advantage of my head, hands, heart, and purse, in getting through the first difficulties of the design, and when they thought they could do without me, they laid me aside."[37]

Against the charge of Franklin and others that Smith was turning the college into an Anglican enclave, Smith sought to demonstrate otherwise. He did so mostly by showing that the leading denominational representation among the faculty came from the Presbyterians, including Vice Provost Francis Alison.[38] After 1758, in fact, when the Presbyterians appeared to have contrived something of a union of Old Side and New Side factions, evidence suggests that Smith began to pay more attention to their challenge than to those of the Quakers and Franklin, now essentially out of the picture. Presbyterians clearly were gaining strength in Pennsylvania. Here as elsewhere that we have seen, the work of George Whitefield had energized many unchurched and indifferent settlers, in

35. Gordon, *College of Philadelphia*, 91–92.
36. *Franklin Papers*, 6:456–57.
37. Gordon, *College of Philadelphia*, 87; *Franklin Papers*, 8:415–16.
38. *Life and Correspondence of Smith*, 1:336–37.

the city and more numerously in the outlying areas. In Philadelphia, further-more, many wealthy Presbyterians had joined the social and economic elite.

The Presbyterian factor complicated academic politics at the college. It complicated it partly because the Presbyterians themselves still presented con-tending factions—the Old Side originals and the rising New Side revivalists, the followers of Whitefield and other partisans of the Awakening. William Smith al-ways thought politically, and he got the Presbyterian picture right. He explained the situation in a 1755 letter to the secretary of the SPG. The letter shows his own prejudices.

> When Mr. Whitefield first came to these parts, among several of his doctrines, many ran away with that of an instantaneous sort of conversion or *new light*, the signs of which were falling into fits, faintings, etc., etc. To such an enthusiastic pitch many well-meaning persons of a warmer temper could no doubt work themselves up, and might, perhaps, mistake their own Enthusiasm for the inward operations of the Holy Spirit. But persons of a cooler and more sedate turn could not believe in the possi-bility of such a sudden change from the most vicious to the most virtuous course of life, unless by a miracle, which was not to be expected in common cases.

Smith went on to fault the New Siders for their "extravagance" and their "igno-rance" and to express the threat posed by "Whitefield's mob," with its domina-tion by "the lower sort." He observed that the New Siders, with their swelling ranks, had been forced to rush young men into the ministry, giving them a poor education at best and "without consulting at least the appearance of humane learning." Smith did say that the recent College of New Jersey might have a good counterinfluence, however. The Old Siders, Smith added, have their greatest disadvantage in the lack of their own seminary.[39]

Smith feared the New Side Presbyterians far more than he did the Old Side. Furthermore, Philadelphia Anglicans and Old Side Presbyterians had reason to cooperate. Both could agree that the city needed a college to compete with Princeton, a major institutional triumph for New Side Presbyterians. So Old Siders then proposed a plan to "ingraft" a seminary of their own onto the Col-lege of Philadelphia. Under this arrangement, students of their religious persua-sion would have the opportunity to read divinity with the minister of the First Presbyterian Church in the city and then take their degrees from the college. The minister in question was Vice Provost Alison. Smith supported the plan and recommended its approval to the SPG. He could be arrogant, but he was also as-tute. He knew that the College of Philadelphia could not survive as a manifestly Anglican college; Anglicans were clearly outnumbered in the city and colony. At one point, he admonished an Anglican cleric, who wanted the college to be explicitly Anglican, that "the people would never have born even the mention

---

39. William Smith to Secretary Samuel Chandler, April 1755, *Life and Correspondence of Smith*, 1:102, 104–5.

of such a design." A deal such as this one took much political pressure off his shoulders.[40] Thus, in 1762, when two Presbyterians joined the trustees, Smith welcomed them and let the public know that he wanted the college to be "wide and catholic."[41]

Notwithstanding, Anglicans and Presbyterians did not trust each other. Smith introduced Anglican forms of worship at the school and persuaded the trustees to have them made standard for prayer services. Francis Alison complained to Ezra Stiles that "the College is artfully got into the hands of Episcopal trustees." He feared the social effects of Anglicanism. "Young men educated here get a taste for the high life," he said, and decide against the modest living of a Presbyterian ministry. On the other hand, Anglicans who saw Presbyterians dominate the faculty expressed their concern. One said that the college was becoming a "mere Presbyterian faction."[42] In 1762, the two parties agreed to hold their representation on the trustees and faculty at the prevailing proportional levels.[43]

The Presbyterian input at the College of Philadelphia takes on greater clarity through the career of a remarkable early leader, Francis Alison. He was born in Leck, County Donegal, Ireland, in 1705. His father was a weaver. Unfortunately, much is missing from the record of Alison's early life. He most certainly went to a Presbyterian academy, most likely the one established by Francis Hutcheson, in Dublin. He attended the University of Edinburgh for an uncertain period of time, earning an M.A. degree there in 1722. He studied moral philosophy with Robert Law, divinity with William Hamilton, and metaphysics with John Stevenson. Alison returned to Ireland to be licensed in the Presbyterian Church, but could not secure a parish appointment. Finally, in 1735, he left for America. Some of his kin had preceded him and settled in western Pennsylvania. Alison himself now became part of the great Ulster migration. In 1743 he established the Presbyterian Latin School at New London that would win him wide recognition in the Middle Colonies. From that position Alison would emerge as the major intellectual figure of the Old Side Presbyterians. He joined the academy as vice provost and kept that position when the College of Philadelphia formed in 1755.[44]

Ezra Stiles called Alison "the greatest classical scholar in America."[45] His learning assured the ascendancy of his career in America, but his personality put

40. Melvin H. Buxbaum, "Franklin and William Smith: Their School and Their Dispute," *Historical Magazine of the Protestant Episcopal Church* 39 (1970): 370–71; William Smith to Secretary Chandler, April 1755, *Life and Correspondence of Smith*, 1:105; Smith to Rev. Dr. Bearcroft, November 1, 1756, *Life and Correspondence of Smith*, 1:143.

41. Gordon, *College of Philadelphia*, 97.

42. Bridenbaughs, *Rebels and Gentlemen*, 61.

43. Gordon, *College of Philadelphia*, 98.

44. Elizabeth A. Ingersoll, "Francis Alison: American *Philosophe*," Ph.D. diss., University of Delaware, 1974, chapter 1.

45. Douglas Sloan, *The Scottish Enlightenment and the American College Ideal* (New York: Teachers College Press, 1971), 74.

limitations on it. He cut something of a rough figure and never projected the gentlemanly and aristocratic bearing that might have gained him large influence in Philadelphia society. "He never did affect the demeanor fit for a salon," writes his biographer. Then too, much of elite Philadelphia society harbored mean prejudices toward the Scotch-Irish in their midst and out on the "wild" frontier where they prevailed. And though Alison often won appreciation from students, few found him very approachable. He appeared a stern and demanding pedagogue, his weighty lectures unrelieved by any wit or levity. One student who lived with Alison for five years at New London said he never saw him smile.[46]

Alison identified clearly with the Old Side Presbyterians. He came from Ulster, where Presbyterian loyalty marked one's public identity. The Scottish settlers transplanted to northern Ireland gave the region a Protestant majority, but they held second-class status nonetheless. English politics and Anglican privilege assured it. Alison, though, never took his Calvinism for granted. He devoted a lifetime to biblical study to secure its intellectual foundation. Alison was also a product of the Scottish Enlightenment, and his Calvinism, as we shall see in his teaching at the college, mixed with the milder religious forms of that movement. Alison asked of different sects only that they have a central faith in Christ and not give priority to human innovations in worship and doctrine. Ben Franklin's daughter reported Alison telling her that God had made the way to heaven so wide that some from all religious persuasions may enter in. To his students at the college, he recommended John Locke's "Letter on Toleration."[47]

Presbyterianism, we have seen, fell into bitter disputes in the 1740s as revivals spread and insurgent New Siders challenged the prevailing authority in the denomination. Their ardent Calvinism notwithstanding, the New Siders had Alison's opposition from the outset. He saw in the group a contentious and partisan spirit that threatened the model Christian commonwealth he described in his college teaching. He did not welcome the emotional revivals and saw in them an anti-intellectual fervor inconsistent with his educational ideals. In disputations with the Awakeners, Alison always appealed to them to use their reason and see the excess in their religious zeal. Nor could Alison accept in the New Siders their obsession with testimony of personal conversion from the ministry. Christ had never made such demands of the church, he insisted. Another factor also sparked Alison's criticism of the New Side. He had hoped that the College of Philadelphia would supply for the Old Side Presbyterians their want in American higher education. He had worked to secure the "ingrafting" of the seminary for that purpose. But as the school produced ministers, he saw them denied churches by the "persecuting, narrow bigots" of the New Side. Some of the students then went off to England and took orders in the Anglican Church, a most

46. Ingersoll, "Francis Alison," 87; Gordon, *College of Philadelphia*, 189–90.
47. Ingersoll, "Francis Alison," 178, 184–85.

unhappy turn of events for Alison. At one point he complained that he had lost three of his best students to the Church of England.[48]

By the end of the 1750s, Presbyterian factionalism was waning, and Alison led the efforts to bring about unity between the two groups. He did so partly because he had long believed that they had more to worry about than the differences between them. Alison himself personally mistrusted both the Anglicans and the Quakers. Toward the Church of England he bore prejudices that date back to the Reformation. It represented to him a religiosity too much given to human forms in its worship, to the neglect of the saving doctrines of traditional Protestantism. Furthermore, English history had made Alison a firm opponent of state religion. Established churches, he believed, inevitably corrupted themselves through their cohabitation with the state. Alison condemned the English Test Act and faulted any church that required for its support "such a notorious infringement of the rights of private judgment." He could justify establishment neither in England nor in the Catholic nations nor in Scotland itself. However much he might resent Quaker politics in Pennsylvania, Alison concurred with their tenets on religious freedom. "No virtuous man," he wrote, "would enter into a social state without having his religious and civil rights secured." The magistrate, he said, owes to all citizens the "sacred right" of judging for themselves and of worshiping according to the best information they can obtain.[49]

From the time of his arrival in Pennsylvania, Alison sided with the Presbyterians and against the Quakers. He had quickly concluded that the Quakers represented a divisive factor in colony politics, and he invoked policies that looked to the collective interest. Here again the western question became the main issue in this concern. Alison respected the Quakers' pacifism, but allowed them no right to exercise it at the expense of others. He credited Thomas Penn with doing much more for the common interest than the Quakers were doing. "Our lives and our fortunes are disposed of by their oaths," he said. The frontier question flared anew when Pontiac's Rebellion broke out in 1763. Quaker reluctance to come to the aid of the westerners led the so-called Paxton Boys into assaults against the Conestoga Indians and a march into Philadelphia when the assembly called for their arrest and trial. The Quakers tried to present the incursion as a Presbyterian rebellion, though it was largely a Scotch-Irish one. Alison continued in the appeal he had made some years before. Although he had no relish for politics, quite in contrast to Provost Smith, he had sermonized in 1756 on "Love of Country." Speaking in Philadelphia, he invoked the social covenant that underlies a government that protects all citizens. Alison urged that all inhabitants of Pennsylvania, and "of every other British colony of America . . . though of different nations, and of different religions and denominations," must unite to preserve the safety of all. Alison called on the government to assist "our friends in distress."[50]

---

48. Ingersoll, "Francis Alison," 406, 440–42, 464, 493.
49. Ingersoll, "Francis Alison," 187–88, 191 (quotation), 193, 65 (quotation).
50. Ingersoll, "Francis Alison," 108–10, 127, 135–36.

At the end of the 1750s and into the next decade, Alison became further embroiled in colonial politics. Things were getting very complicated. Franklin, in alliance with the Quakers, led a movement to make Pennsylvania a royal colony. They had a common bond in their contempt for the proprietor and the political faction that supported him. Making Pennsylvania a royal colony would rid it of Penn's power and influence. It would give the assembly immense powers, too. In 1764 it passed a resolution "praying" King George III "to take the people of . . . [the] province under his immediate protection and government."[51]

This issue aroused the Presbyterians above all. Alison, John Ewing, and Gilbert Tennent, representing Old Side and New Side, joined to stop the quest for royal government. Indeed, in the heavy pamphlet warfare that followed, the opposition was largely Presbyterian-driven, and the angry Franklin called it so. Franklin furthermore found an outrageous irony in the Presbyterians' now coming to the defense of the Pennsylvania Constitution, which he and the Quakers had accused them of undermining for decades. In the 1764 elections, Quakers kept their strength in the outlying areas of Philadelphia, while they lost in the city. Nonetheless, in a surprising move, the assembly forwarded the petition for royal government and assigned Franklin to go to London to secure it. In the end, however, the movement failed.[52]

The bitter struggle over royal government redefined the Proprietary Party, never heretofore a solid coalition anyway. To gain support for the royal colony project, Franklin and the Quakers had to win over some Anglicans. They, too, had their disagreements and divided on the change of government. William Smith, however, saw a big opportunity. He hoped that royal government might at last prepare for an appointment of an American bishop. The cause reemerged in 1764 as a major priority for him. It rallied the Presbyterians even more strongly against royal government, for to a person they considered the bishop project a frightening one. The two issues, in fact, were causing the two Presbyterian factions to forget their differences and they now solidified in the Proprietary Party. That party now virtually, and quite ironically, became a "Presbyterian party," as Alison liked to call it, and he had done more than any other to promote the new Presbyterian unity.[53]

Smith had taken up the bishop issue on the eve of his departure from New York to head the Philadelphia Academy. It spoke to his social and political phi-

---

51. Ingersoll, "Francis Alison," 116; Tully, *Forming American Politics*, 191 (the quotation).
52. Tully, *Forming American Politics*, 194–98.
53. Ingersoll, "Francis Alison," 128–29, 151. Franklin again commented on the shift:

Pleasant, surely it is, to hear that the Proprietary partisans, of all men, bawling for the Constitution, and affecting a terrible concern for our liberties and privileges. They who have been, these twenty years, cursing our Constitution, declaring that it was no Constitution, or worse than none, and that things could never be well with us, til it was new-modeled, and made exactly conformable to the British Constitution. . . . Wonderful change! Astonishing Conversion! Will the wolves then protect the sheep, if they can but persuade 'em to give up their dogs? (Tully, *Forming American Politics*, 198).

losophy. Smith was at that time making a reply to the anti-Anglican attacks of the Reflectors. He did not oppose religious toleration, he said, but insisted that the state must give its authority to one church as a principle of stability in the commonwealth. The American colonies, he urged, dearly needed such stability. To English officials he raised the specter of Calvinist churches in conspiracy to undo Anglican authority.[54] For Alison the prospect of an American bishop was alarming. A bishop in the American colonies, Alison said, would impose a severer ecclesiastical tyranny than in England. For here he would face no checks on his actions. We have no national assembly and no national courts, he said, not even a nobility to stand on equal footing with a bishop. As this issue energized Dissenters all over the colonies, Alison called for united action among them, "a firm union against Episcopal encroachments." He joined with Ezra Stiles of Newport to form the Plan of Union to mark and check the scheme. Smith observed: "The Presbyterians from one end of the continent to the other are attacking the Church about American bishops."[55] One finds it hard to imagine that these two protagonists were coleaders of the same American college.

Despite mistrusts, however, the Anglican Smith and the Presbyterian Alison exercised an effective cooperative leadership at the College of Philadelphia. Many mutual interests joined them. In the political realm, both had an animosity toward the Quakers, no small point in Pennsylvania's political complex. Alison saw Quaker tyranny at its worse in the persecution and trial of his colleague Smith. And he worked with Smith in the charity school scheme. Also, both disdained and feared the growing New Light presence. Each saw in the feverish religiosity of the revivalists an irrational and chaotic presence in a New World environment that needed order and stability. Finally, Smith and Alison had similar Scottish backgrounds, and they shared a near unanimity on the educational purposes of the college and its curriculum.

The College of Philadelphia never became the pioneering institution it might have been. Neither Smith nor Alison shared the utilitarian bent of Franklin. Latin and Greek remained staples of the entire collegiate course. And why not? In Alison the college had a renowned Latin scholar. In Smith, it had a provost who joined classical education to the aristocratic goals he had for the school. The sons of Philadelphia merchants flocked to the college, and Smith envisioned for them a large public role. The city, he believed, must be the vanguard of a civilizing influence amid the backwardness of rural America. Every day, he said, students should have some conversation with one of the ancients, "who charms with all the beauties of his language." Smith took extraordinary measures to bring his students to the attention of the city residents and visitors. He staged oratory events, debates, plays, and other entertainments for his urban

---

54. Carl Bridenbaugh, *Mitre and Sceptre: Transatlantic Faiths, Ideas, Personalities, and Politics, 1689–1775* (London: Oxford University Press, 1962), 152–53.
55. Ingersoll, "Francis Alison," 290–93; Bridenbaugh, *Mitre and Sceptre*, 272 (Alison quotation); Smith to the Secretary of the SPG, May 6, 1768, *Life and Correspondence of Smith*, 1:414.

The Charity School, Philadelphia (later, College of Philadelphia) (Watercolor by Charles M. Lefferts, 1913)

constituency.[56] Smith brought these notions into his first commencement address in 1757. He, a writer of poetry, told the graduates:

> Oh! then, let no part of your future conduct disgrace the lessons you have received, or disappoint hopes you have so justly raised! Consider yourselves, from this day, as distinguished above the vulgar, and called upon to act a more important part in life! Strive to shine forth in every species of moral excellence, and to support the character and dignity of beings formed for endless duration! The Christian world stands much in need of inflexible patterns of integrity and public virtue; and no part of it more so than the land you inhabit.[57]

To the College of Philadelphia Francis Alison brought the Scottish Enlightenment, and he became the bearer of that expression as much as Witherspoon at Princeton. In fact, it arrived earliest in Philadelphia. Alison had studied with Francis Hutcheson during a brief tour at Glasgow University and employed Hutcheson's *A Shorter Introduction to Moral Philosophy* (1747) for his students at the college. Alison used Hutcheson to fortify nearly every aspect of his own Christianity, which he wished to secure on as firm an intellectual foundation as possible. It was methodology as much as ideas that supplied the Scottish advantage to Alison. Hutcheson gave him the confidence to establish religious knowledge on the structure of human nature itself. Alison merged the natural and divine, as the one reinforced the other in an indispensable foundation of truth. Under the Scottish influence, moral philosophy began its long career as the crown jewel in the American college. Alison wrote to Stiles on the subject: "Without this branch of knowledge, we shall ill be able to defend our holy Christian religion; to understand the right of mankind; or to explain and enforce the duties which we owe to God, our neighbors, and ourselves."[58]

Alison had much faith in human reason, but did not endorse the stronger rationalist Christianity of the eighteenth century, such as that found in Samuel Clarke and William Wollaston. By looking to the human constitution, Alison, drawing on Hutcheson, secured a greater empirical basis for religion and metaphysics. Introspection, the epistemological strategy of the Scottish philosophes, provides the most persuasive convictions of an existing God and of a moral imperative that we are obliged to honor in the conduct of our lives, he wrote. The Scottish philosophy opened up to "inward feelings" and the inclinations and instincts of our human nature. The emotions and affections now underscored those moral truths that the conscience furnishes us, Alison asserted. For reason, Alison believed, could never be the sole, secure foundation of religious knowledge. The emotions gave it personal as opposed to abstract apprehension and here they became available for close scrutiny

---

56. Cheyney, *University of Pennsylvania*, 82–83, 87; Gordon, *College of Philadelphia*, 47–49, 154; *Life and Correspondence of Smith*, 2:60.
57. *Life and Correspondence of Smith*, 2:154.
58. Ingersoll, "Francis Alison," 44–45.

and analysis. They supplied a lively and quickened basis for individual spirituality and moral experience.[59]

What may be most surprising about Alison's appropriation of Hutcheson is the American's prominence as intellectual leader of Old Side Presbyterianism. But generally, the Scottish Enlightenment had a mellowing effect in the churches of the Reformed tradition, softening their often harsh Calvinism and raising the status of human nature as a repository of moral truth. Alison reflected this tendency. He insisted that as we discover the rational and ethical dimensions of our nature, we perceive all the more acutely their greater presence in the Almighty. But the discovery, Alison believed, should inspire as much awe as confidence. For true self-knowledge brings awareness of our shortcomings, our distance from divine nature. Alison had an unshakable conviction of original sin in human beings. The more so did he appeal to reason and conscience as the requisites by which we resist the power of a contrary will that would lead us astray. In this sense, moral philosophy reinforced the pulpit instructions of the preacher. It carefully showed the right path of life, and as such won appreciation from many rational and liberal Christian thinkers. But in the case of Alison it also underscored an emotionality of divine dependence consistent with traditional Calvinism.[60]

Alison, it might be said, joined the moral philosopher and the preacher. For the Calvinist in Alison would always find in moral philosophy a crucial differentiation between the natural man and the regenerate man. Moral philosophy will point the way to awareness of our best nature and its model in God, and our own distance from that model. But, for Alison, moral philosophy could not by itself bridge the gap. He turned always to Scripture to assist our faltering reason and to locate our highest obligations. For the major end of man, Alison believed, is perfect obedience to God. Such effort requires perfecting all the faculties of the soul. Moral philosophy can assist in our perceiving these perfections. Alison could therefore give his listeners an argument for their own efforts in salvation. The Scottish moral philosophy thus influenced a moderate Calvinism in Alison, and it gave the Old Side a significant institutional location at the College of Philadelphia.[61]

In other respects, the college looked like a routine facsimile of its colonial counterparts. The day began early with morning prayer. Many students came from the city and returned to homes at night. All had to attend a church of their choice on Sunday. A dull routine would seem to have been in place. School regulations specified punishment for playing ball "in school hours." The curriculum seems cut and dried, and one might go from Harvard to William and Mary and pursue courses sounding very much the same in content.[62] But here and in the other colleges appearances deceive a bit.

---

59. Sloan, *Scottish Enlightenment*, 89–90.
60. Ingersoll, "Francis Alison," 43, 48–54, 201–3.
61. Ingersoll, "Francis Alison," 44, 48, 224.
62. Gordon, *College of Philadelphia*, 191; Cheyney, *University of Pennsylvania*, 72.

However, at Philadelphia and other places an "extra" curriculum existed. Smith's account of his school gives us the best glimpse of it. The school day established "private hours" for the students, in which they were to pursue varied readings. Smith assigned a wide selection of books and journals. His list included *The Spectator* and *The Rambler*, Locke's *Essay on Human Understanding* and Pufendorf on law. He also added Hooker on church polity. To be sure, neither here nor in the regular program did students come to know the great literary figures of their age, but they had a rounded introduction to the modern intellectual world.[63] And of all the colonial colleges, Philadelphia sent the fewest proportion of its students into the ministry.[64]

Smith's political intrigues have won him an unsavory reputation among early American collegiate leaders. But there is more to his record, for in fact his contribution was substantial.[65] Smith represents a phase of the American Enlightenment that derives from the kind of Anglicanism with which he identified. It had little to do with bishops, or church ritual, or Arminian theology. Smith's intellectual interests in fact had less to do with the spiritual life than with the world of nature. He championed and celebrated the progress of the human intellect in the realms of scientific inquiry and the extensions of practical science in the facilitation and greater comfort of daily life. Indeed, for these gains he had the same passion as political rival Benjamin Franklin. Smith had no doubt that science served the greater glory of God. The challenge for religion was for it to keep pace with the advancement of the human mind.[66]

As provost of the College of Philadelphia Smith called for a curriculum that would have students give almost half their time to the study of science. Smith himself set a rare if not singular example of teaching natural science at his college.[67] Smith also contributed to the work of a city in which scientific activity flourished. Philadelphians re-formed the American Society Held at Philadelphia for Promoting and Propagating Useful Knowledge, which had its first meeting in 1766. The American Philosophical Society formed two years later. Even in these activities Philadelphia could not escape political factionalism. The American Society was dominated by anti-Proprietary people; the Philosophical Society was

---

63. William Smith to William Peters, July 18, 1754, *Life and Correspondence of Smith*, 59.

64. Gordon, *College of Philadelphia*, 2:221.

65. One historian who credits Smith's contribution to the American Enlightenment is Henry May, who calls him "the most important leader of the Anglican forward movement, and one of the major figures of the Moderate Enlightenment." Smith was a member of the Royal Society and received honorary degrees from Oxford, Aberdeen, and Trinity in Dublin. See *The Enlightenment in America* (New York: Oxford University Press, 1976), 80 (the quotation)–86.

66. On Smith as an Anglican voice in the Enlightenment, especially in contrast to Samuel Johnson, see John Frederick Woolverton, *Colonial Anglicanism in North America* (Detroit, Mich.: Wayne State University Press, 1984), 209–15.

67. Brooke Hindle, *The Pursuit of Science in Revolutionary America, 1735–1789* (1965; New York: Norton, 1974), 90.

virtually a wing of the Proprietary party.[68] Smith, as one might expect, cast his lot with the Philosophical Society. One incident in particular exemplifies his work for that organization.

David Rittenhouse was a young man whose work was winning him a reputation in Philadelphia. Born in 1732 to parents of German and Quaker background, Rittenhouse grew up on a farm twenty miles from the city, at Norriton. He had a mechanical genius and an impressive grasp of mathematics, physics, and astronomy. These interests took him away from farm work, and he became a skilled clock maker. His talents also led him to build a pocket, metallic thermometer. Now it became his great ambition to produce an orrery—a mechanical model of the universe. These contrivances were fascinating the scientific world and Rittenhouse resolved to surpass all others in his device. His innovation would have the planets revolve around the sun in a vertical plane and would enhance accuracy of representation in all details of the project. Planets would not move at a uniform rate of speed but adhere to Kepler's calculations. Every planet would be placed in its orbit in precise relationship to the others and would show their positions relative to each other at any given time. Rittenhouse dazzled all with whom he discussed his project, including William Smith. So impressed was the provost that he tried to find a place for Rittenhouse's family in the city, but he wanted to do even more for him. He went to the college trustees and arranged for Rittenhouse to receive an honorary Master of Arts degree. Awarding of the degree took place at the commencement events held in November 1767.[69]

Smith's connection to Rittenhouse gave him an advantage when Philadelphians approached a great event that took place on June 3, 1769. For there and throughout Europe scientists and many from the general public looked forward to observing the transit of Venus.[70] Two groups formed in Philadelphia to measure the transit. John Ewing, a Presbyterian minister and member of the college faculty, calculated the time of the transit and presented his data to the Philosophical Society. He also secured considerable financial support, including funds from the anti-Propriety city assembly, for his project. Smith in the meantime teamed up with Rittenhouse, and, true to form, he turned to Thomas Penn for money to assist them. Penn came through in fine fashion. Smith and Rittenhouse set up their telescope in Norriton, where a fascinated public thronged on

---

68. Harold E. Taussig, "Deism in Philadelphia During the Age of Franklin," *Pennsylvania History* 37 (1970): 219.

69. Brooke Hindle, *David Rittenhouse* (Princeton, N.J.: Princeton University Press, 1964), 13–15, 25, 31, 36–37.

70. At this event, Venus passed in front of the sun, visible as a little black dot. It had scientific use for determining the distance of the earth from the sun, from which calculation one might then determine all the other distances in the solar system, at that time known only relatively to each other. The key effort was to measure the time it took for Venus to "contact" the sun and pass over it and to make that measurement from different geographical locations. Or, one could record the exact time of contact at one place and compare it with the exact location recorded at another site. In both instances the data revealed the solar parallax, the angle of the earth's semidiameter from the sun, which could then be expressed in numerical measurement.

June 1. Rittenhouse's weeks of preparation and calculations paid off with the very satisfying data that he and Smith collected that day.[71]

Smith seems never to have had an easy time in his personal relations, and matters with Rittenhouse had one bad moment, too. Rittenhouse continued to work on the orrery, as great expectations grew. As yet, no purchaser had emerged, but that changed when President Witherspoon at Princeton stepped forward in 1770. He went out to Norriton, expressed his high praise for Rittenhouse's construction, and made an offer to buy on behalf of the College of New Jersey. They agreed on the sum of £300 and Rittenhouse had to stipulate that he would not sell another orrery for a lower price. When Smith learned of this transaction he was irate. "I never met with greater mortification," he said. He believed that Rittenhouse was taken off guard, and he saved his greater wrath for Witherspoon, who "had gone too far." Rittenhouse conceded that he had acted carelessly; he meant no deception. Smith and Rittenhouse then observed that no delivery date for the orrery had been specified. They thereupon agreed that Rittenhouse would make a second orrery, keeping the first on hand as a model until he finished the second. Then Princeton would receive the original as arranged.[72]

None of this business dissuaded Smith from his enthusiasm for science and his eagerness to promote the study of it. As Increase Mather might have spoken of American providence in religious terms, Smith did so in reference to science. Indeed, he often made religion the beneficiary of science. "The interests of Christianity," he believed, "will be advanced by promoting the interests of Science." Smith, for all his partisan intrigue in the religious politics of Pennsylvania, hoped that science would bring religion out of its own dark ages and end its divisive role in human history. He regretted, too, that hardened religious prejudice had set its "illiberal system" against the advance of science. Smith could reference science's struggle against "the enormous heap of rubbish and prejudice, which had been piled upon it, during the long long night of ignorance and religious usurpation." Those who bore such prejudice, he said, were "waging war, not only with everything elegant and useful in life, but even with the extension of our common Christianity."[73] Smith addressed the American Philosophical Society (which had merged with the American Society in 1768) in 1773. Again he pleaded for literature and science as the arms of an improving religion in America and cited his belief that science transcended all those religious, cultural, and political factions that divided humanity. Science had the further recommendation, mundane and simple, that it helped all people to live better. These views did not radically separate Smith from the collegiate presidents of the colonial era. But they gave him an advanced place among them.

---

71. Hindle, *Rittenhouse*, ch. 4.
72. Hindle, *Rittenhouse*, 74.
73. Taussig, "Deism in Philadelphia," 226–27; William Smith, *An Oration Delivered Before the Patrons, Vice-Presidents and Members of the American Philosophical Society . . .* (Philadelphia: John Dunlap, 1773), 10.

The College of Philadelphia, in its early years, confronted probably the most factional political structure faced by any of the colonial colleges. That situation clearly set the odds against its becoming what its principal founder had hoped, an institution happily bereft of sectarian influences. And none knew more personally than Benjamin Franklin the failed expectations that attended the founding of the school. His ouster registered the impact of the warfare he had wanted so much to avoid yet had done so much to foster. At the Philadelphia college, the fact of religious neutrality opened the way to religious factionalism and sectarian competition. The first provost of the school, William Smith, had raised expectation that he might lead the school in a new direction for higher education in the colonies. His blueprint in his *College of Mirania* so indicated. But Smith showed himself on arrival to be a thoroughly partisan Anglican, and obnoxious to many as a result. Presbyterianism had a major representative, Francis Alison, as vice provost. Alison's intellectual esteem gave Old Side Presbyterianism a powerful location at the college. A dual religious influence thus prevailed where none was to be dominant.

The charged political situation in Pennsylvania, however, seemed to have the ironic effect of making religion less an intellectual force at the College of Philadelphia than elsewhere. Francis Alison made Old Side Presbyterianism wholly compatible with the milder and nonsectarian expressions of the Scottish Enlightenment. William Smith directed much of his attention to the external arena, the battlefield where Quakers and Proprietors, with their always shifting alliance networks, contended for colonial political control. He did little, in fact, to give the College of Philadelphia an emphatic Anglican identity, as, by comparison, Samuel Johnson did at King's College by a prolific intellectual career on behalf of the English Church. If anything, in fact, Smith made his main contribution to academics at his college in the field of science. Nor could he have effectively rendered the college a solid Anglican outpost. Pennsylvania had a precarious balance of power in its politics. Smith was shrewd enough to know that it had to have some appeal to all factions. He gave it the appearance of neutrality; but neutrality, we have seen, had its perils.

8

❦

Three from the Awakening: Rhode Island College, Queen's College, Dartmouth College

The religious awakenings of the middle eighteenth century challenged all of the colonial colleges we have examined to date. In the case of Princeton, they secured a founding influence. In all the others, however, the movement met rejection, except for Thomas Clap's late and ineffective commitment to the Connecticut New Lights. The revivals had spent their force by 1750. At Princeton, John Witherspoon opened the college to the milder tones of the Scottish Enlightenment. However, the revivals had laid foundations; they had affected individuals and groups who rose to give an institutional locus to their new, fervid religiosity. From these leavening effects emerged the last three of the American colonial colleges. They all formed in the decade that preceded the outbreak of the American Revolution.

Rhode Island College, and its titular successor Brown University, came from insurgent forces that shook New England in the eighteenth century. It is a story of some irony. One hundred years of Puritanism had yielded a Congregational Order in New England measurably altered from its first counterpart. Changes in church polity that had accrued over this time had left here and there some acute pockets of discontent. Many looked back to the original pristine character of the first New England church system, based on an imagined congregational autonomy. The prevailing Standing Order, they said, had become a corrupted one. The revolution they would lead against it therefore looked back in time. It sought to recover the original purity of the churches. To do so meant that these "dissenters" must leave the Standing Order. In doing so, they became Separatists. And some of these became Baptists. A few from this group sought to secure the place of their denomination in the British Empire by establishing the first Baptist university. When they did, they named it Rhode Island College.

Rhode Island College

The Dissenters in question often cited the Half-Way Covenant of 1662. Schisms had occurred in Boston churches and elsewhere after its enactment. Later, however, resentment against the "graceless churches" born of the Half-Way Covenant came from a Puritan Left wing and, in the 1740s, from a critical group of "New Light" partisans. They often pointed to an even worse betrayal—the 1708 Saybrook Platform. This measure, the work of Congregationalists that many New Lights would now scornfully label "Presbyterians," constituted, in their thinking, a wholesale undoing of the original New England polity. Saybrook restricted the ordination and sanctioning of ministers to a clerical association and brought the state into a greater role in ecclesiastical matters. The Awakening of the 1740s seemed to give hope of a return to a polity of autonomous churches. But the Standing Order proved powerful. Radical pietists like Gilbert Tennent and James Davenport renounced their ways and rejoined the established ranks. The true believers then would have to decide if they should commit to a separatist program.[1]

The Separates got their name when events such as that at Canterbury, Connecticut, in 1742 spread to other locations. This town, but recently a frontier post in Windham County, always had radical elements in its ranks. The congregation had witnessed the moral defection and departure of its pastor, and into the void came itinerant evangelicals—Eleazar Wheelock and others. Separatist Elisha Paine also emerged from the Canterbury ranks. A church meeting early the next year resolved to revert to the church discipline specified by the 1648 Cambridge Platform, thus dismissing any authority claimed by the Saybrook Platform. The New Light faction refused any appeal to the consociation when the church failed to agree on a new minister. When the town invited James Cogswell to be a candidate for the position the New Lights protested. They had learned that Cogswell supported the Saybrook Platform, permitted use of the Half-Way Covenant, and did not require public confessions of grace. The New Lights then withdrew from the church and met in a private home. Many a New England church would soon undergo a similar rending of its membership. But the schismatics believed they were not upsetting a legitimate order, only restoring one. The true churches of the elect, constituted of those of demonstrated grace, and institutionally autonomous, they said, looked back to the original Puritan revolution and the essential raison d'etre of New England history.[2]

Studies of the radical Separatists point to other characteristics of the movement and its greater significance. One sees in the group a populist temperament and ideology that would have larger social consequences for New England. Many Separatist leaders assumed a leveling attitude toward authority in the churches. They attacked the ministers for acting arrogantly and disdainfully toward their

---

1. C. C. Goen, *Revivalism and Separatism in New England, 1740–1800: Strict Congregationalists and Separate Baptists in the Great Awakening* (New Haven, Conn.: Yale University Press, 1962), 36–39; William G. McLoughlin, *New England Dissent, 1630–1833: The Baptists and the Separation of Church and State,* 2 vols. (Cambridge, Mass.: Harvard University Press, 1971), 1:345–46.

2. Goen, *Revivalism and Separatism,* 70–71, 164–65.

lay memberships, denying individual believers their special spiritual gifts and prophetic insights. They resented assumptions of a superior learning and higher wisdom in the established clergy. They perceived a haughty bearing in them. The organizations these clergy formed and joined, the radicals said, betrayed a new ecclesiastical tyranny. New Lights sometimes charged the established ministry with "Arminianism." They invoked a primitive Calvinism and made it the reserve of unlearned masses. Thus "the New Lights preached a folk form of Calvinism and their preachers were the folk artists of their day. They brought the rarified intellectualism of Puritanism down to the level of the common man."[3]

However, the Separatist movement also found support among some prominent middle-class people. Paine, for example, was the most prominent lawyer in eastern Connecticut, and his brother Solomon served in the legislature. Most Separatists, it seemed, represented the solid, yeomen citizenry of their rural communities and towns. Often, they came from families who went back to the earliest settlers of their parts and possibly they saw in their Separatist commitments a reconnection to an ancestral trust. Geographically, the movement reflected greater cohesiveness. Although one found Separatist churches in all regions of New England, eastern Connecticut supplied their greatest concentration. It was most recent in its settlement, as King Philip's War cleared the way for white occupation in 1675. Many had come there from Old Plymouth, where separatist habits had long thrived. Windham County in this region had a proximity to Rhode Island and a social intercourse that absorbed that colony's individualism and churchly independence. Historian C. C. Goen writes: "This all adds up to the fact that in the eighteenth-century eastern Connecticut was the home of radical sentiment. There had been little opportunity for conservatism to develop here."[4]

The radical Separatists had some striking figures in their ranks, powerful polemicists. Ebenezer Frothingham was one. He came from Cambridge, Massachusetts, born there in 1719. He found his way later to a pastorate in Wethersfield, Connecticut, in 1747. The Awakening brought him into its ranks and he took it into Separatism. That commitment also brought him a term in prison. For Frothingham, Separatism also signified freedom of religion. In one of his two persuasion pieces, *A Key to Unlock the Door*, Frothingham spoke clearly on this subject: "The main thing which I have in view . . . is freedom, Liberty of Conscience . . . the right of thinking and choosing and acting for oneself in matters of Religion, which respect God and conscience, and to contend for that important privilege, I nor any other person should not be ashamed to do."[5]

A Key and Frothingham's other contribution, *Articles of Faith and Practice*, have an important place in the Separatist literature because they also address issues

---

3. McLoughlin, *New England Dissent*, 353–54; idem, *Isaac Backus and the American Pietistic Tradition* (Boston: Little, Brown and Company, 1967), 45 (the quotation).

4. McLoughlin, *New England Dissent*, 1:347–48; Goen, *Revivalism and Separatism*, 186–87 (the quotation).

5. Ebenezer Frothingham, *A Key to Unlock the Door. . . .* (n.p., 1776), v.

of theology and polity in contention between his group and the Standing Order. In both works, Frothingham rallies Scripture for the Separatist cause. Thus we find the case prepared for only true believers as church members and the argument that their faith may be discerned by the like faithful. We have the tenets of the Cambridge Platform reasserted with the right of a congregation to determine its membership and select its officers without outside involvement or approval. The logic extends to condemnation of ministerial associations, consociations of churches, and ecclesiastical arrangements encumbered by any connections to the civil powers. Frothingham showed that he knew the political fallout in the Separatist movement and he addressed its critics. To those who wondered why his party would divide the churches, he replies that they have ceased to be true churches. They have sold out Puritan standards to Arminian ones, allowing "external morality" to determine church membership, in effect yielding to a covenant of works. As a result, he said, in words so familiar to New Light language, the churches have fallen into a "dead, dry, lifeless form of godliness."[6]

Legal issues compounded the religious ones. Massachusetts and Connecticut imposed compulsory support of the established clergy by means of ministerial rates and church taxes. All families absorbed the taxes, whether they attended the established churches or not. The Awakening, however, had moved the New Lights toward charges of unregenerateness against the ministers. They called them a "hireling clergy" and refused to pay the taxes to support them. Connecticut, however, after the Saybrook Platform went into effect, permitted exemption from these taxes for genuine dissenters—Quakers, Anglicans, Baptists. The law, however, did not apply to Congregationalists and Presbyterians, considered merely whimsical or petulant dissenters when they quarreled with the churches and ministry. The Awakening forced a reconsideration of even this policy, however, and in 1743 it was revoked. Too many New Light parties had sought to exploit it. Connecticut, in turn, became the most aggressive colony in moving against dissenters; "all its institutions were rallied against the hapless Separates." Authorities seized their goods and auctioned them off. They dragged others physically to prison as many cried in loud laments to protest these actions. Eastern Connecticut especially projected a grim scene. Officials in Windham County put a new wing onto the local jailhouse and in 1753 ordered construction of an entirely new prison to accommodate the swelling outlaw ranks.[7]

All the while, New Light Separatism generated new Baptists. Indeed, it changed the face of that tiny denomination, and it took Baptism on a course that would make it the second largest Protestant denomination in the United States by the time of the Civil War. Baptism had begun in England with London's first church of that kind in 1611. Its founders had encountered Mennonites in Holland, to which they had retreated as Separatists three years before, and took from

---

6. Goen, *Revivalism and Separatism*, 129–30; McLoughlin, *New England Dissent*, 1:350–53.
7. Goen, *Revivalism and Separatism*, 129–30; McLoughlin, *New England Dissent*, 1:86, 362.

them their rejection of infant baptism. Neither did they accept baptism by immersion. Also, the London group followed the Mennonites in their Arminianism. They believed in Christ's death as the grounds for the salvation of all people, rejecting the Calvinist doctrine of the elect. These were General Baptists, in
contrast to the Particular Baptists of more emphatic Calvinist leanings. For most
of the seventeenth century the General Baptists had the majority in the denomination.[8]

Particular Baptism began in Rhode Island in 1638 and grew out of American Puritanism. It would have little reinforcement from England, as Puritan
intolerance toward its practitioners discouraged Baptist migration from there
to New England. Orthodox Puritans like Cotton Mather approximated the
antipaedobaptists to the wild men of the European Anabaptist movement.
Mather referred to the "briars of Anabaptisme" and believed it the source of
the worst heresies in Christendom. From it, he contended, came Quakerism,
Familism,[9] Ranterism,[10] and all kinds of Antinomianism. Another Puritan denounced Anabaptism as seductive to the "giddy unstable mind." Particular
Baptism grew, albeit slowly, nonetheless. Its first location in Boston produced
a church that expanded from the nine founders in 1665 to eighty members by
1680. At century's end, six Baptist churches existed in Rhode Island, three in
former Plymouth Colony, and the one in Boston. There were nine in Connecticut. This accruement did not constitute a movement, however. Congregations formed sporadically from the discontents of protesting individuals.
They often disappeared in similar fashion as the authorities suppressed them
one by one, bludgeoning them into silence or exile. Warnings, fines, and whip-
pings were the Baptists' usual lot. As their eminent historian writes, "Throughout the colonial period Baptists were the pariahs of New England society."
They could not vote and could not enter the inner circle of the local economic
and social leadership.[11]

Nonetheless, one by one New Light Separatist churches became Baptist
ones. "Gone to the Baptists" appeared as a recurring entry next to membership
lists of local churches. Some, then and since, have attributed false motives to
New Light Separatists who embraced Baptism. As Baptists, Separatists could
avoid the church taxes. But Massachusetts in 1753 made a provision that none
could claim Baptist status without certification from one of the older Baptist
churches. In both that colony and Connecticut officials played rough with the
Baptists. They, in turn, took up from their New Light predecessors the unrelent-

---

8. McLoughlin, *New England Dissent*, 1:4–5.

9. Religious community founded in Friesland in the sixteenth century by Hendrik Niclaes, formerly Roman Catholic, who claimed to have been chosen prophet and prepared by a special out-
pouring of the spirit. He established the Family of Love, which later moved to England.

10. Name given to members of an Antinomian movement in England in the middle seventeenth
century. They had pantheistic notions of God and appealed to the inner experience of Christ, denying the authority of Scripture.

11. McLoughlin, *New England Dissent*, 1:19, 4–15.

Isaac Backus

ing campaign for separation of church and state and religious toleration in New England. A flood of petitions and pamphlets marked the campaign of Baptists to undo the persecutions by the Standing Order. Intellectually, the Baptist movement began to coalesce. That achievement owed much to the work of its outstanding American leader, Isaac Backus.

Backus was born in 1724. His father Samuel ran a prosperous farm in Norwich, Connecticut. Samuel in turn had been a judge in the region, always quick to apply the law against civil offenders and religious dissenters. Intermarriage with other leading families connected the Backuses to the elite in their area. However, we have a clue to Backus's Puritan orthodoxy in the grandfather's protest against the Saybrook Platform and his dismissal from his church because of it. Young Isaac found his stronger attachment to his mother, the more so as she experienced a rebirth during the Awakening as he did shortly thereafter.[12]

---

12. McLoughlin, *Backus*, 2–6.

The event, in fact, had a big impact in the Norwich area.[13] Whitefield and Davenport aroused audiences in the town. Backus felt that he must seize the power of the moment. He retreated alone to a nearby field and under the shade of a tree poured out his prayers and his tears. He felt the power of God, acute and moving, and perceived the richness of his free gift of grace. "The Word of God and the promise of His grace appeared firmer than a rock, and I was astonished at my previous unbelief. My heavy burden was gone, tormenting fears were fled, and my joy was unspeakable."[14]

Backus accepted a call to minister in Titicut in 1747 and entered a community that the Awakening had already divided. He had not at this point embraced antipaedobaptism. However, it had a compelling logic, and other New Light Separatists took the next step into the Baptist denomination. The doctrine came to define the essence of their pure church ideals. Backus committed himself to an exhaustive scriptural investigation of the question. In the end, he had to conclude that no biblical sanction existed for infant baptism. Further reading in church history also convinced Backus that, as English Baptists had charged, the sacrament had entered the church in the second or third century, a corruption imposed by priests and rulers in their will to power over their subjects. Backus then reached a much more dramatic conclusion. He perceived that infant baptism had a key place in the covenant theology of the Puritans, and he now saw the perversions of that theology. The Puritans had insisted on the continuity of the old covenant with Abraham and the Christian covenant. Backus now perceived that the allegation of such a continuity had permitted the Puritans, all the way down to the prevailing Standing Order, to perpetuate an Old Testament theocracy. From their appropriation of a national covenant the Puritans proceeded, he said, to impose an oppressive regime that sought elimination of all dissent.[15]

At the very time Backus pressed his case he and other Baptists were working hard to give life to a fledgling college in Rhode Island. It had opened two years before. What helped to make that event possible was the fact that by the middle 1760s the Baptists had acquired a certain definition, something more than an ad hoc collection of separating congregations. More than any individual, the prolific Isaac Backus had effected an intellectual coalescence for his denomination. But from such efforts how might a college arise?

---

13. See J. M. Brumsted, "Revivalism and Separatism in New England: The First Society of Norwich, Connecticut as a Case Study," *William and Mary Quarterly* 3rd Series, 24 (1967): 588–612.

14. McLoughlin, *Backus*, 12–14.

15. McLoughlin, *Backus*, 59, 62–63; *Isaac Backus on Church, State, and Calvinism: Pamphlets, 1754–1789*, ed. William G. McLoughlin (Cambridge, Mass.: Harvard University Press, 1968), 33–34. Backus left an extensive written record of Baptist apologetics. One might want to sample in particular his piece *The Bondwoman and the Free* (1756), which one can find in *Backus on Church, State, and Calvinism*, 134–65. We should appreciate the devastating nature of Backus's biblical polemics here. He did nothing less than undermine the New England order as it had existed almost since its founding over a century before. The whole rationale for its civil and ecclesiastical apparatus, and the alliance that had made life so uncomfortable for noncompliers, Backus deprived of legitimacy.

Not easily. In 1765 Backus had responded to an attack by the Rev. Joseph Fish, in a piece he titled *A Fish Caught in Its Own Net*. Fish had accused the Baptists of anti-intellectualism. They had no need for "common" learning, Fish said, and they drew their ministers from the ranks of the unlearned. They have no use for colleges and deigned to send their sons to good schools, he added. Backus cited some examples from his ranks to counter Fish's charge, but he knew he had a problem here.[16] Baptists did not pursue higher education. There had not been a Baptist college graduate in the colonies since 1734.[17] When a meeting of Philadelphia Baptists first raised the prospect of a Baptist college participants were imagining the first of its kind in the British Empire. Many within their ranks thought so ill of the idea that they warned of bad things befalling them if they should pursue it.[18] Backus spoke frankly of the matter in his diary: "And as the Baptists have met with a great deal of abuse from those who are called learned men in our land, they have been not a little prejudiced against learning itself."[19]

The college initiative actually came from the "Western" Baptists in Philadelphia. They had entered the academy ranks in the colonies with the establishment of the Hopewell School in New Jersey, founded in 1756 under the auspices of the Philadelphia Baptist Association. Some Baptists now looked to collegiate status for the denomination. They then had to ponder where to locate a new college. The South had its attractions, especially as only one college existed there. But the recent progress of the Baptists in New England, and especially in Rhode Island, where a tradition of religious toleration added a further recommendation, turned attention to that colony. Furthermore, no college yet existed there.[20]

Rhode Island had not wholly recovered from its early reputation as an outlaw outpost. Roger Williams and Anne Hutchinson had found their way there in the 1630s, banished from the Massachusetts Bay Colony for their radical Puritan ideas. Its religious toleration made it a haven for Dissenters of several varieties, so much so that the orthodox Cotton Mather could refer to it in disgust as "the fag end of creation." Rhode Island and Providence Plantations attracted and nurtured a fractious and independent-minded people into the eighteenth century. The normalizing commercial trends of that later period, however, also affected Rhode Island. Privacy in religion translated into self-interest in economics. And the profit motive exercised a kingly appeal in the region. Cultural and intellectual amenities came slowly, but they did arrive. Rhode Island began to produce its share of architects and painters, silversmiths and other skilled craftsmen. The dress of black slaves, some with powdered wigs and buckled shoes, reflected the high social status of their owners.[21]

---

16. Backus, "A Fish Caught in His Own Net," in *Backus on Church, State, and Calvinism*, 208.
17. McLoughlin, *New England Dissent*, I, 1:491.
18. Reuben Aldridge Guild, *Early History of Brown University, Including the Life, Times, and Correspondence of President Manning, 1756–1791* (Providence, R.I.: Snow and Farnham, 1896), 19.
19. Backus, *Diary*, 2:607n.
20. Guild, *Brown*, 8, 10–11; McLoughlin, *New England Dissent*, 1:509–10.
21. William G. McLoughlin, *Rhode Island: A Bicentennial History* (New York: W. W. Norton, 1978), xiii, 3, 36, 46–47, 68–69.

James Manning

When the Philadelphia Baptists took their plan for a college to the next level they chose James Manning as the first president. He came from Piscataway, New Jersey, his birthplace in 1738. His father James ran a prosperous farm and traced a family line back to the early settlers of the area. The Baptist connection in James's family began with the parents of his mother Grace. James attended the Hopewell Academy, the first student there. He returned to his home after graduation and made a public confession of his faith, thereupon receiving baptism. At the age of twenty he entered the College of New Jersey. His marriage to Margaret Stites in 1759 connected him to a wealthy Baptist family. Her father had served for several years as mayor of Piscataway. Immediately prior to his selection as the college president, Manning received a call from the Baptist church at Warren, Rhode Island, ten miles from Providence. An imposing figure arrived there in 1764. Manning weighed over three hundred pounds.[22]

---

22. Guild, *Brown*, 22–25, 34, 36, 47–48.

At this very time another individual also contemplated a college for Rhode Island. Ezra Stiles, the Yale graduate and future president of that college, had been Congregational minister in Newport since 1755. The broad-minded Stiles thought that Rhode Island might best utilize its religious diversity in a cooperative intellectual effort. A college that united several groups in free inquiry expressed his intention and he was pursuing those plans when the Philadelphia Baptists arrived in 1763 to explore their design. Manning conveyed to Stiles his willingness to cooperate with him, and Stiles proceeded to draft a charter for the new school. All intended that it would express a clear statement on religious tolerance and free inquiry. They would clash, however, on the question of power and control. When Stiles presented his charter to the Rhode Island legislature, that body, stocked with Baptists, balked. They perceived an excess of influence granted to the Congregationalists. Some tinkering was required.[23] Here is the resultant document. (I have followed the editing done by Professors Hofstadter and Smith in their collection; the bracketed words reference the ones taken out of Stiles's draft and the italicized words reference the words inserted into that draft to make the final one.)

> the Trustees shall and may be [thirty-five] *thirty six*, of which [nineteen] *twenty-two* shall forever be elected from the denomination called Baptists [,] *or Anti-Pedobaptists*, [seven] *five* shall forever be elected of the denomination called [Congregationalists or Presbyterians] *Friends or Quakers*, [five] *four* shall forever be elected of the denomination called [Friends or Quakers] *Congregationalists*, and [four] *five* shall forever be elected from the denomination called Episcopalians [:]; and that the succession in this branch shall forever be chosen and filled up from the respective denominations in this proportion, and according to these numbers, which are hereby fixed. . . .
>
> And that the number of the Fellows [(] inclusive of the President [,] (who shall always be a Fellow) [,] shall and [may be] *maybe* twelve; of which eight shall be forever elected of the denomination called [Congregationalists] *Baptists, or Anti-Pedobaptists*, and the rest indifferently of any and all denominations. . . . and they are hereby declared [and established] the first and present Fellows and Fellowship, to whom the President, when hereafter elected (who shall forever be of the denomination called *Baptists or Anti-Pedobaptists*), shall be joined to complete the number.[24]

With only one other change from the original, the completed charter went on to define Rhode Island College as a "liberal and catholic institution" in which "shall never be admitted any religious tests." It guaranteed for all its members

23. Walter C. Bronson, *The History of Brown University, 1764–1914* (1914; New York: Arno Press, 1971), 14–27; Edmund S. Morgan, *The Gentle Puritan: A Life of Ezra Stiles, 1727–1795* (New York: Norton, 1962), 204–6.

24. "Charter of Rhode Island College (Brown University), 1764" in *American Higher Education: A Documentary History*, 2 vols., ed. Richard Hofstadter and Wilson Smith (Chicago: University of Chicago Press, 1961), 1:134.

"absolute and uninterrupted liberty of conscience." It said that all professors and tutors and all other officers except the president may be from any of the Protestant denominations and entitled to all honors and privileges of the college. The charter forbade proselytizing and any religious indoctrination of students.[25] Rhode Island College thus followed other colonial colleges in proscribing religious tests of students but spoke most emphatically in extending the same exemptions to the other officers of the institution.

The new school set up its operation in impromptu quarters in Warren and began instruction in 1765. All knew, however, that the college must soon find permanent headquarters. The corporation acted on the matter the day of the first commencement in 1769. When a committee announced for Bristol County, Warren's location, other interests responded in protest. Newport and Providence petitioned for consideration and made cases for each's peculiar advantages. Finally, the corporation opted to make a contest of it and let competitors raise money for the cause. Now an issue emerged in which all the colony took a lively interest. It soon became clear that two towns had the lead.[26]

In a colony of fifty thousand people in 1765, Newport led other cities with a population of eight thousand; Providence, though growing faster, had four thousand. Newport could recommend itself on the basis of its wealth, fashion, and culture. It exuded elegance. A taste for intellect and culture had taken root earlier with philosopher George Berkeley's efforts, though unsuccessful, to found a college there. Now one could find in Newport fine public buildings in England's latest architectural modes, splendid new churches, parks and shady walks with ornate carriages conspicuously visible. Newport merchants built spacious homes and country villas and endowed them with ample private libraries. These amenities recommended Newport to some. But sensitive Baptists might have had reason to be wary of Newport as their college location. For one, it reflected a powerful Congregational presence and when it came to this denomination Baptists' memories ran deep. Powerful clergy like Ezra Stiles and Samuel Hopkins showed the Congregational influence in Newport. Anglicans, too, abounded here. Many served the Crown as revenue officers and other officials and among the "princely merchants" of Newport one found many Anglicans. Any Baptist observer could also tell you that the Awakening had failed to make an impact in this city. George Whitefield had lamented his inability to deflect Newport's obsession with trade and commerce.[27]

Providence evidenced no less an obsession with commerce. It was rising to leadership in foreign trade, and it connected with the rest of New England. It also made gains in intellectual life, with private schools and libraries. A new sub-

---

25. "Charter of Rhode Island College," 135.
26. Bronson, Brown, 44–46.
27. McLoughlin, Rhode Island, 57, 73, 77; Bronson, Brown, 11–12; Guild, Brown, 116–17.

scription library appeared in 1753. Providence also had religious diversity and, the record showed, a more promising affinity with the Baptists. The city, along with Westerly, had been one of the two centers of Separatist activity in the colony. Gilbert Tennent and Eleazar Wheelock in the Awakening had made a large impression here. Providence also had another advantage. It had the Brown family.[28]

Rhode Island College's beginnings connect directly to the commercial history of colonial America. Chad Brown, his wife Elizabeth, and son John arrived in Boston in 1638. Four years later Brown became the pastor of the first Baptist church in America. The Browns would remain a prominent Baptist family, but known above all for their financial successes. John Brown had seven children and among them James first showed the family's entrepreneurial talents. At age fourteen he became interested in navigation and within the next decade he acquired his own ship. "Captain James," now with his own shop in Providence, engaged in commercial trade with heavy traffic in the Caribbean. Brown became adept at avoiding British trade restrictions and payment of customs owed on his molasses imports. The Captain died in 1739 and younger brother Obadiah took over his trade, and as much as any, now made Providence a challenge to the commercial dominance of Newport in Rhode Island. Obadiah lost his sons in early deaths and now trained the four sons of Captain James. They were Nicholas, Joseph, John, and Moses.[29]

The brothers were a diverse lot. Nicholas displayed caution and a plodding perseverance and guided the family business with a steady hand. Joseph, never enthralled with the business life, took his reflective mind into science, philosophy, and architecture. John was the bold one, never deterred from the most ambitious projects and designs. Moses had the widest range of interests, to the point that commercial transactions wearied him. His practical bent made him a leader in the colony's early industrialization. In 1773, however, he withdrew from the partnership of Nicholas Brown and Company. His wife's death that year led him to redefine his life. The family enterprises had involved both illicit trade with the French colonies and transactions in the African slave trade. That trade now struck his conscience. He freed his six slaves, soon became a Quaker, and threw himself into the work of the Rhode Island Abolition Society.[30]

As much as any individuals in Providence, the Browns took an interest in the new college. Civic pride and colony politics spurred their efforts. The family was teeming with political activity, especially in their efforts in behalf of Stephen Hopkins of their city, whom they had backed several times in his efforts to be

---

28. Bronson, *Brown*, 50–53; Goen, *Revivalism and Separatism*, 90.

29. James B. Hedges, *The Browns of Providence Plantations: The Colonial Years* (Cambridge, Mass.: Harvard University Press, 1952), 1–10.

30. Hedges, *Browns*, 11–17. On the Browns' illicit trade and their involvement in the slave trade, see chapters 4 and 5 respectively.

governor. His election in 1755 broke a long monopoly of Newport in that office.[31] When the corporation opened the location issue to competition Moses
Brown rallied his troops. He helped prepare a petition to the corporation detail-
ing the advantages of Providence. By the end of 1769 the city had come up with
£3,424. Newport, learning of this success, then doubled its efforts and raised a
larger sum. Brown and his brothers, still not to be undone, prepared a handbill
and saw to its distribution around the city. It read:

> Providence, Monday, February 5, 1770. THE Inhabitants of this Town and County
> are desired to meet at the Court-House THIS AFTERNOON, at two o'clock, to
> hear and consider of some effectual Plan for establishing the COLLEGE here. As
> this is a matter of the greatest Consequence, and the Corporation is to meet on
> WEDNESDAY next, a general Attendance is earnestly requested.[32]

When the effort fell short of the Newport total, Brown tried to get the corporation to stop its meeting. The corporation met and chose Providence anyway.

How was that city able to steal the victory from Newport? For one thing,
Manning himself wanted Providence. He lived but ten miles from it and he qui-
etly lobbied on its behalf. He wrote to Nicholas Brown (referencing his brothers also) to convey "a gentle hint" as to how he might yet beat Newport in the
competition, as he expected it to outbid Providence. Here is how he put the
matter: "Now, as I think you have the good of the college at heart more than
they, it will stand you in hand to demonstrate this in the clearest light; and this
you can do by proffering to build the College yourselves." Manning specified
what Brown might detail in terms of the building and the materials to assure
that he would outdo the Newport people. "You will take them here at un-
awares," he said. The Browns alighted on the idea and threw in some of their
own property by deeding it to the college. They proved true to their word.
Workers laid the first foundation stone in May. The building took its design
from Nassau Hall at Princeton and opened for student occupation the following
winter.[33]

Selection of Providence provoked a bitter reaction among the Newport partisans. Some cried "bribery and corruption." Others denounced the Newport
Baptist ministers in the corporation who seemed to defer to Manning and voted
for Providence. Stiles in turn hastened to draw plans for another new college in
Rhode Island and submitted them to the legislature for its appeal. Frightened
representatives of Rhode Island College argued against the need for such a school
and appealed to the liberal character of their own institution. The legislature denied the charter for Stiles's school.[34]

---

31. Hedges, *Browns*, 188.
32. Bronson, *Brown*, 45–46; Guild, *Brown*, 44–46; Hedges, *Browns*, 188, 195–97.
33. Guild, *Brown*, 119, 137–38 (the quotations); Bronson, *Brown*, 54–55.
34. Guild, *Brown*, 124–25, 129; Bronson, *Brown*, 49; Morgan, *Stiles*, 206.

The college now looked more securely toward its future. It had graduated seven students at the 1769 commencement. The enrollment of 21 in Warren in 1770 grew to 41 in Providence four years later. Rhode Island College, reflecting Baptist democratic ideals, broke from the practice of Harvard and Yale and ranked graduates not by their social standing but by alphabetical order.[35] Isaac Backus joined the first group of trustees and gave years of service to the college. Joseph Brown, who had partaken in the observations of the transit of Venus in 1769, became the professor of experimental philosophy. It also acquired a new tutor in 1769, David Howell. He also graduated from Princeton and at Rhode Island taught mathematics and science. He later became professor of law, serving in that role from 1790 to 1824. He represented the new state in Congress during the Confederation years and served as an associate justice of the Supreme Court of Rhode Island.

Manning in turn served the college as president and as an important leader of the Baptists. He took the lead in forming the Warren Association, a defense organization for Baptists and a vehicle for advancing their legal grievances in the New England colonies. For the cause of Baptism was for him the cause of the college. Each would fare as the other did, he believed. He saw around him "the jealous eye with which other denominations behold this infant seminary," and alleged that they do "what mischief they can, by discouraging scholars from coming here." And when Eleazar Wheelock seemed to be turning his Indian school into the new Dartmouth College, Manning worried—another sign of Congregational expansion.[36] But it was now 1771, and, as revolution loomed, Manning, as well as all the college leaders, had another enemy to worry about.

Like other colonial colleges, Queen's had Reformation roots. Protestantism in Europe spread rapidly after Luther's protests in 1517. The Low Countries received Lutheran ideas (and executed their advocates) and Anabaptist agitation, too. Calvinism, however, quickly became the most powerful expression of Protestantism there. It merged with political causes, as when a Dutch independence movement sought to oust the Catholic Spanish King Phillip II. The revolt did succeed, after decades of struggle, in the north provinces, where an independent Holland resulted. Failure of the revolt in the south sent more Calvinists north, and Holland became a major locus of Reformed Protestantism.

The Netherlands gained intellectual prominence in the Protestant movement. Calvinists in the Low Countries met at Antwerp in 1566 and adopted the Belgiac Confession and provisionally the Heidelberg Confession, drafted by two young professors at the university that bears that name. Dutch universities, in fact, became major centers in advancing Reformed theology—Leyden, 1575;

---

35. Guild, *Brown*, 89–90.
36. Guild, *Brown*, 76, 182, 177–78. Manning revealed such fears privately, to Nicholas Brown. See Richard Luftglass, "Nicholas Brown to Isaac Backus: On Bringing Rhode Island College to Providence," *Rhode Island History* 44 (1985): 125.

Jacob Rutsen Hardenbergh

Franeker, 1585; Gronigen, 1614; Utrecht, 1636. Halfway through the eighteenth century most of the American ministers in the Dutch Reformed Church had their training at one of these schools. Dutch Calvinism asserted its hegemony at the 1618 Synod of Dort, where it routed the Arminian intrusion. The Dutch Stadtholders tenaciously embraced and upheld the Reformed commitment.[37]

The great Dutch commercial empire of the seventeenth century included North America. The Church accompanied it, reaching to Asia, the West Indies, and South America as well. The Dutch made scattered settlements in America and then concentrated their strength in New Amsterdam and up from there along the Hudson River. The Church did not take root effectively, however, and religion did not become a defining presence among the American Dutch. Tolerant Holland did not create religious émigrés seeking new pastures. In general, commercial motivations prevailed in the American migration. The Dutch West

---

37. Gerald F. De Jong, *The Dutch Reformed Church in the American Colonies* (Grand Rapids, Mich.: Eerdmans, 1978), 5–9.

India company did make the Church an establishment, but congregational life did not flourish.[38]

The Dutch Reformed Church enjoyed a legal monopoly in New Netherlands. Governor Peter Stuyvesant, son of a minister and "a fiery Calvinist" himself, warned against "dangerous heresies and schisms" and in 1656 issued a decree forbidding public and private religious meetings "except the usual and authorized ones . . . according to the Reformed and established custom." Nonetheless, New Amsterdam did not acquire the Puritan severity that New England did. Drinking enjoyed a wide toleration, even at religious ceremonies, and Sabbath observance was casual at best.[39]

Local church discipline came through the classis, which consisted of a minister and elder from each congregation within a given area. It met quarterly and could license new ministers. At the larger colonial level, church authority in the eighteenth century graduated increasingly to the Classis of Amsterdam, which assigned to itself a protecting role. After the English takeover of New Amsterdam in 1664, it sought to assure the pristine character of the Dutch Reformed Church, particularly in the matter of preserving the Dutch language in the Church. Therein lay some acute future problems.

Queen's College, however, had different religious roots—the pietistic movement of the late seventeenth and early eighteenth centuries. That movement had various expressions—Lutheran piety as influenced by Philip Jacob Spener and Hermann Francke at the University of Halle, Methodism in England, the Dunkers, Count Zinzendorf and the Moravians, the Schwenckfelders, and the various voices within the German and Dutch Reform churches. All had extensions to the American colonies.[40] The last of these locations is most important to this story. Dutch pietism had its earliest voice in William Teelinck, whose popular-style preaching in the early seventeenth century soon induced a more scholarly rendering in the work of Gysbertus Voetius, professor at the University of Utrecht. The movement soon had close ties to English Puritanism, with William Perkins a particular influence. In turn Voetius's work of 1644, *Exercitia et Bibliotheca Studiosi Theologiae*, became recommended reading for Harvard students. Of course, William Ames became a tangible connection between the English and Dutch Calvinists. Jacobus Koelman translated English and Scottish works and, with his animosity toward formalism and ceremony in worship, brought about a more vigorous pietism. Around the German–Holland border pietism flourished most visibly, making Westphalia its main German location. It began to make its way among some German Reformed churches there.[41]

---

38. Sydney E. Ahlstrom, *A Religious History of the American People* (New Haven, Conn: Yale University Press, 1972), 201–4.

39. De Jong, *Dutch Reformed Church*, 34–35, 144–45.

40. See *Continental Pietism and Early American Christianity*, ed. F. Ernest Stoeffler (Grand Rapids, Mich.: Eerdmans, 1976).

41. James Tanis, "Reformed Pietism in Colonial America," in *Continental Pietism and Early American Christianity*, 34–36, 43.

The man who began the Awakening in America came from this region. Theodorus Jacobus Frelinghuysen was born in 1692, the son of a Reformed pastor. The Frelinghuysens had deep roots in Westphalia. Theodorus attended the University of Lingen, now under the influence of Voetius, and here he learned to speak Dutch. Frelinghuysen then took up a pastorate in East Friesland. Here the elector was filling pulpits with Lutheran pietists, inciting opposition from the traditionalists in the area. But Frelinghuysen had only a little time here, for in 1719 he received an invitation to relocate to the Raritan Valley. Anxious to do God's will, he accepted, assuming a move to a nearby place. However, he then learned that he had volunteered to take up work in the New World. Dutch farmers in upper New Jersey were seeking a pastor to supply a want felt by many in their region. Frelinghuysen quickly took on his new assignment with great vigor.[42]

In the Raritan Valley, which today would include towns like Perth Amboy, New Brunswick, and Middletown, Frelinghuysen introduced a program of strict church discipline, puritanical moralism, and "experimental divinity." He insisted that all who sought communion should have experienced a spiritual rebirth. He denied the sacrament to any who had not. Frelinghuysen urged a preparationist process that emphasized an acute awareness of personal sinfulness. This realization lays the ground for inner renewal. For God, said Frelinghuysen, considers "all unconverted as natural men." This group, he warned, includes even they "who lead modest and proper lives, yes, are even outwardly religious." Frelinghuysen formally embraced Calvinism, but he could not deny that God would help those who truly and earnestly sought him. That fact gave the preacher an important initiative, and Frelinghuysen practiced a new method, begun in East Friesland, by which he would draw the new person from the old. In these great efforts the religious awakening in the American colonies began.[43]

The Awakening continued and grew from the connections made by Frelinghuysen. His circle of associates eventually included Presbyterians, most importantly Gilbert Tennent, who, upon his first encounter with Frelinghuysen, saw the power and effect of the latter's new method and took up the practice of it himself. Frelinghuysen invited Tennent to offer English-language services in the Dutch Reformed church, and the two often shared services.[44] All the while, opposition to Frelinghuysen grew among the older Dutch churches, especially those filled by well-established farmers and the burghers in New York City. Frelinghuysen himself had observed that "the largest portion of the faithful have been poor and of little account in the world." Conservative Dutch Reformed ministers feared erosion of the pure language with the English intrusion and with

---

42. James Tanis, *Dutch Calvinistic Pietism in the Middle Colonies: A Study in the Life of Theodorus Jacobus Frelinghuysen* (The Hague: Martinus Nijhoff, 1967), 12–13, 23, 26–31.

43. Tanis, "Reformed Pietism," 49, 53–55.

44. We are told that Frelinghuysen had little confidence in his English and Tennent little in his Dutch, so the two spoke in the common language of their educations—Latin!

it the decay of the formalist Dutch liturgy. "We must therefore," one said, "be careful to keep things in the Dutch way in our churches." But the Frelinghuysen network expanded and in 1739 it now included George Whitefield. When the great evangelist from England sought an opportunity to preach in New York City, Anglican Trinity Church denied him, Anglican though Whitefield was, but so also did the stalwart Dominie Henricus Boel, "on account of his fanaticism." Whitefield did preach in Tennent's church in New Brunswick and, when he returned the next year, crowds gathered in such numbers that this time he preached from a wagon set up in front of Frelinghuysen's church in that town. The conservative among the Dutch churchmen were not amused.[45] However, what his opponents dubbed his "howling prayers" soon had other ministers emulating that style.

As in other denominations, the new measures proved schismatic. The classis tried to discipline Frelinghuysen, but he resisted and replied in a manner it considered "ungentle and bitter." In America, the evangelical insurgency raised another issue, the question of an independent American church. Many believed the American Dutch Reformed Church too dependent on Holland for its ministry and otherwise hampered by the difficulty of communications with the home country. A first inquiry came in 1706, considered three years later by the Classis of Amsterdam, which dismissed the idea in a wholly unencouraging way: "The formation of a classis among you, to correspond to ours at home, is yet far in the future, and we hardly dare to think of it." A follow-up response even said that such a new departure "would be the ruin of the churches of New York." Not until the middle 1730s, in a moment of peace among the colonial church factions, did the Amsterdam Classis take up the matter again, this time with a surprising suggestion that the American churches organize a convention. A New Jersey minister, in turn, recommended formation of a coetus (pronounced "see-tus"), or a group of churches that lacked full classical authority. A 1737 statement of reasons for such a formation mentioned among them the need "to Guard against prevailing errors." The American Coetus won approval, but did not have the right to ordain ministers. This measure came at a time when the American Dutch Reformed Church had far more churches than ministers to serve them. Amsterdam, however, feared an inferior ministry resulting from local ordination.[46]

So long as this problem persisted, however, demands for fuller autonomy would grow. A petition on behalf of an American classis came forth in 1754. Soon the issue reduced to a question of reforming the coetus by granting it new powers. Some Dutch Reformed Church locals opposed the change. In one embroilment of interest to the later college, Dominie Johannes Ritzema faulted the ordination of Jacob Rutsen Hardenbergh, expressing doubt that he could

---

45. Tanis, *Frelinghuysen*, 70 (second quotation), 81–82; Tanis, "Reformed Pietism," 53–54 (first quotation).

46. De Jong, *Dutch Reformed Church*, 175–77, 186, 189–91, 197; Tanis, *Frelinghuysen*, 74 (the quotations).

"translate a single sentence of Latin." Ritzema, watching the gains of the Frelinghuysen wing of the American church, complained that ordination standards had minimized learning in favor of possessing the "spirit" as the favored criterion. Other locals feared inroads of Arminianism if the American Coetus gained the power to ordain.[47]

Dutch Reform factions figured decisively in the college movement. In New York City, the creation of King's College in 1754 agitated local politics, as we have seen. Presbyterians fought against the Anglican takeover, as did the Frelinghuysen wing of the Dutch Church. But some New York Dutch Reformed people did support it, including Ritzema, who would enroll his only son there. This group, however, was also looking for an opportunity. It hoped the college might house a seminary for the Dutch Reformed Church. Such a hope, furthermore, strengthened its resistance to an American classis. The conservatives (mostly located in New York City) wanted to nominate to the college a divinity professor who would uphold their own theological tenets. Such an appointment, some also hoped, would complicate any move by an American classis, should it form, to begin its own college, away from the city. (This anti-coetus group was known as the "Conferentie.") Meanwhile, this Dutch faction also had to deal with the anti-Anglican Triumvirate, the *Independent Reflector* group, now whipping up sentiment against the Anglican designs among the Dutch Reform outside the city. In 1755 the New York consistory won the right to appoint a Dutch professor of divinity at King's.[48]

That event propelled the evangelical faction to act. Leadership in this group fell to Theodore Frelinghuysen of Albany, son of the revivalist, who had died in 1748. He had completed his studies at the University of Utrecht and accepted a call from a church in Albany. He became a champion of the coetus and the cause of colonial ordination. As part of these programs, he included the need for an American university. By this time, the Frelinghuysen faction represented an Americanist party in the colonial Dutch Reformed Church. Creation of an American classis summarized its goals. In this design, however, conservatives again raised the language issue and connected it to the feared erosion of Dutch culture generally. The Americanists in 1747 had won limited authority to ordain ministers. Now, after the concordat of 1755, attention centered on the idea of a new Dutch Reformed college. Frelinghuysen made those intentions clear at a May 1755 meeting of the coetus, which none of the New York people attended. When he spoke of the intended school's instruction, he mentioned the learned languages and liberal arts. He wanted to make the institution a "school of the prophets" to train a new ministry for the Church. Ritzema denounced the resolution of the coetus and called it illegal. Those

---

47. De Jong, *Dutch Reformed Church*, 198–200.
48. David C. Humphrey, *From King's College to Columbia, 1746–1800* (New York: Columbia University Press, 1976), 57–64; De Jong, *Dutch Reformed Church*, 201–2.

who condemned the college idea included many American Dutch Reform ministers native to the Netherlands. The Amsterdam Classis, too, denounced the
idea when Frelinghuysen sailed there to plead the cause in 1759. After two
years of fruitless effort he died at sea on his return home. But the college cause
would not die. Other Dutch ministers took it up, among them Jacob Hardenbergh. By now the issues of college and coetus had brought bitter rancor and
invective to the Dutch factions.[49]

Partisans of the college project turned to the New Jersey governors for support, only to be turned down in succession until in 1766 Governor William
Franklin granted a charter. The college took the name Queen's, in honor of
Charlotte, the Queen Consort. (We neither have nor know the exact details of
this first charter.) A new charter came from Franklin in 1770. It empowered a
board of trustees to establish a college "for the education of youth in the learned
languages, liberal and useful arts and sciences, and especially in divinity; preparing them for the ministry, and other good offices." The college president must be
of the Dutch Church and would also serve as professor of divinity. The charter
also specified that at least one professor instruct the students "in the knowledge
of the English language." Beyond the denominational requisite for the president,
Queens' College had nonsectarian status. The charter specified no religious test
for students or faculty.[50]

Establishment of Queen's College in 1766 confirmed the success of the
Americanist and evangelical movement within the American Dutch Reformed
Church. The coetus had already gone its way independently of the Amsterdam
Classis, even performing its own ordinations. It located itself in New Brunswick,
since the 1740s a center of New Light religious excitements among both the
Presbyterians and the Dutch inhabitants. Jacob Rutsen Hardenbergh became
first president. He had come to New York to study with John Frelinghuysen and
succeeded him upon his death in 1758. (He also married Frelinghuysen's widow
Dinah, though thirteen years her junior.) Now in 1771 the college gained its first
tutor—Frederick Frelinghuysen, grandson of Theodorus Jacobus, son of John,
and stepson of Hardenbergh. Frelinghuysen had graduated from Princeton in
1770. Instruction began in a building acquired by the trustees, the former tavern
"Sign of the Red Lion." And these events did take place amid renewed denominational harmony. A restructuring of the Dutch churches created the General
Assembly, now all but independent of the Classis of Amsterdam. Queen's held
its first commencement in 1774 when it was educating twenty students.[51] The
Awakening thus provided New Jersey its second college. Along the way it was
providing New England its fourth.

---

49. Humphrey, *King's College*, 57–64; De Jong, *Dutch Reformed Church*, 201–2; Tanis, *Frelinghuy-sen*, 90–91.

50. Richard McCormick, *Rutgers: A Bicentennial History* (New Brunswick, N.J.: Rutgers University Press, 1966), 8–9.

51. McCormick, *Rutgers*, 11, 13; De Jong, *Dutch Reformed Church*, 206; Tanis, "Reformed Pietism," 58.

The Reverend Eleazar Wheelock (Oil painting by Joseph Steward, 1796)

It was an unusual combination of personalities, but it worked. One man came directly out of the religious awakening of the eighteenth century, the movement that had already become the fault line of American colonial higher education. He had taken it into missionary educational work among the American natives. The other man came from the social and cultural elite of Portsmouth, New Hampshire, scion of an American Anglican dynasty in upper New England. The establishment of Dartmouth College in 1768 owes to the cooperation and coinciding purposes of these two men—Rev. Eleazar Wheelock and Governor John Wentworth.

Wheelock's family came from England. A great-grandfather, Ralph, was born in Shropshire in 1600 and graduated from Cambridge University, thereupon entering the ministry. He joined the Dissenters and accompanied other persecuted Puritans in their removal to New England. Wheelock settled in Watertown, Massachusetts, then in Dedham, and finally in Medfield. His two marriages produced nine children, including the grandfather and namesake of the Dartmouth founder. One of his sons, Deacon Ralph Wheelock, became a wealthy farmer. He married Ruth Huntington, who in 1711 bore their only son, Eleazar, in Windham, Connecticut.[52]

We have little information about young Wheelock. He entered Yale College in 1729 and shared an academic prize with his later brother-in-law Benjamin Pomeroy. After remaining in New Haven to study theology and earn his M.A. degree, he took a pastorate in Lebanon, Connecticut, and served there in the 1730s. When the religious revivals that shook the colonies at the beginning of the next decade struck Connecticut, Wheelock became an immediate partisan of the cause. Like the other New Lights, Wheelock believed that religion in New England had become listless and formal, having lost the marks of inward conversion that showed true piety. Wheelock considered himself a disciple of George Whitefield, the Tennents, and even of the more controversial James Davenport. From the outset of the revival, Wheelock took an apologetic stance. He wrote to a friend in 1740, "I believe there is vastly less hurt done by some degrees of enthusiasm where there is a fervent love to God than there is by that lukewarmness and coldness that has so generally prevailed among ministers. Witness Brother Davenport's extraordinary success since his intemperate zeal, also the success of the Tenants [sic] and others in the Jersies, not to speak of Mr. Whitefield." Wheelock had close personal ties to the Awakening. Davenport was a brother of Wheelock's first wife (Mrs. Sarah Davenport Maltby). Wheelock's orthodoxy was marked also by his opposition to the Half-Way Covenant, some eighty years after that measure first became controversial. He did, however, uphold the Saybrook Platform of 1708.[53]

Wheelock was nothing if not energetic on behalf of the Awakening. He made two preaching tours of the colony and in one year reported delivering over four hundred sermons. His commitment unavoidably thrust Wheelock into the religious politics of New England. Old Lights resented him, including President Thomas Clap at Yale, who now, recoiling from the specter of Davenport, refused Wheelock a preaching opportunity there. Wheelock wrote to his wife, "Mr. Clap refuses to let me preach in the college or to let other scholars come to hear me. O that God would give him another heart." But Wheelock persisted. He preached at Branford in 1742 and reported "a great shaking" there.[54]

Wheelock received rebuke from the other side as well. Champion of liberal Protestantism Charles Chauncy compiled his massive testimonies against

---

52. James Dow McCallum, *Eleazar Wheelock* (1939; New York: Arno Press and the New York Times, 1969), 2–5; *Memoirs of the Rev. Eleazar Wheelock . . .* , ed. David McClure (1811; New York, Arno Press, 1972), 10–11.

53. Leon Burr Richardson, *History of Dartmouth College* (Hanover, N.H.: Dartmouth University Press, 1932), 21–22, 26; McCallum, *Wheelock*, 5, 8, 31 (the quotation).

54. Richardson, *Dartmouth College*, 22; McCallum, *Wheelock*, 14–15.

the Awakening and published them in his 1743 work, *Seasonable Thoughts on the State of Religion in New England*. He included Wheelock in it. He placed him in the party of Davenport and said that all in it had raised the "commotions" in Connecticut, "where sudden impulses and extraordinary impulses to the Spirit have been more general . . . than in any of the other governments." In Wheelock's case, Chauncy blamed in particular a young Quaker student at Yale, David Ferris, saying that he had early brought Wheelock under his bad influence, capturing Pomeroy and Davenport later. Chauncy quoted a letter to him. "This Ferris was the greatest enthusiast I ever knew," said the writer. He claimed that Ferris, Wheelock, and the others became intimates, all of them "enthusiastic zealots."[55]

Wheelock knew personal tragedy. Three of the six children born to him and Sarah Davenport died in infancy. In 1745 they lost one of the children of her first marriage. She in turn died in 1747, and the next year Wheelock married Mary Brimsmead. He had sent his stepson John to Yale but did not miss the opportunity to preface his arrival by a personal note to Clap. He stated that he felt a bit uncomfortable about the gains at Yale made by Arminianism, which "suit the pride and corruptions of the natural mind." He also chastised the Yale president for a spirit of intolerance in his locking out the revival ministers and in preventing the Yale scholars from attending their preaching. Another son John, product of the second marriage, became a Dartmouth graduate and succeeded his father as second president of the college.[56]

In the aftermath of the Awakening Wheelock began to pursue another interest. In 1756 he wrote to his friend Whitefield expressing his concern for the American Indians—"poor, savage, perishing creatures." He saw the Indians' numbers declining and urged the imperative of converting them, before none remained to convert. God, he believed, had imposed this obligation on the whites, and their failure to fulfill it, Wheelock said, occasioned his letting them loose dangerously and destructively on the land. Wheelock had in mind the creation of an Indian school, which he would establish at Lebanon, Connecticut. He would isolate the Indians, joined by white charity students, from the evil influences in their environment. And while Wheelock could state his mission in clear, religious terms, he could also tie it to the prevailing political situation in North America. The British and French had long competed for Indian loyalty and made alliances with different groups. Wheelock shared with other Protestant leaders a contempt for "the hellish rites of the Jesuits" and

---

55. Charles Chauncy, *Seasonable Thoughts on the State of Religion in New England* (Boston: Rogers and Fowle, 1743), 202, 209–13. Richard Warch reports that Ferris's group of six students at Yale represented an Arminian presence in the college at the time that Clap was trying to uphold orthodoxy. He refers to them as "a coterie of enthusiasts." The Arminian label could not have applied to Wheelock, however (*School of the Prophets: Yale College, 1701–1740* [New Haven, Conn.: Yale University Press, 1973], 169, 169n).

56. McCallum, *Wheelock*, 57–59.

sought to counteract their political influence, too. The British and Americans, he said, would reap more from the work of missionaries and teachers to the Indians than they would from military defenses. This point he always pressed upon Sir William Johnson, British superintendent of Indian affairs.[57]

Wheelock set up in the school an instructional program heavily religious and classical in nature. The native youth were to receive a rapid entry into the foundations of Western civilization; no distinction in subject prevailed between the two races in the school. Critics like Charles Chauncy would have preferred an exclusive concentration on English. The language issue, however, proved the least of Wheelock's worries. More vexing was the character of the Indians themselves. In a despairing mood, Wheelock wrote to George Whitefield in 1761, "None know, nor can any, without experience, well conceive of, the difficulty of educating an Indian. They would soon kill themselves with eating and sloth, if constant care were not exercised for them at least the first year." They sit always on the ground, he said, and they shun clothing provided for them. Wheelock reported additional frustrations in his efforts to keep liquor away from the Indians.[58]

The school attained fame in the colonies and England in part from the achievements of Indian student Sam Occum. He became a gospel preacher and the first of his race to preach in England, where he arrived in 1766. There he attracted large audiences and made a great impression. Dissenting ministers issued invitations to Occum to preach in their churches. Wheelock also used the native's talents to attract funds for the school, most importantly from the Earl of Dartmouth, who also influenced a contribution from King George III. Wheelock also used the situation to establish a Board of Trustees for the school, with Dartmouth as its president. In making these arrangements, the Indian school officials took advantage of Dartmouth's late priorities. The Englishman had taken an interest in the Methodist movement and become a follower of Whitefield. Now he joined this special work of American Dissenters.[59]

All along, Wheelock preserved a commitment to the revivalist side of American Protestantism. He has not left a large record of his intellectual life, but an address given at the ordination of Benjamin Trumbull in 1760 places Wheelock clearly in the New Light camp. He appropriately chose for the occasion a sermon on preaching. Wheelock set an Edwardsean standard for the preaching ministry: "They must set before sinners the wretchedness, seriousness, and necessities of their state by nature. Without a conviction of this, in vain are the glories of the mediator set before them. They can feel no such comeliness or excellency in him, as will attract their love, and work in them an esteem of him." For people, he said, have a native aversion to God's truth and the conviction of their

---

57. McCallum, *Wheelock*, 75–76, 79; Richardson, *Dartmouth College*, 27; Wheelock to Johnson, June 1761, in *Memoirs of Wheelock*, 227.

58. McCallum, *Wheelock*, 84 (the quotation)–85, 90; *Memoirs of Wheelock*, 32–33.

59. Richardson, *Dartmouth College*, 9–11; *Memoirs of Wheelock*, 44–46.

sin. So the preacher must lay open that sickness so that they know and feel their true state—"miserable and poor, and blind, and naked." Said Wheelock, "Fear is the only principle that moves the sinner in the business of his salvation." Wheelock, however, decried a prevailing state in which the ministry itself had lost the relish for these expostulations. It had relinquished the sense of urgency about these matters and preached a vague doctrine of salvation by hope. Too much preaching now, Wheelock lamented, averted the painful subject of human depravity.[60]

Thematic of the New Light ministry, too, Wheelock stressed the greatness of God's love. And he linked it to a sensitivity to sinfulness. For only from that perspective may we grasp the great, undeserved gift that God rendered humanity, "a perishing, polluted, apostate, sinking world." Wheelock thus stood against the liberal trend in American Protestantism. It had softened the sense of sin and neutralized a corrupt human nature, he judged. He faulted "such preaching as represents man as being morally clean by nature, not the subject of spiritual death, nor a child of wrath." Such advocacy, he said, "though it well suits the pride of carnal hearts" finds no favor with God and deprecates Christ's great atonement for the human race. Then Wheelock made the classic New Light accusation: those who have not the spirit in them cannot be the purveyors of God's message of deliverance. They cannot bring others to the imperative of spiritual renewal had they not keenly felt it themselves. "It is not likely they will have either the skill, or zeal, to make such representations of the glories of Christ, or sinners' perishing need of him, as are most suitable, and likely to persuade them to come to him."[61] Wheelock said, with less of the accusatory strains, and without the invective, what Gilbert Tennent had said in 1740.

In 1768 Wheelock decided to move the Indian school and make it a college. He had not yet determined the place of its relocation. Not all associated with the school, however, approved the change. Occum wrote to Wheelock expressing his fear that the school would lose its special character as an Indian institution. "I am very jealous," he said, "that instead of your seminary becoming alma mater she will be too alba mater to suckle the Tawnees."[62] Wheelock, though, felt frustrated by the school's progress as measured against his ambitions for it. As to its new site, he had not ruled out Connecticut or Massachusetts. A remarkable turn of events, however, would place the new Dartmouth College in New Hampshire.

Settlements of present-day New Hampshire had begun in the 1640s and were reinforced by the party of Rev. John Wheelwright and other Antinomian exiles banished in the Anne Hutchinson affair. Exeter, Portsmouth, and Dover were early townships that acknowledged the authority of Massachusetts. In 1680 New Hampshire became a royal colony. The vast timberlands of the region as-

---

60. Eleazar Wheelock, *The Preaching of Christ, an Expression of God's Great Love to Sinners* . . . (Boston: S. Kneeland, 1760), 6, 8–9.
61. Wheelock, *The Preaching of Christ*, 13, 19–20.
62. *Memoirs of Wheelock*, 46; Richardson, *Dartmouth College*, 114 (the quotation).

Governor John Wentworth (Pastel by John Singleton Copley, 1769)

sured a growing economy for the colony, and it became a key exporter. Its political history would have a special significance for Dartmouth College, and in the eighteenth century that story involved New Hampshire's most powerful family, the Wentworths.

They came from Alford, England, a market town in eastern Lincolnshire on the North Sea. William, born in 1616, was the first of the Wentworths to cross the Atlantic to America. His family had a distant connection to the more powerful English Wentworths that included Sir Thomas, earl of Stratford, executed in 1641 for loyalty to King Charles I. This Wentworth formed ties with Rev. Wheelwright and moved with him to New Hampshire in 1637. Here he married and settled in Dover. The later Wentworths included Samuel, lieutenant governor of New Hampshire from 1717 to 1730. This person especially consolidated the family's economic and political power. He exercised his authority in granting townships, and both family and wealthy Portsmouth merchants gained by his favors. Samuel Wentworth, in turn, became the leader in the movement for New

Hampshire's separation from Massachusetts, a move that would have given him even more power in making land grants.[63]

Leadership in the independence effort fell to Samuel's son Benning, after the father's death in 1730. Benning pursued the effort vigorously and Governor Jonathan Belcher of Massachusetts dubbed him the "rascal." Benning Wentworth, born in 1696 and a graduate of Harvard, had entered into the mercantile business, in Boston and then in Portsmouth. He formed close ties to Theodore Atkinson and entered politics through election to the House of Representatives. He was appointed governor of New Hampshire in 1741. A biographer has written of Benning Wentworth: "More than anyone else, Benning Wentworth was responsible for making the Wentworth name nearly legendary in New Hampshire. He literally ruled the province for twenty-five years, the longest reign of any governor in the history of England's American colonies."[64]

The Wentworths had become stalwarts of the Anglican Church. That connection also applied to Benning's brother, younger by thirteen years, Mark Hunking Wentworth. He too became a merchant and with an eventual monopoly of the mast trade in the 1740s had the greatest wealth of all Portsmouth. He had married Elizabeth Rindge, and in 1637 she gave birth to son John. He was to be the key player in the Dartmouth story. John graduated from Harvard in 1655, a classmate and longtime friend of John Adams. John Wentworth returned to Portsmouth and entered his father's business.[65]

John Wentworth first learned of the Connecticut Indian school and its plans to become a college when he was in England. His sojourn of 1763 to 1767 included a stay at Bath where he made the acquaintance of Nathaniel Whitaker. The latter came as envoy both from Eleazar Wheelock and Mark Hunking Wentworth who sought Wentworth's support for the school. Further solicitations came from Sam Occum, also part of the English fund-raising effort. John Wentworth took a particular interest in the project when he learned that Wheelock now sought a new location for the school. Wentworth made a financial pledge to it. Furthermore, as he had become governor in 1766 and prepared to return to New Hampshire to begin his term, he promised Whitaker the grant of a township if Wheelock would relocate the school to New Hampshire.[66]

When Eleazar Wheelock called on John Wentworth in Portsmouth, late in 1767, he came to a town splendid in wealth and culture. Benning Wentworth had set the pace.

> Over the years, through Wentworth's baronial gateway and along the stately driveways came shining coaches drawn by high-stepping horses, bearing the governor's

---

63. Paul W. Wilderson, *Governor John Wentworth and the American Revolution: The English Connection* (Hanover, N.H.: University Press of New England, 1994), 15, 17.
64. Wilderson, *Governor John Wentworth*, 17–18.
65. Wilderson, *Governor John Wentworth*, 20, 23, 32, 37.
66. Wilderson, *Governor John Wentworth*, 85–86.

friends, relatives, and political visitors. Sitting beneath Wentworth family portraits, on elegantly upholstered chairs, using the finest china and silver, Wentworth guests were served the best cuisine the province had to offer, complemented by wines imported from Europe.[67]

Cosmopolitan interests prevailed among many citizens of Portsmouth. The province had its first newspaper, the *New Hampshire Gazette*, started by Daniel Fowle of Boston. He also opened a bookshop that offered the works of Shakespeare, Addison, and Locke and the wide repertoire of English notables. Many prominent Portsmouth merchants had private libraries of their own, and, in 1750, inspired by the example of Ben Franklin, the town began a subscription library. Theater also came to town when a successful petition to the governor led to construction of a playhouse. Not all Portsmouth welcomed the new worldliness of the town, however. A counterpetition warned that stage entertainment would have a pernicious influence on the morals of the young, giving them "an idle turn of attachment to pleasure and amusement." Religious taste got intermixed in these judgments. Congregational clergy took offense at Anglican high living as exemplified by the Wentworths.[68]

Wheelock came to Portsmouth to remind Wentworth of his earlier promise to the school. The governor received the minister cordially and promised faithfulness to his commitment. Wentworth, though, had motivations of his own in supporting the new college. Wheelock had promoted the school to him by emphasizing the interest of the western farmers, those out in the Connecticut River Valley. They wanted new ministers to serve their towns. Wentworth in turn had a keen interest in developing the region through new settlement. A college would be an attraction. Even a college only for Indians, he believed, would have its use, as many potential settlers, he believed, feared relocation to New Hampshire because of Indian problems. The college might allay those fears. He had a personal sympathy for the natives besides. The wealthy of Portsmouth, too, took an interest in the college. They believed its existence would increase the value of various land holdings around the colony. Finally, the colonial legislature also made a small contribution to the school, designated by Wheelock for location in Hanover on the Connecticut River.[69]

But the deed was not quite done. Wheelock had to secure a charter for the college and had doubts about his ability to attain one. He had not told Wentworth that the Indian school was under the control of a board of English trustees that included Lord Dartmouth, and that board, Wheelock knew, did not want to relinquish its control. Should the governor doubt his authority to grant a charter, Wheelock suggested, he might inquire in England and learn the truth. So

---

67. Elizabeth Forbes Morison and Elting E. Morison, *New Hampshire: A Bicentennial History* (New York: Norton, 1976), 58.
68. Wilderson, *Governor John Wentworth*, 42–44; Morisons, *New Hampshire*, 58.
69. Wilderson, *Governor John Wentworth*, 126–28; *Memoirs of Wheelock*, 61–62.

Dartmouth College

Wheelock had to turn to Portsmouth friends, Congregational ministers mostly, and sound out Wentworth on the idea. They learned that he had no qualms, and Wheelock set about preparing a charter. Into it he introduced a major change— creation of an American board that left the English one with no power. Wheelock and Wentworth headed the new board. So far so good. But then Wentworth introduced a troubling factor.[70]

The New Hampshire governor proposed to include on the board of the new college the bishop of London. Everyone knew Wentworth to be a strong Anglican who had supported the Church in predominantly Congregationalist New Hampshire. Now some suspected sinister designs on the part of the governor, possibly even an intention to turn the college into an Anglican institution. A letter to the bishop, virtually outlining an Anglican future of this kind, implied such intentions. The governor's proposal worried Wheelock considerably. His anxieties reflected those of many throughout the colony in these years before the American Revolution. As relations with the mother country worsened, the fears of an American Anglican bishop took on a conspiratorial perspective; many feared a plot. Wheelock made those fears known to Wentworth and contemplated moving the school to another location. Wentworth assuaged him, however, by showing that his proposal had useful political purposes. He wished to use the appointment, he said, to overcome English opposition toward establishment of another dissenting college in the colonies. Furthermore, he intended to have the bishop sit only on the English board. Wheelock felt greatly relieved, even overjoyed, and he offered to name the school after Wentworth. The governor declined. Now the charter went into final form, letters patented in the name of George III were issued, and Wentworth affixed the seal of the governor on the charter, dated December 13, 1769. In his interest in the school and support of it, the new college probably had no greater friend in New Hampshire than Governor Wentworth.[71]

Wheelock named the college for the Earl of Dartmouth. He had long shown an interest in Wheelock's work with American Indians, and Wheelock kept a correspondence with him, at one point sending the earl an Indian artifact, elaborately described in his letter. The school opened in 1770 and graduated its first students in 1773, in which year it had eighty attending. Its curriculum was standard in every way as Wheelock extended a commitment to classical studies that he had brought even into the education of Indians. Dartmouth College attracted a large portion of its students from Connecticut, in part because President Clap at Yale had won such a reputation as an opponent of the Awakening.[72] His late switch had little impact. Dartmouth now stood as New England's second school

---

70. Wilderson, *Governor John Wentworth*, 128–29. See also Jurgen Herbst, *From Crisis to Crisis: American College Government, 1636–1819* (Cambridge, Mass.: Harvard University Press, 1982), 128–31.
71. McCallum, *Wheelock*, 171–72; Wilderson, *Governor John Wentworth*, 129–31.
72. Richardson, *Dartmouth College*, 134, 119.

of New Light identity. Its successful beginning owed much to the collaboration of a pious minister and a wealthy Anglican stalwart. But revolutionary days now quickened. They would put the fruitful alliance in severe jeopardy.

The various expressions of religious intensity that we call the Great Awakening, whether they deserve so precise a label or not, did cause division and faction in American colonial Protestantism. What this chapter demonstrates is how readily these effects found institutional expression in the creation of three new colleges. With the initial breakthrough in the College of New Jersey's creation in 1746, Rhode Island College, Queen's College, and Dartmouth College constitute those four schools among the colonial nine that derived from the Awakening. But each was particularized within the Awakening. Queen's became the second to have an "ethnic" identity (after the Scotch-Irish influence at Princeton), but it represented an Americanist segment within the larger Dutch-American population and the Dutch Reformed Church. Rhode Island College was the achievement of a New England faction that spun away not only from the Standing Order in Connecticut and Massachusetts but also from the non-Separatist mainstream of New England Congregationalism that did embrace the Awakening. That group found its collegiate extension in Dartmouth College. All four schools reflect the continuing vitality of the Calvinist intellectual impact on colonial America, the Reformed tradition finding institutional location beyond the legions of churches that subscribed to it.

9

Harvard II: A Liberal Turn

The events of 1707 pointed Harvard in a new direction. Taking it there would be another matter. The new president enjoyed high personal esteem; the college's historian called him "The Great Leverett." But Leverett added little to the college's intellectual history, as he published virtually nothing. Under his leadership, Harvard underwent no significant curricular change.[1] Whereas the college presidency has had center stage in this history so far, now a shift occurs. Harvard's history entered a new era when, from a surprising source, it gained opportunities to establish two professorships. The pattern would develop at other colleges, and professors who held these places of distinction now took on new intellectual prominence at their institutions. The Hollis professorships in religion and science are the anchor points of Harvard's intellectual life in the middle era of the eighteenth century. As the forces of liberal Christianity and the Enlightenment spread in New England, and as the religious revivals challenged the standing order in Massachusetts, the Hollis professors best help us chart Harvard's uneasy path.

The old order was out of power but it was by no means dead. It still had strong voices among the overseers, and on the outside it had the remaining voice of the Mather dynasty, always vigilant. One issue that troubled Cotton Mather concerned the religious identity of the college under Leverett. The president used some Anglican works in his religious instruction, and Mather feared a liberal direction in theology. He and others among the orthodox also feared a cozy nexus between Leverett and the royal governors, inferring a "Tory" turn in the college's political situation.[2] Mather often confided his thoughts and fears to his

---

1. Samuel Eliot Morison, *Three Centuries of Harvard, 1636–1936* (Cambridge, Mass.: Harvard University Press, 1942), 54, 57.
2. Morison, *Three Centuries,* 64.

diary. He vexed at the presence of William Whiston's[3] works in the Harvard library, for this English thinker had embraced non-Trinitarian Christianity. Mather offered his own views of the Trinity as antidote to the "wretched poison" given out by Whiston, with a special intention "to defend the students in our college from the corruption."[4]

Sometimes Mather avowed even more direct action. In 1716 he wrote, "I will get further books, which I think will be of great use for the interests of piety and orthodoxy in the college, into the hands of the students there."[5] Eight years later, however, Mather worried about a continuing conspiracy "among our wicked Church of England men," who designed, as he put it, "to get our college into their hands."[6] Nor did the general trend of Harvard education please him. He saw its religious core gradually dissolving into curricular surrogates, especially ethics, "a vile form of paganism," that now surpassed Scripture as the greater authority for moral instruction.[7]

Meanwhile, Harvard came under censure from another source. In Boston young Ben Franklin had already won notoriety for his satirical barbs against the religious establishment. Now he took on the college. In 1722 he had "Silence Dogood" take her fanciful pilgrimage to the "Temple of Learning." She discovers a place where poverty screens out multitudes of would-be scholars, where learning, in its many forms, seems to occupy places of splendor, but proves upon inspection to be formless and hollow. "Idleness" and "Ignorance" keep the classics in a neglected state, their mastery by the students, "dunces and blockheads," but a pretense. Out of the college march its graduates, some to become mechanics, more to have no useful pursuits at all. The largest group treks into "The Temple of Theology," lured by money. They are last seen copying lines from Tillotson.[8]

Leverett died in 1724. Cotton Mather expected to get the call to succeed him,[9] but the corporation looked elsewhere. It called on Samuel Sewall, who declined, leaving Mather again hopeful. But Benjamin Colman then got the nod. Colman saw the political situation at the school and perceived the orthodox aligned against him. So he too declined. Finally, the corporation invited Benjamin Wadsworth, minister of the First Church in Boston and a Harvard graduate of 1690. He did not relish political fighting either, but duty drove him to accept. Mather seethed. He had already concluded that the college had declined into dissipation and confusion. He felt meanly slighted. "The Corporation of our miserable College do again (upon a fresh opportunity) treat me with their ac-

---

3. Whiston (1667–1752), a Cambridge graduate and heterodox Anglican who moved in the direction of Arianism, eventually becoming a Baptist. He wrote *A New Theory of the Earth* in 1696, which explained the Mosaic account of creation by naturalistic, Newtonian principles (see below).

4. *Diary of Cotton Mather, Volume II, 1709–1724* (New York: Frederick Ungar, n.d.), 186 (March 1712/13).

5. *Mather Diary*, 350 (May 1716).

6. *Mather Diary*, 703 (March 1724).

7. *Mather Diary*, 357 (June 1716).

8. Benjamin Franklin, "Silence Dogood, No. 4," in *The Papers of Benjamin Franklin*, ed. Leonard W. Larabee (New Haven, Conn.: Yale University Press, 1959), 36 vols. 1:15–17.

9. *Mather Diary*, 723 (May 1724).

customed indignity and malignity," he wrote. He found solace only in the thought that this outcome just might be the will of God.[10]

Two years before Leverrett's death, Harvard received an unusual windfall. The wealthy London merchant Thomas Hollis had been communicating with Benjamin Colman. Impressed that Harvard had entered a liberal and tolerant era, Hollis decided to endow a divinity professorship there. Hollis was a Baptist and trusted Harvard to have a welcoming posture toward his denomination and others. He had already given scholarship money and books to the college and now in 1722 offered this handsome bequest. The president and fellows of the college could make the appointment to the new chair, provided "that none be refused on account of his belief and practice of adult baptism."[11]

In drafting guidelines for the chair, however, Hollis and some collaborators expressed their own preference for an individual "of sound and orthodox principles." In this wording, the overseers, and particularly the conservatives among them, saw an opportunity. They understood "orthodoxy" to mean Congregationalist and Calvinist. Consequently, when Edward Wigglesworth gained appointment to the chair, he had to swear allegiance to William Ames's *Medulla Theologicae*, even at this late date the standing symbol of intellectual orthodoxy. He had to promise conviction as to the doctrines of the Holy Trinity, predestination, special and efficacious grace, and the divine right of infant baptism. Thus quite disingenuously did Harvard receive and execute the generous gift of Thomas Hollis.[12]

Edward Wigglesworth occupied the first Harvard professorship in 1722. It would be his until his death in 1768. Wigglesworth came from Cambridge itself, the son of Michael and Sybil Sparhawk Wigglesworth, he a pastor and writer of the great Puritan poem, "The Day of Doom." Young Wigglesworth graduated from Harvard in 1710. Colman recommended him to Hollis as "a man of known and exemplary piety, literature, modesty, meekness, and other Christian ornaments." Apart from the loyalty sworn to the Hollis Chair standards, Wigglesworth must have secured a reputation for orthodoxy quite on his own. Yale College, but one year after the shock of the Anglican apostasy, invited him to succeed Timothy Cutler as rector. Wigglesworth declined. In the years ahead, Wigglesworth's "orthodoxy" would face many tests and undergo revisions. He showed himself to be a man of immense learning, and many of his essays lay out, in prolix and ponderous display, both sides of a theological argument. But his fairness often betrayed indecisiveness. Many could not determine exactly where he stood. During Wigglesworth's tenure in the divinity chair, the intellectual turmoil of the eighteenth century came home to Harvard. In the Boston/Cambridge area, one found both factions of the rival cultures that warred in that era—liberal Christianity and Calvinism. Through Wigglesworth, Harvard took a middle course.[13]

George Whitefield came to New England in 1740. Controversy followed him here as it did everywhere else, and Whitefield invited it. He preached in Boston

10. *Mather Diary*, 730 (June 1724), 774 (November 1724).
11. Morison, *Three Centuries*, 6.
12. Morison, *Three Centuries*, 67; *National Cyclopedia of American Biography* (NCAB), 9:237.
13. NCAB, 9:237; Richard Warch, *School of the Prophets: Yale College, 1701–1740* (New Haven, Conn.: Yale University Press, 1973), 128, 130.

Edward Wigglesworth

and then toured surrounding towns. He visited Cambridge in September of this year and recorded in his journal, which always found its way quickly into press, his observations of people and institutions. Harvard was an irresistible target, he found. He described it as "not far superior to our universities in piety." Given the reining Arminianism at Oxford and Cambridge, Whitefield intended no compliment in this comparison. He went on to record that "bad books are become fashionable among the tutors and students. Tillotson and [Samuel] Clarke[14] are read, instead of Shepard, Stoddard, and such-like evangelical writers." Whitefield connected Harvard to the prevailing religiosity in the Boston area and that, too, he found deficient. "I am persuaded," he wrote, "the generality of preachers talk of an unknown and an unfelt Christ." He furthermore blamed the ministers for the

14. Clarke (1675–1729), English rational theologian, critical of deism but sympathetic to some of its notions. His work, *Scripture-Doctrine of the Trinity* (1712) put him in the Arian camp.

low state of religion among the people. The "congregations," he said, "have been so dead because they had dead men preaching to them." Whitefield found Boston a place of visible wealth where the form of religion prevailed but not its power. He decried the "jewels, patches, and gay apparel" in fashion among women. All seemed "too much conformed to the world."[15]

In this unlikely place, Whitefield enjoyed immediate and great success. Most of the ministers welcomed his rejuvenating effects, including even Benjamin Colman of the Brattle Street Church. He applauded "the great additions made to our churches" and thanked God "for the great and good work of his grace" wrought by Whitefield. The highly respected Colman gave the revival much credibility.[16]

Harvard College responded to the fervor as some tutors and several students took on new commitments, many holding all-night religious services. Nonetheless, the president and faculty saw every reason to fear Whitefield. Edward Holyoke had become president in 1737 and under him a twenty-year program of curricular modernization began. Harvard courses had new textbooks as instructors discarded those judged obsolete.[17] Whitefield, however, took it upon himself to encourage the students to join the religious awakening. He used the pages of the Boston *Gazette* in 1742 to address them openly, and to warn that "learning without piety will only render you more capable of promoting the Kingdom of the Devil." He urged the students to tread in the steps of "your pious forefathers."[18]

By 1744, Harvard authorities had had quite enough of Whitefield's disparagements and interventions. The president and faculty drafted testimony against Whitefield and it was anything but subtle. Whitefield's activities, it said, tended greatly "to the detriment of religion, and the entire destruction of the order of these churches of Christ." The testimony tried particularly to expose Whitefield's work as bogus and inauthentic. The Harvard group also called Whitefield "an enthusiast, a censorious, uncharitable person, and a deluder of the people." He has given satisfaction "to many an enthusiast among us since the year 1740," the document stated. He has caused his followers to mistake their physical agitations for the true work of the Spirit. He was himself an enthusiast, for by "enthusiast," was meant a person who acts according to dreams, or persuasions and impressions. The testimony cited passages from Whitefield's journal to that effect and noted that "sometimes he speaks as if he had communications directly from the Spirit of God." Here was rank heresy both to orthodox Puritanism and rational Christianity. Whitefield, as charged, had "a vain conceit of his own worth and excellency" and responded only to the dictates of "his own heated brain."[19]

15. George Whitefield, *Journals*, [1740], in *The Great Awakening: Documents of the Revival of Religion, 1740–1745*, ed. Richard L. Bushman (Chapel Hill: University of North Carolina Press, 1970), 30–31.

16. Edwin Scott Gaustad, *The Great Awakening in New England* (New York: Harper and Brothers, 1957), 51–52.

17. Morison, *Three Centuries*, 89.

18. "Whitefield Responds, *Boston Gazette*," in *The Great Awakening* (Bushman) 38.

19. "The Testimony of Harvard College against George Whitefield," in *The Great Awakening: Documents Illustrating the Crisis and Its Consequences*, ed. Alan Heimert and Perry Miller (Indianapolis: Bobbs-Merrill: 1967), 341–44, 346.

Naturally, the Harvard spokesmen resented most of all Whitefield's intrusions into college matters. "But his arrogance is more flagrant still, that such a young man as he should take upon him to tell what books we should allow our students to read," they wrote. Whitefield's reputation had preceded him to Cambridge and the Harvard people knew of a publication he had issued the year before when he had engaged the Anglican commissary Alexander Garden of South Carolina in an intensive debate. Whitefield published *A Letter . . . wherein he Vindicates his Asserting that Archbishop Tillotson knew no more of Christ than Mahomet*. In it he accused the Church of England of abandoning the Calvinist principles upon which he insisted it had been founded. Harvard took umbrage at Whitefield's offense to a favorite divine. Even Increase Mather, its document replied, had spoken well of the great Tillotson.[20]

Harvard had entered into a significant religious discussion. Whitefield, on the occasion of his return to Boston two years later, offered a rejoinder. His reply demonstrated how differentiated were the two understandings of religious life and experience now circulating in mid-eighteenth-century New England. Whitefield bristled at the charge of "enthusiasm," but could not ignore it. Did he act according to dreams, as Harvard charged? Whitefield denied any indiscriminate faith in dreams, but he did say that dreams can have providential meaning. One may act on them after cautious consideration. Did Whitefield have any intimate communication with God? Harvard had charged that he presumed to act, like the prophets, from direct inspiration from God. Whitefield did not claim a like status, but he did not discount a direct inspiration. He wrote, "This I affirm, that I would not have undertaken to preach the gospel . . . had I not been fully persuaded that I had a degree of that spirit, and was admitted to a degree of that holy and familiar converse and communion with God, which the prophets and apostles were favored with, in common with all believers." Whitefield also defended the manner of his preaching, especially his itinerary. All of Protestantism, from the Reformation on, would have been nothing without this strategy, he said. Finally, Whitefield threw out this challenge to Harvard: "Gentlemen, I profess myself a Calvinist as to principle, and preach no other doctrines than those which your pious ancestors and the founders of Harvard preached long before I was born. And I am come to New England with no intention to meddle with, much less to destroy the order of the New England churches, or turn out the generality of their ministers."[21]

The matter did not end here. This time Harvard appointed its heavy artillery to come back at Whitefield. It turned to Wigglesworth. Wigglesworth published a letter of over sixty pages in which he fortified every one of the points that Harvard had made against Whitefield and refuted the evangelist's rebuttal to the charges. In fact, he began by saying that in the two years since the initial charges Whitefield had done nothing to change Harvard's opinion of him. Again Wigglesworth called him an enthusiast. Some people, he said, might think this

---

20. "Testimony of Harvard College," 346–47.
21. George Whitefield, *A Letter to the Rev. the President, and Professors, Tutors, and Hebrew Instructor, of Harvard College in Cambridge, In Answer to a Testimony Published by Them . . .* (Boston: S. Kneeland and T. Green, 1745), 3–6, 21–22 (quotations on pp. 11 and 21–22).

charge trivial, but the history of the Church, he insisted, showed the damage of enthusiasm. For the enthusiast is consumed by a conviction of a direct influence of the holy spirit. He tolerates no guidance or correction and his actions become reckless. Thus, said Wigglesworth, we have had the horrors of the Anabaptist Reformation, with Thomas Munster and his violent followers. More recently, English history discloses the riotous spirit of the Fifth Monarchy Men.[22] Wigglesworth gave a full chronicle of their activities. For Wigglesworth, enthusiasm went hand in hand with Antinomianism and opened the way to social anarchy and defiance of responsible authority.[23]

Wigglesworth reviewed other charges made against Harvard, but he had a particular concern to defend the institution itself from Whitefield's aspersions. He knew that the itinerant had hurt the college's reputation and its opportunity to raise money. He asked Whitefield why he wanted to slander the college. Wigglesworth insisted that the liberal books had no place in the college curriculum, did not have the endorsement of the college, and, furthermore, had not even been checked from the library. No one had signed for Tillotson or Clarke, he said, from 1732 to 1741. No, the popular items, he pointed out, were Owen, Baxter, (Samuel) Willard, Howe,[24] and Watts, and locals like Thomas Shepard and Solomon Stoddard. (Interestingly, Wigglesworth misspelled Shepard as "Shepherd"; Whitefield got it right.) Whitefield had also charged that the tutors did not pray with the students nor seek to determine the state of their souls. To this charge, Wigglesworth replied resourcefully. "We have a duty," he said, "to examine our own hearts," but he doubted the obligation to examine others'. He asked Whitefield, "Would you turn our living quarters into Romish confessionals?"[25]

Wigglesworth asserted that Harvard defined the ideal of a religious institution in the proper sense. He rejected Whitefield's charge that it and Yale had become seminaries of paganism. But Whitefield seemed clearly to be forcing Wigglesworth into a defensive position and a conservative posture. Wigglesworth conceded that Harvard did not adhere to its old ideals as much he would like. "And yet we may with great truth, and without any immodesty, affirm, that the knowledge of the only true God, and of Jesus Christ whom he has sent, is earnestly recommended to the students as that, in comparison whereof they ought to account all things as but loss and dung."[26]

Furthermore, Wigglesworth now felt compelled to defend not merely the religious character of Harvard but its Calvinist identity, specifically. His reply to Whitefield has this significant statement: "We assure you, sir, that the same

---

22. Or Fifth Monarchists. They were active in the years 1649 to 1661 and constituted a quasipolitical religious party that aspired to reform Parliament and the government in the expectation of Christ's imminent return. They had support from Baptists and Quakers, among others. Fifth Monarchists derived their name from Daniel 2:44 and the prophetic dream of King Nebuchadnezzer. They formed the New Model Army, but Cromwell imprisoned some hundred of them, along with four thousand Quakers, and the movement faded.

23. Edward Wigglesworth, *A Letter to the Reverend Mr. George Whitefield by Way of Reply to his Answer to the College Testimony Against him and His Conduct* (Boston: T. Eliot, 1745), 3–5, 58–59.

24. John Howe (1630–1705), English Puritan clergyman and chaplain to Oliver Cromwell. He authored *The Living Temple of God*, published in 1724.

25. Wigglesworth, *Letter to Whitefield*, 30–31, 29.

26. Wigglesworth, *Letter to Whitefield*, 27.

doctrines are at this day preached at Harvard College, which were preached by our pious ancestors. We have no quarrel with you so far as you are a Calvinist in principle. And if you had never preached any other doctrines than those of Calvinism, or of the doctrinal articles of the Church of England, we should not have taken any exceptions at the matter of your preaching."[27] How curious. Are we to understand Wigglesworth as really making a plea for Harvard Calvinism? If so, he must be understood as defying the major intellectual trends of the day and placing the college athwart the theological currents issuing from some of the prominent pulpits in his own area. The matter, though, was not quite so simple.

One more item about the exchange between Whitefield and Harvard—its personal invective. Whitefield used damning and polemical words in describing Harvard. Wigglesworth, in making his reply on the college's behalf, came off no more charitably. He judged Whitefield's notion that the faithful are directed by God to be so outlandish as to consider it "full proof that you, sir, are at all times not so directed."[28] Whitefield had said he had intended to leave the colonies and the controversy behind, had not illness prevented him. To which declaration Wigglesworth replied, "We observe, that you are comfortably recovered, the season of the year is inviting to travel, and yet you are not quite gone, three months after the date of your letter."[29] Finally, Wigglesworth wanted Whitefield and the world to know that "these things, sir, I have written in the name, and at the direction of the Rev. President of Harvard College."[30]

Whitefield wanted to set Harvard in a new direction, or more properly an old one. Other forces of change, however, were now emerging. As they affected Harvard, they would have different social and intellectual implications than those posed by the Awakening. Soon Boston would be the major seat of the liberalizing tendencies in New England Congregationalism, and Harvard would gain a reputation for academic liberalism, too. Ahead lay the Unitarian takeover of 1804 and the electrifying reform measures of Charles W. Eliot after 1869. The picture suggests a smooth evolution, but reality shows otherwise if we look further at the career of Harvard's professor of divinity. He met the challenge the Awakening brought from the right; how might he confront the one posed by the liberals?

Charles Chauncy, a stalwart among the liberals, was born into a long-established Boston family. He could look back to the great-grandfather who fled England, under duress, because he took Puritan offense at the King's Book of Sports. He came to Plymouth and established his pulpit there in 1638. This Charles Chauncy, as earlier described, became Harvard's second president. The fourth Charles in this line was born in 1711, attended the Boston Latin School, and matriculated at Harvard in 1717. He loved studies, did not aspire to the pulpit, and hung around the college as long as he plausibly could. Finally and reluctantly he entered the ministry. Here by all accounts he was all reason and intellect, shunning emotional preaching. In-

27. Wigglesworth, *Letter to Whitefield*, 58.
28. Wigglesworth, *Letter to Whitefield*, 13.
29. Wigglesworth, *Letter to Whitefield*, 62–63.
30. Wigglesworth, *Letter to Whitefield*, 61.

deed, we learn much about Chauncy by noting his stark aversion to impassioned sermonizing. It is said of him that he prayed God he would never be a powerful, dramatic preacher and that God wholly answered his prayers.[31]

The First Church of Boston that Chauncy joined as assistant pastor to Thomas Foxcroft had already signaled the signs of change that disturbed traditionalists in Boston. The church, known as "Old Brick," conveyed a mild religiosity. It saw itself in competition for wealthy members with the Brattle Street Church and with King's Chapel, which symbolized the growing appeal of Anglicanism in this venerable Puritan city. Under Chauncy, more changes would occur. In 1731 First Church abandoned the requirement of a personal testimony of religious experience as a criterion of church membership, and in 1736 it voted to offer baptism to all adults. Chauncy himself became prominent in the city. His position gave him a seat on the Harvard Board of Overseers, and until his death in 1787 he took an active interest in the college.[32]

Much of Chauncy's reputation derived from the new role he took on in 1740. When the Awakening came to New England, Chauncy immediately became its most outspoken and thoroughgoing critic. He did everything he could to discredit it. He visited sites of the revival and he solicited damning accounts of the gatherings. In late 1742 he entered into a controversy surrounding Samuel Mather, in trouble with his congregation because he held liberal religious views. When Jonathan Edwards issued his powerful manifesto in defense of the revivals, Chauncy took him on, publishing his *Seasonable Thoughts* as a direct rebuttal in 1743. He had already entered the fray the year before with his *Enthusiasm Decried and Cautioned Against*.

Chauncy saw himself above all as the champion of a rational Christianity. The Awakening defied everything he meant by that ideal, and he used words like "a bad temperament of the blood and spirits" and "the blind impetus of a wild fancy" to describe the forces that controlled the New Lights. He assaulted the new preachers for "the disregard they express for the dictates of reason" and took offense when they faulted the ministers for their "carnal reason." Chauncy urged his readers: "Make use of the reason and understanding God has given you. . . . Next to the Scripture, there is no greater enemy to enthusiasm, than reason. 'Tis indeed impossible a man should be an enthusiast, who is in the just exercise of his understanding; and 'tis because men don't pay a due regard to the sober dictates of a well-informed mind, that they are led aside by the delusions of a vain imagination." In short, act like a human being and not like "the horse or mule."[33]

Chauncy tried valiantly to make this point. The Awakening troubled him most in its notion of the "new creature" that emerged from the conversion process. It appeared that the new creature lived on a new and high emotional state of existence, revitalized and powerfully transformed from a previous state. But for Chauncy a major end of religion was to place the emotions in subordi-

31. Charles H. Lippy, *Seasonable Revolutionary: The Mind of Charles Chauncy* (Chicago: Nelson-Hall, 1981), 3–5.

32. Lippy, *Seasonable Revolutionary*, 6–10.

33. Charles Chauncy, "Enthusiasm Decried and Cautioned Against," in *The Great Awakening* (Heimert and Miller), 231–32, 246 (the quotation).

nation, to curb all the destabilizing forces that contain human life at the level of animal existence. He could thus ask, "Is it reasonable to think, that the divine spirit, in dealing with men in a way of grace . . . would give their passions the chief sway over them? Would not this be to invert their frame? To place the dominion in those powers, which were made to be kept in subjection?" Chauncy insisted, in contrast, that "one of the most essential things necessary in the new-forming Men, is the reduction of their passions to a proper regimen." He sustained this plea throughout his *Seasonable Thoughts*, a document described as "the first comprehensive statement of the new American rationalism."[34]

Liberal Congregationalism seems to have had social connections and that possibility raises some questions. Chauncy spoke for the internal order that true religion induced, but he spoke for social order, too. Some historians have seen an alliance of liberal Christianity and social conservatism.[35] With Chauncy they can make a good point. He represented one of Boston's wealthiest churches, and his collaborators in the discrediting of the Awakening constituted New England's "Social Register" of the day, it has been noted.[36] Chauncy recoiled from the revival because it brought disruption to the church order of New England. It sowed seeds of discontent, rebellion, and schism.[37] Worse, though, it led always in the direction of the lesser social classes and thus had threatening effects beyond mere ecclesiastical disorder.

Chauncy opposed the passions in religion and had no doubt that the devil used them for evil purposes. He feared the passions of "the vulgar" especially and set them against the good order and the "proper spheres" that society must uphold. But good order, said Chauncy, "is the strength and beauty of the world," and men must not "transgress the limits of their stations." Powerful upheavals such as the Awakening had the contrary and dangerous tendency. The more he studied the situation the more Chauncy condemned it. He abhorred the laughing and singing he saw at the revival services. He denounced the "coarse converse" he heard between God and the converts, so close and familiar to God had these deluded souls in their imaginations projected themselves. In addition, Chauncy did not set comfortably with the millennial theme in the Awakening, citing Jonathan Edwards specifically. Millennial ideology, he believed, always promoted radical politics and social revolt. To top off his case, Chauncy chastised the Awakeners for encouraging women to participate in their services. Had not the apostle instructed women to keep silent in the churches? he asked.[38]

Boston had another liberal spirit in Jonathan Mayhew. In this case, Enlightenment thought carried into political liberty as Mayhew became first a staunch defender of Congregational independence against Anglican plans for American bishops and then a spokesman against British imperial policies. May-

---

34. Charles Chauncy, "Seasonable Thoughts on the State of Religion," in *The Great Awakening* (Heimert and Miller), 297; editors' introduction to Chauncy, 292.

35. See especially Alan Heimert, *Religion and the American Mind: From the Great Awakening to the American Revolution* (Cambridge, Mass.: Harvard University Press, 1968).

36. Editors' introduction to Chauncy, 292.

37. Chauncy, "Enthusiasm," 236–37.

38. Chauncy, "Seasonable Thoughts," 298, 294, 302; idem, "Enthusiasm," 241.

hew died in 1766, but his short career in the ministry had made him widely known and by no means supported even by his fellow clergymen. Like Chauncy, he came from an old Massachusetts family. Thomas Mayhew had come from Wiltshire, England, in 1631 and established missionary work among the Indians as a family tradition. The fourth generation Mayhew, Experience, was an active intellect who clearly influenced his son in a liberal direction. Jonathan, born in 1720, entered Harvard in 1740, and became, like Chauncy, another student of Wigglesworth. At Harvard, despite a habit of troublemaking, Mayhew found much else to stimulate his thinking. By all appearances he quite thoroughly absorbed the modernizing curriculum under Edward Holyoke. Newton, Locke, and William Wollaston (*The Religion of Nature Delineated*) and a good dose of moral philosophy marked the new intellectual directions.[39]

Mayhew had an initial welcoming view of the Awakening, impressed by its startling effects. As Harvard turned against it, however, so did he. In 1744, he received a fellowship for further study at the college and it kept him within its confines. Three years later came a call from the West Church, occasioned by the departure of its minister to England for Anglican ordination. After Mayhew received ordination at West Church, he renewed his Harvard connection by study toward his master's degree.

The West Church was a landmark of the new Boston. The western section of the city had been growing rapidly for two decades, a refuge for those, with money, fleeing the North End and relocating into imposing new homes in this area. Two prominent merchants, Hugh Hall and Harrison Gray, arranged for construction of a new church, opened in 1737, and paying its new minister the largest salary of any minister in the city. Visitors would soon comment on the "high dress" of ladies in this "genteel congregation." Prominent parishioners from West Church have left their likenesses for us in John Singleton Copley portraits. Mayhew's biographer makes astute comments about the church that now called the young Harvard man to his new post:

> More than any other in Boston it was the church of ambitious and often self-made men who lived by their wits, who were cosmopolitan in their business and social worlds, and who were impatient of restraining traditions. Such men had come to respect success more than social status, and, consciously or not, they now regarded religion as the chief bulwark of private property and Christian freedom as the freedom to pursue profits. Mayhew's task was to adapt the Puritan heritage to this segment of commercial Boston.[40]

Calvinism to this group would have been a right-hand glove placed on the left hand. But that was no problem for Mayhew. His father, among whose library books he had an early education, had set the family against Calvinism with his 1744 publication, *Grace Defended*. A careful critique of Calvinist notions, it brought Experience Mayhew to the brink of Arminianism.

---

39. Charles W. Akers, *Called into Liberty: A Life of Jonathan Mayhew, 1720–1766* (Cambridge, Mass.: Harvard University Press, 1964), 5–7, 9, 23, 26–27.

40. Akers, *Called into Liberty*, 45, 47, 53–54 (the quotation).

His son seems clearly to have taken it over the brink. In 1740, Boston had but a handful of Arminians—liberal and anti-Calvinist ministers. They did not apply that name to themselves and would seldom do so even in the following decades as their numbers swelled. The technical matters in this issue may be less important than the more visible identity of this liberal party in the social complex of Boston. There remained in the New England liberals a residue of old Calvinist notions like original sin, though it could be but barely glimpsed in the extreme rationalists like Chauncy and Mayhew. Mayhew's *Seven Sermons*, published in 1749, showed that he had absorbed English Arminian ideas thoroughly. And as he was attacked even by moderates in Boston, he saw his book gain celebrated acceptance in England. Liberal and scholarly Anglicans did not see any new ideas in Mayhew; they did see a new liberal voice coming out of the once mighty Calvinist fortress of New England.[41]

The liberal ministers did not address their congregations in terms of the conundrums of mysterious grace. They might have said with Mayhew that "Christianity is principally an institution of life and manners; designed to teach us how to be good men, and to show us the necessity of becoming so." A Bostonian elite that justified itself in public service and civic virtue could endorse Mayhew's assertion that "the whole tenor of our Lord's preaching was *moral*." They would welcome Mayhew's description of "practical religion"—"the love of God, and a life of righteousness and charity."[42] These values, however, implied the role of a leadership class. Mayhew did not find these elevated virtues among the masses, who offered society no hope of improvement. He resented the New Lights' appeal to these groups and the pretensions they assumed in their newly gained redemption. Historian Alan Heimert finds only condescension in Mayhew, not a benign, liberal spirit. When Mayhew says, for example, that "he that was born like the wild asses-colt must need continue to be so; or, at best come to maturity, and grow up into an ass himself," he sees rank elitism and acute class-consciousness.[43]

Edward Wigglesworth lived amid the contending religious factions of his day. He felt them acutely and favored neither of them. He spoke for Harvard against the Awakening but gave no welcome to Arminianism either. He once dismissed a work of Experience Mayhew as "a medley of Arminianism and Pelagianism."[44] On the other hand, if social class issues fueled the prevailing antagonisms, Wigglesworth took little note of them. In his published record he appears almost apolitical. Wigglesworth instead concentrated on intellectual matters. More than any thinker of his day he sought painstakingly to find his way through the divisive theological issues. Here he played the role of ac-

---

41. Akers, *Called into Liberty*, 75–76.
42. Akers, *Called into Liberty*, 74.
43. Alan Heimert, *Religion and the American Mind*, 47.
44. Akers, *Called into Liberty*, 65. Pelagianism: Christian heretical sect of the fifth century that challenged St. Augustine's notions of grace and predestination. The monk Pelagius believed that individuals have a natural ability to resist evil, and he thus rejected original sin.

ademic professor and public intellectual, as many of his Harvard lectures became published essays. Furthermore, Wigglesworth, for an unknown duration, gave public lectures on Tuesdays. New England took an interest in him, but it had a very hard time discerning exactly where he stood. This fact may explain why Wigglesworth, for all his erudition and intellect, has suffered scholarly neglect.

Wigglesworth offered his most important piece two years before his death. It is the best measure of his role in the religious conflicts and, with a few glimpses backward, we may examine it closely to see that role. For over three decades, Wigglesworth had been setting forth the rival views of Calvinists and Arminians. Here he did so again. He took up the issue of reprobation. Arminians had long pressed on Calvinists the point that if God wills the damnation of individuals then he must be the author of their sin, for his willingness is to that extent the cause of their fall. At the outset, Wigglesworth conceded nothing to the Arminians and restated familiar Calvinist ideas. A determination of the divine will, he said, does cause some men to be condemned, and for eternity. God, therefore, is "antecedently determining" the condemnation, such that his will is either the moral or physical cause of it. We also say, he added, that if God chose, he could prevent this outcome, but he chooses not. God knows our future condition beforehand, Wigglesworth wrote, because no other conclusion agrees with the fact of God's omniscience.[45]

Nonetheless, Wigglesworth insisted, these facts do not make God the author of sin. To clarify his position, Wigglesworth outlined two alternative views and then introduced a third. He put the matter thus: "Whether God had ordained certain men to condemnation upon a foresight of their ungodliness and infidelity? Or whether the ungodliness and infidelity of men are in consequence of their having before of old been ordained to condemnation, and follow such an ordination necessarily?" The Arminians, Wigglesworth said, take the first position. They contend that God intended to create all men free and rational and in doing so foresaw what actions they would take and the use they would make of their liberty. Thus all people receive "sufficient assistance" from God, but they must decide whether or not they will use it. On the other hand, what Wigglesworth called the "Supralapsarian" position, the strong Calvinist one, denies this opening to free will and personal decision. God's foresight is a determination, otherwise it is an imperfect foresight, which cannot be of God. The Calvinists also deny, said Wigglesworth, that we can accept the offer of grace at will. Such a human discretion compromises the will and power of God and subjects both to human agency.[46]

Wigglesworth, in typical fashion, conceded some merit to both sides. He did assert, however, that both sides made a common error in putting election and reprobation on the same footing; that is, assuming that they both alike must be free or determined. Wigglesworth then introduced the position of the

45. Edward Wigglesworth, *The Doctrine of Reprobation* . . . (Boston: Richard and Samuel Draper, 1763), 12–13.
46. Wigglesworth, *Reprobation*, 14–17, 23–26.

"Sublapsarians."[47] It rejects the notion of the stronger Calvinists that God determines "immediately and by a determinative influence" the actions of men,
whether good or evil. The weaker Calvinist position, which Wigglesworth supported, is uncomfortable with God's creating a creature incapable of right action. That idea reflects badly on the character of God, he said, and it destroys
the difference between natural and voluntary agents. Wigglesworth also labeled the Supralapsarian position unbiblical, finding its origin in the thirteenth century with Aquinas. Wigglesworth could not let go the grip of
Calvinism, however, and did say that God does foreknow. "For if God does determine men to their sinful actions," he wrote, "he must either foreknow what
they will do when he don't determine them, or he must be ignorant before
hand of the great part of the actions of mankind." Wigglesworth then insisted,
unpersuasively, that foreknowledge does not make things certain and pleaded
for a difference between an effective and a permissive decree.[48]

Wigglesworth described an alternative Sublapsarian position, which he endorsed. He said, in effect, that God does foresee and thus does ordain the condemnation of the wicked, but he gives the possibility of a redemption to others.
Thus reprobation and election do not stand on the same footing. The Sublapsarians, he wrote, "maintain that the ordaining of certain men from eternity to
condemnation was upon a foresight of their ungodliness and infidelity, though
on the other hand, they deny that any were elected to everlasting life upon foresight of their faith and obedience." These two things, he insisted, "stand upon as
different a foot as possible." They are the difference between an effective and a
persuasive decree.[49]

Here Wigglesworth built on an important statement he had made in 1741,
at the beginning of the Awakening. He gave two public lectures at Harvard on
the sovereignty of God and even then was seeking a medium between strict
Calvinist determinism and Arminianism. God, he said, could have glorified his
justice by rightfully destroying all humanity, given its reprobate state, or he could
have glorified his mercy by seeing to the salvation of all. However, Wigglesworth
wrote, God takes "a middle way." He decides to leave some individuals to their
own devices, giving them the hope of salvation. Many of these will chose the
darkness over the light, however, and God may see fit to withdraw his blessings
from them. Wigglesworth clearly stayed within the original Calvinist framework

---

47. Wigglesworth, it seems, was extrapolating the contending views in his discussion from an
older and still ongoing debate, that between Supralapsarians and Infralapsarians, sometimes called,
as here, Sublapsarians. Essentially the question centered on the logical order of God's eternal decrees.
The former view held that God, contemplating a yet unfallen human race, chose some to receive
eternal life and at the same time rejected all others. It thus would suggest that God's decree of election logically preceded his decision to permit Adam's fall. Sublapsarians contended that God's resolve to permit the Fall logically preceded his decree of election. In attacking Supralapsarianism
Wigglesworth quite plausibly was also undermining the more strenuous Calvinism of Theodora Beza,
who upheld that view. But none of the Reformed creeds upheld Supralapsarianism. The main charge
against it is that it would have God condemning man to damnation before he contemplates them as
sinners. See Phillip R. Johnson, "Notes on Supralapsarianism and Infralapsarianism,"
http://www.gty.org/~phil/.
48. Wigglesworth, Reprobation, 31–33, 37 (quotation)–38.
49. Wigglesworth, Reprobation, 38–44, 48 (the quotation).

here and had said at the outset of his talks that he feared the influence of some English thinkers who were moving toward doctrines of universal salvation. Wigglesworth qualified a strict Calvinism, to be sure, but he based his talks on a favored passage of the Calvinists, Romans 9:18: "Therefore hath he mercy on whom he will have mercy; and whom will he hardneth." To some God gives an opportunity, of which many may not take advantage. Wigglesworth did, however, make an opening to the Arminian position through this distinction. He thus concluded that "so notwithstanding anything in the decrees of God, there may be a certain connection between striving to enter into the straight gate, and admission into it." Hence, he said, we have "a middle way" between Calvinism and Arminianism.[50]

In his 1763 essay, Wigglesworth culminated a career of theological adjudication. He exhibited learning marked by inconclusiveness, except to conclude that matters were often difficult, and that truth did not rest with either side. In 1738, for example, he had taken as his subject the imputation of Adam's sin to his posterity. Does Adam stand for all mankind? Wigglesworth could not let go the Calvinist conjoining of the two and thus would not yield to the Arminians in their call for individual judgment of human beings based on each one's free will. On the other hand, he warned Calvinists not to be so quick to condemn all people "before they have been guilty of actual sin." Wigglesworth produced a laborious ninety-page essay as he expounded and assessed the rival views. In the end, he pleaded for "mutual charity" on both sides. Too much, he said, was at stake, for any side to commit to dogmatic conclusions.[51]

The history of Harvard's second Hollis professorship further charts the course of the college's intellectual direction in the eighteenth century. The good Baptist made his second bequest in 1727 and thereby created the Hollis professorship in mathematics and natural philosophy.[52] The event had something to do with the ambition and enterprise of a young scientist from Boston, for it was Isaac Greenwood who urged Hollis to endow the chair and who then secured the first appointment to it. Greenwood had graduated from Harvard in 1721, a student of Thomas Robie, a Royal Society member in 1725 by virtue of his work in astronomy. Greenwood had caught

---

50. Wigglesworth, *The Sovereignty of God in the Exercise of His Mercy* (Boston: Rogers and Fowle, 1741), 6n, 15, 27 (quotation); idem, *Reprobation*, 28–29.

51. Edward Wigglesworth, *Enquiry into the Truth of the Imputation of the Guilt of Adam's First Sin to His Posterity* (Boston: J. Draper, 1738), 8, 10–11, 89 (the quotation)–90.

52. So that no ambiguity would induce the confusion that followed the religion professorship, point 12 in the "Rules for the Hollis Professorship of Mathematics" specified: "At the same time and place and in the same presence he [i.e. the designated professor] shall declare himself to be of the Protestant reformed Religion as it is now professed and practiced by the churches in New England commonly distinguished by the name of Congregational, Presbyterian or Baptist and that he will comply with the same" (*Publications of the Colonial Society of Massachusetts. Harvard College Records, Part V, Documents, 1722–1750*, ed. Robert W. Lovett [Boston: Colonial Society of Massachusetts, 1975], 596). In addition to the several branches of mathematics, the endowment commanded instruction in what we properly understand to be science, to wit, "a system of natural Philosophy and a course of experimental . . . the principles of astronomy and geography, viz. The doctrine of the spheres, the use of the globes, the motions of the heavenly bodies according to the different hypotheses of Ptolemy, Tycho Brahe, and Copernicus."

the public's eye when he entered into the heated debate about smallpox inoculation. He wrote a satirical essay on the subject, mocking the enemies of Cotton
Mather, who urged the new protective measures. Greenwood studied for the ministry, but on a visit to London made Hollis's acquaintance. He returned to Boston
and began a series of public lectures in science.[53]

Greenwood championed Newtonian science and helped introduce it to a
New England public audience. His short treatise A *Philosophical Discourse* em-
braced a strictly mechanical view of the universe, an even more secular account
than Newton's himself.[54] Greenwood also reshaped the mathematical curriculum
at Harvard and, with his large following, improved instruction in that subject in
New England schools. Greenwood, however, fell victim to his own bad habits.
He could not resist the bottle and his intemperance impaired his usefulness at
Harvard. The authorities removed him from the chair in 1738.[55]

The post fell to a young and promising recent graduate of Harvard, one
who would hold the chair until his death in 1779 and earn a record of solid
achievement in American colonial science. John Winthrop IV was born in
1714, son of Chief Justice Adam Winthrop and great-grandnephew of Massachusetts' first governor. He earned B.A. and M.A. degrees from Harvard in
1732 and 1735. He studied with Greenwood at the college but had an earlier
influence from the writings of Cotton Mather. Winthrop was an enthusiast for
science. He acquired an impressive collection of scientific works, one of the
biggest in colonial America. He significantly built up Harvard's collection of
scientific apparatus. There also he introduced differential and integral calcu-
lus to his classrooms. Winthrop observed the transit of Mercury in 1740 and
1743 and saw his reports published in the Royal Society transactions. On Benjamin Franklin's nomination he became a member of the Royal Society. The
transit of Venus in 1761, as all colonial scientists knew, would yield key data
for calculating the distances of the planets. Winthrop used his influence to get
public money and travel to Newfoundland, taking Harvard equipment with
him. He supplied the singular study of this event from colonial America.
Winthrop eagerly took on a public role as well. When frightful events such as
earthquakes and comets aroused public worry, Winthrop used the Harvard
chapel to enlighten local audiences on modern science's understanding of
these events. And on both these subjects Winthrop contributed to modern
scientific knowledge. Ezra Stiles said of him, "I believe he had not his equal
in Europe: he was a perfect master of Newton's *Principia*—which cannot be
said of many Professors of Philosophy in Europe." Winthrop served on occasions as acting president of Harvard but declined invitations to have that position permanently.[56]

53. Raymond Phineas Stearns, *Science in the British Colonies of America* (Urbana: University of Illinois Press, 1970), 443, 446, 455.

54. Isaac Greenwood, *Course of Philosophical Lectures with a Great Variety of Curious Experiments Illustrating and Confirming Sir Isaac Newton's Laws of Matter and Motion* (Boston? 1726?).

55. Stearns, *Science in the British Colonies*, 453–54.

56. Theodore Hornberger, *Scientific Thought in the American Colonies* (Austin: University of Texas
Press, 1945), 49–51 (quotation); Stearns, *Science in the British Colonies*, 643–44; Brooke Hindle, *The
Pursuit of Science in Revolutionary America, 1753–1789* (1956; New York: Norton, 1974), 84, 99–101.

John Winthrop IV

Winthrop's reports on earthquakes and comets have particular interest for this study. They confronted a large historical literature—religious and scientific—and a persistent folklore that surrounded these events. As Harvard's spokesman for science, Winthrop defined its intellectual direction and brought students and public alike into a modern cosmology. Winthrop found himself addressing the attitudes and fears that had long accompanied these surprising and frightening events. What did modern science teach us about them? Did they confirm the wrath and dire warnings of an angry God? Did they have anything to do with God at all?

The year 1755 brought fear to people in Europe and North America. The famous earthquake of November 1 destroyed Lisbon, Portugal, and inspired Voltaire's satire of benevolent worldviews in his *Candide*. A lesser quake shook New England on November 18, with successive shock waves felt from Nova Scotia to Western Maryland. The events caused a Boston minister, Thomas Prince, to reissue a publication from nearly thirty years ago, two sermons in which he explained the earthquake of 1727. Prince, one of the ministers of the South Church, represented the religious viewpoint thoroughly. What he said caused Winthrop to make a careful reply and set the record straight.

Prince titled his two sermons "God Shakes the Earth Because His is Wroth." He searched for biblical events (Isaiah 24:1; 2 Peter 3; Revelation 20) in which great shakings of the earth address the ways of a sinful people. Prince described natural settings for earthquakes. Caverns and hollow places in the earth, he said, fill up with sulphurous mineral particles, such as those in the clouds, which are the natural causes of thunder and lightning. When put into motion they strike against each other and fly off with "amazing violence." Prince cited the familiar example of gunpowder to illustrate. Now if these particles "have not a speedy vent," said Prince, "they will tare and rend away all before them." They will heave and raise the earth until they force their own exit and will sink whole mountains and buildings when they do so. Prince concluded, "Thus has the most high God, in the very composition and frame of this earth . . . made sufficient provision for such dire convulsions."[57]

Our considerations must not stop here, however, Prince urged. Secondary causes do not suffice for the full explanation of earthquake occurrences. For we must not assume, he said, that these forces act of themselves "without design or reason." Prince feared a deistic reading of earthquakes and other dramatic natural phenomenon, a reading that would have God create material substances for only general ends and without a "continuing directive influence on them." We must not, in other words, assign natural things any independence from God, for such thinking would deny God's "continual providence." Prince attributed to God a creation with forethought, a consistent Calvinist understanding of God's ways. "Having therefore most wisely laid the universal train in his mind," Prince wrote, "He creates a vast variety of things as a means in which he pleases to work, in the fittest times and places to fulfill his designs." Prince made God a great coordinator, causing unrelated things to interact with each other with purpose, ignorant of the "wonderful laws" by which they are governed. To be sure, God chooses to work by way of what we perceive as natural laws, except "in some extraordinary cases where his usual manner of working cannot reach his designs." Thus we live also in a universe of occasional miracles.[58]

Finally, Prince insisted that earthquakes have providential significance. In his own times they conveyed God's warnings to a people lapsing into "security," the kind of religious coolness or even indifference that a segment of the New England ministry had long decried. "Let us then have a care of returning to our former security," Prince said, "and let us bare [sic] in our minds a lively sense of our continual danger. Let our flesh still tremble for fear of God, and let us be ever afraid of his judgments." As God reveals himself in nature, Prince argued, then it must follow that calamitous natural events must reflect his wrath. Of these events, earthquakes, coming without warning and destroying in a moment, show the extreme of that wrath. For our only defense, Prince urged, we must look to our own current sinfulness, and he specified false worship, Sabbath neglect, drunkenness, whoredom, malice to neighbor, pride, and jealousy.[59]

57. Thomas Prince, *Two Sermons on Psalm XVIII, 7* (Boston: D. Henchman, 1727), 4–5, 9–11. This is the front page title, listed in the Evans collection by the one cited in text. Quotations on pages 10, 4.

58. Prince, *Two Sermons*, 12–13.

59. Prince, *Two Sermons*, 16 (the quotation), 17, 26.

John Winthrop did not know of Prince's reissuing of these sermons, nor of his adding an appendix in which he attributed earthquakes to electricity, when he addressed the subject after the events of 1755. Winthrop interrupted his science course at Harvard in November to relocate to the college chapel, there to address his students and a public audience. On the mind of all was the shaking of the earth that had "so recently spread terror throughout New England," as Winthrop acknowledged. For such an occasion, Winthrop could muster the rhetorical power of a minister addressing his flock, as this passage from his first lecture reveals.

> Imagine then the earth trembling with a huge thundering noise, or heaving and swelling like a rolling sea—now gaping in chasms of various sizes, and then immediately closing again; either swallowing up the unhappy persons who chanced to be over them, or crushing them to death by the middle;—from some, spouting up prodigious quantities of water to a vast height, or belching out hot, offensive and suffocating exhalations; while others are streaming with torrents of melted minerals:—some houses moving out of their places; others cracking and tumbling into heaps of rubbish; and others again, not barely by whole streets, but by whole cities at a time, sinking downright to a great depth in the earth, or under water:—on the shore, the sea roaring and rising in billows . . . vessels driven from their anchors, some overset and lost, others thrown up on the land.[60]

By so hellish a picture Winthrop showed his sympathy with those brought to great fear by the recent quake. But he was also skillfully preparing them for an entirely different understanding of this phenomenon.

For Winthrop then settled into a mode of detached analysis, offering, by way of careful observations, a natural explanation of earthquakes. He told his audience that we may best understand these events as an undulatory motion within the earth. In short, Winthrop was advancing the wave-length theory of earthquakes, a pioneer explanation in this subject. He spoke from various reports coming from around New England, noting that buildings rocked by the quake moved farther at the top than below, throwing off objects a greater distance there. Said Winthrop, "This perfectly agrees with the idea of an *undulatory* motion of the earth." He cited as familiar examples for his listeners the rocking of a cradle or the motion of a boat at sea when agitated by a high wave. Winthrop kept his explanation close to home by citing the breaking off of a spindle at Faneuil Hall in Boston.[61]

For the underlying causes of earthquakes Winthrop referenced the same forces that Prince did. He demystified them a bit, however, by saying that these chemical materials are not much different from what a scientist could produce in a laboratory, that is, some highly flammable materials, solid and liquid, that could be ignited. The resulting vapors could force themselves to any avenue of escape, "heaving up the earth over them" and making "that kind of progressive swelling undulation, in which we have supposed earthquakes commonly consist." And given the volatile and explosive conditions underneath the earth,

---

60. John Winthrop, *On Earthquakes* (Boston: Edes & Gill, 1755), 8–9.
61. Winthrop, *On Earthquakes*, 10–12.

Winthrop said, we should not wonder at the power of the events; but we might wonder that we have no more of them than we actually do.[62]

Winthrop wanted his audience to have a different emotional grasp of earthquakes than did Prince. Prince saw them properly evoking a just fear of an angry God. Winthrop saw them as the work of a wise and benevolent creator. He drew on recent scientific speculation that the violent upheavals in the earth have the effect of replenishing the supply of minerals there. Here a God with foresight has acted to create a self-perpetuating process by which the earth restores its nourishing elements. Again Winthrop went for the example near at hand. As a farmer must every year break and prod the soil "in order to fit it for the purposes of vegetation," such a loosening of the earth "may promote even the growth of vegetables on its surface." Volcanoes, for example, have induced the great soil fertility in the areas around Ætna and Vesuvius, he informed.[63]

Winthrop stated in his lecture that he addressed only the physical causes and natural ends of earthquakes—the benevolent, *general* ends they served. He did not speculate here on their moral ends, though he had no doubt "that the laws of nature were established, and that the operations of nature are conducted, with a view, *ultimately*, to *moral* purposes, and that there is the most perfect coincidence, at all times, between God's governance of the *natural* and of the *moral* world." But in a footnote insertion in the published lectures, Winthrop made a clear differentiation of his religious understanding and that of Prince and his kind of Puritanism. For, Winthrop observed, it seemed to be the conventional wisdom that a truly religious understanding of earthquakes is one that brings to our attention the workings of a powerful, intervening God and alerts us to his wrath. Any other view, Winthrop noted of this conventional wisdom, would apparently detract from a proper religious understanding of such calamitous events. But Winthrop disagreed. An understanding of earthquakes that foregrounds their long-term benevolent effects, he said, should yield an equal awe of God, but a less terrifying one. He wrote:

> The idea here exhibited, while it exalts the wiseness and goodness, does not in the least detract from the majesty, or from the justice, of God. And the terror, which an earthquake never fails to carry with it, will be sufficient to secure the interests of religion, so far as they are to be secured by the influence of fear; even though such a phenomenon be represented in the most favorable light that truth will admit of.[64]

The inserted footnote must have been a response to the appendix update that Prince made in the reprinting of his 1727 sermon.[65] In that appendix, Prince, seizing on the great, new public interest in electricity, and referencing "the sagacious Mr. Franklin," now offered another theory. Because we know the

---

62. Winthrop, *On Earthquakes*, 23–24, 26.
63. Winthrop, *On Earthquakes*, 27–28, 30.
64. Winthrop, *On Earthquakes*, 29, 29n.
65. Eleanor M. Tilton, "Lightning Rods and the Earthquake of 1755," *New England Quarterly* 13 (March 1940): 88. The author writes, "Perhaps this was an addition prompted by reading Prince's effusions." I believe this was certainly the case.

earth's atmosphere to be charged with electricity, he said, and because we know that "iron-points" (i.e., lightning rods) draw electricity from it, then a place of high assemblage of the iron-points will be proportionately more susceptible to lightning destruction. Therefore Prince had another warning to sound: "In Boston are more erected than anywhere else in New England; and Boston seems to be more dreadfully shaken [by the recent quake]. O! Is there no getting out of the mighty hand of God. If we think to avoid it in the air, we cannot in the earth. Yea, it may grow more fatal."[66]

Prince's further ventures into science enraged Winthrop. He added his own appendix in the printed edition of his lectures, directly answering Prince in this matter of electricity. In a dispassionate scientific discourse, he showed that Prince had wholly misconstrued contemporary knowledge of electricity. When turning to Prince more personally, his language became more charged. He called Prince's theological conclusions "pathetic" and likely to have the dangerous consequences of dissuading people from taking just measures for their own precaution against lightning strikes. For such fears of incurring divine wrath were "perfectly groundless and chimerical."[67] The debate did not end there. Prince took his case to the Boston *Gazette* where Winthrop again replied. The matter grew in heat but not in further enlightenment.[68]

Opportunity for public enlightenment came again for Harvard's eminent scientist three years later. The year 1758 brought the return of Halley's comet and with it fears and folklore that always found expression when these celestial wonders made their appearance. Once more, Winthrop interrupted his course of instruction at the college and laid his ideas before a public audience. The occasion offers another measure of intellectual direction at Harvard. This one requires some background perspectives.

We associate modern cosmology with the achievements of Sir Isaac Newton in the late seventeenth century. But Newton represented no headlong rush into the rational and secular view of things. As Sarah Schechner Genuth has described, Newton inherited and somewhat perpetuated the provincial intellect that shaped his early life. Religion also figured in Newton's motivations. In presenting a universe of order and regularity, Newton looked back to the pristine religiosity of the ancients, corrupted since then by various expressions of polytheism and astronomy. Philosopher-priests of all kinds had made the skies the repositories of spirits and gods, Newton said, and had gained a political control by imposing on believers a variety of charms and superstitions. Many of these blasphemous elements, such as reliquaries, ghosts, and demons, found their way into historic Catholicism and its alliance with divine-right monarchy. The solution was to give comets and the solar system a greater autonomy and to shift their intellectual domain from politics to science.[69]

---

66. Tilton, "Lightning Rods," 87.
67. Winthrop, *On Earthquakes*, 36.
68. John Winthrop, *A Letter to the Publishers of the Boston Gazette, etc. Containing an Answer to the Rev. Mr. Prince's Letter. Inserted in said Gazette, on the 26th of January 1756 Boston?* [1756], 1–7. For selections from Prince's letter, see Tilton, "Lightning Rods," 91.
69. Sarah Schechner Genuth, *Comets, Popular Culture, and the Birth of Modern Cosmology* (Princeton, N.J.: Princeton University Press, 1997), 133, 138–40.

Harvard, by Burgis, 1743

But that shift did not negate for Newton the reality of an intricate, benevo-lent universe wrought and maintained by an omniscient deity. For Newton did more than establish the regular trajectories of the comets. He made their very composition part of a brilliant system by which a designing God gives the universe the means of its perpetuation. Thus Newton found it quite plausible that the comets' vapors, as they dissipate and scatter throughout the universe, find their way, by gravitational attraction, to the planets. As such, they supplied the vital fluid this system required. They furnish the essential oceans needed by the earth. And they do much more. In a passage intended for a later edition of the *Principia*, Newton speculated that "the vapors which arise from the sun, the fixed stars, and the tails of comets, may meet at last with, and fall into, the atmospheres of the planets by their gravity, and there be condensed and turned into water and humid spirits; and from thence, by a slow heat, pass gradually into the form of salts, and sulphurs and tinctures, and mud, and clay, and sand, and stones, and corals, and other terrestrial substances." Here a system, based on the "perpetual interchange of all things," shows a God who disposes all things "in the best order." And all without divine intervention.[70]

Winthrop often referred to Newton as the "great philosopher," and his un-derstanding of comets will bear comparison with Newton's. It is instructive to know then of Newton's own private feelings about comets, notions often con-veyed in letters to friends. For Newton did not entirely move beyond the folk

---

70. Genuth, *Comets*, 145–46.

wisdom of the day on that subject. That wisdom often described the cleansing effects of comets. Nor did Newton separate the moral history of the world from the physical. Divine wrath intermixed with divine benevolence, he believed. Comets could destroy worlds. They could reconstitute the universe, preparing new sites for creation and ushering in the millennium. Thus even Newtonian science reflected the popular mind of the seventeenth century. "What Newton did was redescribe popular beliefs in sophisticated, natural philosophical terms."[71]

Edmond Halley also wanted to take cosmology out of the hands of priests and turn it over to scientists. Halley studied the comet of 1682 and, checking the dates of previous comets, concluded that the world was witnessing one comet on a cyclical course. He thus predicted the return of this one in 1758. Halley held catastrophic views of the heavens and earth. He thus believed wholly that an ancient deluge had covered the earth, but he wanted more than simple biblical narrative to confirm the fact. God, he believed, worked through natural causes, and an extraterrestrial cause, such as a comet, gave the best explanation for the events in question. Also like Newton, Halley attributed cleansing and healing effects to comets. They might strike the earth and cause a rejuvenation of the earth's surface, the better to sustain life. Such a collision would destroy all inhabitants, but it would prepare the sustenance of future races.[72]

Winthrop again read his lectures in the Harvard Chapel, in April 1759. They gave learned accounts about the constitution of comets, with considerations of the projection of their tails and the intensity of their appearances. Winthrop said he welcomed the progress made in the study of comets since Tycho Brahe in the sixteenth century. Too long, he believed, these heavenly appearances had not attracted serious study. Their apparent, irregular appearances had caused people to dismiss them as prodigies and omens of dreadful calamities. Now, Winthrop said, modern knowledge has imposed on them a regularity akin to the planets.[73] And as we have a new scientific understanding of these remarkable events, we should also, Winthrop told his listeners, have a better religious understanding of them.

Winthrop did not disavow a connection between the moral and physical history of the earth. Such grand and unusual events as comets, he said, arouse mankind from a natural slumber and a turning away from God. A universe of absolute uniformity conduces to a forgetfulness of God's presence.[74] Winthrop knew, as did a portion of his audience certainly, of the writings of William Whiston. In 1696 he had argued that a comet had formed the earth and later brought about the biblical flood. From the publication of his *A New Theory of the Earth* in this year and through numerous works that followed, Whiston gave comets emphatic religious meanings, even suggesting that they might house hell itself.[75] Winthrop did not dismiss the speculations of the "ingenious and learned Mr.

71. Genuth, *Comets*, 153–55.
72. Genuth, *Comets*, 157, 159, 162, 164.
73. John Winthrop, *Two Lectures on Comets* (Boston: Green & Russell, 1759), 10, 22.
74. Winthrop, *Two Lectures on Comets*, 38.
75. Genuth, *Comets* 190, 193.

Whiston" and conceded that comets furnished credible causal explanations for such events as the flood. He further stipulated, "Indeed, according to the laws of nature, particularly those of gravity, it is not possible but that the near approach of a comet to a planet, either in its descent to the sun or ascent from him, should draw after it a train of dangerous, if not fatal consequences."[76]

Nonetheless, as in the case of earthquakes, Winthrop wished to put the most benevolent cast on the subject of comets. "It seems most probable," he spoke, "that comets are designed to be some way or other serviceable to the planetary worlds." He cited Newton and concurred with him. Comets' vapors, diffused throughout the solar system, supply "the most spiritous part of our air" and re-nourish our world. Winthrop thought comets might refuel the sun, so close do they pass by it; eventually they may fall into it, with like effects. Winthrop wanted to detach comets from the unwarranted and unnecessary fears that had long accompanied their appearances. He asked his audience to ponder how rare, in fact, were disasters caused by comets. They constantly streak the skies, but we have only the possible distant Flood as a mark of their destructiveness, he ob-served. The God who contrived these phenomena also assured their good effects. "The foresight of that great Being," wrote Winthrop, "which has hitherto pre-vented such disorders, will continue to prevent them, so long as He sees it fit the present frame of nature should subsist."[77] Winthrop urged his audience to see comets as a scientist does, and not with "unphilosphical eyes." Too long have "idle and superstitious fancies" and "times of ignorance" prevailed, he insisted. To react with panic to the appearance of these natural events, he concluded, be-trays a weakness "unbecoming a reasonable human being."[78]

Edward Wigglesworth and John Winthrop, two of the Hollis professors, best de-fine Harvard's intellectual place in the middle eighteenth century. We have seen Wigglesworth's uneasy location, opposing the fervor of the Awakening, but fault-ing liberal theology. Winthrop is not necessarily easy to place, but he clearly car-ried Harvard further in the direction of the Enlightenment than did Wig-glesworth. Thus, through its professorship in religion, Harvard moved cautiously; through its professorship in science, it moved more resolutely.

It has been suggested that Winthrop's references to God place him solidly in an old Puritan tradition; or, as one historian has said, Winthrop's "scientific piety" stood "aligned with the traditional Puritan beliefs of his day."[79] But this judgment cannot stand. To take some measure of the traditional Puritan beliefs of his day, we might look again at Winthrop's rival Thomas Prince. Their differ-ences go beyond the intellectual ones we have already recorded. Prince gradu-ated Harvard in 1707, at a time when the liberal insurgency was beginning to re-define Harvard's identity. After ten years in London, Prince returned to Boston and joined the Mather party in its resistance to William Brattle, John Leverett,

---

76. Winthrop, *Two Lectures on Comets*, 42–43
77. Winthrop, *Two Lectures on Comets*, 42–43 (quotations).
78. Winthrop, *Two Lectures on Comets*, 40, 43.
79. Louis Graham, "The Scientific Piety of John Winthrop," *New England Quarterly* 46 (March 1973): 112–18.

and Benjamin Colman. He preached the funeral sermon for Cotton Mather and called for a renewal of the Mather political influence. In the ensuing years, Prince worked to revitalize the old Puritan covenant with its unique New England focus and its doctrine of the elect. Furthermore, for Prince, this restoration would include a political state with an obligation to uphold true religion. Prince published his celebration of the early Puritans, *Chronological History*, in 1736. His introduction welcomed his readers: "You will doubtless take a noble and useful pleasure, in reviewing the names and actions of your predecessors, that you may imitate their virtues."[80] One as sensitive as Prince was to the decline of his own New England from those past superior days might well look at comets and see signs of God's wrath. Nor should we be surprised that Prince and Joseph Sewall helped to make the South Church a key locus of the Awakening in Boston. Prince published the magazine *Christian History* to chronicle and encourage the "surprising and . . . extensive revivals."[81]

No restoration ideology pervades whatever there may be of a "scientific piety" in John Winthrop. If anything, the religious dimension in Winthrop's thought looks for a new religiosity for New England. He wanted to discredit the old fears generated by the orthodox piety and he wished to dislodge those fears from the public's understanding of natural events such as earthquakes and comets. One should not doubt the sincerity of Winthrop's references to God and the place of God in Winthrop's scientific intellect. But Winthrop clearly saw a god of first causes, not a god of providential activity. Thus in his letter to the *Gazette*, Winthrop stressed that "the main business of natural philosophy is, to trace the chain of natural causes from one link to another, till we come to the First Cause."[82] So much for Winthrop's public pronouncements. In his classroom, the model of a mechanical universe prevailed. A young John Adams was there for the opening of Professor Winthrop's course on experimental philosophy, April 1, 1754, in Old Harvard's second floor classroom. Winthrop used the opening lecture, Adams recorded in his journal, to show the students the "meaning, nature, and excellence" of natural philosophy. The teacher explained that all physical objects, from the great heavenly bodies to the minutest particles of matter within them, are all regulated by the same mechanical laws. Here in the classroom a different first cause prevailed. As Adams noted from the lecture, "The First Cause, and indeed the alpha and omega of natural phenomena, is motion, there being an utter impossibility that any effect should be produced in a natural way without motion." Adams valued his learning from Winthrop. He attributed to him, above all his Harvard professors, a profound and lasting influence.[83]

---

80. John Van de Wetering, "Thomas Prince's *Chronological History*," *William and Mary Quarterly* 3rd Series, 18 (1961): 547–51 (the quotation is on p. 550). The work in question is Prince's *A Chronological History of New England* (Boston: Kneeland & Green, 1736).

81. Edwin S. Gaustad, "Society and the Great Awakening in New England," *William & Mary Quarterly* 3rd Series, 11 (1954): 575. The sermon tract is Prince, *Civil Rulers Raised Up* (Boston: Gerrish, 1728).

82. Winthrop, *A Letter*, 2.

83. *The Earliest Diary of John Adams*, ed. L. H. Butterfield (Cambridge, Mass.: Harvard University Press, 1966), ix–x, 60 (the quotation).

Part II
POLITICS, REVOLUTION, AND INTELLECTUAL CULTURE

10

⟪⟫

The Colleges and the
Revolution: New England

The American colonial colleges grew amid the intellectual warfare of the seventeenth and eighteenth centuries, and they contributed to it. The nine institutions studied to this point each partook of denominational struggles, sometimes within those denominations to which they belonged, sometimes within
the contests for power and influence that set Protestant groups against each
other in this period. Usually, in fact, these histories reflected both intramural and
intermural conflict. Partisan confrontation was nothing new, then, when the
American colleges entered the revolutionary years of the 1760s and the events
that carried the colonies into war against England in the next decade.

That war turned the colleges into patriot schools. In 1760, on the news of
King George II's death, the six colleges then existing had almost outdone each
other in memorializing the departed monarch. Some held special services; others offered orations.[1] Five years later, however, college students were wearing
homespun to announce support of American boycotts of British goods. Thirteen
years later, students swore off drinking tea, again to protest British policy. At
some schools, undergraduates formed their own militias, drilled on the college
premises, and made themselves visibly defiant of the mother country. Indeed, the
war came to the colleges. Seven of the nine would have to suspend instruction
as British troops took over their buildings. Some relocated to other quarters to
avoid the presence of war. Others suspended commencement ceremonies. Enrollments plummeted. The lives of those who took the revolutionary fervor to
heart would change. From the American colleges came fifty-five graduates who

---

1. John F. Roche, *The Colonial Colleges in the War for Independence* (Millwood, N.Y.: National University Publications, 1986), 12.

affixed their names to the Declaration of Independence. Nineteen of these served in the Second Continental Congress.[2]

The concluding two chapters will explore the collegiate connections to American political thought and the advent of the American Revolution. They will survey briefly the events that made that connection in the most tangible way, that is, the direct impact of the war on the colleges. They will also examine a less certain connection—the colonial academic experience and the creation of an American intellectual culture in the revolutionary decades of the 1760s and 1770s. For the revolutionary era was that as much as anything—a period that flourished with new ideas about politics, statehood, and citizenship. The colleges produced presidents who addressed the political events of the day and the larger significance of the rebellion. They produced graduates who took their educations and plunged by word and deed into revolutionary politics. Some of these individuals launched careers that took them to the highest offices of the new nation. This review must, of course, be a selective one. Individuals other than those included here could readily extend a large subject that we must here limit to some prominent individuals and events. Nonetheless, evidence abounds of an academic role in shaping Americans' ways of thinking about themselves as a people and as political players situated in an historical moment. The colonists in the 1760s were compelled to think politically, to confront questions about government, authority, and rights, as they had not been so necessitated before. Many who took on that challenge, and who became American leaders, drew on learning, reinforced by reflection and personal experience, from their collegiate days.

Harvard College had entered its liberal era under the presidency of John Leverett. But its liberalism never reigned uncontested, as we have seen, and when President Edward Holyoke succeeded Benjamin Wadsworth on his death in 1737, the new leader seemed anxious to renew the spirit of Leverett. The curriculum underwent extensive modernization. A more open atmosphere prevailed well before the revolution, and Harvard life became animated with political discussion. Even before Holyoke and under his administration, students' commencement theses took on such questions as these: "Is unlimited obedience to rulers taught by Christ and His Apostles?" (1729), "Is the Voice of the People the Voice of God?" (1733), "Is it Lawful to resist the Supreme Magistrate, if the Commonwealth cannot otherwise be preserved?" (1743), and "Does Civil Government originate from Compact?" (1743, 1747, 1751, 1761, 1762). These topics all received attention before passage in 1764 of the Sugar Act. The intensifying political focus later led Harvard historian Samuel Morison to write, "It is probably more than a coincidence that so many of the New Englanders who took a leading part in the American Revolution had their education under [Holyoke]."[3]

2. Roche, *Colonial Colleges*, 25–26, 83, 125.

3. Samuel Eliot Morison, *Three Centuries of Harvard, 1636–1936* (Cambridge, Mass.: Harvard University Press, 1942), 83, 90–91.

One contribution came from the liberal ministry that graduated from Harvard. Their record in bringing Puritanism out of its "glacier" era and into the Enlightenment climate of the eighteenth century stands uncontested. Less certain, however, is its record respecting the American Revolution. To such a formidable reader of the religious literature as Alan Heimert, the liberal Congregationalists (who go by "Arminians" and "Liberals" in his rendering) made at best a dubious contribution to the revolution. In his justly renowned book *Religion and the American Mind: From the Great Awakening to the Revolution*, published in 1968, Heimert described the Liberals, such as Jonathan Mayhew and Charles Chauncy, as recoiling from the religious and social excesses of the religious Awakening, and committed to order and stability in the social complex. Reason should rule in society as it should in religion, they believed. "Well into the 1770s," wrote Heimert, "the end and aim of Liberal political thought was the preservation of the ordered tranquility of colonial society." The Liberals, in Heimert's assessment, posed the standards of neoclassicism against the Christian standards of the revivalists (or "Calvinists" as Heimert labels them) and had clearly more materialistic measures of colonial well-being than the Awakeners, committed as the latter were to a moral regeneration and renewed spirituality in America.[4]

Jonathan Mayhew came from Harvard's memorable class of 1743. No minister seemed less hesitant than he in moving from pulpit to politics. He made the West Church of Boston not only the vehicle of his liberal theology but a theater of political protest as well. New Englanders had long associated Arminianism, the kind articulated by Mayhew, with Anglicanism. Mayhew, however, wanted to sever that bond and forge a liberal Congregationalism. His ministerial career began when his predecessor at the West Church left it to go over to Anglican King's Chapel in Boston. Until his untimely death in 1766, Mayhew preserved ties with Harvard. He served on the Board of Overseers and in 1765 gave the Dudleian Lecture at the college. Furthermore, he nurtured its intellectual growth. Mayhew oversaw the continuing contribution of books made to Harvard by his good friend Thomas Hollis. Through Mayhew's agency, Harvard amassed the collection that nourished Arminian theology and Whig political thinking among its students.[5]

Those who did not hear Mayhew's sermon of January 1750 in person soon heard of it by word of mouth. Many would remember it for a long time. John Adams later wrote that "I read it, til the substance of it was incorporated into my nature and indelibly engraved on my memory."[6] The sermon made Mayhew doubly notorious—for his theology and for his politics. What prompted his address was something that had troubled and annoyed him. Some Bostonians, he noted,

---

4. Alan Heimert, *Religion and the American Mind: From the Great Awakening to the Revolution* (Cambridge, Mass.: Harvard University Press, 1968), 240, 245–46, 251–52, 254 (the quotation), 273, 276.

5. Charles W. Akers, *Called into Liberty: A Life of Jonathan Mayhew, 1720–1766* (Cambridge, Mass.: Harvard University Press, 1964), 82, 144, 195, 146.

6. Akers, *Mayhew*, 93.

especially among its growing Anglican population, had annually solemnized the execution of the Stuart King Charles I in 1649. (Later, after royal appointee Francis Bernard became governor, he hung portraits of Charles II and James II in his office.) Mayhew titled his sermon *Concerning Unlimited Submission and Non-resistance to the Higher Powers*, and he used it to make some choice remarks about Charles I.

First, however, Mayhew addressed some theoretical matters. He used an introductory passage, Romans 13:1–8. The verses in question would seem to set down pretty clearly a general mandate for all to obey the constituted political powers, "for the powers that be are ordained of God." Whoever resists established power, therefore, resists God. Nor did Mayhew contest these foundational notions. He was not one to disrespect authority as such. But Mayhew could not allow these principles to beg the question, on what grounds might one justify resistance to the magistrate? When the magistrate abuses his authority, he answered. Mayhew cited examples from Julius Caesar to Charles I to illustrate. For rulers, said Mayhew, have no authority from God to do mischief; they have only an emissary role to execute God's laws and God's plans.[7]

Mayhew pronounced no ideas unfamiliar to generations of Protestant thinkers from the time of Calvin. Nor, for that matter, did he formulate any response that might not have already been taken up in Harvard commencement exercises in recent decades. Mayhew, nonetheless, used language that added Arminian notions and Whig political ideology to standard Protestant prescription. Rulers, he said, must have as their main concern "the good of human society." And government could have no other end, he insisted. Mayhew's God, in his Arminian construction, had an emphatically benevolent character. Mayhew could not quite join his Puritan predecessors in seeing the state as the needed restraint on a fallen and depraved human nature, a tether for an animal that always yields to its expansive instincts. Government does derive its legitimacy from God, Mayhew agreed, but that God is a rational and caring deity who wishes only good for his subjects. And so must the magistrate reflect such qualities. So also must human laws, for "laws attempered and accommodated to the common welfare of the subjects must be supposed to be agreeable to God's will . . . whose tender mercies are over all his works." Any government that does not adhere to such solicitations warrants resistance, and the people may, with God's blessing, act to undo it.[8]

These reflections prepared the way for the heavily ad hominem turn of Mayhew's sermon. For the West Church minister wished to assert that in every way the resistance against King Charles had legitimate ends. Mayhew launched into a litany of abuses that he cited against the king—from his oppressive taxation to his designs with the papacy. The connection of Charles to his larger thesis was clear:

---

7. Jonathan Mayhew, "Concerning Unlimited Submission and Nonresistance to the Higher Powers," [1750], in *Pamphlets of the American Revolution, 1750–1776*, ed. Bernard Bailyn, 4 vols. (Cambridge, Mass.: Harvard University Press, 1965), 1:215, 221–22, 228.

8. Mayhew, "Unlimited Submission," 226, 228 (the quotation), 230–32.

"Even God himself," Mayhew wrote, "does not govern in an absolutely arbitrary and despotic manner," as did Charles I. Mayhew chastised the New England Anglicans who venerated the tyrant and who would see him as a saint and martyr. Mayhew thereby recalled to his parishioners the rightness of the Dissenters' cause and their holy fight against royal and ecclesiastical despotism.[9]

Mayhew had just begun his political fight. The 1750 sermon raised the matter of Anglican complicity in royal abuses of power. In 1763 and afterward the issue became a fixation with Mayhew. On this matter above all could Mayhew demonstrate the dislocation of Arminianism and rational Christianity from Anglicanism. Thomas Secker had become archbishop of Canterbury in 1758 and shortly thereafter announced his hopes for a renewed effort to establish an American bishopric. For Mayhew that idea raised the specter of a new breed of High Churchmen, interconnected with the swelling ranks of royal officials in the colonies. The prospect also led Mayhew to reflect, in the manner of all the Harvard graduates who took up the American cause in the 1760s, on the significance of the Puritan escape from Anglican tyranny. For even those products of liberal Harvard took from their school a sense of its historical significance in the lives of the first generation of American Puritans. Harvard connected them to a special past—to a history of refuge from oppression, to the righteous cause of Dissenters from the Church of England. Speaking on invitation before the Massachusetts Council in 1754, Mayhew had said, "Our ancestors, though not perfect and infallible in all respects, were a religious, brave, and virtuous set of men, whose love of liberty, civil and religious, brought them from their native land into the American deserts." Thus did Mayhew give historical depth to the current, raging bishop issue. When he accused the Society for the Propagation of the Gospel (SPG) of violating its own announced intentions to bring the non-churched into Anglicanism and of seeking instead to take over all of New England, he created a picture that was all of a piece with an extended warfare of Puritan and Anglican.[10]

When Mayhew died, his older friend Charles Chauncy, of Harvard's class of 1721, took up the anti-bishop cause, and with a vengeance. He engaged Anglican spokesmen in some of the most intense newspaper warfare of the day just on this issue. Chauncy even used the Harvard campus, the setting of his Dudleian Lecture in 1762, to make the case for anti-episcopacy. He tried to show that neither Scripture nor history supported the Anglican claim for bishops as opposed to presbyters.[11] Chauncy could just as readily as Mayhew invoke Puritan history for his cause. He did so in a 1770 sermon in his First Church of Boston. He urged

9. Mayhew, "Unlimited Submission," 238–39; Akers, *Mayhew*, 87.

10. Akers, *Mayhew*, 171–72, 178, 185; Jonathan Mayhew, A Sermon . . . [1754], in *The Wall and the Garden: Selected Massachusetts Election Sermons, 1670–1775*, ed. A. W. Plumstead (Minneapolis: University of Minnesota Press, 1968), 301.

11. Edward M. Griffin, *Old Brick: Charles Chauncy of Boston, 1705–1787* (Minneapolis: University of Minnesota Press, 1980), 127–28, 131, 135–35; Carl Bridenbaugh, *Mitre and Sceptre: Transatlantic Faiths, Ideas, Personalities, and Politics, 1689–1775* (London: Oxford University Press, 1962), 100–3, 202–4, 294–95.

his audience to remember the prayerful habits of their "pious forefathers," whom God delivered from their afflictions, as he had once done the same to the Israelites. He wanted contemporaries to remember the examples of humility in the first Puritans, who though conscious of their sinfulness, nonetheless trusted in God. Chauncy also rehearsed the trials of the forebears, "oppressed in England" and wearing "the ecclesiastical yoke of bondage"—the fines, imprisonments, and banishments imposed by a cruel church–state alliance. Citing the colonies' service to an ungrateful Crown in the late war against the French, Chauncy urged now that renewed tyranny demanded that they turn to God once again.[12]

That prescription, for Chauncy and other liberals, endorsed liberty, not mass democracy. Nor did it necessarily lead to a call for independence from England. Mayhew's political pronouncements reflected religious liberals' caution, their conservative instinct when it came to politics. Mayhew recoiled from the violence of the Sons of Liberty in their reaction to the Stamp Act, and he even wrote apologetically to Thomas Hutchinson after the lieutenant governor's house fell to the wrath of the Boston crowd.[13] Chauncy, too, decried the "mobbish actions" of August 1765.[14] Mayhew did rejoice at the repeal of the Stamp Act and issued, in the year of his death, 1766, one of the mostly widely read of the revolutionary addresses. In it, he cited as influences on his thinking both the classical tradition—Plato, Demosthenes, Cicero—and the English Whig writers—Milton, Locke, and Benjamin Hoadley. He acknowledged the great tradition of English law, which king and Parliament had themselves violated in passing the Stamp Act. He upheld the "natural rights" doctrine that protected Americans and English alike. The British violations, however, Mayhew said, had reduced the Americans "to a state of slavery." Ultimately, though, he wanted both sides to draw back, as Parliament had done with the repeal of the Stamp Act. He censored those in Boston who "had the effrontery to cloak their rapacious violences with the pretext of the zeal for liberty" and called for renewed respect and order among the colonists.[15] Another Harvard product, however, showed little respect.

Samuel Adams had the same Harvard education as Mayhew, graduating three years prior to him in the class of 1740. Adams was a Boston product, born there in 1722, where his father had a prosperous brewery and successful mercantile business; he had even acquired a comfortable estate. The elder Adams also served as deacon of the Old South Church. Young Sam knew politics early on. His father turned the family home into a gathering place for active Bostonians. Here local justices of the peace, selectmen and state representatives, and mem-

12. Charles Chauncy, *Trust in God, the Duty of a People in a Day of Trouble* (Boston: Daniel Kneeland, 1770), 8, 12–13.

13. Akers, *Mayhew*, 205–6.

14. Griffin, *Chauncy*, 141.

15. Jonathan Mayhew, *The Snare Broken, A Thanksgiving Discourse* [1766], in *Political Sermons of the Founding Era, 1730–1885*, ed. Ellis Sandoz (Indianapolis: Liberty Fund, 1991), 240–41, 252.

bers of the General Court came to discuss the business and politics of the day. With this bit of a head start, Sam entered Harvard at the age of fourteen. His formal education to date had prepared him for the entry exam on Tully and Virgil and for the Latin writing test. His father's social standing placed him sixth in a class of twenty-three.[16]

By no means did Adams leave politics behind when he entered the college. Besides the classical curriculum, Adams also took an interest in the English political writers that had established the rich Whig tradition of the last century. Adams and his Harvard friends also discussed the Glorious Revolution and the issues it raised about the powers of kings and the rights of elected assemblies. John Locke supplied intellectual fare for any who wanted to take up the subject of individual rights and the origins of government. Following procedure, Adams graduated Harvard and returned three years later to pursue his M.A. degree. Politics had now become his consuming interest. He intensified his reading in Locke, James Harrington, and Samuel Pufendorf. It was Adams who in 1743 had taken the affirmative in the proposition: "whether it be lawful to resist the Supreme Magistrate, if the Commonwealth cannot otherwise be preserved."[17]

But another influence was also at work on Adams, though it is more difficult to measure precisely. In his undergraduate years at Harvard Adams saw the outbreak of the religious Awakening in Boston and all around New England. We have seen how many Harvard students welcomed it, as did at first even some liberal ministers like Benjamin Colman. The Awakening had visible effects. Adams remembered: "Young men and women cast off their finery and walked along the fashionable Boston Mall . . . wearing the somber dress seen in the heyday of Puritanism." Adams approved. All his life he held a respect for his Puritan ancestors. He regularly attended the Old South Church. The Awakening thus impressed him most favorably. Later in 1749 he read Jonathan Edwards's *Account of the Life of the Rev. Mr. David Brainerd*, the Yale student expelled for his religious zeal and a heroic figure among the New Lights of New England and elsewhere. Adams never gave much attention to religious ideas. He did not interest himself in Brainerd or Edwards because of their Calvinism. What he seemed to take from the Awakening was its moral earnestness, its improvements in self-discipline, its social modesty, even its leveling effects, its respect for common people and common ways. In one like Adams, these effects could forge revolutionary affectations.[18]

After Harvard, Sam entered his father's businesses but found no love either for brewing or finance. Indeed, a joint venture with him in a land bank badly hurt the family. The passion for politics thrived through it all, though. Now

---

16. William M. Fowler, Jr., *Samuel Adams: Radical Puritan* (New York: Longman, 1997), 11, 14–15; John C. Miller, *Samuel Adams, Pioneer in Propaganda* (1936; Stanford, Calif.: Stanford University Press, 1960), 4, 8–9.

17. Fowler, *Samuel Adams*, 16–17, 25–26; Miller, *Samuel Adams*, 15.

18. Fowler, *Samuel Adams*, 29, 56; Miller, *Samuel Adams*, 6–7 (the quotation).

younger faces appeared at the family discussion groups, and with some of these Sam embarked on a venture of his own. The collaboration was a new journalistic outlet, the *Independent Advertiser*, launched in 1748.

Adams's writings in this publication show a Puritan strain, mixed with classical, republican judgments. The Awakening had spent its force, and now Adams and his colleagues saw a reigning materialism in New England. They warned against it. Growing wealth and luxury, they said, were eroding the "good old New England spirit." Affluence, they also feared, would corrupt the spirit, wearing away the love of liberty. When Puritanism declines, the *Advertiser* said, "our morals, our constitution, our liberties must needs degenerate." Adams's historical reach went back even further. As John C. Miller wrote, "In the *Independent Advertiser*, he repeatedly revealed the influence of his classical education— Plutarch, Cicero, and the Roman historians. Characteristically, he used the decline of Rome as a 'dreadful example' of what New Englanders might expect if they lost the puritan virtues, and he drew a close comparison between the best days of the Roman republic and the early period of New England settlement." Adams sounded views that he would hold the rest of his life. He passionately urged that Americans look to the models of pre-imperial Rome and pre-mercantile New England, adhering to a simple way of life and exemplifying a "Christian Sparta." Many described Sam Adams as the "Cato" of the American Revolution.[19]

These sentiments had not yet spoiled in Adams a true admiration and respect for England. Like so many Americans, he saw in the English constitution a secure preserve of natural rights. He treasured the English common law tradition. But he also had a sense of how fragile liberty could be. Adams shared with the Whig philosophers a great mistrust of power, especially in the hands of kings. All the more indispensable, then, was a virtuous and vigilant citizenry. From Rome to old New England to David Brainerd in the Awakening, the *Advertiser* summoned up models of public virtue. Adams would find an easy alliance with the "black regiment," the New England clergy, in the years of the American Revolution.[20]

Massachusetts politics had become a warfare of "Country" versus "Court" party politics. Adams emerged as a major voice of the Country group, allied with James Otis and others. He was visibly a "man of the people" in dress and demeanor, affecting a "genteel poverty," it was said. By the early 1760s Adams had made himself well known to the tavern crowd of Boston. Here among the "tippling, nasty, vicious crew" "Sam the Publican" found the social set that would forge the Sons of Liberty and would fight the Crown and its tax collectors. "Adams dearly loved a pot of ale, a good fire, and the company of mechanics and shipyard workers of radical political opinions." But his own middle-class status

---

19. Miller, *Samuel Adams*, 18–19.
20. Fowler, *Samuel Adams*, 28–29; Miller, *Samuel Adams*, 36–37.

and Harvard education gave him suasion with merchants, bankers, and clergymen. He forged a remarkable and effective alliance for the cause of American independence.[21]

That alliance also took shape in cooperation with another Harvard graduate, James Otis, Jr., who, in the early part of the 1760s, led the emerging popular
party in the agitation against Great Britain. Otis came from a distinguished family in Barnstable, where his father won recognition as a lawyer and representative to the colonial assembly. James was born in 1725 and the father, seeking to
gain a high status for his son from education, sent him to Harvard for that purpose. There James absorbed the classical curriculum in a manner that anticipated
the character of his later politics. He came to admire leaders like Brutus,
Cromwell, and the English parliamentarians who fought the Stuart kings. In all
he praised their resistance to tyranny. And a local incident at this time gave him
a cause. A Harvard student who used disparaging language in speaking about the
college president and tutors won a dismissal for his words. Otis took up his case
and denounced the Harvard administration as a "miserable, despicable, and arbitrary government." Later he would use similar words to describe the British
government.[22]

Another influence emerged at Harvard. Like Adams, Otis found great excitement in the visit of George Whitefield in 1740. With other students they
formed a group that prayed, sang psalms, and discussed religious issues. The
Awakening thus widened the undergraduate's interests, and he gave himself to
concentrated reading, even during his vacations. Otis carried that concentration
into the years after his graduation in 1743 and acquired a second degree from
Harvard in 1746. He might have given his life to study of the classics, but his father pressed him into a legal apprenticeship. Otis took up his own practice in
1748, first at Barnstable and then in Boston. In 1755 he married an heiress from
that city.[23]

Otis added dramatically to his growing renown with the events of 1761. The
matter concerned writs of assistance. The customs service used these devices, ob-
tained from the court of exchequer in England, to make unspecified searches of
Boston ships. Boston merchants, deeply resentful of the practice, engaged Otis to
represent them in the Massachusetts Superior Court. Otis made the most of the
occasion and the language he employed in his speech[24] has captured historians'
attention. "This writ," he began, "is against the fundamental principles of law."
He traced the writs back to the reign of Charles II, "when star chamber powers

21. Fowler, *Samuel Adams*, 54, 63; Miller, *Samuel Adams*, 19–21, 38–40 (the quotation).

22. John J. Waters, Jr., *The Otis Family in Provincial and Revolutionary Massachusetts* (Chapel Hill:
University of North Carolina Press, 1968), 111–12.

23. Waters, *Otis Family*, 112–13, 125; Clifford K. Shipton, *Sibley's Harvard Graduates: Biographical
Sketches of Those Who Attended Harvard College*, 18 vols. (Boston: Massachusetts Historical Society,
1960), 11:247.

24. We do not have an original transcript, just the reconstructed version originally derived from
notes taken by a young John Adams.

and all powers but lawful and useful powers, were pushed to extremity." More significantly, Otis asserted that Parliament could not violate certain natural and fundamental limitations of its authority. "As to Acts of Parliament: An act against the Constitution is void; an act against natural equity is void." Otis thus articulated notions that would form the foundations of American constitutional thought.[25]

Otis's action, in an event that sparked the American Revolution, has placed him in the tradition of John Locke. But Otis drew on a wide learning, and other sources entered into his political thinking. Thomas Hobbes had a particular influence; however, Otis was deprived of a larger influence in the revolutionary movement because of the manner in which he utilized the philosopher. Otis later became erratic and irrational in his behavior as he fell increasingly into madness. But in the middle decade he remained a bright intellect who sought carefully to solve the major political problems between the colonies and the mother country. He agreed with Hobbes on the important question of sovereignty, that it must have a location in the state, and for Otis that meant the legislature. So when Otis published his pamphlet *A Vindication of the British Colonies* in 1765 he made concessions to parliamentary authority that shocked and even enraged his friends. His defense came at the time of the hated Stamp Act. Although Otis denounced the act as crude and impolitic he acknowledged Parliament's power to enact it. Otis did insist that the colonies had a right to representation in Parliament and spoke for such an arrangement. In truth, he feared separation. "God forbid these colonies should ever prove undutiful to their mother country!" he wrote. Americans enjoyed rights in sufficient quantity under English protection, he believed, and separation would bring only the "blood and confusion" of warring petty states. That concern explains the clear diminution of natural rights emphasis in the later Otis, and his growing irrelevance to the American drive to independence.[26]

Otis thus did not apply his Harvard learning like Adams did in making key differentiations between America and England. However, for a time in the 1760s the two Harvard graduates forged the "Otis–Adams group" that shaped that drive.[27] One person especially became the focus of their wrath, the lieutenant governor of Massachusetts, Thomas Hutchinson. He, too, was a Harvard product, but he illustrates a much different experience. Hutchinson's family had deep roots in New England, beginning with his famous ancestor Anne, who sparked the Antinomian crisis in the 1630s. A bright boy, Thomas entered Harvard before the age of twelve and graduated in 1727. He found a great joy, apparently,

---

25. "James Otis' Speech against the Writs of Assistance," in *Documents of American History*, ed. Henry Steele Commager (New York: Appleton-Century-Crofts, 1948), 45.

26. James R. Ferguson, "Reason in Madness: The Political Thought of James Otis," *William and Mary Quarterly* 3rd Series, 36 (1979): 197–202.

27. Robert Middlekauff used that term in his study *The Glorious Cause: The American Revolution, 1763–1789* (New York: Oxford University Press, 1982), 170–71, 179, 194, 201–2.

in reading English history. He studied further for the law and entered the long-established commercial business of the Hutchinsons. His major biographer describes him as "cautious and temperate in everything he did," "an accumulator, a slow relentless acquisitor." He displayed a Puritan moderation in his habits, but showed little of the religious dimension of that New England habit. Religion signified for him personal rectitude and a healthy social influence, no more. It never affected Hutchinson with moral or emotional power. He had both a fascination for and fear of his noted ancestor, for her life demonstrated to him the destructiveness of religious extremism. Hutchinson would have preferred the Church of England, with its rational and tolerant ways, but liberal Congregationalism sufficed.[28]

Hutchinson was a man of great learning, but one cannot easily say how Harvard shaped his career.[29] To be sure, it was not always ideology that defined the animosities between Hutchinson and the Otis–Adams group. In a controversial move, Governor Francis Bernard had appointed Hutchinson chief justice of Massachusetts, reneging, it was charged, on a promise to appoint James Otis, Sr.[30] Personal politics thus fueled the rivalry. But real differences existed. Hutchinson seemed to read history through his personality and everywhere saw the excesses of emotion and unreason. Where others saw great moral issues at stake, as did Otis in his 1761 speech on the writs, Hutchinson saw only the letter of the law. Those like Sam Adams and, as we shall see, John Adams, who could draw on their Puritan heritage, who could read Roman history and fear the consequences of wealth and empire, never spoke meaningfully to Hutchinson. These patriots could endow ordinary events with passion and ideological significance. Hutchinson could not. So powerful expressions like the Stamp Act resistance could appear to him only as the work of unruly street gangs and the demagogues who manipulated them. Even the passion for liberty, he said, "must work anarchy and confusion" unless some external force checked it. For Hutchinson the loyalist that check was the British government.[31] In August 1765 the Sons of Liberty, Sam Adams's group, systematically demolished the splendid home of the Massachusetts lieutenant governor.

In Sam's younger cousin John Adams we have the most instructive example of the combining influences of Protestant Christianity and classical letters in shaping the revolutionary thought of this era. Adams concludes this look at the Harvard legacy.

---

28. Bernard Bailyn, *The Ordeal of Thomas Hutchinson* (Cambridge, Mass.: Harvard University Press, 1974), 20, 25 (the quotations), 21–23, 26.

29. In his authoritative biography of nearly four hundred pages of narrative, Bailyn gives only one paragraph to Hutchinson's Harvard years.

30. On this and other family feuds, see John J. Waters and John A. Schutz, "Patterns of Massachusetts Colonial Politics: The Writs of Assistance and the Rivalry between the Otis and Hutchinson Families," *William and Mary Quarterly* 3rd Series, 24 (1967): 543–67.

31. Bailyn, *Thomas Hutchinson*, 33, 71–73. As Bailyn shows, Hutchinson could site Locke and other thinkers readily, but he did so to support the imperative of balance between liberty and authority, not to uphold the strange notion of natural rights (see pp. 101–2).

John Adams came from a lower rung on the social ladder than did Sam. Nor was John a city boy like his cousin. Father "Deacon" John Adams earned a living as a farmer and cordwainer, and though a respected citizen he had no ancestors among the regional elite. He had married Sarah Boylston and in 1735 they became parents of a boy to whom they gave the father's name. They reared the son in the local ways, attending church faithfully and seeing young John through the Braintree Latin School. John did not take to formal learning and looked forward to an outdoors life. Intellectual interest had little to do with his going off to Harvard College in 1751. He certainly did not anticipate the great transformation the four-year experience would bring in him.[32]

Adams discovered a love of learning, and the record of his years after Harvard reflects it in several ways. He kept a remarkable diary, a neglected literary record, full of interesting reflections and judgments about himself and life. He was at once a young man driven to read and study relentlessly, but always reprimanding himself for slack in his intellectual pursuits. One sees in him a Puritan personality ("I am constantly forming, but never executing good resolutions"[33]) and that reputation stayed with him through all his career. A year out of Harvard we find him anxious but resolute: "Oh! That I could wear out of my mind every mean and base affectation, conquer my natural pride and self-conceit, expect no more deference from my fellows than I deserve, acquire that meekness, and humility, which are the sure marks and characters of a great and generous soul."[34] And Adams could impose such standards on others, too. In 1759 he recorded a day in which he sat in a tavern by the fire. He read a book while the others there played cards. The scene troubled him. "What pleasure," he wrote in his journal,

> can a young gentlemen, who is capable of thinking, take, in playing cards? It gratifies none of the senses, nor sight, hearing, taste, smell, feeling. It can entertain the mind only by hushing its clamors. Cards, backgammon are the great antidotes to reflection, to thinking, that cruel tyrant within us. What learning, or sense, are we to expect from young gentlemen, in whom a fondness for cards, etc., outgrows and checks the desire of knowledge?[35]

But we miss the true young Adams, fresh from Harvard, if we see only a Puritan critic. For he was most assuredly an enthusiast for the modern world, and above all its intellectual excitements and new directions in science. He exuded a Newtonian wonder at the universe. Another journal entry, the year after his leaving Harvard, reads: "Thus we see the amazing harmony of our solar system. The minutest particle in one of Saturn's satellites may have some in-

---

32. John Ferling, *John Adams: A Life* (Knoxville: University of Tennessee Press, 1992), 10, 12, 16.

33. *Diary and Autobiography of John Adams*, ed. L. H. Butterfield, 4 vols., *Diary, 1755–1770* (Cambridge, Mass.: Harvard University Press, 1961), 1:6.

34. *Diary and Autobiography of John Adams*, 1:7–8.

35. *Diary and Autobiography of John Adams*, 1:77.

fluence upon the most distant regions of the system. The stupendous plan of operation was projected by him who rules the universe, and a part assigned to every particle of matter to act, in this great and complicated drama."[36] At Harvard, John Winthrop IV had left a mark on Adams—an admiration for the new science and an excitement about its improving effects. Adams would remember with particular enthusiasm a clear night in Cambridge when he mounted a rooftop and gazed through Professor Winthrop's telescope to view the satellites of Jupiter. When Winthrop's experiments in electricity brought denunciations from the superstitious, who thought the work an impious effort to rob God of his thunder, Adams decried their ignorance.[37] When Adams looked about him, he concluded, too, that his own country bore the welcome signs of an improving age. A continent but recently the home of savages and wild beasts, he recorded, now evidenced everywhere the progressive marks of the European settlers.[38]

Adams applauded the same modernizing trends in religion. For a while after graduating from Harvard, in 1756, he taught school in Worcester. There he came into the company of some free thinkers, but Harvard had prepared him for them. If he did not share their deist credo he did certainly embrace a liberal Protestantism that now flourished among the New England educated classes.[39] Adams's intense reading program in these years found him immersed at one point in Francis Hutcheson's *A Short Introduction to Moral Philosophy*. Almost certainly Harvard's opening to this major voice of the Scottish Enlightenment took Adams in a liberal direction in religion and moral philosophy.[40] He also studied the English latitudinarians and British moralists, copying extracts from John Tillotson, Joseph Butler, and Samuel Clarke.[41] All these activities induced in Adams a recoil from Calvinism, which he could not uphold in face of the modern intellect. At least within a year after Harvard Adams had decided that moral truth may come to us either by the constitution of the human brain or by supernatural revelation; by whatever means it registered the efficacious work of the "Supreme Being" in facilitating our moral conduct. By the same account, however, the doctrine of original sin could not bear Adams's scrutiny. He accepted an argument of the religious liberals that this doctrine made God the author of sin and exculpated human beings from moral judgment of their wrongdoing. Original Sin, and the eternal damnation that followed had the further fault, Adams believed, of making it better for most people that they had never

---

36. *Diary and Autobiography of John Adams*, 1:24.

37. *Diary and Autobiography of John Adams*, 1:61. The comments are marginal notes that Adams made while reading Winthrop's *Lectures on Earthquakes* in 1755; David McCullough, *John Adams* (New York: Simon and Schuster, 2001), 35.

38. *Diary and Autobiography of John Adams*, 1:34.

39. C. Bradley Thompson, "Young John Adams and the New Philosophic Rationalism," *William and Mary Quarterly* 3rd Series, 55 (1998): 264.

40. *Diary and Autobiography of John Adams*, 1:2.

41. Thompson, "Young John Adams," 268.

been born.[42] Adams did continue to believe in an active and vigilant God, even a God of miracles. He found such faith wholly consistent with a rational religion.[43]

Adams had thought of going into the ministry. He feared, though, that his Arminian bent would work as a prejudice against him. He had seen it happen to other pastors that he knew.[44] Now he thought of the law. He was reading heavily in that subject and in political theory, recording his reflections in journal commentary. The *Independent Whig* of Trenchard and Gordon received his attention.[45] He read Justinian, Pufendorf, and Hugo Grotius, among others.[46] Adams wanted to be a lawyer, but feared that his desire to do so came from a lust for fame; his Puritan conscience admonished him. Gradually, however, Adams convinced himself that law constituted a form of public usefulness, or that he, at least, could make it so. "The study and practice of law," he wrote, "I am sure does not dissolve the obligations of morality or of religion."[47] In his study of law with James Putnam, Adams found much personal and intellectual satisfaction. Law, he believed, was the vehicle of reason. Its practice would give him more gratification than the life of the ministry.[48]

Law practice also intensified Adams's political activity. He wrote publicly on the subject and recorded his thoughts in his diary. Then came the "momentous" year of 1765, as he put it. British policy regarding the colonies vexed and troubled him. He wrote on Christmas day that year: "At home. Thinking, reading, searching concerning taxation without consent."[49] In reaction to the Stamp Act he had already concluded that the action showed the frightening power of the British government and its ability to destroy individual liberties. "And if this authority is once acknowledged and established, the ruin of America will become inevitable," he wrote.[50] Also, very early in the same year, Adams and some colleagues formed the Sodalitas Club. It defined its purpose as the study of law and oratory. Its members would meet every Thursday evening and discuss a selected legal text from a list of classic works. The club began by taking up the feudal law. Adams seized on the subject, and his immersion in it greatly clarified his political understanding. Now the issues of the day emerged in larger meaning for him. He presented his thoughts, formulated even before the Stamp Act, to the Sodalitas group. Then he offered them to the world as his *Dissertation on the Canon and the Feudal Law*. He had become a revolutionary.

---

42. *Diary and Autobiography of John Adams*, 1:42; see also, *Papers of John Adams*, ed. Robert J. Taylor, et al., 10 vols. (Cambridge, Mass.: Harvard University Press, 1977), 1:49.
43. *Diary and Autobiography of John Adams*, 1:11.
44. *Papers of John Adams*, 1:13, :21.
45. *Diary and Autobiography of John Adams*, 1:7.
46. *Diary and Autobiography of John Adams*, 1:44, 174
47. Ferling, *John Adams*, 18; *Diary and Autobiography of John Adams*, 1:143.
48. *Diary and Autobiography of John Adams*, 1:117.
49. *Diary and Autobiography of John Adams*, 1:273.
50. *Diary and Autobiography of John Adams*, 1:264–65.

Toward the end of the *Dissertation* Adams wrote, "There seems to be a direct and formal design on foot, to enslave all America."[51] He had prepared his audience for this viewpoint by outlining a long period of history. Adams saw the canon and feudal law as the critical vehicles by which the powerful European states and their ominous alliances with the Church had contrived to secure their oppressive rule. Both flourished amid religious superstition and blind loyalty to the civil powers. The clerical offices of the Roman Catholic Church received most of Adams's invective. That form of Christianity, he believed, could thrive only by its own manufactured superstitions, evidenced in its absurd assertions on behalf of the sacraments. By the claims of transubstantiation, he said, the Roman clergy foisted on the populace "a state of sordid ignorance" and a "religious horror of letters and knowledge." The feudal states were only too happy to see such a mentality perpetuated, for they could all the more easily facilitate "a blind, implicit obedience to civil magistry."[52]

This contribution by Adams to the literature of the American Revolution reflects one part of his Harvard legacy. He saw history as a struggle between intellectual light and darkness. He described the Protestant Reformation as an intellectual breakthrough against Catholic superstition, and he maintained that in England above all it did its good work. The good work came not from the Church of England but from the Puritans who rebelled against it. "They had become intelligent in general, and many of them learned," he wrote. He celebrated the knowledge of the classics among the first New Englanders, their acquaintance with poets, historians, and philosophers. Harvard and Yale, the schools of the Puritans, reflected that love of learning, Adams said. He wrote of the Puritans, "Their civil and religious principles, therefore, conspired to propagate and perpetuate knowledge. For this purpose they laid very early the foundations of colleges, and invested them with ample privileges and emoluments."[53] He further credited the Puritans with breaking from the ecclesiastical pomp and ritual of the High Church, of rejecting the same forms in government, by which the English state had secured its own worship by the masses. Adams compressed much thematic history in one of the passages in the *Dissertation*. The Puritans, he said,

> knew that government was a plain, simple, intelligible thing founded in nature and reason and quite comprehensible by common sense. They detested all the base services, and servile dependencies of the feudal system. They knew that no such unworthy dependencies took place in the ancient states of liberty, the republics of Greece and Rome: and they thought all such slavish subordinations were equally inconsistent with the constitution of human nature and that religious liberty with which Jesus had made them free.[54]

---

51. John Adams, *A Dissertation on the Canon and the Feudal Law*, in *Papers of John Adams*, 1:127.
52. Adams, *Dissertation*, 1:112–13.
53. Adams, *Dissertation*, 1:114, 118.
54. Adams, *Dissertation*, 1:117.

In making historical sense of his country, Adams, as this passage suggests, also drew upon another source. His Harvard education had inspired in him a profound love of classical literature, invoked, as noted, in the *Dissertation* in its connection with ancient republicanism. His immersion in this culture was almost life-long. At Harvard he began an enduring association with Sallust, the Roman historian of the first century BCE and the subject of his 1755 commencement disputation. Sallust filled the pages of Adams's commonplace books at Harvard. When he persuaded himself of the legal profession's merits he gained assurance knowing that his was "a field in which Demosthenes, Cicero, and others of immortal fame have exulted before me." When the Sodalitas Club formed, it gave prime attention to Cicero. Adams admired in James Otis's 1761 speech its "promptitude of classical allusions."[55]

As Carl Richard has shown in his study of the classics and the Founders, Adams could render any situation, personal or public, in a classical parallel. Thus in 1763, vexed at party factions, he likened himself to Xenephon: "If engagements to a party are necessary to make a fortune, I had rather make none at all, and spend the remainder of my days like my favorite author, that ancient and immortal husbandman, philosopher, politician, and general, Xenephon, in his retreat." More importantly, in the crisis years of the 1770s, Adams upheld ancient history against the colonial policy of the Britons. Greece, he said, ruled its colonies benevolently; they all became distinct and independent commonwealths. Rome of the republic allowed its colonies to govern themselves by their own laws. Adams compared Thomas Hutchinson, now in 1771 royal governor of Massachusetts, to Caesar: "Caesar, by destroying the Roman Republic, made himself a perpetual dictator; Hutchinson, by countenancing and supporting a system of corruption and tyranny, has made himself governor." In 1775 Adams could not have been more explicit. "The imperial crown of Great Britain," he wrote, "was introduced in allusion to that of the Roman empire, and intended to insinuate that the prerogative of the imperial crown of England was like that of the Roman Empire." History, for Adams, was always a lesson book.[56]

For the ten years preceding Adams's pronouncement, Boston and Harvard had seethed with revolutionary fervor. Resistance to the Sugar Act in 1764 and stronger defiance of the Stamp Act in 1765 placed Boston under virtual siege. British officials and British troops gave it the appearance of an occupied city. Faced with such a menace, the House of Representatives refused to meet, so Governor Francis Bernard convened the body at Harvard College in Cambridge. The legislature met in the Holden Chapel on the campus, and in 1770 the council also arrived, holding meetings in the Harvard library. Here students could

55. Carl J. Richard, *The Founders and the Classics: Greece, Rome, and the American Enlightenment* (Cambridge, Mass.: Harvard University Press, 1994), 21, 30, 60, 61.
56. Richard, *The Founders and the Classics*, 57, 75, 100.

Ezra Stiles

supplement their ordinary curricular fare by hearing the earlier Harvard graduate, James Otis, berate the British government for its iniquitous policies toward
the colonies. Meanwhile, students had formed their own militia; you could see
them in long blue coats as you passed near the campus.[57]

The early morning guns at Lexington green on April 19, 1775, brought the
imperial conflict into open warfare. Almost immediately, the necessities of war
turned the Harvard campus into barracks for the patriot soldiers. Harvard
yielded three of its buildings to American soldiers and soon became a hospital
for the troops as well. President Samuel Langdon prayed with the soldiers on
the campus. The overseers, meanwhile, appraised the situation and decided to
relocate the college to Concord, twelve miles to the west of Cambridge. It reopened there in October and there it functioned for eight months. No commencement exercises took place from the time of the Boston Port Act of 1774

---

57. Morison, *Three Centuries of Harvard*, 98–99, 137, 141.

until 1781 as the war approached an end. Student enrollments fell throughout the war.[58]

Harvard received a new president in 1774, the Reverend Samuel Langdon. Born in 1723, Langdon came out of family poverty in Boston, attended Harvard from 1736 to 1740, and earned B.A. and M.A. degrees there. Langdon was always a patriot. In Portsmouth, where he was a teacher and then minister at the Congregational church, Langdon served as the New Hampshire chaplain to the regiment that assaulted Ft. Louisbourg in 1745. In the 1760s he took up the cause of Congregational unity with Ezra Stiles. Langdon greatly disliked the Church of England and joined the unity movement so that the Calvinist churches in New England would have a solid front against its sinister designs. For Langdon the cause of no taxation without representation was the same as the cause of no bishop in the colonies. Langdon's appointment had clear political reasons for he was a known Whig, friend of Sam Adams and others in the revolutionary cohort. Harvard treasurer John Hancock helped secure him the presidency. Langdon has received little credit for his administrative career at Harvard, and he left in 1780 under a cloud.

Langdon did, however, contribute a remarkable piece to the literature of the revolution. He presented it shortly after his arrival, and just six weeks after the fighting at Lexington and Concord. Langdon not only put Harvard publicly on the side of the colonies and their independence, he also left us with one of the great thematic summaries of their cause. His statement occurred a full year and more before Thomas Jefferson stated the American brief against Great Britain in his famous declaration of 1776.

As did so many voices of the revolution, Langdon cited the British Constitution, the once great pride of Americans, as the source of their liberties. But it now lay in ruin, he lamented, corrupted and abused by Parliament and king, by men "whose aim is to exercise lordship over us." The consequence: "British liberty is just ready to expire." And what were the signs of this late tyranny? Langdon anticipated Jefferson: "fleets and armies sent to our capital"; troops in the night who seize colonialists' weapons; the attempt to establish popery in their midst (a reference to the 1774 Quebec Act); a flood of "vile dependents"—officers, bureaucrats, and ministers—placed among the colonists to deplete their public funds.[59]

Langdon drew on historical parallels to shed light on the current crisis. He turned first to ancient Israel where a nation sunk in sin gave rise to political rulers who used placements and bribery to enhance their personal power. God did not deign to save his people because they had turned from him. True religion had given way to "mere ceremony and hypocrisy," he complained. What alone

---

58. David Robson, *Educating Republicans: The College in the Era of the American Revolution, 1750–1800* (Westport, Conn.: Greenwood, 1985), 100.

59. Samuel Langdon, *A Sermon . . .* , in *The Wall and the Garden*, 357–58.

could save Israel—a reformation in religion and morals—the people could not bring on. And only had they done so would God have seen fit to save them. Langdon urged this example as an historical model of Anglo-Saxon Britain and contrasted it with the present time. For Puritans, too, once had benevolent rulers and officers. "They were fathers of the people and sought the welfare and prosperity of the whole body. They did not exhaust the national wealth by luxury and bribery." But Britain had become "a mere shadow of its ancient political system." It now gloried only "in vast public treasures lavished in corruption." So much had the spoils of empire debauched a once noble land, said Langdon, that it now lay subservient before its rulers. Such was the "corrupted, dying state" of Great Britain.[60]

Langdon's sermon not only invoked moral republicanism in the fashion of the American Whig patriots, it also looked to a revitalized religion in America. American republicans usually cited early Rome against Great Britain to posit American innocence and virtue against decadent England. But latterday Calvinists like Langdon tended more demonstrably to document Americans' own sins. Indeed, Langdon might have given little comfort to Harvard liberals, for rational Christianity did not provide the standards for the moral and spiritual recovery that he wished to see in the colonies. This Harvard president sounded like Increase Mather. "We have rebelled against God," he told his audience. "We have lost the true spirit of Christianity, though we retain the outer profession and form of it. . . . The worship of many is but mere compliment to the deity, while their hearts are far from him." Langdon even added that this learned generation had allowed the gospel to yield to "a superficial system of moral philosophy." And finally citing the "sins of America," Langdon, like all the voices of Harvard patriotism, invoked the Puritan memory:

> Have we not lost much of that spirit of genuine Christianity which so remarkably appeared in our ancestors? . . . Have we not departed from their virtues? . . . Have we not made light of the gospel of salvation, and too much affected the cold, formal, fashionable religion of countries grown old in vice and overspread with infidelity? . . . Have we not, especially in our seaports, gone much too far into the pride and luxuries of life? . . . And have not even these young governments been in some measure infected with the corruptions of European courts?

And so the recitation went on. Langdon looked to a moral and religious recovery among his countrymen, for then they might hope for God's assistance. And they may yet escape enslavement.[61]

In general, one finds in the Harvard language of the revolution a certain retrospection. This institution had found its way, never easily or smoothly, but

60. Langdon, *A Sermon*, 362–65. Quotations on pp. 364–65.
61. Langdon, *A Sermon*, 364 (first quotation), 367 (second quotation), 368.

persistently, away from its Puritan Calvinist origins. In religion and science it opened to the liberal directions of the eighteenth century and its milder, rational environment. However, Harvard's Puritan origins, and indeed the heroic age of New England beginnings, now reemerged in memory during the revolutionary decades. They reemerged not as any kind of Calvinist recovery, but as mythology. Puritan history in the age of the Stuarts spoke out again to latter-day Harvard Puritans to present them with models of tenacity, defiance, and commitment in the face of oppression. We have seen here that political leaders like Sam and John Adams were more inclined even than religious leaders to invoke that ancestral heroism. Through careers that immersed them in the classics and the study of law, Harvard served also to reconnect the revolutionary generation to the Puritan founders that now inspired their struggles against tyrannical England.

In the years of the American Revolution Yale College, "school of the prophets," became Yale, school of patriots. In 1765 it reacted immediately and defiantly to the Stamp Act. A tutor, Richard Woodhull, organized students for protest. Seniors issued an announcement: "The Senior Class of Yale College have unanimously agreed to make their appearance at the next public commencement . . . wholly dressed in the manufactures of our own country." (They also asked their parents to pay for the homespun!) Nor were the faculty indifferent. Professor of Divinity Naphtali Daggett (soon to be president ex tempore) excoriated the Stamp Act and used the pages of the *Connecticut Gazette* to denounce collector Jared Ingersoll. When war came in 1775, Yale students formed their own militia. Graduates of the New Haven school supplied a large portion of Connecticut's militia. Four from Yale signed the Declaration of Independence, and Yale alumnus Nathan Hale issued long-remembered patriotic words as he died at the hands of the British in 1776. Yale did have Loyalists among its graduates, but they constituted an unhappy few. One denounced his alma mater for its dangerously republican spirit and its "utter aversion to [Anglican] bishops." Thomas Gage of the British army labeled Yale "a seminary of democracy."[62] He did not intend a compliment.

As with Harvard, Yale's connection to the revolution related also to intellectual history. This situation turns our attention to a phenomenon known as the New Divinity movement. It flourished in New England, but above all in Connecticut, and all of its major voices had links to Yale College. The New Divinity emerged in the aftermath of the Awakening. Some New Divinity people remembered the Awakening for its social effects—a remarkable new commitment to good and right living, sprung from a new religious seriousness and spirituality. Joseph Bellamy, a major figure, recalled that in the early 1740s the courts in Con-

---

62. Brooks Mather Kelley, *Yale: A History* (New Haven, Conn: Yale University Press, 1974), 83 (the quotation)–88; Roche, *Colonial Colleges*, 20, 62, 12.

necticut were closed and the taverns shut up. The law of God, he said, reigned above the law of men. Social harmony prevailed. New Divinity men were Calvinists ("the hyper-Calvinist wing of the New Light movement," as Joseph Conforti labels them) and attributed the gains of the Awakening to a revitalized Reformed theology, armed to allay a spreading Arminianism.[63]

The New Divinity now spread rapidly. By the end of the revolution it occupied probably half of the Connecticut's Congregationalist pulpits and had greatest strength in the northwest region of the state. The opening of the back country in western New England, especially after the ending of the war with France in 1763, sent Yale graduates to the small towns there. With their New Divinity affiliations, they formed an "intellectual counterpoise" to the secular and liberal culture of eastern New England, where a Harvard influence prevailed. Also, their location mostly in small towns and rural villages gave a social prejudice to their movement. Bellamy would recall that at Yale he and his New Light companions stood apart from the upper-class representation of the Old Light students.[64]

Also, some among the group, and Bellamy especially, profoundly mistrusted the new commercial order emerging in the American colonies. Bellamy did not like the signs of it in Connecticut. Amid the pressure of social change, the new morally intense Calvinism of the New Divinity men promised to be a stabilizing force in their communities. Old Lights and Arminians, with their locations in the urban and commercial centers, did not speak kindly of the New Divinity men. Ezra Stiles said that, for all their education, they remained unrefined in manners and conduct. Liberal William Bentley called them "Farmer Metaphysicians" who might flourish in the backwoods but lacked the dignity to win acceptance in cultured environs.[65]

Theological matters weighed even more heavily in the New Divinity controversies. The Old Calvinists, as one party, upheld the traditional Puritan standards of the federal, or covenant theology. New Divinity ministers, as another party, had problems with the old Calvinism. They had seen many in New England, reacting as they did against its harsh doctrines respecting election and damnation, turned into Arminians. The New Divinity men, however, did not shy from battle with the liberals and sought instead to strengthen Calvinism by way of modifying it. They won the label "consistent Calvinists." All claimed the mantle of Edwards although with him also they made some key alterations. Old Calvinists would call the New Divinity men heretics. Nonetheless, the efforts of

---

63. Heimert, *Religion and the American Mind*, 182; Joseph Conforti, *Samuel Hopkins and the New Divinity Movement: Calvinism, the Congregational Ministry, and Reform in New England between the Great Awakenings* (Grand Rapids, Mich.: Christian University Press, 1981), 3.

64. Conforti, *Hopkins*, 40–42, 58; Mark Valeri, *Law and Providence in Joseph Bellamy's New England* (New York: Oxford University Press, 1994), 11–12.

65. Richard D. Birdsall, "Ezra Stiles versus the New Divinity Men," *American Quarterly* 17 (1965): 251; Heimert, *Religion and the American Mind*, 133, 344–45 (the quotation); Conforti, *Hopkins*, 9–10.

the New Divinity produced what one author has called "the first indigenously American school of Calvinism."[66]

The New Divinity men believed that the federal theology bred Antinomianism and neglect of moral action. Justification, that is, induced smugness and comfort, dissuading those in the covenant of grace from attention to the moral law. They saw that consequence among the extreme New Lights in the Awakening. But moral behavior and obedience to the law took on a new urgency for the New Divinity ministers in the 1750s and 1760s. They saw in the new commercial centers of New England a decline of the communalism and social ethic of old New England, yielding now to an aggressive and antisocial individualism as the entrepreneurial spirit flourished in the new towns. New Divinity preachers gave sermons resounding in moral hyperbole and reflecting a profound fear of social change. Hence, too, the overwhelming rural location of the New Divinity exponents. Partisans took to their pulpits, and the New Divinity message rang out through farming and small-town New England well into the nineteenth century.[67]

A summary of New Divinity theology will show that it had an overriding concern with individual moral accountability and moral recovery in the public life of New England. The New Divinity men promoted that concern by careful reconstructions of Calvinist orthodoxy on such issues as the atonement, original sin, and moral agency (free will versus determinism). They believed that God not only permitted sin, he willed it. The existence of sin demonstrated all the more dramatically the triumph of grace out of it. Against the contention of the Old Calvinists that Christ provided a limited atonement that saved only the elect, New Divinity men argued that Christ's sacrifice made salvation possible, but not necessary, to those whom God gave sovereign grace. In the older Calvinism New Divinity men saw an encouragement of Antinomianism because entry into the covenant of grace, they asserted, did not demand a subsequent obedience to the law. Bellamy thus expressed disbelief that anyone could assert that "Christ came down from heaven and died, to purchase this abatement of the law of God, and procure this lawless liberty for his rebellious subjects." Hence the subtle theological fine-turning by the New Divinity had the dramatic effect of liberating both God and man from the stricter terms of the older covenant upheld by the Puritans and their intellectual descendants.[68]

---

66. William Breitenbach, "The Consistent Calvinism of the New Divinity Movement," *William and Mary Quarterly* 3rd Series, 41 (1984): 241, 245; Joseph A. Conforti, "Samuel Hopkins and the New Divinity: Theology, Ethics, and Social Reform in Eighteenth-Century New England," *William and Mary Quarterly* 3rd Series, 34 (1977): 573 (the quotation); idem, *Hopkins*, 63.

67. Conforti, "Hopkins," 574n, 588; see also, Kenneth A. Lockeridge, "Social Change and the Meaning of the American Revolution," *Journal of Social History* 6 (1973): 423–24.

68. Breitenbach, "New Divinity," 247–50 (the quotation). Bellamy said that Old Calvinists who considered Christ as "paying the whole debt of the elect" were tempted to believe "that Christ has done all their duty, so that now . . . they have nothing to do with the law—no, not so much as to be their rule to live by,—but are set at full liberty from all obligations to any duty whatsoever." 249; Conforti, *Hopkins*, 66.

Samuel Hopkins made the greatest strides among the New Divinity ministers in revising Edwards. Born in Waterbury, Connecticut, in 1721, Hopkins, against the general New Divinity pattern, grew up in a family of some means and social distinction. He entered Yale in 1737 and became a serious student, graduated Yale in 1741, then studied with Edwards. He remained his lasting friend until Edwards died in 1758. Hopkins would spend a quarter-century preaching in the backcountry before a relocation to Newport in 1770. In sermons and writings Hopkins painstakingly revised the Old Calvinism, often in a manner that its exponents judged obscurantist and downright metaphysical. Hopkins thought Edwards's ideas of beauty and true virtue, stressing "love to being in general" (i.e., Edwards's notion of the full immersion of the self in the totality of God's creation), too amorphous and abstract. Edwards made of moral truth a species of esthetics, Hopkins objected, and rendered his system ineffective as a spur to individual accountability. Hopkins, that is, wanted to move virtue from Edwards's location of it in the affections to a practice in right actions. The Newport minister gave a systematic rendering of these ideas in 1773 with the publication of *An Inquiry into the Nature of True Holiness*. Virtue now took the form of "evangelical activism." Hopkins encouraged a moral regeneration in New England. Politics was not exempt from the call.[69]

Hopkins also brought the judgment of rural New England against the modernity of worldly and commercial Newport. Its public sins were manifest, he believed. Newport flourished as prime player in the slave trade and maker of the rum used to secure its human victims. Commercial Newport symbolized for Hopkins, fearfully, what America might become. Hopkins preached to his church on the evils of the slave trade and published *A Dialogue Concerning the Slavery of the Africans* in 1776. He dedicated the work to the Continental Congress. Hopkins urged the end of the trade "not merely from political reasons; but from a conviction of the unrighteousness and cruelty of that trade and a regard to justice and benevolence." Hopkins in this issue consciously took the Edwardsian ethic and gave it a targeted social application, for "disinterested benevolence," he said, must include a love that would liberate slaves.[70]

This matter directly related to the issues in the American Revolution, Hopkins believed. Patriots who cited all the moral outrages committed by the British government must also extend demands of benevolence to the slaves in their own country. Too many patriots, however, he said, stood condemned as hypocrites, for failure to do so. Indeed, Hopkins even made antislavery a sign of conversion and to that conversion placed the hope of American triumph in its war against its evil enemy. He believed that the social transformation that the Awakening had failed to achieve the revolution would secure. The moral extravagances of American

69. Conforti, *Hopkins*, 21–22, 30–31; idem, "Hopkins," 573, 585, 575–76, 583.

70. Conforti, *Hopkins*, 112–17. In Newport, most of the slave-owning families belonged not to Hopkins's Second Church but to Ezra Stiles's First Church (p. 127).

life, from tea drinking on the lower scale to slavery on the upper, would meet their undoing if the revolution carried through the moral regeneration it promised to effect.[71]

The New Divinity recourse to the moral law governed the views of its other spokesmen on the American Revolution. If Hopkins represented a strenuous voice of the New Divinity, Joseph Bellamy stood for its militant wing. Bellamy, born in Cheshire, Connecticut, in 1719, came from a family with deep roots but not high social standing in Connecticut. He entered Yale College and there, as news of the religious stirrings in Edwards's Northampton spread, he found his first and lasting identity with the New Light factions in that colony. He also studied with Edwards, then earned an M.A. degree in 1735. He became in Connecticut one of the strongest champions of the revivals of 1740 and received invitations to preach in several New Light pulpits. At this time, Bellamy adhered to an un-embellished Calvinism and took on an organizational leadership in resisting the legislative efforts by Connecticut, in its Old Light political domination, to re-strict the evangelicals. He soon made his church at Bethlehem in western Con-necticut the major center of the New Divinity influence.[72]

In the late 1740s Bellamy took a significant turn. He had by then seen the worst aspect of the Awakening, an excessive enthusiasm and a supreme self-assurance that spilled over into Antinomianism. Old Light Congregationalism, to be sure, had made too much of a corporate religiosity, he believed, satisfied with moral and financial loyalty to the churches and overlooking internal re-newal. He had furthermore come to associate Old Light formalism and legalism with Arminianism, whose gains he feared greatly. Thus uncertain, Bellamy sus-pended his commitments and engaged in a concentrated period of reading—Shaftesbury, Hutcheson, Hume—works much removed in tone and spirit from his old copies of Ames and Willard. But he emerged rearmed and resolved to up-hold Calvinism in a new way, with a focus on God's law as the central element of the Christian faith. There resulted his *True Religion Delineated* (1750). Here and in sermons in the following years, Bellamy challenged liberal religion on every front. He meant to defend "experimental religion" against formality on the one hand and enthusiasm on the other. He and others among the New Divinity group showed that true virtue, or benevolence, implied a love of God, but also an acquiescence to the divine will. Bellamy, by inscribing moral philosophy into Calvinism, brought right action to the forefront of his preaching. Individuals must adhere to the law. History, he also asserted, illustrated everywhere that God punishes a people who ignore the law while he upholds those who live in right-eousness.[73]

---

71. Conforti, *Hopkins*, 128, 130.
72. Valeri, *Joseph Bellamy*, 10–13, 15, 17–18.
73. Valeri, *Joseph Bellamy*, 41–42, 44, 49–54; idem, "The New Divinity and the American Revo-lution," *William and Mary Quarterly* 3rd Series, 46 (October 1989): 746–50.

Bellamy in a famous sermon in 1762 posted a litany of social abuses: "luxury, idleness, debauchery, dishonesty, gay dressing, extravagant high living." These evils had all become prevalent since the Awakening had subsided, he observed, as had also the resurgence of Arminianism. The pattern was unmistakable, for Arminian gains centered in the social worlds of the wealthy and powerful in Connecticut, their urban and market cultures. New luxuries and the easy credit that made them accessible led people, Bellamy said, to "spend their time in idleness, their substance in taverns, in gay dressing, in high living." He described a people under judgment for failure to obey God's laws. Bellamy became a major personality in the anti-Calvinist assaults of the liberals, Mayhew and Chauncy in particular. Bellamy, though, cast a wide net in his moral excoriations. In only a few years, New Divinity men would turn their social prejudices into anti-British ones.[74]

Bellamy turned increasingly in the 1760s on the British government. He preached a politics of benevolence—for the people and for their rulers. The latter, he urged, must rule by "a benevolent, generous frame of heart" to earn in return the love of their subjects. Bellamy had the occasion to pronounce these views, in his Bethlehem pulpit and in numerous election day sermons. In the 1760s he turned critically against the British government for its violations of these maxims. King, Parliament, and royal officials, he warned, must reform themselves and turn from their "arbitrary and tyrannical" habits and from a politics of self-interest that neglected the public weal. They must spread "brotherly love" to all the colonies, he said. All officers of the colonial government, too, he insisted, must enforce laws that promote "virtue." Bellamy also accused the British of holding a particular prejudice. They persecute us, he said, "because we are Puritans."[75]

Levi Hart and Jonathan Edwards, Jr., added more New Divinity voices to the American cause. Hart, a Yale graduate in 1760, preached in Preston, Connecticut. When the war broke out he issued a string of revolutionary sermons and from his pulpit called for divine vengeance against George III and "the venal House of Commons." British policies, he argued, justified American rebellion. The younger Edwards felt similarly. He was a Princeton graduate in 1765 but studied with Hopkins and then with Bellamy. From his pulpit in 1774 Edwards denounced the Coercive Acts and called for Connecticut people to support the Continental Congress. The news from Lexington and Concord the next year rallied Edwards further. He called on Americans to take up arms and train to fight. Submission to Crown and Parliament was nothing less than treachery, Edwards affirmed.[76]

Neither Hart nor Edwards nor Bellamy appealed to New England's social covenant in their revolutionary pleas. They did not assign American a providential

---

74. Valeri, *Joseph Bellamy*, 78, 86–89 (the quotation), 118. Valeri notes, however, that Bellamy lived in the finest home in Bethlehem.
75. Valeri, *Joseph Bellamy*, 155; idem, "New Divinity," 753, 741, 767.
76. Valeri, "New Divinity," 741–42.

role in history or consider the nation elect of God. They had separated that much from the federal theology of the Old Lights. Instead they upheld a universal law and measured the British actions against it. Their neo-Calvinism posited a human government and a divine government, the latter one of perfect benevolence. Human government could never match the divine in virtue, but when men who ruled fell far away from the divine standards, they said, their subjects must defy their oppression and rebel. New Divinity ministers did warn that rebels must look to their own house, too. Enslavement of Negroes made the colonists a culpable people. New Divinity men called for a moral reform at home. By the middle of the 1770s, however, Bellamy was giving overwhelming attention to the sins of England. He and others in the New Divinity party wanted Americans to swear off all British imports, the luxury and finery of a bloated empire and a curse to America's moral aspirations. Surveying the whole imperial scene, Bellamy concluded that the British Empire "is ripe for destruction."[77]

Yale College also had an Old Light connection, and its most direct, personal one to the American Revolution, in Ezra Stiles. Stiles stood aloof from the New Divinity movement and in fact, as noted, often disparaged it. Nonetheless, he played a critical role in trying to overcome religious factions in New England and to unify its Congregational churches. That role also made him a revolutionary. Stiles had graduated from Yale in 1746, pursued private study, then served as tutor at Yale from 1749 to 1755. That year he answered a call to Newport and began a twenty-year ministry that would make him an eyewitness to the war. He came back to his alma mater in 1778 as the new college president. There, too, he would see the war up close and personal.

Yale well prepared Stiles for his critical role. He graduated from the school of Thomas Clap where he could see Puritan orthodoxy at every turn. At the same time Stiles had access to the finest collection of liberal thinking in America, the acquisitions that Yale had made in the 1730s. So when he graduated from Yale, he remembered, he "stood on the precipice . . . of deism." Sometime after his Newport arrival, though, Stiles moved in a conservative direction and returned to the Old Lights. His sermons focused more on divine grace. The humanist ethics of virtue that had carried him to this point now appeared insufficient to him. It did not sound the depth of corruption in the human heart, he believed, and it did not bring the atonement of Christ into significance. Stiles urged less emphasis on moral excellence and more for a right notion of saving grace.[78]

This concern was turning the Old Light Stiles back to the original Puritan divines. He urged recovery of the doctrines of "our pious ancestors" and fear for "the tremendous torments of damnation." Now Stiles, in correspondence with

---

77. Valeri, *Joseph Bellamy*, 150, 140 (the quotation)–41; idem, "New Divinity," 757–58, 763–64, 767. In Connecticut, revolutionary patriotism was most evident in the areas of New Divinity strength (p. 151).

78. Christopher Grasso, *A Speaking Aristocracy: Transforming Public Discourse in Eighteenth-Century Connecticut* (Chapel Hill: University of North Carolina Press, 1999), 230–48.

Edward Wigglesworth, was recommending Thomas Hooker and William Perkins, the latter still a viable model for evangelical preaching. "I am in principle with the good old Puritans," he wrote to a friend in 1770. But Stiles's new appreciation of the ancestral faith had another source. More and more in the decades of turmoil with England the old New Englanders recommended themselves to him for their love of liberty, for their long and bitter struggle against ecclesiastical and state oppression.[79]

But even before the Sugar Act and the Stamp Act raised American anger against England, Stiles had entered the conflict from another side. He had been considering the matter of church unity among the different branches of New England Protestantism. He had seen the furor of the Awakening dissolve, and with it some of the old hostilities. The Americans and British had just achieved a great victory over the French. Stiles, welcoming a mood of reconciliation and accord, now looked for a common constitution for the churches. In 1762, before a small audience in Bristol, Rhode Island, Stiles delivered an address that historian Carl Bridenbaugh labeled "one of the most remarkable sermons ever preached in colonial America." Stiles titled it *Discourse on the Christian Union.* Charles Chauncy in Boston and Francis Alison in Philadelphia hailed its publication. Chauncy even reported that seven hundred copies from the house of Edes and Gill had sold out and no more could be had.[80]

The sermon was remarkable indeed, if for nothing but its sheer ambition. Looking beyond a history racked by intellectual and political turmoil, Stiles sought to recall Protestants to their common unity. He surveyed points of doctrine; he took up recent intellectual trends, even showing how Jonathan Edwards and John Locke each helped to affirm traditional Protestant notions about freedom and responsibility for sin; he passed over classic fights among Calvinists and Arminians with a wave of the hand. Then he came to an explosive issue—the matter of ordination. Stiles made a polite gesture to the Anglicans ("in justice to our Protestant episcopal brethren") that nonetheless concealed a lethal weapon. For Stiles meant to come down unequivocally on the side of presbyterian ordination as the essential foundation of Protestant consensus. "We agree," he wrote, "in the sufficiency and validity of presbyterian ordination. This was the ordination practiced by the apostles, and among the primitive Christians of the first and second centuries," he claimed.[81]

Problematically, this foundation read the Church of England out of any place in the new union. For all true Protestants, Stiles wrote, concurred in presbyterian ordination—except Anglicans. (He said nothing of Quakers and Baptists.) Stiles maintained that, no matter how confusing the early terminology

---

79. Edmund Morgan, *The Gentle Puritan: A Life of Ezra Stiles, 1727–1795* (New York: Norton, 1962), 174–75.

80. Bridenbaugh, *Mitre and Sceptre,* 4–5.

81. Ezra Stiles, *Discourse on the Christian Union* . . . (Boston: Edes and Gill, 1762), 30 (second quotation), 33 (first quotation).

about bishops and presbyters, episcopacy, as since practiced, had no sanction in Scripture. As if this reading were not condemnatory enough, Stiles proceeded to a political consideration. Episcopacy, he said, had always found an ally in a powerful state. It had always rendered itself subservient to kings and magistrates. Only a polity that assured congregational autonomy, Stiles responded, could prevent this co-option. The more so, he believed, could we now appreciate the great achievement of English and New England Puritans. They avoided the evil of complete and indiscriminate toleration, on the one hand, while yet protecting the churches from ecclesiastical and state domination on the other. He said of the New England congregations that "there is no body of churches in the Protestant world more nearly recovered to the simplicity and purity of the apostolic age. . . . In general our churches appear to me to be nearly on the same footing with the primitive churches." New England Congregationalism, in short, protected "the precious jewel of religious liberty."[82]

Stiles's sermon had the appearance of a learned treatise. But it was a political manifesto as well. Stiles's effort was clearly self-serving. Isaac Backus and New England Baptists would find it flawed to the core. But these were partisan times, and Stiles himself would now take on a very partisan role. He had learned of, and been persuaded by, reports of a vast conspiracy by England to subvert the American colonists. New taxation, alteration of colonial charters, and the planting of bishops—all these punitive actions would soon be visited on Americans, he feared. Stiles heard these rumors in 1764. The Sugar Act followed immediately and the Stamp Act the next year. In fact, though, Stiles had already taken on the bishop issue. Following an initiative that came from Old Side Presbyterian Francis Alison and other Philadelphians, Stiles, beginning in 1755, established a network of correspondence that ran the whole coast of America. It had the singular purpose of alerting all of the colonies to Anglican designs. The effort made Stiles "one of the master minds in defense of colonial dissent" and the "executive secretary of the anti-Episcopal forces." Stiles did more than write letters. He rode the circuit in New England to bring its ministers into a Plan of Union. He had no doubt, as he wrote in a 1766 letter, that thwarting Anglican designs "will require as vigilant and spirited a defense as the first hundred years of the Reformation." We are not surprised to learn that the first meeting of the Union, in 1767, took place at Yale College. There it convened again two years later.[83]

All the while, Stiles used pulpit and epistle to denounce the British imperial policies and he encouraged the American resistance—the tax protests, boycotts, pamphlets, and newspaper pieces. When news of the Stamp Act reached Newport, Stiles made it his sermon subject. In language familiar to a New England audience, he likened the colonies to the old Israelites. God submits them to a trial of tribulation. They should look to their own hearts and purge their own

---

82. Stiles, *Christian Union*, 30–33, 95–96 (the quotation).
83. Bridenbaugh, *Mitre and Sceptre*, 188, 244–45, 274–76 (quotation on p. 275); Morgan, *Gentle Puritan*, 241–43.

sins, he said. God will see them, his latter-day chosen people, through their ordeals, Stiles assured. But he left no doubt that England had become tyrannous and corrupt. He contrasted a surfeit British government, top-heavy with bureaucracy, against the simple norms of the American states. All the events of the day, Stiles urged, pointed to separate directions for the two peoples. The Stamp Act merely showed the extent of alienation between them and the imperative of American independence. "Henceforth," he wrote, "the European and American interests are separated, never more to be joined."[84]

Stiles watched the events of the revolution with an obsession. He sought out reports from battles. He recorded in his diary the news that came his way. Twice he went to the American encampments outside Boston. He turned all he gathered into sermon subjects. He never doubted the righteousness of the American cause but, to be sure, he never neglected to remind Americans of their own sins. The British navy's ravaging of the coastal towns must have something to do, he said, with "the vice and wickedness" one finds in those towns. Newport itself saw the war firsthand. The British had moved in there in December 1776. Many had already left the city when in February the next year the Stiles family, too, departed. They removed to Portsmouth, New Hampshire. An opening had occurred at the church there because its minister, Samuel Langdon, had departed awhile back to become president of Harvard.[85]

Portsmouth would not long be his home. There soon came to him an offer from the Corporation of Yale College to become the school's new president. Stiles pondered it. Friend Samuel West urged him not to accept; Charles Chauncy insisted he must. Months later Stiles saw his way to answer the call of his alma mater. His letter of acceptance listed reasons why he ought not to accept so imposing a challenge, but then he acquiesced; he would answer "the will of God, the ordering of heaven, and the call of divine Providence." So he prepared to depart for New Haven.[86]

By this time Yale College had joined the patriotic movement. Naphtali Daggett, professor of divinity, had become acting president in 1766. His predecessor Thomas Clap had remained wholly aloof from imperial politics, but Daggett showed no such indifference. He entered the fray, as noted earlier, in 1765 when he responded to the Stamp Act with a series of newspaper attacks under the pseudonym "Cato." Daggett held stamp distributor Jared Ingersoll in contempt and attributed sinister designs to the British government in its enacting the tax legislation. Daggett had the same views as Stiles and Alison respecting the design for an American Anglican bishop, convinced as he was that civil and ecclesiastical tyranny went hand in hand.[87]

---

84. Morgan, *Gentle Puritan*, 223, 226–27, 268 (the quotation)–69.
85. Morgan, *Gentle Puritan*, 278–89, 284.
86. *The Literary Diary of Ezra Stiles*, ed. Franklin Bowditch Dexter, 3 vols. (New York: Charles Scribner's Sons, 1901), 2:252, 268 (the quotation).
87. Robson, *Educating Republicans*, 49.

Yale College in 1778 enrolled 132 students. The war had taken a toll, though fighting had not yet come to the seaport. Yale in fact was experiencing significant and exciting change. Beginning in the late 1760s a movement emerged to change the educational program of the college. Two Yale graduates had become tutors and wished urgently to have Yale's curriculum expand to include modern literary subjects. John Trumbull (1767) and Timothy Dwight (1769) were poets and aspired to literary careers. They helped Yale students stage plays (illegal ones) and so inspired them that the corporation responded to their requests for new instruction in history, rhetoric, and belles lettres. Here and at other colleges student literary societies emerged. The other aspirants, Noah Webster and Joel Barlow, graduated Yale in 1778. Patriotic sentiments flourished in all these Yale literati as the beginnings of an American literature stirred in New Haven.[88] In 1776, Yale seniors heard Timothy Dwight give his valedictory address. Both reason and Scripture, he said, assured that America would be the scene of God's millennial kingdom, a glorious Christian empire.[89] Dwight became an army chaplain in the war, served a ministry at Fairfield, Connecticut, and succeeded Stiles as Yale president in 1795.[90]

The war came to New Haven on July 5, 1779. President Stiles looked out from the steeple of the college chapel, telescope to his eye, and saw a large British fleet out in the waters. He soon saw more than two thousand British troops debark. He reacted quickly. He had his family leave New Haven and he closed the college. Some of the students departed quickly for home, but a good seventy or so hastily formed their own militia to fight the British, Stiles's son Ezra, Jr. helping to lead the unit. The regular militia and town volunteers joined them. Former president ex tempore Daggett sniped at the British and soon fell captive to the invaders.[91]

To the Stiles diary reports of the New Haven events we owe much of our knowledge of what happened there. He even drew a map of the scene. He reported the "ravage and plunder" given the town by the British and the damage they did even to what they left behind. Stiles chronicled the offensive with patriotic indignation:

And next morning soon after the evacuation I returned to town, and visited the desolation, dead corpses, and conflagrations. It was a scene of mixed joy and sorrow—plunder, rapes, murder, bayoneting, indelicacies toward the sex, insolence, and abuse and insults towards the inhabitants in general, dwellings and stores just setting on fire at E. Haven in full view, etc., etc., etc—joy and rejoicing that the buildings had escaped the flames in the compact part of the town.[92]

---

88. Kelley, *Yale*, 82; Kenneth Silverman, *A Cultural History of the American Revolution* (New York: Thomas Y. Crowell, 1976), 221–22, 402.

89. Grasso, *A Speaking Aristocracy*, 333.

90. Yale, of course, did not produce only patriots. Where Harvard had its Thomas Hutchinson, Yale had its Jared Ingersoll.

91. Kelley, *Yale*, 93–95.

92. Stiles, *Diary*, 2:351, 354, 357 (the quotation).

In early 1780 Stiles called for a February reopening of the college, but that date saw no alleviation of its financial crisis. The steward had no money to buy food, and the continental currency had no purchasing power besides. Finally, in July Yale reopened, with 116 students back. All the while, Stiles followed the news of the war eagerly and recorded it in his journal. Reports from Yorktown thrilled him, he drew a map of the scene as he imagined it, and when the battle ended, he consulted with one of Washington's men, present at the event, and then modified the map according to his testimony.[93]

The American Revolution signified to Ezra Stiles a moment of divine and world import. In 1783, the year of the Treaty of Paris that formally concluded the war, Stiles appeared before the Connecticut state legislature in Hartford and delivered an election sermon. It wrung with patriotic optimism.

> This great American Revolution, this recent political phenomenon of a new sovereignty arising among the sovereign powers of the earth, will be attended to and contemplated by all nations. Navigation will carry the American flag around the globe itself, and display the thirteen stripes and new constellation at Bengal and Canton, on the Indus and Ganges, on the Whang-ho and the Yang-tse-kiang; and with commerce will import the wisdom and literature of the East. That prophecy of Daniel is now literally fulfilled . . . there shall be a universal traveling to and fro, and knowledge shall be increased. This knowledge will be brought home and treasured up in America, and being here dignified and carried up to the highest perfection, may reblaze back from America to Europe, Asia, and Africa, and illumine the world with truth and liberty.

In Yale's president, American patriotism and love of learning found a happy union.[94]

As in Cambridge and New Haven, the war came home to Providence, Rhode Island, too. In late November 1776, British commander William Howe dispatched General Henry Clinton, with four thousand regulars, to Rhode Island. He took with him a flotilla of ships, staffed by six hundred men, and he had instructions to seize Newport. Clinton was reinforcing an already substantial British force in the colony, which had plundered nearby towns. Inhabitants judged resistance futile and the British quickly occupied the capital. Fifteen miles away, President Manning at Rhode Island College could look out at the large British encampment that stretched to the perimeters of the campus at Providence. He heard "the horrid roar of artillery" and witnessed "scenes of carnage," even as he "was sitting in my house and lying on my bed." The Rhode Island militia itself relocated to Providence, dispersed the students, and took over the college buildings.

---

93. Stiles, *Diary*, 2:570.
94. Stiles, *The United States Elevated to Glory and Honor*. . . (New Haven, Conn.: Thomas & Samuel Green, 1783), 52.

Manning, who had tried so valiantly to get the fledgling college on its feet, now had to announce its closing.[95]

Patriotic fervor had already taken root in Providence and at the college. At its first commencement in 1769 Manning donned a suit of "American manufacture" symbolizing his support of the American boycotts. All seven graduates dressed with similar patriotic show. In 1775 three students petitioned Manning to hold the graduation exercises in private, forsaking the usual great public event. They cited requests of the Continental Congress; they also rendered their plea in fervent patriotic language: "Deeply affected with the distress of our oppressed country, which now, most unjustly, feels the baneful effects of arbitrary power, provoked to the greatest height of cruelty and vengeance by the noble and manly resistance of a free and determined people." So speaking, the students made their request. Manning gave his ready approval: "Be assured that we shall most heartily concur in this, and every measure which has been, or may be, adopted by the grand American Congress, as well as the legislature of this colony, in order to obtain the most complete redress of all our grievances." He urged the need for Americans to regain "those liberties and privileges, both civil and religious, which the Almighty Father of the universe originally granted to every individual of the human race."[96]

In fact, however, the American Revolution had made Manning a troubled man. He did not welcome the rebellion and throughout the war he expressed in letters his hopes for an early end and a renewed peaceful relationship with the mother country. Behind Manning's ambivalence lay the continuing problems of the religious denomination that ran his college. For unlike any other of the American schools, Rhode Island College confronted a dual challenge in the war. Like them, it faced the enmity and real presence of British power. But Rhode Island College, and the Baptists for whom it existed, also faced the power of New England's Standing Order, the established Congregational churches in Massachusetts, Connecticut, and New Hampshire. That confrontation had shaped the early history of the college and now the role its leaders played in the revolutionary years.

Matters between the Baptists and the Standing Order had grown only worse since the opening of the college in 1765. The laws against which Baptists protested had not changed. The legislation of 1727 had exempted Anglicans, Quakers, and Baptists from taxes to the Congregational churches, but that regulation nonetheless insulted Baptist principles of strict separation of church and state. The law requiring certificates to exercise the exemption annoyed the Baptists and gave colony officials opportunities to disqualify them. Social stigma attached to being a "certificate man." Baptist parents complained that their children were outcasts. Often Baptists could not buy land; towns feared declining

95. Roche, *Colonial Colleges*, 109; Reuben Aldridge Guild, *Early History of Brown University, Including the Life, Times, and Correspondence of President Manning, 1756–1791* (Providence, R.I.: Snow & Farnham, 1897), 294.

96. Guild, *Brown University*, 286–87.

property values from their presence. Penalties against refusing to pay taxes could be severe—imprisonment, loss of a cow, loss of land. Sometimes people mocked the Baptists' peculiar religious beliefs. A river baptism might be the occasion for a callous individual to take a pig into the water and dunk it mockingly. Outside Rhode Island, life did not go easily for the Baptists.[97]

The events of the American Revolution inspired the Baptists to take up their case with renewed energy. They had witnessed the civil disobedience of Americans against the Stamp Act in 1765. Readily, they read the revolutionary pamphleteers with their language of natural rights and individual liberties. They saw in the case of the colonists against England their own cause against the Standing Order. And in making it, they consciously copied the cry of Boston's Sons of Liberty: "no taxation without representation." In 1773, New England Baptists decided on their own course of civil disobedience; they would go to jail so that the world would know the unjust lot that was theirs. Isaac Backus stated the Baptist position precisely: "Many who are filling the nation with the cry of LIBERTY and against oppressors [in England] are at the same time themselves violating the dearest of all rights, LIBERTY OF CONSCIENCE." The Sons of Liberty quoted John Locke on the Second Treatise of Government. Backus quoted Locke's *Letters Concerning Toleration*.[98]

Professor McLoughlin identifies two groups of Baptists in the 1770s. One represented an educated segment of that community, urbane and somewhat cosmopolitan. The "Western" Baptists, who played so important a role in establishing Rhode Island College, figured largely in this group, which included President Manning. Although they protested the policies of the Standing Order, they wanted to get along with it. Manning had many friends among the New England clergy. In fact, he never took up pen in public cause against the establishment. John Davis, a trustee of the college, also belonged to the "western brethren." Many in this group wanted their new college to lend a higher prestige to Baptists, to associate them with learning and humane letters, to help them rival the Congregationalists in cultural achievements. The rural Baptists, the second group, were a more feisty lot. They held a militant attachment to their principles. They wanted no intercourse with paedobaptists. They had come out of the Separatist movement in New England, moved away from the Standing Order and into Baptist polity and practice. The rural Baptists had their strong voice in Backus, who, like them, had never gone to college.[99]

The protests of 1773 coincided with the publication of Backus's plea for religious freedom, one of the great documents on that subject in American literature. Backus had seen his mother, brother, and uncle all go to prison for refusal to pay the religion tax in Connecticut. He now worked on committees and wrote

---

97. William McLoughlin, "Massive Civil Disobedience as a Baptist Tactic in 1773," *American Quarterly* 21 (Winter 1969): 711–12, 721.
98. McLoughlin, "Massive Civil Disobedience," 710, 719.
99. McLoughlin, "Massive Civil Disobedience," 716–17.

incessantly to win political reform for his denomination. Backus also spoke as a trustee of Rhode Island College and as a Massachusetts minister. His substantial essay, called "An Appeal to the Public for Religious Liberty," built on a Calvinist perspective, the inherent sinfulness of the human race and its alienation from God. So dividing man from God, Backus also posited a radical dualism of state and church. "The forming of [a] constitution, and appointment of the particular orders and officers of government is left to human discretion," Backus wrote. "Whereas in ecclesiastical affairs we are most solemnly warned not to subject to ordinances, after the doctrines and commandments of men." The churches, he urged, utterly corrupt themselves when they permit their income to be the doings of kings and magistrates. They neglect Jesus' urging that his kingdom is not of this world. And, addressing his New England readership, Backus recalled for them the history of tyranny that grew from kingly domination of the English church. He reminded that audience how that tyranny had driven "our fathers" to seek refuge in this new land. No listener could have missed his point.[100]

Leading Baptists from around the country came to Providence in 1774 to attend the Rhode Island College commencement. The event shows how the college had become a focus for the national Baptist community. The Western Baptists at the meeting then perceived an opportunity. The Boston "Tea Party" of the year before had driven the British to their strongest retaliatory measures yet, collectively known as the Coercive Acts, which included closing of the Boston harbor. Colonists responded out of sympathy for Bostonians and a need for collective action, and they organized the first Continental Congress, to meet in Philadelphia in September. The Baptists now prepared to take their own case to the highest national level. They would send a delegation to Philadelphia to present it before the new congress. Backus and Manning prepared for the trip.

President Manning made the formal presentation of the Baptists' grievances to the Congress while the Baptist group arranged for the distribution of Backus's "Appeal to the Public" to each of the delegates. Manning argued that the emerging struggle with Great Britain had political and religious liberty as its goals. Religious conscience, he argued, could not be put at the mercy of fallible human legislators. "The merciful Father of mankind," he said, was "alone Lord of conscience." Nor did Manning spare details. He reviewed the legislative history of Massachusetts to document the long list of discrimination and abuse. To the enlightened delegates, he also cited "the great Mr. Locke" and the doctrine of natural rights. Certainly, the Baptists captured a larger audience for their case.[101] The New Englanders, however, had no intention of giving ground. Delegates like Sam Adams, John Adams, and Robert Treat Paine showed themselves distinctly

---

100. Isaac Backus, "An Appeal to the Public for Religious Liberty," in *Political Sermons of the Founding Era*, 332, 335 (the quotation), 338.
101. Guild, *Brown University*, 276, 279; William McLoughlin, *Isaac Backus and the American Pietistic Tradition* (Boston: Little, Brown, 1967), 129–31 (the quotation).

unsympathetic. They dismissed the matter as a petty quarrel over a small amount of money.[102]

In fact, the Baptists' strategy may have impaired their cause. When the group arrived in Philadelphia they were joined by supporting Quakers, who shared the Baptists' views on established religion. The Quakers, however, had made known their sympathy to the Crown and contributed heavily to the ranks of Loyalists in the Middle Colonies. The connection did the Baptists no good. Nor did it help that some of the New England Baptists had said that they might even appeal to the king for redress of grievances. In New England the Baptists and Rhode Island College began to get a bad rap. Some called the college loyalist in its sympathies. Ezra Stiles confided anger toward the Baptists to his diary. Their appeal to the king, he said, would injure the revolutionary cause. It would leave the struggle to the Congregationalists in the North and the Anglicans in the South. Stiles resented the Baptists for singling out New England as the source of their oppression, while they fared worse under the Anglicans elsewhere. The next year he censored President Manning in particular. He labeled him "a Tory, affecting neutrality." At every turn, Stiles charged, Manning had shunned patriotic expression, refusing even to pray for Washington's troops. Manning, said Stiles, the "gentle Puritan," "expressed the heart of the bigoted Baptist politicians."[103]

Manning was no Tory, but he could not see the war in quite the patriotic terms that his fellow religionists did, including his colleague Backus, who had no difficulty pledging full support to the American cause. Individuals who ascribed to the revolutionary events the preparation for a new Kingdom of God, Manning believed, had misconstrued things. Such millennial expectations, he said, gave too much spiritual meaning to secular affairs, for the kingdom in question would not be of this world. In fact, Manning even lamented that the revolution had caused a turning away from religion. A revival in the area was flourishing on the eve of April 19, 1775, he reported; then news of Lexington and Concord arrived. Religion had languished ever since, as Manning reported nineteen months later. Increasingly, the war made Manning a man of sorrow. In 1779 he looked out at a population near starvation. He wrote to Moses Brown importuning his help in the face of dire need.[104]

By this time the college had been closed three years. Its buildings had served as housing and hospital for American soldiers. In 1780, Congress, in recognition of its service to the nation, voted compensation for damages and occupation of the college buildings. Two months later Manning summoned Baptists to Providence and presented plans for the reopening of the school. Again the war intervened, however, as Manning received instructions to turn the college into a hospital for French troops. In this role it served until May 1782. By that time the

---

102. McLoughlin, *Backus*, 132; Roche, *Colonial Colleges*, 37.
103. Stiles, *Diary*, 1:474–75; 2:23.
104. Guild, *Brown University*, 296–97. On Backus and the war, see McLoughlin, *Backus*, 134–35, 137.

institution had taken steps to affirm its American identity. It had removed the king and queen of England from the college seal and prepared a new one, made of silver, marking the institution's entry into its American era.[105]

One would have had every reason to expect Dartmouth College to march in patriotic step with Harvard and Yale. It was a Congregational school. Its President, Eleazar Wheelock, had risen from the ranks of the religious Awakeners. They often projected their combativeness, their moral resolve, and their intolerance of anything ungodly against the corrupt British and their oppressive imperial measures. New Light ministers often envisioned vast historical patterns, going back to Israel and Rome, and down through the Stuart era in England, that explained the lapse into despotism now evidenced by a decadent England. And indeed, Wheelock had patriotic feelings. He had wholly identified with the Americans and British in their triumph over the "anti-Christian" Catholic French. He could sermonize at times against the "wanton butcheries" of the British. What, though, do we have, ultimately, from Dartmouth? Tepid responses, equivocation, naive gestures toward reconciliation of the two sides. Dartmouth becomes a virtual non-player in the ranks of collegiate patriotism. Why?[106]

The key lies in politics, and precisely in New Hampshire colonial politics. At Harvard, Yale, and Rhode Island, intellect created politics. At Dartmouth, politics trumped intellect. A previous chapter noted the remarkable alliance of minister and politician, of the Reverend Wheelock and the Governor John Wentworth, that helped create the college in 1768. The alliance also relied upon connections that both partners had made in England. The popular Wentworth had longstanding family connections there and had resided at the Wentworth-Woodhouse estate in Yorkshire for nearly three years in the middle 1760s. He had formed a close, personal friendship with Charles Watson-Wentworth, the marquis of Rockingham, a pillar of English politics and in 1765 head of the new government appointed by George III. Two years later Wentworth received his appointment as royal governor of New Hampshire. Wheelock, too, had used English connections in establishing his college, which bore the name of the Earl of Dartmouth. Lord Dartmouth joined the new British ministry in 1765 in the key position as head of the Board of Trade.[107]

The English connections influenced Wentworth's governorship in every issue. He saw himself as an official of the Crown, as indeed he was. He took office amid the growing hostilities between the colonies and England, but resolved to do his best in preserving, among New Hampshire citizens, a feeling of loyalty and obedience to English authority. The hostile posture taken by Massachusetts peo-

105. Guild, *Brown University*, 333, 335, 337.

106. David McClure and Elijah Parish, *Memoirs of the Rev. Eleazar Wheelock. . .* (1811; New York: Arno Press, 1972), 323; Heimert, *Religion and the American Mind*, 454.

107. Paul W. Wilderson, *Governor John Wentworth & the American Revolution: The English Connection* (Hanover, N.H.: University Press of New England, 1994), 58–59, 63.

ple to the south troubled him considerably. He greatly feared a contagion moving into New Hampshire. But Wentworth, of course, had American friends, too.
In 1770 he accepted an invitation to Harvard, his alma mater, from which he
had graduated in the same year as his friend John Adams. In Cambridge, William
Brattle held an elegant dinner for the New Hampshire governor. Afterwards the
large party went over to the college, to which, as noted earlier, the Massachusetts
legislature had removed. Certainly Wentworth must have wondered how these
two peoples—the British and the Americans—could ever divide.[108]

In fact, the American Revolution never made sense to John Wentworth. The
painful truth of escalating hostilities, however, became increasingly evident. To be
sure, New Hampshire had been quiet in these years and Wentworth congratulated
himself on that fact. Then in 1770, four months before Wentworth's visit to Harvard, the "massacre" in Boston occurred. Now anti-British feelings surged through
New Hampshire. In the interior of the province, towns like Exeter became places
of disaffection and protest. Laborers—mechanics, artisans, and lumbermen—fortified the ranks of the Sons of Liberty and found a fondness for rioting. Congregational clergymen also raised rebellious voices. The best-educated in the colony and
the most prestigious, they lent their pulpit oratory to the growing revolutionary
sentiments. One by one, towns voted to support the boycott of British goods. Four
years later, British reaction to the Boston Tea Party provoked more hostility in
New Hampshire. In May the assembly approved formation of a committee of correspondence with the intention of demonstrating the colony's willingness "to join
all salutary measures . . . for saving the rights and privileges of the Americans."[109]

For all these activities, however, New Hampshire remained probably the
most conservative of the New England colonies. Loyalists concentrated in fair
numbers in the seacoast counties of Rockingham and Strafford, areas of greatest
wealth. British officials and colony officers under the extensive patronage reach
of Wentworth augmented Loyalist ranks. Sometimes Loyalist opinion broke out
in public expression. The town council in Hinsdale denounced "false patriots"
who, they said, disguised their personal ambition and factional interest in the
language of rights. Citizens of Francestown that year resolved to "show our dis-
approbation of all unlawful proceedings of unjust men congregating together as
they pretend to maintain their liberties."[110] Wentworth, however, felt events
crowding in on him.

What Wentworth said in 1774 ("Certain I am that Britain and America have
reciprocal affections, which neither can give up"),[111] Eleazar Wheelock could
have said also. He always felt himself an American patriot, but his pronunciations
on the conflict in process, and into the war, always conveyed qualifications. He

---

108. Wilderson, *John Wentworth*, 136–39, 161–62.
109. Wilderson, *John Wentworth*, 178, 226–27; Elizabeth Forbes Morison and Elting E. Morison, *New Hampshire: A Bicentennial History* (New York: Norton, 1976), 66–67.
110. Wilderson, *Wentworth*, 222, 238; Morisons, *New Hampshire*, 66–67.
111. Wilderson, *Wentworth*, 236.

announced his support of the boycott. But the thing annoyed him, and in 1774 he sought to secure clothing for the school through an intermediary. Wheelock could not wholly sympathize with colonial grievances against England. He believed them excessive and dangerously provocative. He neither endorsed nor understood the extreme reactions of the colonists; the radical wing of the patriot cause suggested to him intemperance and unreason. In a 1775 letter he assessed the work of some local revolutionaries, three months before the outbreak of war.

> There appears to be at and about Coos, a large combination, who under pretense of defending the cause of liberty, are furiously acting in direct opposition to those who are soberly contending for it. They seem not to be contending for those constitutional rights [i.e., under the British Constitution], which we have quietly enjoyed heretofore, but to break up the very constitution itself, and all the invaluable privileges we have had, and enjoyed under it. Some of them appear to be inspired to a great degree, but not from on high, nor with a spirit that disposes them to an imitation of the meek, patient, and humble Immanuel.[112]

Wentworth for his part did not make it easy for himself. His family had a long history in the Anglican Church, and in fact the Church owed its beginnings in New England to the family. In 1769 Wentworth picked up a scheme begun by his uncle Benning. He contrived to arrange for appointment of an Anglican minister each year in the colony. To this end he invoked the help of the Society for Propagation of the Gospel as he would use its reserved lots in the towns. He would begin by appointing a chaplain to his own office. The plan also fit into Wentworth's larger hopes that he could build up allegiance to royal authority in New Hampshire. He knew the risks, to be sure, and in his correspondence for the effort he urged "caution, prudence, and secrecy." It probably matters little that the plan never really took off (only one minister arrived). It did matter that the Congregationalists in New Hampshire knew what the governor was up to.[113]

Then in 1774 Wentworth made a bigger mistake. British General Thomas Gage in Boston needed barracks for his British troops but knew that local artisans would provide no help in building them. So he asked colonial royal governors to help. Wentworth responded. He gathered carpenters at Portsmouth and then dispatched them to Boston. He tried to keep the purpose of the arrangement secret, but soon the scheme became widely known. Again Wentworth was making an effort to bolster royal authority. Furthermore, he took his royal office seriously. He acted, however, at the very time that Portsmouth and other New Hampshire towns were contributing large sums for the relief of Boston. Other communities swore their allegiance to the Continental Congress. Wentworth could see in these actions only the rising tide of "popular tyranny." Now that

---

112. James Dow McCallum, *Eleazer Wheelock* (1939; New York: Arno Press and the New York Times, 1969), 196–97; Wheelock, *Memoirs*, 330 (the quotation).
113. Wilderson, *Wentworth*, 170–71.

tide, in reaction to the carpenters' affair, turned against Wentworth himself. Citizens at Portsmouth labeled him "an enemy to the community."[114]

In the wake of this incident, Wheelock wrote Wentworth a curious letter. And lucky for him that it did not go public. What he said in effect was that he saw nothing wrong in the governor's sending the carpenters. He could "not see what injury the building of those barracks will be to Boston, or to the cause of liberty which is so justly dear to them." Wheelock observed that New York had sent eighty-seven carpenters, so why should some from New Hampshire not take advantage of the situation? And again Wheelock faulted the excesses of those who now were "making a public bustle and clamor" about the incident. Wheelock could think only of the consequences to himself. The all too zealous patriots, he said, would soon bring down upon themselves, and others ("us, the infant settlers of your frontier") the fury of a merciless British army. Wheelock's letter conveyed his profound ambivalence about the expanding conflict. He concluded, "This part of your province is as unanimous and warm (according to their ability) for the defense of that liberty which is threatened, as any part of the continent, and when duty calls, will be as active to do their part; but at the same time are firmly attached to your person, and esteem the past silence of this province, in the controversy, and your Excellency's friendship for your people."[115]

Wheelock did think he could help the cause of reconciliation. He would take advantage of Dartmouth's status as an Indian school by dispatching James Dean, who as a youth had been naturalized among the Oneidas and who had graduated from Dartmouth in 1773, to secure the alliance of all the tribes in the Six Nations with the Americans. It was an ambitious, and naive, hope. But Wheelock feared the worse should war break out. He envisioned massive Indian raids against northern New England and a relocation of American troops away from other scenes of the war to defensive outposts in the north.[116]

Both Wentworth and Wheelock feared that excess on one or both sides would produce a fatal war. Lord Dartmouth, too, in England, championed reconciliation, and even expressed to Wentworth his willingness to support some new kind of union between the colonies and England. Wentworth urged moderation on the part of the British and wished for the return of the Rockingham Whigs to stabilize this by now inflammatory situation.[117] When the guns fired at Lexington and Concord in April 1775, Wheelock reacted bitterly against the British. He wrote to a friend a letter that indicated that in private correspondence, aside from his communications with Wentworth, Wheelock strongly sympathized with the colonists. His letter denounced the British actions as "horrid murders and savage butcheries inhumanly committed under pretense of ordering rebels to obedience."[118]

114. Wilderson, Wentworth, 241–42; Morison, New Hampshire, 70; McCallum, Wheelock, 198.
115. McCallum, Wheelock, 197–98.
116. Wheelock, Memoirs, 328; McCallum, Wheelock, 202.
117. Wilderson, Wentworth, 186, 244.
118. Roche, Colonial Colleges, 69.

One other episode indicates Wheelock's inability to act decisively in the revolution. Seven months after Lexington and Concord Wheelock observed a "day of thanksgiving" in Hanover. He had read that Connecticut had proclaimed the date of November 16 for the observance, and he believed it had done so in response to a request from Congress. It then became known that Congress had specified November 30 for the event and great public pressure now urged Wheelock to make another observance. Wheelock replied, though, that he saw no reason to repeat the observance. A hostile reaction formed against him. The town of Exeter, for example, denounced him as a Tory and an enemy to America. So Wheelock used the day of November 30 to offer a sermon, to be preached at the college, in which he would explain fully why he had acted as he did. He titled his sermon "Liberty of Conscience." It's an impressive piece of equivocation.[119]

Wheelock made his conduct look like an act of sacred principle. He noted that others had urged him to go along with the public clamor for revolution, if only to save his reputation. Some offered to bring in a minister to observe the event in the college hall at Dartmouth. But to hold the day of thanksgiving, merely out of obedience to Congress, to acquiesce in the demands of the "zealous liberty men," Wheelock said, would be "an open affront to the King of Zion." Wheelock used for his text John 18:36, "My kingdom is not of this world." So doing, Wheelock adhered throughout his sermon to a radical dualism. He defined the kingdom of God as one strictly spiritual and having to do only with the "inner man." The kingdoms of men, he said, have to do only with the "outer man." So arguing, Wheelock insisted that "we do violence to these distinctions when honoring worldly authority above godly." Wheelock thus judged it "an open affront to Jesus Christ to repeat what we did a fortnight ago, by keeping this day as an anniversary thanksgiving, purely and only out of obedience and respect to civil authority, or advice of the Congress."[120]

The sermon abounds in confusion. Wheelock maintained that humans have natural rights that are derived from "the God of nature." "And none has the right to take them away." Then he added that it is not so in Christ's kingdom—there is no such thing as a natural right in this spiritual kingdom. "None has right so much as to be, or do, or enjoy the least thing in this kingdom," he said, "but by grant from Christ, and they have it only in and by his right."[121] Wheelock never elaborated his meaning. Did he believe that Christians, or perhaps the "elect" among them, lived outside the secular state? He surely would not endorse such Antinomianism. And where stood those rights granted by "the God of nature"? Were not the British violating them? Wheelock had said as much. So should not Americans react? Calvinists had long employed a dual kingdom theology, but they never failed to give the state its due and to insist on obedience to it so long as rulers did not vio-

---

119. McCallum, *Wheelock*, 200–1.
120. Eleazar Wheelock, *Liberty of Conscience*. . . (Hartford, Conn.: Eben. Watson, 1775), v–viii, 13–15 (the quotation), 17.
121. Wheelock, *Liberty of Conscience*, 16.

late the laws of God. Surely Wheelock did not mean to exclude the Continental Congress from Americans' loyalty. And Wheelock himself had observed the *first* day of thanksgiving when he thought it was Congress's request.

Wheelock avowed no disrespect to Congress and its "wise and prudent counselors." Nor, he proclaimed, did he fault the Continental Congress for effectively having destroyed the British Constitution, revered by Wheelock, while it still professed to restore the union of England and America. And yet he felt compelled to raise the point. So seeming to exonerate himself and uphold his patriotism, Wheelock nonetheless delivered a sermon that was anything but an endorsement of the American cause as it was defined in Philadelphia in 1775.[122]

By the time Wheelock delivered this sermon, his good friend and supporter Governor Wentworth had departed New Hampshire, virtually an outcast among a people that once revered him. The colony's last royal governor would not return. Wheelock himself was already declining in health. The war that he dreaded had come. The man he hoped could prevent it had gone. For the rest of the war he worked for the American cause. But he was running out of strength and running out of money. He wished for a pension, that he might buy a little wine and a little chocolate, as his physicians prescribed. "I wait upon God to provide me in these respects," he said. Wheelock penned these words to a friend in March 1779; he died a month later.[123]

Harvard, Yale, and Rhode Island College contributed to the literature of the American Revolution more than did Dartmouth, pulled as it was to its sponsoring colonial government and the alliance forged between President Wheelock and Governor Wentworth. One might expect that Wheelock, a powerful voice of the Awakening, might otherwise have better defined the patriot cause in northern New England. What the other schools demonstrate to us is the long reach of Puritan Calvinism down to the era of the revolution. We do not see it whole at that time. Rather, we see an extensive heritage selected, adopted, refined, even reformulated for contemporary political application, especially as latter-day Puritans mixed and merged their religious heritage with the classical learning of their collegiate experiences. Harvard, Yale, and Rhode Island personnel—presidents, board members, graduates—all could search the historical and intellectual record and derive from it—as ideology or mythology—the ingredients for patriotic expression. Harvard Congregationalists, Yale Congregationalists, and Rhode Island Baptists could all claim a Calvinist foundation. That heritage could make them, at various times, rivals or even enemies. Yale people saw Harvard going astray. Rhode Island people saw a record of oppression from both of these groups. Yet all three could read the record for their own purposes, and all did so in a manner that helped shape an American political culture.

---

122. Wheelock, *Liberty of Conscience*, 19–20.
123. McCallum, *Wheelock*, 205.

11

⁓

The Colleges and the Revolution: South and Middle

Shortly before he became governor of Virginia in 1779, Thomas Jefferson drafted three radical measures for the new state. One promoted freedom of religion. Another dealt with education, specifically, the creation of an extensive public school system for Virginia. The third proposed radical reforms for the College of William and Mary. Behind the convergence of these three concerns lay a recent history that raised them all to a matter of urgency in the mind of the young politician. Virginia, after all, was in the middle of a war. So what was it about the revolution, and about the college in the course of its events, that compelled Jefferson into these legislative initiatives? The answer is the complex interconnection of college and colonial politics. In the case of America's second oldest college, institutional history took a profound political turn in the era of the American Revolution. We might expect as much. Here lay a college but a short walk from the colony capital, a capital that seethed with revolutionary ideas and emotions in the 1760s and 1770s.

We need to pick up the story in the 1750s, however. Matters between the Anglican Church and its ministers and the aristocratic political leadership of the colony were coming to a head. Anglican clergymen in Virginia still had low esteem in the eyes of the populace and a low social standing besides. The Church of England had never sent its best there, and the people knew it. Many in the clerical ranks had never succeeded in the Anglican ministry at home; they were "peddlars turned into priests," as one Virginian put it, or "a beggarly clergy" in the judgment of another. It was a clergy, furthermore, that had long smarted under the thumbs of the aristocracy, whose powers in the local vestries assured its domination over the ministers.[1]

---

1. Rhys Isaac, "Religion and Authority: Problems of the Anglican Establishment in Virginia in the Era of the Great Awakening and the Parsons' Cause," *William and Mary Quarterly* 3rd Series, 30 (1973): 6–7.

By 1750 many in this group had lived too long with these controls and disparagements. A new mood of self-assertion emerged. The Reverend John Camm spoke for the disaffected ministers in asking, what would be the condition of the Church of England in its home country if the preacher risked his job every time he mustered the courage to fault a leading parishioner?[2] Camm merits our attention, for he was not only an Anglican leader in Virginia but had just become a professor of divinity at William and Mary. Born in England, Camm graduated Trinity College, Cambridge, and came to the colony in 1745. The next year Camm and other clergy, with College of William and Mary personnel in the vanguard, found their cause. The House of Burgesses had passed the first of two measures known as the Two Penny Acts. Clergy were then receiving their salaries in the form of allotments of tobacco. But poor harvests had raised the price of this product, placing many of the colony's poor with their backs to the wall. The burgesses consequently intervened, and the ministers saw a potential bonanza fade from reality. Salaries had long been a grievance with them. They had addressed the burgesses this year and met rebuff. The second act three years later intensified their embitterment. Now the clergy were to receive payment at the fixed rate of twopence per pound. A fiery young Patrick Henry made the case against the ministers in the House of Burgesses and also made a bitter enemy of Camm, who took up the Parsons' Cause, as it has been called. Camm, in fact, took their petition all the way to England. Henry rose to boiling point against the clergy's defiance of the colonial statute. He rebuked these "rapacious harpies" who would, he charged, "snatch from their honest parishioner his last hoecake." Jacob Rowe, Anglican clergyman and new professor of moral philosophy at the college, said that if any of the "scoundrels" in the legislature who supported the two-penny legislation sought communion from him he would refuse them.[3]

William and Mary College could not escape this conflict; indeed, it found itself in the thick of it. In part, it inherited that implication. Its charter gave the Corporation of the College the power to hold and manage its revenues, but a lay governing board, called the Visitors, had the power to select the president and faculty and to make the statutes for its structure and its rules of operation. The Visitors, eighteen in number, also elected their own head, the rector. The college in turn had a direct political function in the colony, for it could send its own representative to the legislature. The Visitors, generally embracing those aristocrats that had dominated the Anglican clergy through the parish vestries, had no sympathy with that group in the Parsons' Cause. They had no sympathy either for those faculty at the college who supported the ministers.

2. Isaac, "Anglican Establishment," 10.

3. Henry Mayer, *A Son of Thunder: Patrick Henry and the American Republic* (Charlottesville: University Press of Virginia, 1991), 64–65; Susan H. Godson et al., *The College of William and Mary: A History, Volume I, 1693–1888* (Williamsburg, Va.: King and Queen Press, 1993), 90, 95.

Consequently, they fired every one of them, including Camm. So Camm went to England carrying a second protest, and on this one he had success. He returned in 1763 holding an Order-in-Council reinstating him and his allies and winning back pay besides.[4]

That ploy won him no favor with the Visitors, of course. They then created the statute of 1763, joined in the effort by Governor Francis Fauquier, who held Camm in contempt, so much so that he told his servants and slaves not to let him into the Governor's Palace anymore. The new law virtually destroyed all faculty autonomy, bringing it and the president under strict supervision. Again the faculty, over the course of a four-year fight, responded, replying that the act violated the original charter and once again taking its case to England. In this effort Camm joined with new president James Horrocks, who had been professor of humanity. (The Visitors had made him president because as a faculty member he alone had sworn an allegiance to the statutes, but he made his peace with Camm and now turned against the Visitors.) Camm and Horrocks sought a new charter from the Crown. Power soon shifted in their favor. Fauquier died in 1768 and that year Horrocks became commissary. His alliance with Camm faded, but all this resistance to the Visitors and the House of Burgesses had left Camm and the clergy as marked men in the colony—enemies, even traitors.[5]

Some historians have seen in the Parson's Cause controversy the stirrings of sentiments that would rekindle in the events that led to the American Revolution. Anticlericalism became associated with an emerging Whig ideology that would promote republican political ideals. One individual in this early conflict exhibited such notions. The fight against the ministers found a leader in the House of Burgesses, Richard Bland. His work evidences William and Mary College's role, even before Jefferson, in influencing a liberal political leadership in the colony.

The Bland ancestry in the colonies went back to 1654 to Theodorick Bland. The family rose in stature, and later Richard Bland, Sr., sold family lands to William Byrd I, who thereby established his Westover estate. Richard Bland, born in 1710, studied at William and Mary, began a legal career in 1746, and then served on the Board of Visitors. He became known as an immensely learned individual and "the most active member of America's oldest legislature." His actions in the Parsons' Cause made him the major polemicist against the ministers, writing *A Letter to the Clergy of Virginia* (1760) and *The Colonel Dismounted* (1764), pamphlets that required Camm to write rebuttals. Bland carried his political commitments into the era of the revolution. The year after passage of the Stamp Act he wrote *An Inquiry into the Rights of the British Colonies*. He secured

---

4. Robert Folk Thomson, "The Reform of the College of William and Mary, 1763–1780," *Proceedings of the American Philosophical Society* 115 (1971): 188, 190.

5. Thomson, "Reform," 191, 194; Isaac, "Anglican Establishment," 16; Godson et al., *William and Mary*, 97, 106.

his philosophy solidly in John Locke, fortified by other Whig writers and the ancient classics, especially Thucydides and Tacitus.[6]

Meanwhile, a familiar, and always divisive, issue was emerging in Virginia—
the American bishop controversy. This issue, the effort to establish such an office in the colonies, had heretofore been a northern initiative. Southern Anglicans had reacted with only indifference to it. But in 1766 Samuel Johnson,
president of King's College, recognized that the bishop prospect had no hope of
success without southern backing. He then approached Virginia Anglicans and
found his way to Camm, such was his reputation as an ardent Anglican. Johnson
presented the matter to Camm as a device needed to stay the tide of insurgent
Presbyterians in the colonies. He found a ready ear in Camm, who in turn took
the matter to Horrocks, now the college president. Camm also issued An Appeal
to the southern clergy to ignite interest in the bishop cause. Horrocks pursued
the matter by calling for a convention of the Virginia clergy, to be held in June
1771, an action for which Bland accused him of eyeing the prize himself. Also,
it appeared that William and Mary's role in the campaign might gain additional
force from the arrival of two young Anglican ministers, who now joined the college faculty. Samuel Henley, new professor of moral philosophy, and Thomas
Gwatkin, new professor of mathematics, had arrived in Williamsburg in 1770.[7]

Camm took the lead in drafting a proposal for the convention, but it hardly
had an auspicious beginning. Only eleven of some one hundred clergy even
bothered to respond to the invitation. Then Camm could get only an eight-to-
four vote on behalf of his proposal. Worse for him, and to the surprise of many,
Henley and Gwatkin joined the dissenters and clearly made known their strong
opposition to the bishop plan. Both thought the petition dangerously inflammatory. It would circumvent the established political offices of the colony, an "indecent" action, they said. The movement, then, they feared, could have only
alienating effects between the colonies and the mother country, thus threatening "the very existence of the British Empire in America." Henley labeled the
bishop idea "a hobby horse no less pregnant with mischief than the insidious gift
to Troy." When Anglicans in New York and New Jersey faulted the two faculty
members for their action, Gwatkin issued a lengthy reply. He, and Henley even
more so, were often given to fiery invective and biting sarcasm. Gwatkin said
that he opposed all episcopates, and he saw in this "new fangled episcopate" a
merely political device that had no spiritual dimension to it whatsoever. Thus,
in Virginia, the strongest pleas for and against an American bishop issued from
the William and Mary campus. The matter had no support in the Virginia legislature, which, in fact, specifically resolved an expression of thanks to Henley and

---

6. Clinton Rossiter, "Richard Bland: The Whig in America," William and Mary Quarterly 3rd Series, 10 (1953): 33–79; Carl J. Richard, The Founders and the Classics: Greece, Rome, and the American Enlightenment (Cambridge, Mass.: Harvard University Press, 1994) 76, 82.

7. Carl Bridenbaugh, Mitre and Sceptre: Transatlantic Faiths, Ideas, Personalities, and Politics,
1689–1775 (London: Oxford University Press, 1962), 317–18; Godson et al., William and Mary, 119.

Gwatkin for their opposition to the idea. By this time, too, the issue had entered the public domain through an extensive and angry pamphlet warfare.[8]

Political tensions at William and Mary swelled in the early 1770s as the colonies moved toward revolution. Loyalist personalities at the college considered their institution an arm of the Crown and the Church and the noblest extension of England into the colonies. The Visitors, however, had several members who were taking the lead in condemning British imperial policy. They made things unpleasant for Tories at the college. Horrocks left Virginia and returned to England in 1771 after the bishop effort fizzled. He died there two years later. Camm won election as president but cooled his political passions upon assuming the office. (Perhaps, too, marriage had mellowed him. In 1769 at age fifty-one, bachelor Camm married the fifteen-year-old Elizabeth Hansford, by whom he would have five children.) Henley and Gwatkin showed themselves loyal to the king and constituted the main Tory presence in the faculty. Whig sentiments, however, gained almost year by year. After the news of Lexington and Concord reached Virginia, some of the college students volunteered to join the new continental army, including future American president James Monroe. That year, 1775, Henley and Gwatkin departed and, with royal governor Lord Dunmore, also returned to England. Two years later, patriots gained control of the Visitors, bringing Edmund Randolph, Benjamin Harrison, and Thomas Jefferson to those offices. Camm refused to recognize the revolutionary government in Virginia, and the Visitors removed him from office, he too returning to England that year. They put in the presidency the rising star of the William and Mary campus, the young professor James Madison.[9]

Madison was born near Staunton, on the rim of the Virginia frontier, in 1749. He early on knew the two future American presidents from this region—his cousin and like-named James Madison, and Thomas Jefferson. Young James entered William and Mary in 1768 and established an exemplary academic record, especially in science. He prepared for the law by study with George Wythe, but decided to dedicate himself to his favorite academic subject. Through Jefferson's good offices he became William and Mary's professor of natural philosophy in 1773.[10]

---

8. Arthur Lyon Cross, *The Anglican Episcopate and the American Colonies* (1902; Hamden, Conn.: Archon Books, 1964), 232–33, 235; Ray Hiner, Jr., "Samuel Henley and Thomas Gwatkin: Partners in Protest," *Historical Magazine of the Protestant Episcopal Church* 37 (1968): 42 (Henley quotation); Bridenbaugh, *Mitre and Sceptre*, 319–21; Thomson, "Reform," 198; George William Pilcher, "The Pamphlet Warfare on the Proposed Virginia Anglican Episcopate, 1767–1775," *Historical Magazine of the Protestant Episcopal Church* 30 (1961): 266–79.

9. John F. Roche, *The Colonial Colleges in the War for American Independence* (Millwood, N.Y.: Associated Faculty Press, 1986), 74, 133–35; Hiner, "Henley and Gwatkin," 49–50; Cross, *Anglican Episcopate*, 231n; Godson et. el., *William and Mary*, 85, 107.

10. Charles Crowe, "The Reverend James Madison in Williamsburg and London, 1768–1771," *West Virginia History* 24 (1964): 270–72. [Note: the dates cited in the title are misleading; the terminal date is 1777.]

Bishop James Madison

The year before, as a student, Madison delivered a remarkable address at the college. Virginia would soon know that this young Anglican was an American patriot to the core, and would soon be the most prominent Whig voice on the campus. Madison's oration reverberated with Lockean notions, virtually recapitulating the contract theory of government. Thus, he said, when man leaves the state of nature and enters into society, he entrusts those natural rights, his birthrights, that his original condition bequeaths him, to the state. The foundation of government, nonetheless, remains "the will of the people." Citizens, Madison said, should be vigilant about those rights, lest they allow themselves to become slaves. Madison's address celebrated liberty. "Tempered by reason," he said, "civil liberty becomes the parent of every social blessing, invigorates the mind, gives it a bold and noble turn."[11]

---

11. James Madison, *An Oration in Commemoration of the Founders of William and Mary College* . . . (Williamsburg, Va.: William Rind, 1772), 6–8 (the quotation).

As did so many public addresses of the day, Madison's had an historical ret-rospect. However, whereas New Englanders turned to their Puritan ancestors to make the connections between their struggles and that of their contemporaries against British tyranny, the Anglican Madison looked to a different source for the comparison. Using the occasion of an anniversary celebration of the college, Madison hailed "our royal founder" King William as England's salvation from the oppressive Stuart kings. For under the last Stuart, said Madison, "the voice of law was heard no more. Vice rioted with impunity, perjury received its sanction from regal authority, the perversion, nay, the abolition of justice triumphed under the auspices of Jefferies and James." Religion, too, said Madison, lay corrupted by the monarch's hand. Then "Britain awoke, as from a dream, waved the standard of freedom," and found its salvation in William. He "brought on the auspicious day," said Madison. "His influence dispelled each fear, renewed the laws, eman-cipated religion, burst each mental fetter, and set reason free." The lesson was clear. English people could strike back at despotic kings. George III should take note.[12]

Madison's appointment set the stage for major change at William and Mary. It made possible the thoroughgoing reforms that Jefferson would send three years later to the Visitors. We last took note of Jefferson as he graduated from William and Mary in 1762 and embarked on a course of reading for the legal profession under the tutelage of George Wythe. Wythe contrived a rigorous program. Jef-ferson submitted to a seven-hour morning regime that had him reading "ethics, religion, and natural law," including Cicero, Locke, Condorcet, Lord Kames, and Francis Hutcheson's *Introduction to Moral Philosophy*. Rebounding from a lunch break, the young scholar then took on politics: Locke, Sidney, Joseph Priestley, Montesquieu, mixed with some economics from Thomas Say. He read Scottish historian William Robertson on Charles V and other writers on English and American history. He saved the evenings for belles lettres, criticism, rhetoric, and oratory.[13]

But it was Edward Coke, the great English jurist, who constituted the heart of Jefferson's reading for the law. Wythe had cut his legal teeth on Coke. And Jefferson would have no easy time with this legal scholar. (He wrote to his friend John Page in 1762: "I do wish the devil had old Cooke [sic], for I am sure I never was so tired of an old dull scoundrel in my life."[14]) Wythe had derived from the master a sustained critique of the Stuart monarchs that would furnish him with revolutionary sentiments in the ensuing years. And this understanding of Coke facilitated Jefferson's rendering of English history as well as the Saxon myth that he came to embrace.

12. Madison, *An Oration*, 9; see also, Charles Crowe, "Bishop James Madison and the Republic of Virtue," *Journal of Southern History* 30 (1964): 58–70.

13. Willard Sterne Randall, *Thomas Jefferson: A Life* (New York: HarperPerennial, 1994), 56.

14. *The Papers of Thomas Jefferson*, ed. Julian P. Boyd, Volume I: *1760–1776* (Princeton, N.J.: Princeton University Press, 1950), 5.

As explained by Jefferson biographer Merrill Peterson, the Saxon myth posited the roots of democracy in the early Saxons of Germany, who carried them in their migration to the British Isles. The Norman conquest of the eleventh century supplanted these seedling institutions with monarchy. English history thereafter followed a cyclical pattern as different groups sought to restore the Saxon legacy, making some gains, and then yielding to the resurgent tides of royal despotism. Thus, as Peterson summarizes:

> The recurring struggle thenceforth characterized English history. Magna Charta opened a new epoch by restoring, substantially, the original constitution. Usurpation ever threatened, however, and under the Stuarts in the seventeenth century English liberty and self-government were again destroyed. The Long Parliament, the Commonwealth, the Restoration—these turbulent chapters were brought to a close by the Glorious Revolution of 1688. Alas, corruption and vice and new forms of oppression—standing armies, septennial parliaments, ministerial influence—soon spoiled the promising new epoch. In the eyes of belligerently libertarian Englishmen of the eighteenth century, salvation lay in return to the track of the ancient constitution.

And such was Jefferson's commitment to the Saxon myth that any challenge to it vexed him considerably, as particularly in his long struggles with the English histories of the Scotsman David Hume.[15]

When the Stamp Act hit the colonies in 1765, Jefferson became wholly obsessed with politics. At the capital he and fellow law students stood outside the burgesses' chamber and listened enthralled as Patrick Henry excoriated the British. They heard the cries of "treason, treason!" as some shocked and outraged legislators recoiled in horror at Henry's denunciations. Jefferson, as was his nature, turned the political challenge defined by Henry into an intellectual challenge for himself. He now took up a massive reading project, one that would join philosophy to politics. He read Viscount Bolingbroke, his most valuable source, for in him Jefferson found confirmation of his religious deism and his growing critique of the institutional church as the corrupted institution of Christianity. Jefferson's own career took a political advance in 1768 when he won election to the House of Burgesses. Virginia governor Lord Botetourt had that year dissolved the legislature that would now meet in defiance of him. His action, legal but arrogant, prompted Jefferson's new resolve to move from political study to political action. Just six years later he won deserved renown for his writing of A Summary View of the Rights of British America and, of course, two years later the Declaration of Independence.[16]

With respect to the college, however, it was the subject of religion and the church that most underscored Jefferson's efforts to redesign the academic program and structure of William and Mary. Jefferson shared the general disdain of

---

15. Merrill D. Peterson, *Thomas Jefferson and the New Nation: A Biography* (New York: Oxford University Press, 1970), 57–61. The quotation is on p. 58. Douglas L. Wilson, "Jefferson vs. Hume," *William and Mary Quarterly* 3rd Series, 46 (1989): 49–70.

16. Randall, *Jefferson*, 76–78, 85–86, 119.

the Virginia aristocracy for the Anglican ministry in the colony. He had already come to define the church–state alliance of England as a problem factor in the whole range of imperial issues. The connection thwarted Virginia's political autonomy, he believed, and perpetuated its subservience to England. It yielded up from the colonial ministry aggressive and ambitious clergy like Horrocks, of whom Jefferson said "with this gentleman I believe no farther than I can see." Jefferson wanted to undermine the connection and did so by examining the historical record, looking for the constitutional foundation of Anglican privilege in English law. He found none and argued so in his piece "Whether Christianity is a Part of the Common Law." Jefferson took on some noted legal scholars—Sir Matthew Hale and Sir William Blackstone—in making his case. He searched the records for the five hundred years before Magna Carta and could find no evidence of incorporation and nothing more than the codification of the Ten Commandments and their inscription into the common law under King Alfred in the ninth century. Jefferson's readings in English history had already led him to conclude that the laws of England and America were distinct and separate, and that the colonies were tied to England only by king and not by Parliament. He had now completely undermined Anglican authority in Virginia.[17]

Jefferson's religious beliefs and his now emphatic views of church–state relations would lead to authorship of his famous bill for religious freedom in Virginia. But the submission of that bill in 1779 acquires a significant context when we review Jefferson's almost simultaneous efforts to construct a system of public education in the state and to reform the College of William and Mary. The college issue brought the other two into a critical juxtaposition.

At the college, James Madison had helped prepare the way for Jefferson's reforms. Madison, as noted, assumed his professorship at William and Mary in 1773. Two years later he departed for England and there received ordination in the Anglican Church. He pursued his scientific interests while abroad and achieved an admirable record in his field. But Madison never abandoned his passionate interest in politics. He had discussed the subject at length with Jefferson and Wythe in Williamsburg, and in England news of the war's outbreak regenerated his patriotism. He believed that American colleges would play a principal role in the new national mission and he wanted to be part of it. He returned to Virginia in the summer of 1776. The very next year the new Board of Visitors made Madison president of the college, a position he would hold until his death in 1812. In 1790, Madison became Virginia's first Anglican bishop. But for now, he welcomed the opportunity to work with Jefferson in making William and Mary an instrument of republicanism.[18]

Revolutionary events had quickened Jefferson's thinking about education in America. In 1776 he undertook not only the formidable challenge of preparing

17. Peterson, *Jefferson*, 60; Randall, *Jefferson*, 135–37, 203; *Papers of Thomas Jefferson, Volume 1*, 61 (the quotation).

18. Crowe, "Bishop James Madison," 272–78.

drafts for the new Virginia state constitution, but he also worked with Wythe, George Mason, and Edmund Pendleton on the Committee to Revise the Laws of the Commonwealth. Jefferson took on the subject of education himself and from his efforts came one of the most famous statements about public education in America, the preamble to Jefferson's "A Bill for the More General Diffusion of Knowledge." Jefferson's eloquent language summarized the key point in his thinking: public education is a bulwark against tyrannical government. A wise and informed citizenry, he wrote, alone can prevent those abuses to which any form of government may succumb. Jefferson then went on to detail his plan for a layered structure of public education in the new state. At a time when public education simply did not exist in the American South, Jefferson's document constituted a bold new vision and remains a landmark in the historical literature of American education.[19]

Jefferson's bill dealing with William and Mary followed. He conceded in his document that the college had not answered the expectations of the public. He wanted to secure its more certain financial support by the legislature, and he sought a structural reconfiguration, too. Jefferson proposed to reduce the Board of Visitors to five and to have them appointed by the legislature, annually. All English connections, religious and legal, would now be severed, including the "canons or constitution of the English church as enjoined in [the original] charter." So zealous was Jefferson, in fact, to disconnect William and Mary from its ecclesiastical past and to secure it as a state-affiliated public institution that he imposed a troubling restriction on the faculty, who, the bill prescribed, "before they enter on the execution of their office . . . shall give assurance of fidelity to the commonwealth, before some Justice of the Peace."[20] A test oath, in short.

Jefferson's proposed curricular reforms have attracted most of the interest in this document. He specified establishment of eight professorships. The new education would highlight ethics, mathematics, and science, and bring into new and higher prominence history, the modern languages, and the fine arts. The schematic chart that Jefferson included in his bill inscribed an expansive array of course subjects within the eight major fields. Thus under ethics he included the law of nations, under fine arts gardening and architecture, under law common law and ecclesiastic law and the law of commerce, under mathematics acoustics and astronomy, and under language Anglo-Saxon, Icelandic, and Hebrew. Jefferson also made an unprecedented break from a Eurocentrist curriculum. His bill read: "The said professors shall likewise appoint, from time to time, a missionary, of approved veracity, to the several tribes of Indians, whose business shall be to investigate their laws, customs, religions, traditions, and more particularly their

---

19. Lawrence Cremin, *American Education: The Colonial Experience, 1607–1783* (New York: Harper & Row, 1970), 438–40; *Papers of Thomas Jefferson, Volume 2, 526–35*; Randall, *Jefferson*, 303–5. This plan was not put into place until 1796.

20. *Papers of Thomas Jefferson, Volume 2, 538–40*.

languages, constructing grammars thereof."[21] Finally, gone from the reconstituted college was the professorship in religion.

Jefferson prepared to see his proposed statute through the Virginia legislature, but in the meantime a letter arrived to him in early 1779. It came from Samuel Stanhope Smith, then rector of an academy in Virginia. He was the son-in-law of John Witherspoon of Princeton and later president of that college. Smith took great interest in what Jefferson was trying to do in his plan for the diffusion of knowledge. "The nature of the design," he told the author, "must recommend it to every lover of leaning and of his country." It recalled the wisdom of antiquity, he added, "when legislation and philosophy were always connected, and but different parts of the same sage characters." But Smith also said that he foresaw trouble. He and Jefferson knew that Virginia now flourished with many different religious groups, each jealous of its own interests. The emerging contest, Smith specified, will center on Anglicans and Presbyterians. Smith referenced Jefferson's making William and Mary the capstone of the public school structure in the state, whose officials had, as he understood the matter, the power to prescribe the instructional programs for the lower schools.[22] All was at stake, then, in control of the college. As it was now constituted, that is, as an Anglican-dominated school, Smith warned that Presbyterians would fight the scheme tooth and nail. To be sure, Smith wrote as a Presbyterian himself, but he had genuine interests in helping Jefferson secure the noble goals of his plan. "The partiality of sects," he wrote, "ought to have no place in a system of liberal education. They are the disgrace of science and would to heaven it were possible utterly to banish them from the society of men."[23]

We do not have Jefferson's reply to Smith. But Jefferson knew only too well how effectively Smith had placed his remarks. Smith was saying that so long as the Anglican Church had a privileged place in Virginia then so would the college remain an extension of Anglican influence. The issue of establishment was very much alive in Virginia at the time that Smith wrote. In 1776 George Mason had prepared the draft for the new Virginia Bill of Rights. Patrick Henry wrote the important sixteenth provision stating the principle of religious freedom. Religion, the provision said, should be directed by "reason and conviction"; it could not be secured through force or violence. The bill of rights therefore said that "all men are equally entitled to the free exercise of religion, according to the dictates of conscience." Article 16, however, eluded the question of establishment.[24] Baptists therefore protested the document on this point. Jefferson and

---

21. *Papers of Thomas Jefferson, Volume 2*, 540 (the quotation)–42.

22. Jefferson's words on the matter said that an overseer shall be appointed, over every ten schools, and will ascertain that "any general plan of reading and instruction recommended by the visitors of William and Mary College shall be observed" (*Papers of Thomas Jefferson, Volume 2*, 528–29).

23. *Papers of Thomas Jefferson, Volume 2*, 247–48.

24. "The Virginia Bill of Rights," in *Documents of American History*, ed. Henry Steele Commager, 4th ed. (New York: Appleton-Century-Crofts, 1948), 104.

John Witherspoon

the young James Madison of Orange County wanted complete disestablishment
of the Anglican Church in Virginia. Anglican landed gentry still prevailed in the
legislature, however, and the more radical reformers could secure only the repeal
of all acts that suppressed dissenters and a bill that exempted them from paying
taxes to support the Anglican clergy. Nonetheless, Anglicanism remained the established church in Virginia, however much the meaning of that term had now
shifted.[25]

 Jefferson evidently replied to Smith, for Smith's second letter thanked him
for correcting some misunderstandings in the first. Smith did reassert that he had
never found the case for established religion convincing. His letter suggested endorsement of a "religion of nature," by which, he said, God first instructed the
human race; the state should then be content to let each group decide how to
put that religion into worship as it sees fit. Smith had hoped that "the enlight-

---

25. Randall, *Jefferson*, 290–91.

ened sentiments of the age" would have brought the Christian groups into a tol-erant unity. Now the situation in Virginia grew worse, he feared, and "I foresee a contest between these two parties." And he feared that the Anglicans would cling tenaciously to what power remained to them. Herein the problem with the college: despite Jefferson's reforms, Smith feared, they did not assure dislocation of the Anglicans as the controlling force. That perception would deny to the leg-islation, valuable as it was, the needed support to secure it.[26]

Of course, Jefferson needed no further persuasion to commit to complete dis-establishment. But we have the suggestive fact that Jefferson placed his famous bill for establishing religious freedom before the Virginia legislature just six weeks after Smith wrote him his urgent letter. And Jefferson, one should notice, won election as the new governor but three days before Smith wrote him, though he had not yet assumed his office. He penned in the bill his passionate convictions for intellectual freedom and the evils in all efforts, and most dangerously of the state, to curtail it. The bill prescribed that no person shall suffer any restrictions in choice of worship and endure no compulsion to support any religion. Nor should any civil penalties inhere in the profession and advocacy of any religious faith. It would take until 1786 for Jefferson to secure the legislative victory he sought for this bill. But he considered its triumph one of the great accomplish-ments of his life.[27]

Jefferson had one thing more to do to square the college reforms with the American Revolution. The creation by Jefferson, as provided in his William and Mary bill, of the first law professorship in the United States had much logic to it. In his Summary View of 1774 Jefferson outlined a legal crisis that had emerged between the colonies and England. Statutory laws, he indicated, had evolved from the different colonial legislatures. Jefferson did not then claim superiority of these laws and acknowledged that colonial legislation had legitimacy only within the larger parameters of the British Constitution. He did assert, however, that George III had wantonly abused his right of veto in a manifestation of con-tempt toward the colonies. "For the most trifling reasons, and sometimes for no conceivable reason at all," Jefferson wrote, "his majesty has rejected laws of the most salutary tendency."[28] He thus became concerned with the legitimacy of colonial law, and in Virginia, as noted, he worked, upon independence, for a complete rewriting of the Virginia statutes. Indeed, that work represented for him the major achievement and opportunity of the independence that revolu-tion sought to secure.

Just as logical was Jefferson's wish to have George Wythe occupy the new pro-fessorship. His former mentor had risen to a place of highest prominence in Vir-ginia law, and his occupying the new position would give it maximum prestige,

---

26. *Papers of Thomas Jefferson*, Volume 2, 253–54.
27. *Papers of Thomas Jefferson*, Volume 2, 545–46; Randall, *Jefferson*, 292–94.
28. From the *Summary View* in *Papers of Thomas Jefferson*, Volume 1, 129–30.

Jefferson believed. Wythe has frustrated biographers by leaving so few records. We do know that his father, Thomas Wythe III, had represented Elizabeth City County in the House of Burgesses. He married Margaret Walker, who profoundly influenced young George's early intellectual growth. Wythe learned the law mostly on his own and no evidence substantiates earlier assertions that he attended William and Mary. In 1746, he gained the right to practice in the county courts and rose rapidly in rank thereafter. He had mastered immense learning in classical scholarship, and his reputation spread for this achievement as well. Wythe won election to the house in 1754 and in 1758 became William and Mary's representative to that body. With passage of the Stamp Act, he became an early partisan of the patriot cause. Wythe served as a delegate to the Continental Congress in 1775 and signed the Declaration of Independence the next year.[29] He began his professorship in Richmond in 1779, where the capital had moved. From there Jefferson wrote the next year to Madison:

> Our new institution at the college has had a success which has gained it universal applause. Wythe's school is numerous. They hold weekly courts and assemblies in the capitol. The professors join in it; and the young men dispute with elegance, method, and learning. This single school by throwing from time to time new hands well principled and well informed into the legislature will be of infinite value.[30]

Almost to the end of the revolution William and Mary had escaped the military disturbances of the war. To be sure, the college struggled with loss of income and declining enrollment, but not until 1781 did Lord Cornwallis's southern campaign bring the battles close to Williamsburg. At that time William and Mary became the last of the colonial colleges to undergo military occupation. In June British forces marched to the capital and held the town for a month. Cornwallis made Madison's house his army headquarters.[31] The college closed for a year, but in November Cornwallis surrendered his forces to General Washington. As events moved toward that culminating scene of the revolution, President Madison gave a thanksgiving day address at Botetourt County. He painted a bright future for the United States, a nation providentially blessed.

> America has become the theater, whereon the providence of God is now manifested—America is now holding forth the display of divine power, which shall excite the wonder and gratitude of posterity. . . . America! . . . shall long invigorate the heart of virtue, shall long instruct the astonished world, that perseverance in the cause of justice, in the defense of those rights which God hath given, will ever find a protecting guardian in the ruler of the universe.[32]

---

29. This information is summarized from chapters I to II of Richard B. Kirtland, *George Wythe: Lawyer, Revolutionary, Judge* (New York: Garland Randall Publishing, 1986).
30. *Papers of Thomas Jefferson, Volume 3*, 507.
31. Roche, *Colonial Colleges*, 119–20.
32. Reverend James Madison, *A Sermon Preached in the County of Botetourt* . . . (Williamsburg, Va.: n.p., 1781), 11.

Nothing more clearly indicated that William and Mary College had moved away from its Anglican past and taken on an American identity. But the transition here also offers an instructive history. The experience of the English Church in the southern American colonies did not produce a heroic age from which patriots, like the collegiate generations in New England, could draw. But also, the liberal and rational intellectual tradition in Anglicanism did not inspire in America sustaining loyalty to the Church; it seems in fact to have conspired against institutional affection for it. With some irony, then, this liberalism, when merged with the lessons of the ancient classical authors, English Whigs, and the Saxon myth, led Virginians to turn against England and its American church. In doing so, they severed their college from its Anglican roots.

When future president of the United States Woodrow Wilson spoke at the sesquicentennial of Princeton College in 1896 he made his theme "Princeton in the nation's service." He looked to the institution's future, but he could summon the past, too. Its historian could rightly call Princeton "a school of statesmen." Patriotism had early been a part of its outlook. Samuel Davies found millennial themes in the Seven Years' War, and Samuel Finley, especially in a memorable piece titled *The Curse of Meroz* in 1757, called for unwavering support for the British and American cause against the French. Princeton produced an impressive number of graduates who made political life their calling and who served visibly in the formative years of the nation. One became president of the country, four served in the Continental Congress, twenty-one entered the United States Congress and twenty-one the Senate. Fifty-six became state legislators, three became justices of the United States Supreme Court, and another was attorney general. They all had studied with President John Witherspoon, whom Garry Wills has called "probably the most influential teacher in the entire history of American education." He adds, "There are times when the Constitutional Convention must have looked like a reunion of Princetonians." Witherspoon turned Princeton from a school of ministers into a school of politicians.[33] The transformation involved him, as well as the college and its graduates, in the complexity of New Jersey colonial politics. Nearby Queen's College also committed to the patriot cause in the revolution. It, too, found itself caught in the matrix of colony politics. Struggling institution though it was, it furnished personnel zealous for the success of the rebellion.

Witherspoon's arrival at Princeton from Scotland in 1768 coincided with the early events of the revolution. He landed in Philadelphia just as news came from Boston that merchants there had signed a non-importation agreement and that citizens had gathered at Faneuil Hall and resolved to defend their liberties "at the utmost peril of their lives and fortunes." The college community that soon greeted him was already charged with political fervor. Student speakers at the September

---

33. Thomas Wertenbaker, *Princeton: 1746–1896* (Princeton, N.J.: Princeton University Press, 1946), 76, 115–16; Garry Wills, *Explaining America: The Federalist* (New York: Penguin, 1981), 18, 19 (the quotations).

commencement exercises took on topics like "Civil Liberty" and "Patriotism." Two years later Witherspoon's son James, speaking in Latin, defended resistance to tyrannical kings, while John Ogden defended the non-importation agreements as "a noble example of self-denial and public spirit." Frederick Frelinghuysen, future instructor at Queen's College, urged the importance of American economic independence from Great Britain.[34] Particularly memorable were the commencement events of 1771. Here the two Princeton graduates Philip Freneau and Hugh Henry Brackenridge offered their patriotic salute, A *Poem, on the Rising Glory of America*. Princeton thus joined Yale in contributing to an early nationalistic literature.[35]

When Witherspoon came to Princeton it had 115 students. He sought a larger school and a national influence for the college. Witherspoon traveled widely and made important contacts in his effort, especially in the South. And "the President never returned empty-handed." He won financial contributions for the college and made valuable connections. In Virginia he met the Lees, the Madisons, and the Washingtons. Increasingly, the contacts had profound political implications. In the summer of 1774 New England delegates passed through Princeton on their way to the first meeting of the Continental Congress. Silas Deane visited the college, and then John Adams arrived. Adams and the president discussed the political situation and shared each other's company at the nearby tavern. Adams recorded his impression that the Scotsman was "as high a son of liberty as any man in America." And the president seemed to reflect the spirit of the campus. That winter the students had held a "tea party," burning the steward's supply of the stuff and hanging Massachusetts governor Thomas Hutchinson in effigy.[36]

A student who arrived at Princeton in 1769 tells us much about the school, and its president. James Madison came from Orange County. In 1663 one John Madison had gained six hundred acres of land and passed on his holdings, now four times greater, to his son John twenty years later. Ambrose Madison, one of the grandchildren, expanded his holdings to the Piedmont area and there built Montpelier. But he died young and left his wife to manage the estate, which she did effectively. James Madison, their son, grew up in this region. This James Madison married Nellie Conway, and next year the couple had their first son, named for the father. So the future American president came from a family well established, to be sure, even if it and the other prominent families of this region were less aristocratic and less wealthy than those of the Tidewater. James Madison, Sr., served as a justice of the peace and vestryman in the Anglican Church. He owned over a hundred slaves and brought two thousand acres of Montpelier under cultivation.[37]

34. Varnum Lansing Collins, *President Witherspoon: A Biography*, 2 vols. (1925; New York: Arno Press & The New York Times, 1969), 1:118–19; Ralph Ketcham, *James Madison: A Biography* (New York: Macmillan, 1971), 37.
35. Kenneth Silverman, *A Cultural History of the American Revolution* (New York: Thomas Y. Crowell, 1976), 232–35.
36. Collins, *Witherspoon*, 1:127–28, 157, 165–66; Wertenbaker, *Princeton*, 57.
37. Irving Brant, *James Madison: The Virginia Revolutionist* (Indianapolis: Bobbs-Merrill, 1941), 22, 27, 29, 31; Douglass Adair, *Fame and the Founding Fathers: Essays by Douglass Adair*, ed. Trevor Colbourn (New York: Norton, 1974), 124–25.

Colonel Frederick Frelinghuysen

James Madison, Jr., grew up the eldest of twelve children. "Besides inherited wealth and position," wrote Douglass Adair, "he had an advantage far more important—a first rate-brain." His part of Virginia, however, offered few outlets for the life of the mind. Guns and horses interested the men folk; some of whom took pleasure in such debasing indulgences as cockfighting. The social life was more the measure of the good life—the balls, the barbeques, the riding parties. But young Madison always found a way to nourish his intellect. Happily for him, he made his way in 1762 to Donald Robertson's school where he had a thorough introduction to the classical languages, French, algebra, and geometry. He studied philosophy, too. Here above all he discovered the essays of Joseph Addison, and they inspired in him a love for writing. Madison copied essays from *The Spectator* into his commonplace book. Furthermore, the pieces helped define his own early standards: moderation in life, good manners, aversion to fanaticism of any kind, morality enhanced by wit, virtue in the public arena. In 1767 Madison took on studies with Reverend Thomas Martin, who in fact came to Montpelier to teach the other Madison children, too. Martin was a Princeton graduate. There lay Madison's next step.[38]

One in Madison's circumstances would have been expected to select the College of William and Mary for a college education. That school, however, faced many problems in 1769 and furthermore had a reputation as a resting place for the spoiled sons of the Virginia aristocracy. As such, it did not appeal to Madison. He had shunned the gambling, drinking, and horse racing ways of the Virginia elite. His fragile health also stayed him from Williamsburg and the "sickly season" of the summer months. Also, Madison had already embraced principles of religious freedom and Princeton was known for adhering to them. President Witherspoon was winning a good reputation in Madison's area of the country as well. Perhaps Madison knew also of the great additions the new president had brought with him from Scotland as his gift to the college library. If not he soon discovered them—Milton, Sidney, Locke, John Trenchard, and Thomas Gordon. There was plenty in this collection to nurture young revolutionary intellects. And to Princeton in 1769 traveled James Madison, accompanied by Thomas Martin and his brother, and a slave named Sawney.[39]

Madison came to the College of New Jersey a determined student. He gained approval for an accelerated program, in part because at age seventeen he was an "old" freshman. He would graduate in a little over two years. His application to his studies nearly destroyed his health. Nonetheless, he flourished. Literature had the greatest appeal to him, especially in the new extracurriculum that had emerged at Princeton and at other colonial colleges. He became an early member, perhaps even a founder, of the American Whig Society, one of the many student groups that emerged on American campuses in the two and a half years before the revolution.[40] Madison had a gift for polemic and satire (and for the off-color) that he readily employed against the bitter rival of the Whigs, the Cliosophic (or Cliosophian) Society. This group, which had a large portion of

---

38. Brant, *Madison*, 50; Ketcham, *Madison*, 40–41; Adair, *Fame and the Founding Fathers*, 124–26. The quotation is on p. 125.

39. Ketcham, *Madison*, 23–24, 38–39; Brant, *Madison*, 70.

40. Brant, *Madison*, 78–80, 86; Ketcham, *Madison*, 35. We know of the existence of student societies at the colonial colleges, but little about their activities. James Machlan provides this list of their origins in his essay "The *Choice of Hercules*: American Student Societies in the Early 19th Century," in *The University in Society*, Vol. II, *Europe, Scotland, and the United States from the 16th to the 20th Century*, ed. Lawrence Stone (Princeton, N.J.: Princeton University Press, 1974), 486.

1750	Flat Hat Club	William and Mary
1750	Critonian	Yale
1753	Linonian	Yale
1765	American Whig	Princeton
1765	Cliosophic	Princeton
1768	Brothers in Unity	Yale
1770	Institute of 1770	Harvard
1771	Pronouncing	Rhode Island College
1776	Phi Beta Kappa	William and Mary
1781	Social Friends	Dartmouth

New Englanders and projected a more "puritan" attitude, had to contend with the social superiority of the Whigs, heavily represented by southerners and Pennsylvanians. A paper war raged at Princeton as one group went after the other. Often the faculty had to intervene as the warfare found its way into the chapel services. The Whigs called their rivals "Tories," not because of any political implication on their part (for both groups embraced American patriotism), but because the epithet was the most condemning they could concoct. We glimpse the flavor of these student groups in this literary offering by Madison, "A Poem Written Against the Tories," in 1772. (The names cited refer to members of the rival Cliosophians.)[41]

> Of late our muse keen satire drew
> And humorous thoughts in vollies flew
> Because we took our foes for men
> Who might deserve a decent pen
> A gross mistake with brutes we fight
> And [goblins?] from the realms of night
> With lice collected from the beds
> Where Spring and Craig lay down their heads
> Sometimes a goat steps on the pump
> Which animates old Warford's trunk
> Sometimes a poisonous toad appears
> Which Eckley's yellow carcuss bears
> And then to grace us with a bull
> Foorsooth they show McOrkles skull
> And that the Ass may not escape
> He takes the poet Laureat's shape
> The screech owl too comes in the train
> Which leaped from Alexander's brain
> Just as he scratched his grizzly head
> Which people say is made of lead
> Come noble whigs, disdain these sons
> Of screech owls, monkeys, & baboons
> Keep up you[r] minds to humourous themes
> And verdant means & flowing streams
> Until this tribe of dunces find
> The baseness of their groveling mind
> And skulk within their dens together
> Where each one's stench will kill his brother

Life with the Whigs established Madison's early circle of friends at Princeton. He became particularly close with William Bradford as their informative correspondence after graduation confirms. Bradford was the son of the well-known "patriot

---

41. *The Papers of James Madison, Volume 1, 16 March 1751–16 December 1779*, ed. William T. Hutchinson and William M. E. Rachal (Chicago: University of Chicago Press, 1962), 65.

printer" of Philadelphia. Like Madison he would later return to Princeton for further study with Witherspoon. The work inclined him toward the law and to patriotic activity as well. He served eleven years as attorney general of Pennsylvania and then accepted President Washington's offer to become the second
attorney general of the United States in 1794.[42] Madison also knew Freneau, one
of the most zealous of the Whig Society members. He came from a Presbyterian
family in New York City, which had relocated to Monmouth County, New Jersey. He entered the college as a sophomore, so impressed with his ability was
President Witherspoon. He could be "vicious to the point of cruelty" when it
came to assailing the Clios. The American Revolution inspired his best work and
he joined that cause to his antislavery feelings. He fought in the war. The Madison connection became important to him later when Secretary of State Jefferson
in 1791 asked him to begin a party newspaper, the *National Gazette*, to rival the
Federalist voice the *Gazette of the United States*.[43]

   The fourth member of this circle, Hugh Henry Brackenridge, had a shifting
and mostly indifferent career after Princeton. Born in Scotland, he came to the
colonies with his family, who settled in York County, Pennsylvania. He always
had Presbyterian connections, but had no fighting faith and at times his religious
views bordered on skepticism. He went in the direction of law and politics and
won elections to political office in Pennsylvania. He supported the constitution,
disapproved the Whiskey Rebellion, but never convinced the powerful Federalists that he was really one of them. He did continue in literature, but much of
what he wrote had little influence and no staying power. He authored the pica-
resque novel *Modern Chivalry* in 1792, often considered his greatest literary
achievement.[44]

   Madison, however fatigued by his intensive academic program, returned
shortly after graduation for more study. The readings he undertook with President
Witherspoon now worked an important transition. Politics surpassed literature as
his consuming passion. He had previously heard Witherspoon lecture on political
writers, a wide range of them, in fact, and he began to see that the state might be
a vehicle of virtue and moral influence as much as literature. Now he could study
the writers close up. Politics began to assume in his outlook a greater weightiness
than belles lettres. Two letters to Bradford in late 1773 and early 1774 explain
Madison's shifting interests. In the first he says, "The principles and modes of government are too important to be disregarded by an inquisitive mind and I think
are well worthy of a critical examination by all students that have health and
leisure." In the next, "I myself used to have too great a hankering after those
amusing studies. Poetry, wit, and criticism, romances, plays, etc., captivated me
much; but I began to discover that they deserve but a small portion of a mortal's

   42. Gary S. DeKrey, "William Bradford, Jr.," in *Princetonians, 1769–1775: A Biographical Dictionary*, ed. Richard A. Harrison (Princeton, N.J.: Princeton University Press, 1980), 185–91.
   43. "Philip Morin Freneau," in *Princetonians*, 149–56.
   44. "Hugh Henry Brackenridge," in *Princetonians*, 138–45.

time, and that something more substantial, more durable, and more profitable, be-
fits a riper age." At the end of 1774 voters in Orange County elected Madison to
its Committee of Safety. The Continental Congress had called for these elections
to enforce the ban on trade that it had prescribed. Now in the most personal way
for Madison, the American Revolution was under way.[45]

Madison's new interest thus took him back to Virginia. The College of New
Jersey and Queen's College had to confront the political situation in New Jersey.
West Jersey still bore the stamp of its Quaker beginnings; it had greater homo-
geneity, a more rural cast, and larger farms than the other. East Jersey had a Puritan tone, more diversity in religion and ethnicity, and the beginnings of a commercial economy. The proprietary group still had economic and political
ascendancy and had come to constitute New Jersey's most powerful elite as it also
dominated the colonial legislature. That fact, though, was giving rise to a democratic insurgency resentful of this condition. New Jersey also had divided regional cultures. West Jersey operated in the orbit of Philadelphia, East Jersey in
that of New York City. Indeed, the colony had not even a newspaper of its own.
About two hundred religious congregations existed there in 1775 of which there
were fifty Presbyterian, forty Quaker, thirty each of Baptist and Dutch Reformed,
and twenty Anglican.[46]

New Jersey had been slow to respond to the British imperial measures of the
1760s, but was by no means indifferent to them. Much loyalist sympathy existed
in the colony, but increasingly in the next decade popular resentments against the
British intensified and local governments acted. The establishment of the Continental Congress and then the news of Lexington and Concord led to the creation
in New Jersey of three provincial congresses that bypassed the elected legislature.
The first met in May 1775 in Trenton. The Quakers made their absence conspicuous. The most zealous anti-British expressions came from the delegates from
Somerset County, including especially John Witherspoon. Frederick Frelinghuysen, a Princeton graduate and now instructor at Queen's, won election as an assistant secretary of the group. Overall, Presbyterians dominated the Congress.
Their contingent also included William Livingston, the Yale graduate who had
formed part of the Triumvirate that agitated against Anglican control of King's
College in the 1750s. Livingston had married a New Jersey woman and moved to
Essex County in 1772. He had since taken up another Presbyterian cause—the resistance to appointment of an Anglican bishop. Livingston represented the rising
tide of political influence from Presbyterians in New Jersey.[47] Their influence became even more visible after war broke out. As Thomas Fleming wrote, "The

---

45. Ketcham, *Madison*, 43, 55 (the first quotation) 63; *The Writings of James Madison*, 49 vols., ed.
Gaillard Hunt (New York: G. P. Putnam's Sons, 1900), 1:20 (the second quotation).

46. Larry R. Gerlach, *Prologue to Independence: New Jersey in the Coming of the American Revolu-
tion* (New Brunswick, N.J.: Rutgers University Press, 1976), 6, 22; Thomas Fleming, *New Jersey: A
Bicentennial History* (New York: Norton, 1977), 49; John E. Pomfret, *Colonial New Jersey: A History*
(New York: Scribner, 1973), 218.

47. Pomfret, *Colonial New Jersey*, 253; Fleming, *New Jersey*, 51.

Presbyterians ran the Revolution in New Jersey, controlling all aspects of it, from the distribution of political jobs to the appointment of New Jersey officers in the Continental Army."[48]

A second Provincial Congress met in January 1776 in New Brunswick. The third took place in June that year, also in New Brunswick. Now the matter of independence dominated the meeting, with a clear majority for the first time in favor. Witherspoon and Jacob Green, Presbyterian minister in Hanover and a trustee of the College of New Jersey, were stating the case for independence most forcefully. The agenda also called for electing delegates to the Continental Congress where New Jersey, slow to act, yet had no voice. The meeting chose Richard Stockton, a Princeton graduate of 1748 and now a trustee of the college; Witherspoon, "the most radical"; and three others. Four of the five were Presbyterians. The Congress instructed New Jersey's representatives to uphold all just rights and liberties of America and if necessary to support the independence of the "united colonies." As a result, all signed the Declaration of Independence.[49]

The Dutch in New Jersey had both loyalist and patriot adherents, but seemed to be moving more emphatically to the American side. Generally, the division reflected the familiar ones that had prevailed in the Dutch Reformed Church in this colony and in New York. Among the Loyalists of New Jersey one found members of the conservative Conferentie wing, or the "orthodox" Dutch that had resisted the Americanization movement that had created Queen's College. This group had its regional strength in Bergen County in East Jersey. The liberal coetus group supported independence. It had its strength where its movement had begun in New Jersey, in the Raritan Valley. When revolution broke out, a veritable civil war prevailed among the Dutch. Ministers like John Henry Goetschius, influential in starting the college, and Dirck Romeyn, a Princeton graduate, faced many difficulties from resentful Loyalists. In Bergen "whole families were divided in their allegiance, and neighbor suspected neighbor." The British suspected patriot ministers, too, hunted them down, and destroyed their churches.[50]

Queen's College had none of these divided loyalties. It joined wholeheartedly in the American quest for independence. Dominie Jacob Hardenbergh, trustee, faculty member, and temporary president, supported the revolution from the beginning. He served in the provincial congresses and in the new state legislature. Hardenbergh preached and wrote in favor of independence. He rankled the British to the point that they put a price on his head.[51] John Taylor also connected Queen's to the American cause. He graduated from Princeton in 1773, a member of the Cliosophic Society there. He became the first tutor at Queen's,

48. Fleming, *New Jersey*, 62.
49. Pomfret, *Colonial New Jersey*, 260–61; Gerlach, *Prologue to Independence*, 324, 337.
50. Pomfret, *Colonial New Jersey*, 228–29, 272, 280–81 (the quotation).
51. David W. Robson, *Educating Republicans: The College in the Era of the American Revolution, 1750–1800* (Westport, Conn.: Greenwood, 1985), 114.

joining his friend Frelinghuysen. At Queen's Taylor helped reshape the curriculum and involved students in forming their own literary group, the Athenian Society, which focused on contemporary issues. The versatile Taylor also trained his students in military science and when a "minute man" regiment formed in New Brunswick, Taylor became its captain. The next year, 1776, the state convention made Taylor a first major. When the British occupied New Brunswick, they forced the closing of the college. Taylor then gave full time to military service, joining some Queen's students in that commitment. In 1779 the trustees of Queen's urged his return to New Brunswick. He responded, and in October reopened the school. Another relocation soon followed, but after 1780 Taylor could give his full attention to the college, which he did until 1790.[52]

Taylor's friend Frederick Frelinghuysen graduated from Princeton the same year as he. After his father's death in 1774, his mother married Jacob Hardenbergh. His study with Witherspoon had influenced Frelinghuysen to go into law, a change from his original intention to enter the ministry. Instead, though, he joined Taylor as classes opened at Queen's in October 1771, still continuing his legal studies with Richard Stockton. Politics also claimed his time. He served on the Committee of Safety and the Committee of Correspondence in Somerset County before his work with the Provincial Congress. Frelinghuysen also joined the local Minute Men and saw action at Morristown and Middlebrook Heights in 1777, and at Monmouth Courthouse the next year. After the declaration of American independence, he helped write the new constitution for the state of New Jersey. At the same time, he patrolled Hunterdon and Essex counties arresting Loyalists. He was elected senator from New Jersey in 1793. Frelinghuysen maintained a long loyalty to Queen's. He became a trustee and even served as tutor again in 1784.[53] So Queen's cast itself on the patriot side with no tensions. It changed its name to Rutgers College in 1825.

The political situation in New Jersey faced the additional complication of a Loyalist royal governor. William Franklin was Ben Franklin's illegitimate son. The fact haunted him all his life and he tried to compensate for it by gaining approval and a secure identity through association with the "best" people. His father also tried to compensate by giving William all the advantages he could. He would raise him like a gentleman, provide him the best education, and endow him with material abundance. That resolve eventually found young Franklin, a handsome and charming man, studying law with Joseph Galloway. Father and son were very close, for the most part. William joined in the famous kite experiment of 1751. He early championed his father's schemes on behalf of an expanding British empire, also. That nationalism he kept when later Ben lost his. In 1757 the two went to England. The trip sealed their closeness but also that of William with England.

---

52. "John Taylor," in *Princetonians*, 111–14; Richard P. McCormick, *Rutgers: A Bicentennial History* (New Brunswick, N.J.: Rutgers University Press, 1966), 16–18.

53. "Frederick Frelinghuysen," in *Princetonians*, 78–83; Gerlach, *Prologue to Independence*, 279.

The rest of his life he would agonize as the pressure of events tested his dual loyalties—to America and to England. His trials began in 1763 when he found himself appointed the new royal governor of New Jersey.[54]

One of the East Jersey proprietors said of Franklin's appointment that the news came "like a thunderbolt." They expected trouble from him, for they assumed that his Pennsylvania background and his father's alliance with the Quakers would lead Franklin to favor West Jersey interests. Franklin himself made a gesture of independence from the Eastern elite by establishing his residence in Burlington, in "a magnificent three-story house" facing the Delaware River. He soon built an impressive private library as well for he wished to be a cultural as well as a political leader in the colony. Presbyterians in New Jersey soon came to resent him, however. They suspected that he tried, three years later, to take over the College of New Jersey. Franklin was Anglican, converted by his devout wife, and he openly supported the Society for the Propagation of the Gospel (SPG). On the other hand, he never championed the bishop cause. The Presbyterians in New Jersey knew also what an enemy Benjamin had made of their fellows in Pennsylvania. They never endeared themselves to William.[55]

Franklin kept his faith to the very last that colonists and mother country could overcome their problems. He saw them as mutual partners in a great empire. Every year showed the growing unreality of that faith. Franklin blamed both sides. He knew from his first visit to England that Englanders had belittling views of the colonists, unwarranted ones. Better communications could help. On the other hand, he saw New Jersey politics yielding increasingly to a dangerous populist trend. He never understood the fury of the patriot mobs, as in January 1770 when club-wielding protestors went after the proprietors and shut down the courts in Monmouth. Governor Franklin saw only an improper assault on authority. He grew alienated from the colonial assembly. Franklin had a paternalistic view of government. Elected officials should responsibly shape public opinion, he believed; they should not follow it. But in the revolutionary years, in New Jersey, the elected legislators reflected more and more the electorate that put them in office. In his effort to straddle the differences of the colonialists and England, however, Franklin incurred the wrath of the home leadership as well. Lord Hillsborough in 1767 gave him a dressing down, accusing Franklin of disobedience in favoring the assembly. Though devastated by the rebuke, Franklin cited England's offenses, defended the assembly, and exonerated himself.[56]

By 1775 Franklin knew that he had lost control of things. Lexington and Concord finally convinced him that no reconciliation was anymore possible, though he continued to blame both sides and hated to see revolution come because of an event in Massachusetts that he labeled an "unlucky incident." By De-

54. Sheila L. Skemp, *William Franklin: Son of a Patriot, Servant of a King* (New York: Oxford University Press, 1990). Summarized from chapters I–II.

55. Skemp, *William Franklin*, 46, 51, 82; Wertenbaker, *Princeton*, 48.

56. Skemp, *William Franklin*, 54, 91–95, 109–10, 163.

cember 1775 Franklin was almost all that remained of the royal government in New Jersey. Then a half-year later the third Provincial Congress moved on the governor. The meeting charged that Franklin had defied the Continental Congress in his efforts to uphold royal authority in New Jersey. It denounced him as "an enemy to the liberties of this country" and called for his arrest. Sam Adams came from Philadelphia to New Jersey personally to tell the Provincial Congress that the Continental Congress would not interfere with efforts to unseat Franklin. On June 19 Franklin heard a knock on his door. He was being summoned to the Provincial Congress for interrogating. Franklin immediately challenged his captors, questioning their authority. Two days later, however, Franklin rode in a coach, heading a somber parade to government headquarters. Samuel Tucker began the questioning and then yielded to the next inquisitor—the president of the College of New Jersey. Witherspoon had been in on this action from the outset, serving on the committee to arrange for the arrest and deposition of the governor. Now Witherspoon, by all reports, unleashed an intemperate assault on the governor, assailing his political beliefs and his personal habits as well. He mocked his pretensions of gentility, whereas all knew his bastard circumstances. The president's arms flailed as the humbled Franklin sat before him. It was not Witherspoon's finest hour; the governor deserved at least more respect. And thus ended royal government in New Jersey. That August the first state assembly met to elect the first state governor. William Livingston won in a run-off vote against Richard Stockton. Significantly, the meeting took place at Nassau Hall on the Princeton campus.[57]

What had brought John Witherspoon to this critical turn in New Jersey history and to a heightened political activism on his part? Although he arrived to America amid the political turmoil of taxation and representation, Witherspoon, however clear his sympathies, did not speak out on political matters. He carefully shunned the subject in the pulpit. For a long time he insisted that Great Britain needed a better understanding of the Americans. Like William Franklin, he hoped that such understanding would resolve the conflicts. But hope turned to anger in Witherspoon as British policy worsened in ignorance and deepened in oppression. He wrote in 1776, "Nothing is more manifest, than that the people of Great Britain, and even the king and ministry, have been hitherto exceedingly ignorant of the state of things in America. For this reason, their measures have been ridiculous in the highest degree, and the issue disgraceful."[58]

In the meantime, Witherspoon became more and more involved in local politics, both religious and secular. After entertaining the guests en route to the first Continental Congress in 1774, Witherspoon could not resist going there himself—no more than he was able to resist joining the battle to save Britain from the Jacobites years ago in his native Scotland. There he commingled with

---

57. Skemp, *William Franklin*, 166, 191, 207–12; Pomfret, *Colonial New Jersey*, 260, 264; Gerlach, *Prologue to Independence*, 333; Collins, *Witherspoon*, 1:209–12. Collins gives an account defensive of Witherspoon.

58. Collins, *Witherspoon*, 190.

Nassau Hall

John Adams, Richard Henry Lee, and others, then preached at a city church. Witherspoon had also prepared for the Congress his *Thoughts on American Liberty*—nine propositions he wished it to endorse. They included a commitment to non-importation and nonconsumption, a call to all the colonies to ready their militia for fighting, and a plan of union for the common colonial defense. Another resolution read, "To declare firm resolve never to submit to the claims of Great Britain, but deliberately to prefer war with all its horrors, and even extermination, to slavery." Witherspoon meant to do his share. He returned home, there to take up service in the summer of 1775 on the Somerset County committee of correspondence.[59]

Witherspoon had a like agenda for American Presbyterians. Meeting with the Synod of New York and Philadelphia, which he had helped to create, Witherspoon, in summer 1775, chaired a committee to design a pastoral letter to be read in American Presbyterian churches. Here Witherspoon used milder language. He encouraged loyalty to the king, but support for American unity and the Continental Congress. The document, however, saw war as virtually unavoidable, so it asked for days of prayer and fasting, and for valor and nobility on the field of battle. Witherspoon with this activity made himself the premier Presbyterian leader in America. He would be the only minister to sign the Declaration of Independence.[60]

By that time, Witherspoon had abandoned separation of pulpit and politics. As late as September of the previous year he had spoken of the pressing events only in veiled allusions. At the Princeton commencement in September Witherspoon addressed the subject of "Christian Magnanimity." He began by referencing the "present state," which everyone must admit to be "a continual trial of the faith and constancy of a Christian." And it was not a time for timid souls, he said. Some "infidels," Witherspoon warned, see Christianity as a religion of meekness, humility, and submission to affliction. They hold up for emulation the heroic models of pagan Greece and Rome as alternative ideals. Witherspoon offered instead Christian magnanimity. By this quality Witherspoon meant the attempt to do great and difficult things, to aspire after prized and valuable possessions, to encounter dangers with resolution, to struggle against difficulties with perseverance, and to bear sufferings with fortitude and patience. It sounded like a prescription for revolutionary times. Witherspoon assured that whereas the human passions lead often to tyranny and violation of others, religion ennobles the passions and gives them a higher direction. Christian magnanimity had that recommendation.[61]

Six weeks earlier at Princeton, and on the occasion of Congress's designation of a general fast to be observed in all the colonies, Witherspoon delivered a

---

59. Collins, *Witherspoon*, 166–67, 162–63, 177.
60. Collins, *Witherspoon*, 176; Gerlach, *Prologue to Independence*, 274.
61. John Witherspoon, "Christian Magnanimity: A Sermon," in *The Works of John Witherspoon*, 3 vols., ed. John Rodgers (Philadelphia: William W. Woodward, 1800), 1:600–5, 610.

political sermon. It had the title "The Dominion of Providence over the Passions of Men." "You are all my witnesses," Witherspoon told his audience, "that this is the first time of my introducing any political subject into the pulpit." But the matter had become urgent, he said. "The cause in which America is now engaged," Witherspoon insisted, "is the cause of justice, of liberty, and of human nature." The last reference became particularly important for his message. "The Dominion of Providence" reflects Scottish and American Presbyterianism.[62]

Wisdom in politics, Witherspoon argued, begins in knowing human sinfulness. He wished his audience not to lose sight of that fact. Witherspoon particularly scorned the polemicist Thomas Paine in this matter. The radical deist Paine had made the false and contrived doctrine of original sin an intellectual system used by tyrants to uphold hereditary monarchies and their attending cruelties. For Witherspoon, though, original sin was a not an invention; it was a reality. He assailed Paine's ideas as expressed that year in his pamphlet *Common Sense*. Witherspoon stated, "Others may, if they please, treat the corruption of our nature as a chimera: for my part, I see it everywhere, and I feel it every day. All the disorders in human society, and the greatest part even of the unhappiness we are exposed to, arise from the envy, malice, covetousness, and other lusts of men." These lusts, warned Witherspoon, fill the records of history as one group seeks to annihilate the other, driven as it is by its mad passions. Witherspoon, however, took his text from Proverbs 76:10 ("Surely the wrath of man shall praise thee; the remainder of wrath shalt thou restrain"). He wanted to show that God foils the cruel passions. The Christians survive and outlast the Romans. The Protestants of the Reformation ("when true religion began to revive") endure their persecutors. England triumphs over brutal Spain on the providential winds of 1588. Puritan dissenters defy the malevolent Stuarts and bring vital religion to New England. Witherspoon wanted his audience to know that the very cruelty, the hatred of oppressors, proves to be their undoing. The dominion of providence over the passions of men has good and godly effects.[63]

Providential aid, Witherspoon believed, coincides with a people's internal reformation. As the wrath of man demonstrates our corruption, he said, a conviction of sin begins redemption. "Nothing can be more absolutely necessary to true religion," Witherspoon exhorted, "than a clear and full conviction of the sinfulness of our nature and state." He also warned that a people can become lax, indifferent to their true state, amid times of prosperity and comfort. Then God may act to awaken them from this ease. Witherspoon wished to test these propositions against the "the present state of the American colonies, and the plague of war." He had no doubt that this situation was thematic of his sermon. "The ambition of mistaken princes, the cunning and cruelty of oppressive and corrupt

---

62. John Witherspoon, "The Dominion of Providence over the Passions of Men," in *Political Sermons of the Founding Era, 1730–1805*, ed. Ellis Sandoz (Indianapolis: Liberty Fund, 1991), 549.

63. Witherspoon, "Dominion of Providence," 536 (the quotation), 538n, 543–44.

ministers, and even the inhumanity of brutal soldiers, however dreadful," Witherspoon maintained, "shall finally promote the glory of God."[64]

Witherspoon conveyed emphatically his convictions that the American cause met the standards of just rebellion. It had its motivations in justice and liberty. He urged that Americans preserve their pure character, that a strong public interest transcend all petty and personal ones, that the social classes and the provincial factions not blind them to "the absolute necessity of union." Americans should also look to "the national character and manners" for the means of promoting "public virtue, and bearing down impiety and vice." Profligacy, the president warned, prepares a nation for destruction, no matter what its form of government. Witherspoon urged his audience to discipline themselves through work, to practice frugality "in your families, and every other article of expense," to observe temperance in eating, moderation and decency in dress and home. Vital religion, good and honest living, would assure success in revolution.[65]

Witherspoon's address, one of the most severe of any of the American college presidents in the revolutionary era, illustrates a recurring point—the manner in which the college leaders and collegiate graduates of this era selected at will from diverse pasts. Richard Sher, in a careful study of this document, argues that Witherspoon's rhetoric and construction came directly from a tradition of the Scottish jeremiad. Both the Moderate and Popular religious parties in Scotland used it, and it dated back to the days of John Knox and the Scottish Reformation. It reverberated with themes of God's displeasure with the nation, as now spewed forth from American pulpits. When Witherspoon arrived at Princeton in 1768 he saw the occasion to make Francis Hutcheson, voice of the Scottish Enlightenment, the vehicle of his moral philosophy teaching and intellectual defense against both idealism and materialism. Now, in the imperial crisis of the 1770s, Witherspoon returned to the religious tradition from which he came and applied it to the cause of revolution.[66]

Witherspoon rustled the feathers of many at home and abroad with his strong talk. A Glasgow publisher who read subversion in it printed copies of the "Dominion of Providence" only to denounce it. He considered it an affront that clerical influence sparked revolutionary notions in the colonies and labeled Witherspoon the worst example of that abuse. He had blended "the most rebellious sentiments with the most sacred and important truths," the critic wrote. An Edinburgh editor bristled at "Dr. Silverspoon," and labeled him "Preacher of

---

64. Witherspoon, "Dominion of Providence," 535, 540.
65. Witherspoon, "Dominion of Providence," 549, 551–57.
66. Richard B. Sher, "Witherspoon's *Dominion of Providence* and the Scottish Jeremiad Tradition," in *Scotland and America in the Age of Enlightenment*, ed. Richard B. Sher and Jeffrey R. Smitten (Edinburgh: University of Edinburgh Press, 1990), 46–53. Witherspoon himself had preached a jeremiad ten years before his coming to America, in the midst of the Seven Years' War. He said: "Affliction springeth not out of the dust. National calamity is not the rigor of an arbitrary tyrant, but the wise chastisement of a gracious father, or the punishment of a righteous judge" (p. 55).

Sedition in America." Even Adam Ferguson, one of the Scottish thinkers whose works Witherspoon admired, had harsh words for him.

> It is the fashion to say that we have lost America. . . . I am in great hopes that nothing will be lost, not even the continent of North America. We have 1200 miles of territory occupied by about 300,000 people of which there are 150,000 with Johnny Witherspoon at their head, against us—and the rest for us. I am not sure that if proper measures were taken but we should reduce Johnny Witherspoon to the small support of Franklin, Adams and two or three more of the most abandoned villains in the world, but I tremble at the thought of their cunning and determination opposed to us.[67]

A New York Loyalist, taking to the pages of the *Gazette*, expressed his offense at Witherspoon's boasting of "the spirit of liberty" at Princeton. And in New Jersey, Witherspoon earned the implacable enmity of the leading Anglican, Thomas Bradbury Chandler—minister of St. John's church in Elizabeth, arch-Loyalist, and monarchist.[68]

Of all the colonial college presidents Witherspoon made the most personal contribution to the revolution. His influence in American politics, as noted, extended also to the many students who came from his tutelage at Princeton, most importantly James Madison. Many have speculated about the connection and most suggestively in making the links from Witherspoon's Scottish connections to Madison's own political thinking. In fact, the Scottish connection began for Madison before his days at Princeton. Donald Robertson, who ran the school Madison attended, had his education at the universities of Aberdeen and Edinburgh. He exposed his students to an expansive curriculum that "in form resembled that of the first three years of the University of Edinburgh when Robertson was a student there." Robertson evoked in Madison a philosophical bent. At the age of fifteen he drafted a critique of Lockean epistemology.[69]

Madison secured much of his reputation from his contribution to the political thinking of the founding era, especially in his contribution to *The Federalist*, the essays by Madison, Alexander Hamilton, and John Jay. Madison's famous paper, the tenth essay, dealt with factions. It has been much discussed and analyzed. Historians such as Roy Branson, Douglass Adair, and Garry Wills have seen the direct influence of the Scottish Enlightenment, whose connection Madison made at Princeton through the teaching of Witherspoon as well as the collection of Scottish books that he brought with him to Princeton. Madison would revise Witherspoon in at least one significant way, but it is also true that his consideration of factions begins with his Princeton years.

As Madison traveled with his party to Princeton in 1769, the group stopped in Philadelphia where they visited the Bradfords. The city impressed him. Here

---

67. Collins, *Witherspoon*, 2:35 (Ferguson quotation), 1:227, 230–31, 145.
68. Gerlach, *Prologue to Independence*, 237.
69. Brant, *Madison*, 60–61 (the quotation); Wills, *Explaining America*, 13–14.

was a place of many religious affiliations, and yet all denominations lived toler-ably well together. A few years later, after he and William Bradford had left the college, Madison wrote him in Philadelphia, "I want again to breathe your free air." Madison had grown up an Anglican and his family attended services regu-larly. He developed early on, however, a distaste for established religion and chose Princeton in part because it imposed no sectarian loyalties on students. The Whig Society that Madison joined at Princeton had taken its name from "The American Whig" pen name of William Livingston, already known for his role in the *Independent Reflector* and its fight against religious establishment. The entire experience at Princeton seems to have confirmed Madison in his views on church and state. He speculated that had the Church of England enjoyed in all of America the privileges it had in Virginia, it would have effected a slavish men-tality everywhere. He wrote Bradford in 1774, "Religious bondage shackles and debilitates the mind, and unfits it for every noble enterprise, every expanded prospect." Madison had been observing the trials of the Baptists in Virginia and made a sympathetic plea for them. He believed the Church too influential in colony politics and too closely tied to the Crown. After independence, Madison joined with Jefferson in trying to disestablish the Church of England.[70]

Madison's first reflections on factions began within the religious situation of the American colonies. His education in Scottish thought enabled him to reach his later full consideration of the subject, as expressed in the tenth *Federalist*. The Scottish intellectuals influenced Madison in two ways. First they provided him a model and a methodology for the study of human society. Madison would follow the Scottish thinkers in expanding the religious factions he first knew to include predominantly economic ones. J. G. A. Pocock has written: "The great achieve-ment of the Scottish School of sociological historians was the recognition that a commercial organization of society had rendered obsolete much that had been be-lieved about society before it." The individuals Pocock had in mind were Adam Ferguson, David Hume, Adam Smith, and John Millar. Madison had read their works under Witherspoon's direction at Princeton. Witherspoon viewed much of history as a moral drama, as conveyed in the sermon he gave in 1775. Madison, who had never used a predominantly religious or theological framework for his studies, easily followed the Scots' alternative. They aspired to a scientific study of society. To Hume, history did not disclose any dramatic trajectory or regulating cycles. "Mankind," he wrote, "are so much the same, in all times and places, that history informs us of nothing new or strange in this particular. Its chief use is only to discover the constant and universal principles of human nature."[71]

The Scottish affiliation somewhat removed Madison from both the Lock-ean and republican models for the new America and even from Witherspoon.

---

70. Ketcham, *Madison*, 27, 58; Brant, *Madison*, 51; *Writings of Madison*, 19, 21–23 (the quotation).
71. Roy Branson, "James Madison and the Scottish Enlightenment," *Journal of the History of Ideas* 40 (1979): 237 (Pocock quotation); Ketcham, *Madison*, 43; Adair, *Fame and the Founding Fathers*, 95 (Hume quotation).

Witherspoon himself followed Locke in key respects. He accepted the Lockean idea of the social contract, "that men are originally and by nature equal, and consequently free." Witherspoon also joined Lockean liberalism to his Calvinist faith. He never separated ethics from religion.[72]

Madison, however, saw America more like Hume did, not as a retreat to a state of nature but the beneficiary of well-constructed government and its incorporated protections for individuals. Branson summarized the Scottish perspective. "The thinkers of the Scottish Enlightenment," he writes, "suggested an alternative to the idea that change meant revolution of government and a return to nature. The Scots even challenged the Lockean concept of individuals in a state of nature consenting to an original contract creating society." That shift in perspective led Madison to a focus on groups as primary and individuals as secondary in the dynamics of the social complex.[73]

In the tenth *Federalist* Madison made the argument that a republican system of government could flourish within a large state. Much in the debate surrounding the establishment of the new constitution involved this question. Negative opinion could site theorists like Montesquieu, who had made a formidable case against that proposition, and both Whig and Tory partisans in English politics. Supporters of the constitution had to show that individual freedoms could withstand the presence of a large government and that such governments were not necessarily oppressive. By the middle of the 1780s Madison and other Federalists had recent history on their side, or so they believed. They had seen the new states yield to narrow interests groups and a mean and provincial factionalism.

David Hume had given much attention, and descriptive diagnosis, to party and faction. He did not share the moral repugnance to them that others did and he wanted to study them in a more detached way. Ferguson in turn saw factions as useful agents of a healthy social competition. He wrote in his *Essay on the History of Civil Society* that amidst the contentions of party and faction the public interest does manage to thrive, "not because individuals are disposed to regard it as the end of their conduct, but because each, in his own place, is determined to preserve his own." "Liberty," Ferguson concluded, "is maintained by the continued differences and oppositions of numbers, not by their concurring zeal in behalf of equitable government." If we see here a version of Adam Smith's more renowned "invisible hand" we should not be surprised. Smith wanted to show that factions, however potentially dangerous, could also do good; they could even innovate and reform.[74]

---

72. John P. Diggins, *The Lost Soul of American Politics: Virtue, Self-Interest, and the Foundations of Liberalism* (New York: Basic, 1984), 165–66; James H. Smylie, "Madison and Witherspoon: Theological Roots of American Political Thought," *American Presbyterians* 73 (1995): 159.

73. Branson, "Madison and the Scottish Enlightenment," 239, 242.

74. Adair, *Fame and the Founding Fathers*, 104; Branson, "Madison and the Scottish Enlightenment," 248–49. By the time of the movement for a new constitution, to which Madison contributed significantly, he had subjected the republican ideology of the revolutionary era to a thoroughgoing skepticism. See Gordon Wood, *The Creation of the American Republic, 1776–1787* (Chapel Hill: University of North Carolina Press, 1969), 410–11.

In following the Scottish thinkers, Madison moved considerably out of the orbit of American republicanism, as had many of the Federalists promoting the new constitution. He did not appeal to a moral idealism of civic duty; he had more the perspective of the worldly sociologist who accepted the inevitability of factions but sought to contain their worst tendencies. When he concluded that a large state made the best guarantee for that effect he again reflected Scottish opinion. Hume for one found no allure in the small republic theory. The opposite, he said, was more persuasive. It may be more difficult to establish a republican government in a large domain, Hume argued, but it is easier to maintain it. In writing his tenth *Federalist* Madison had Hume ready at hand. Readers of Madison's famous essay will see familiar words in Hume's *Essays, Moral, Political, and Literary*: "In a large government, which is modeled with masterly skill, there is compass and room enough to refine the democracy. . . . The parts are so distant and remote, that it is very difficult, either by intrigue, prejudice, or passion, to hurry them into any measures against the public interest."[75] Compare Madison: "Extend the sphere and you take in a great variety of parties and interests; you make it less probable that a majority of the whole will have a common motive to invade the rights of other citizens; or if such a common motive exists, it will be more difficult for all who feel it to discover their own strength and to act in unison with each other."[76] To this extent had Madison carried forward and adapted his Scottish learning to the ideas of the new Constitution of 1787. The education that began with the Scottish books Witherspoon brought to Princeton eventually surpassed Witherspoon's own use of them. Adair could say of Madison, "The most creative and philosophical disciple of the Scottish school of science and politics in the Philadelphia Convention was James Madison."[77]

In November 1776 John Witherspoon, on learning of the approaching British army, assembled the Princeton students. Somber and a bit shaken, Witherspoon spoke to them of the crisis at hand and then sent them home. The Redcoats arrived on December 7 and took over campus and town. Nassau Hall became a prison for local citizens suspected as rebels. Soldiers took over the students' quarters, plundered the library, and greatly damaged the building. Three days into the next year, however, the British units retreated in haste. George Washington had executed his brilliant Christmas eve crossing of the Delaware, advanced into Trenton, and, eluding General Cornwallis, moved to Princeton. The army moved on Nassau Hall, sending a cannonball that blasted a portrait of George II inside. Some of the troops remained at Nassau Hall for five months and also disgraced themselves by their own destructive behavior. Cornwallis passed through Princeton; he was on his way to nearby New

---

75. Adair, *Fame and the Founding Fathers*, 98–100. Madison had the 1758 edition of the *Essays* available to him. See Adair, p. 100n. The original may also be found in Hume's essay "Idea of a Perfect Commonwealth" in David Hume, *Essays and Treatises on Several Subjects, In Two Volumes, Volume First, Containing Essays, Moral, Political, and Literary* (1742; Edinburgh: James Walker), 508.

76. *The Federalist Papers*, ed. Clinton Rossiter (New York: The New American Library, 1961), 83.

77. Adair, *Fame and the Founding Fathers*, 97.

Brunswick. General William Howe arrived there in July and closed Queen's College.[78]

By the middle 1760s, King's College in New York City showed signs of realizing the hopes of its founders. It looked like a bastion of Anglican strength and identity. It had a faculty solidly loyal to the Church of England. Churchmen had strength on the college board. King's students came from the city's elite—its wealthiest and most powerful political families. Some of its graduates, like Samuel Auchmuty, Jr., and Thomas Barclay, had become stalwarts of the colonial Church. King's officials boasted to England that their school provided the mother country with "an instrument" for "cementing the union between Great Britain and the colonies." In Myles Cooper, King's had a president who felt no compunction about habitually toasting Archbishop William Laud, of sacred Anglican memory. However, Cooper worried. He saw the rising tide of Presbyterianism in the colonies, and growing numbers of Methodists and Baptists, too. "Every Dissenter of high principles, upon the Continent," he said, "is our enemy." He saw conspiracies against the college everywhere. But Cooper hardly knew the depths of his problems. King's College was producing its own enemy within, a group of student patriots. King's would provide for the American Revolution and the creation of the United States Constitution none less than John Jay, Gouverneur Morris, and Alexander Hamilton.[79]

No college more directly felt the impact of the revolution than did King's. That fact derived from the religious politics of the institution and from King's place in the political and social culture of New York City and the larger colony. New York had special characteristics. One historian has described it as "the closest approximation to an aristocracy in America" and similar to England for that reason. The colony had both its upstate elites and its city elites. King's College found itself in a city of three-storied brick houses, connected to one another, with spacious gardens set behind them. Lavish Georgian mansions announced the residences of the most famous names—Oliver DeLancey, Peter Van Brugh Livingston, Pierre Van Cortlandt, and others. The city aristocracy had black slaves, maids, and footmen. It exuded a mildly hedonistic air, enjoying without any Puritan unease their lavish meals and expensive wines. New York culture was pragmatic and rational. Its city folk accepted a religion that generated little emotionalism and appealed more through its rational and esthetic forms than its demands for critical introspection by its adherents. New York could thus display an aggressive materialism, a pervasive drive to advance in worldly comfort. One found in New York little of New England's moral angst. Its social life could thus exude a crass commercialism, its politics a visible corruption.[80]

---

78. Wertenbaker, *Princeton*, 59–61.

79. David C. Humphrey, *From King's College to Columbia, 1746–1800* (New York: Columbia University Press, 1976), 139–43, 151, 199. The quotations are on pages 141 and 142.

80. Max M. Mintz, *Gouverneur Morris and the American Revolution* (Norman: University of Oklahoma Press, 1970), 32 (the quotation)–35; Alan Tully, *Forming American Politics: Ideals, Interests, and Institutions in Colonial New York and Pennsylvania* (Baltimore: Johns Hopkins University Press, 1994), 247–48.

Myles Cooper (Detail; oil painting by John Singleton Copley)

New York politics has confounded historians. Dynastic connections and rivalries dominated in the colonial era.[81] In the recent decades the rivalry focused on the James DeLancey and Philip Livingston factions. That competition did not reproduce the ideological warfare and patterns of political faction familiar to the eighteenth century, such as "Court" and "Country" partisanships.[82] Both factions in New York had elite leaderships that forged alliances with whatever groups they could to stay in power or get there. Economic differentiation helps little in understanding these factions. One difference, however, stands out. The Livingston party consisted heavily of religious Dissenters, while the DeLancey

---

81. See Patricia U. Bonomi, *A Factious People: Politics and Society in Colonial New York* (New York: Columbia University Press, 1971).
82. See Tully, *Forming American Politics*, for a weighty analysis, especially pp. 224–56.

faction had a preponderance of Anglicans. The religious divisions did not always matter, but in such an instance as the founding of King's College in the earlier 1750s they crystallized. (Recall William Livingston and the Triumvirate from the earlier chapter on King's.) Later, every member of the Livingston coalition sided with the patriot cause in the revolution, while the DeLanceys contributed heavily to the Loyalists.[83]

In New York, religious politics had a life of its own. By the middle 1760s the Anglicans felt their privileged position threatened. The newspaper warfare that had raged in the previous decade, with King's College the major focus, renewed. Worried Anglicans in 1766 formed a convention. Its leaders constituted the institutional elite of that denomination in New York—William Bradbury Chandler, Samuel Seabury, Charles Inglis, Cooper, and Auchmuty. In a memorandum concerning the founding, the convention told the SPG of its commitment to the bishop cause, but it also cited the threat posed by aggressive Presbyterians and "their pernicious designs" against the Church. The convention announced its intention to exercise a vigilance of its own "to watch all their publications . . . and to obviate the evil influence of such as appeared to have a bad tendency by the speediest answers." The Anglicans then took to the presses. Chandler published in 1767 his *Appeal to the Public in Favor of the Church of England in America.* William Livingston responded for the Presbyterians with a series that bore the heading "The American Whig." Cooper, Chandler, and Inglis retaliated with a package of articles titled "A Whip for the American Whig." Both series appeared in the New York *Gazette.* Inglis labeled the American Whig "an insolent, audacious attack" on Chandler, full of "low witticisms, buffoonery, falsehoods, and blunders." Livingston made an attack on Inglis in turn, one that the Anglican said "abounds with the lowest scurrility." The war of words lasted three years.[84]

Anglicans did look beyond their churches for institutional strength in their cause. They could find it at King's College. It had, first of all, Myles Cooper. No colonial college had a more fiercely Loyalist president. He stood for Anglican faith and Anglican politics, and these loyalties made him an enemy to the rebellion. To King's College Anglicans like Cooper the very notion of rebellion, or even lack of deference to authority, seemed alien postures. The "health of the state," wrote Cooper, "requires a regular and due subordination of its members to the governing power. . . . Let every man then be contented with his station, and

---

83. James S. Olson, "The New York Assembly, the Politics of Religion, and the Origins of the American Revolution, 1768–1771," *Historical Magazine of the Protestant Episcopal Church* 43 (1974): 21–23, 26–28. William Smith, Jr., did become a Loyalist.

84. Leopold Leinitz-Schurer, "A Loyalist Clergyman's Response to the Imperial Crisis in the American Colonies: A Note on Samuel Seabury's Letters of a Westchester Farmer," *Historical Magazine of the Protestant Episcopal Church* 44 (1975): 107–19 (the quotation); Clarence H. Vance, "Introductory Essay," in *Letters of a Westchester Farmer,* ed. Clarence H. Vance (White Plains, N.Y.: Westchester County Historical Society, 1930), 68–69, 72–74; John Wolf Lydekker, *The Life and Letters of Charles Inglis . . .* (London: Society for Promoting Christian Knowledge, 1936), 72–74, 77–79. The Inglis quotations are on pages 77 and 79.

faithfully discharge his attendant duties." Whether in religion or politics, Cooper believed, the populace should eschew "wild, visionary, enthusiastic notions"— notions like natural rights, which any malcontent could cite against the restraining laws of the government. In Cooper's judgment, Americans rested safe and protected under the most benign regime in the world, the British government and its noble constitution. Only "clever radicals" could argue otherwise, he said. New York patriots resented such unctuous pronunciations. Cooper's name made a list of the six "most odious" Loyalists in New York on a handbill issued when the revolution broke out in 1775.[85]

Cooper placed a protégé at King's when he appointed John Vardill to teach classical languages beginning in 1772. Vardill was no less shy than his mentor in speaking out politically, and he even became a mouthpiece for Cooper. Vardill, a graduate of King's, could see in both the religious and political Dissenters of the day only "unbridled licentiousness." He, too, celebrated colonial obeisance to the Crown. In speaking of the American relation to England, Vardill employed the familial analogy. "The authority of the one," he said, "should be the beneficial authority of a parent; and the obedience of the other, the liberal obedience of a child." Vardill became now a campus apologist of the home regime as he issued authentic conservative dicta: "No man loves liberty more than I do, but of all tyranny I most dread that of the multitude." Vardill had a special contempt for the Presbyterians and in 1773 gave President Witherspoon of Princeton a thorough dressing down. During the revolution he became a British spy.[86]

Charles Inglis completes the Anglican circle of King's College. He became acting president in 1771 when Cooper went abroad to England. Inglis came to America around 1754 from Ireland, where he was born in 1734. He represented a long line of Scottish Anglicans. We know little of his early life and education. He settled in the Lancaster, Pennsylvania, area and soon took on a missionary project with the Delaware Indians. Inglis always spoke for the needs of the Church in the colonies, beginning with an early letter to the SPG, sent from Dover, in which he made a plea for Anglican bishops. He married in 1764 and removed to New York City for reasons of his wife's health. Inglis encountered a late stage of the revivalist movement in the colonies and recoiled from it in horror. Another letter to the SPG thus decried the ways of "a mad enthusiast" and his unaccountable influence on his hearers. That specter of social disorder renewed Inglis's campaign for bishops. He made his first connection with King's College when Cooper joined him on a mission to the Mohawks, Cooper looking for new students for King's from this group of natives. At the time of his appointment as interim president, Inglis was the associate minister at Trinity

85. Humphrey, *King's College*, 221, 223; Bruce Bliven, Jr., *New York* (New York: Norton, 1981), 48.

86. Humphrey, *King's College*, 150, 151, 221, 215 (the quotation); Janice Potter, *The Liberty We Seek: Loyalist Ideology in Colonial New York and Massachusetts* (Cambridge, Mass.: Harvard University Press, 1983), 3.

Church. It tells us something of this church–college connection, for Inglis seems to have had no teaching function at King's while serving as the church leader. The identification with Trinity sufficed to get him the job.[87]

New York has long had the reputation of a mostly loyalist colony, perhaps the most reluctant to take up the cause of independence and support the rebellion. A closer look, however, encounters a more complicated record. In fact, New York responded as quickly, and as angrily, as any colony with the first decisive measures of the British government in 1764 and 1765. The New York legislature immediately denounced the Sugar Act as illegal and its proclamation became "one of the major state papers of the entire revolutionary era," having an impact on other colonies that followed. The next year New York merchants made their city the first to react to the Stamp Act by establishing non-importation agreements. In New York, too, the crowds got into the action. In October 1765 the mob hung the royal lieutenant governor Cadwallader Colden in effigy, sacked the home of a British major, and swarmed the city, destroying property. The situation quieted for a few years and New York became less conspicuous on the road to revolution. Soon, however, a major contest emerged: who would control the rebellion in New York colony?[88]

That question became acute in New York in 1773. That year England imposed its infamous Tea Act on the colonies. The Boston Tea Party, held in response to it, is legendary. But New York, too, had a tea party. Early in the next year the New York Assembly protested the Tea Act. In April a city mob, encouraged by the action taken in Boston, boarded the ship *London* and there the "Mohawks" dumped eighteen cases of tea into the harbor. When news arrived in May that England had closed the port of Boston, radicals called for a public meeting to be held at the Fraunces Tavern in the city. When the word got out, the "moderates" got activated. They had been politically aloof to date, but they now realized a great fear—the possible mob takeover of city politics. So they too enhanced the crowd at the Fraunces, which could not contain all who wanted to partake. The throng relocated to the Exchange. Elections there produced a Committee of Fifty (soon Fifty-One). The vote represented a defeat for the New York's Sons of Liberty, the radical faction. Colden opined that they were "in disgrace." One of the moderates who had stolen the movement from the radicals was the young John Jay. Next month, when the committee elected a moderate delegation, including Jay, to the Constitutional Convention, the radicals resigned. Michael Kammen summarizes the significance of these developments: "Ultimately, the likes of John Jay, Gouverneur Morris, and Robert R. Livingston came to regard separation [from England] as inevitable; they determined to keep the new government under men of their own social class and political outlook."[89]

---

87. Lydekker, *Life and Letters of Charles Inglis*, 1–2, 9, 12, 29, 31, 51–52, 76, 96, 133, 135.

88. Michael Kammen, *Colonial New York: A History* (New York: Scribner, 1975), 349, 352.

89. Kammen, *Colonial New York*, 342–43 (the quotation); Mintz, *Gouverneur Morris*, 43; Frank Monaghan, *John Jay: Defender of Liberty* (New York: Bobbs-Merrill, 1935), 51; Philip Ranlet, *The New York Loyalists* (Knoxville: University of Tennessee Press, 1986), 41–43.

We last saw Jay as a student at King's in the 1760s. He finished there in 1764. After three more years of reading for the law he gained a master's degree from the college. Now all was set for his ascending career and his advance into the higher social circles of the city. The pattern befit his family's standing among the prominent urban merchants. In 1770 Jay helped to form the Moot Club, a group of attorneys that included William Livingston, William Smith, Jr., John Morin Scott, and Robert R. Livingston, with eighteen members in all. They met at city taverns—the King's Arms, the Queen's Head, and the Fraunces. Jay also joined the Social Club, "the best of the New York clubs." In April 1774 he married into the Livingston clan through his union with Sarah Van Brugh Livingston, daughter of William.[90]

Jay had spoken hardly at all on politics until the events of 1773. The tea riots in New York City sent him into action. He joined the ranks of the moderates and got himself elected to the Committee of Fifty and then to the delegation from New York to the Philadelphia convention in autumn 1774. He did not at that time support American independence. He represented what David Humphrey (following Alfred Young) calls the "conservative Whig" faction, to which King's College made a significant contribution. For as Humphrey notes, the conservative Whigs that came from King's had more in common then with the New York Loyalists than they did with the patriot radicals. Most of that group of popular Whigs later became anti-Federalists while the likes of Jay and Hamilton helped write the Federalist Papers and the Constitution of 1789. The conservative Whigs had a commitment to hierarchical politics. They deeply mistrusted populist and radical republican tendencies. This much King's had given them. They all could echo the sentiments of John Vardill about the tyranny of the multitude. They could also warn, with Myles Cooper, that Americans ought not to focus too much on external threats to their liberties "lest we become enslaved by tyrants within." Jay's group on the Committee of Fifty-One consisted entirely of merchants with the exception of three lawyers, he among them. As Jay's biographer writes, "This group of fifty-one worked toward a double purpose: to settle the quarrel with England along dignified, conservative lines and to exclude the unenfranchised, led by the extreme radicals, from further political influence."[91]

Fall 1774 found Jay in Philadelphia for the meeting of the Continental Congress. A man of but twenty-nine years of age, he nonetheless soon had great influence. Right away he engaged the volatile Patrick Henry on the matter of colonial independence from Great Britain. Henry gave a moving speech. He urged nationalist feelings on the delegates. "The distinctions between Virginians, Pennsylvanians, New Yorkers, and New Englanders, are no more," he said. "I am not a Virginian, but an American!" Jay rose to overrule those sentiments. He

---

90. Monaghan, *John Jay*, 42–43, 46.
91. Monaghan, *John Jay*, 30, 38, 42–43, 46, 52 (the quotation); Humphrey, *King's College*, 210–12, 216; Ranlet, *New York Loyalists*, 41.

thought them premature. He stated that the colonies might still use their influence to repair the faults in the prevailing system; it was not yet time for a new
government. Jay found more embroilment when appointed to the committee to
draft an address to the people of Great Britain. He served with his father-in-law
William Livingston and Richard Henry Lee. Lee, the most radical, and Jay, the
most conservative, soon stood at odds with each other. Lee wrote the draft and
submitted it to a cool reception by the convention. It deferred action, giving Jay
an opportunity to write a position paper of his own. Livingston presented it, and
it won immediate acclaim. Most of the delegation assumed that Livingston himself had written it. Thomas Jefferson gave it his highest praise. Indeed, Jay's *Address to the People of Great Britain* appeared almost simultaneously with Jefferson's
Summary View of the Rights of British Americans.[92]

Jay's *Address* begins with a revealing salutation, "Friends and Fellow Subjects."
But it conveys honest, and indeed quite radical, American sentiments. It opens:

> When a nation, led to greatness by the hand of liberty, and possessed of all the glory
> that heroism, munificence, and humanity can bestow, descends to the ungrateful
> task of forging chains for her friends, and instead of giving support to freedom, turns
> advocate for slavery and oppression, there is reason to suspect she had either ceased
> to be virtuous, or been extremely negligent in the appointment of her rulers.

Then Jay made clear why he employed the term "fellow subjects." He turns it on
the British people to whom he appeals in the address. He pleas for commonality
and equality of British and Americans. "Why then," Jay asks,

> are the proprietors of the soil of America less lords of their property than you are of
> yours? Or why should they submit to the disposal of your parliament, or any other
> parliament or council in the world, not of their election? Can the intervention of
> the sea that divides us cause disparity in rights? Or any reason be given why English
> subjects, who live three thousand miles from the royal palace, should enjoy less lib-
> erty than those who are three hundred miles distant from it?[93]

Like Jefferson's declaration two years later, Jay cited American grievances.
He specified the multiple ways in which England had controlled the colonies'
trade, "drawing from us the wealth produced by our commerce." It had taken
American money and placed British soldiers in the colonies, he wrote. It had
squandered expenses on "court favorites and ministerial dependants." It had deprived Americans of "the inestimable right of trial by jury" and removed cases
from American jurisdiction all together. Jay also cited the Tea Act and the closing of Boston port. He referenced the "dissolute, weak, and wicked governors"

---

92. Monaghan, *John Jay*, 58, 60–61.
93. John Jay, *Address to the People of Great Britain*, in William Jay, *Life of John Jay: With Selections
from His Correspondence and Miscellaneous Papers*, 2 vols. (1833; Freeport, N.Y.: Books for Libraries
Press, 1972) 1:465, 467.

imposed by the Crown on the colonies, and suspension of their own legislatures. He proclaimed that Americans had been loyal beyond reason, but he warned that "we will never submit to be hewers of wood or drawers of water for any ministry or nation in the world."[94]

When the news of Lexington and Concord in 1775 reached New York City it ignited another round of violence. Things got to their worst on May 10, and King's College was in the thick of it. President Cooper had recently received a letter—he was one of five Loyalists to get one—warning that his "repeated insults" toward the patriots had placed him in severe jeopardy. He and his cohorts had better "fly for your lives, or anticipate your doom," the epistle said. Cooper did leave and took cover on a British warship in New York harbor. He returned later. Around midnight a crowd of angry patriots descended on the college. They broke down the gate and came looking for Cooper. The buckets of tar they carried and the feathers in sacks announced their intentions. A King's student heard of the imminent crisis and got his friend to speed with him to the president's house. They reached the front steps just as the crowd arrived. The student ordered it to halt. The patriots recognized him as one of their own and heeded his order. He could not contain the more fiery spirits among the mob, however, as they broke into the home. Cooper, nonetheless, had gained just the few moments he needed to make a retreat, half-dressed, through a rear exit. He made his way to the Hudson River and the protection of a friend and next day boarded a British ship. Shortly thereafter he found permanent exile in England. The student rescuer was the young Alexander Hamilton.[95]

The mob wanted yet another trophy—one James Rivington. Rivington had gained notoriety as the publisher of *Rivington's New York Gazetteer*, or what the patriots called the "Lying Gazette." For Rivington held and publicized strong Tory views. The Committee of Fifty-One had already begun an investigation of him. Again, intervention by two friends saved a Tory. For a while, Rivington had the sufferance of the patriots, but then he resumed his attacks. In November, Isaac Sears, one of the most radical of the Sons of Liberty, organized a mob of Connecticut rebels. They crossed into New York, demolished Rivington's press, and melted it down for bullets. Shortly thereafter, Rivington left for England.[96]

These events further estranged the conservative Whigs and the radicals. One who came to the defense of Rivington was the young attorney Gouverneur Morris, who pleaded for lenient treatment. Morris had experienced his political awakening only the previous year, in the New York City "Tea Party." There he confronted the spectacle of an aroused populace, and he graphically expressed the general fear that defined the moderates. "The mob begin to think and reason," he wrote. "Poor reptiles! it is with them a vernal morning, they are struggling to cast

94. Jay, *Address*, 468–75 (the longer quotation).
95. Humphrey, *King's College*, 153; Nathan Schachner, *Alexander Hamilton* (New York: D. Appleton-Century Company, 1946), 41.
96. Mintz, *Gouverneur Morris*, 50, 52.

off their winter's slough, they bask in the sunshine, and ere noon they will bite, depend on it. The gentry begin to fear this." Morris wanted a quick repair of matters with England, lest the American situation yield more and more to the rabble. "I see, and I see it with fear and trembling, that if the disputes with Britain continue, we shall be under the worst of all possible dominions," Morris warned. "We shall be under the domination of a riotous mob."[97]

Upon his graduating from King's College in 1768 Morris began his studies for the law with William Smith, Jr. He absorbed Pufendorf, the newly available Blackstone, and other names in an expansive list. Smith undoubtedly influenced Morris's growing distrust of popular government, but seems not to have passed on his extreme anti-Anglicanism, still alive from the days of the *Independent Reflector*. Morris joined The Moot in 1774 and like his fellow alumnus entered the more exclusive set of New York City, also joining the Social Club. The events of 1773 forced Morris to choose sides. He would go with his country against England, but not with the Sons of Liberty. He felt their patriotic zeal, but not their political radicalism. Morris could recall one of his student addresses at King's, in which he had counted himself among those who "can boast the glorious title of free born American." He would watch his mother side with the Loyalists, as a brother-in-law did also. But when the news came from Lexington, Morris became patriot; he won election from Westchester to a proposed Provincial Congress of New York. He joined the conservative Whigs.[98]

By this time New York was experiencing not only political drama but intellectual warfare as well. That subject brings us to the third of the King's College patriot triumvirate—Alexander Hamilton. It is by any measure a remarkable story. It might be said of Hamilton that of all college students in colonial America he partook the most intensely and most directly in the American Revolution while a student. And he did so in the most comprehensive way—with pen and sword. Hamilton also rounds out a thematic intellectual portrait, for his views well articulated the conservative Whig politics that King's made as its special contribution to the revolutionary movement.

Most readers will know something of Hamilton's background. He came to the British colonies of North America from the Caribbean. John Faucette, a French Huguenot, landed on the island of Nevis in 1685. He became a wealthy physician and married a woman twenty years younger than he. They had three daughters, of whom Rachel was the youngest, born in 1736. Mary Faucette left the faltering marriage. Rachel was soon pursued by one John Michael Levine, a Danish-Jewish planter from St. Croix. She married this much older man, then deserted him, leaving behind a four-year-old son. Rachel encountered James Hamilton, and they cohabitated, shunning the legal complexities of attaining a divorce for her and marriage for them. A son Alexander became the first prod-

97. Mintz, *Gouverneur Morris*, 44.
98. Mintz, *Gouverneur Morris*, 25–27, 29, 37–40, 47.

uct of this union, probably in 1757. Another son followed, James, in 1762. Failing in business and his marriage becoming acrimonious, James Hamilton deserted the family. Rachel died in 1768. Such were the inauspicious beginnings of Alexander Hamilton.[99]

Without mother or father, and eleven years old, Hamilton took work as an apprentice to Nicholas Cruger, one of the wealthiest merchants on St. Croix. When Cruger left the island four years later he entrusted the business to the young Hamilton. A letter that Hamilton wrote—a vivid account of the powerful hurricane that had struck the Caribbean—gained him the attention of some powerful political, business, and church people, who resolved that such literary talent must not languish. Hamilton went off to New York City, still connected to Cruger's affairs there. He had a year of tutelage in Elizabeth Town, New Jersey, then, per the intentions of his sponsors, prepared to apply to college. He inquired first at Princeton and then at King's where Myles Cooper acceded to Hamilton's demands to pursue an accelerated program of studies.[100]

From the beginning at King's Hamilton flourished. He fell into a circle of students with like-minded literary interests. They formed a society to expand those interests beyond the formal curriculum. Their passion was by no means only aesthetic. When the city exploded in 1773 with the politics of tea, the students engaged the whole gamut of imperial issues. And they took up the partisan cause of the patriots. Here at Anglican King's College a resolute coterie of students vilified King George. Hamilton himself went public. Seizing time between his studies of science and classical languages, he composed a speech, one he labeled "Defense of the Destruction of the Tea." *Holt's Journal* published it and then gave Hamilton additional outlets on its pages. In July 1774 the young King's scholar took to the outdoors. To a gathering in "The Fields," and to an audience stocked with the Sons of Liberty, he responded to the calls of his friends ("Give 'em a speech, Alexander"). Hamilton mounted the platform. The student laid forth a litany of abuses, enumerating the crimes of the Crown against the colonies. Spectators began to turn to each other, asking "Who is he?" "A collegian," one said. "Then all voices joined in a roar of approval as the boy of seventeen, flushed and conscious of his powers, descended from the platform." He had experienced a great success.[101]

What had made young Hamilton so outspoken a patriot? Certainly, like any collegians of his era, Hamilton could absorb from the classical curriculum a good deal of republican ideology. Jefferson may be the best example of one who did so. But republicanism rarely emerged unalloyed. Jefferson incorporated Lockean language into the Declaration of Independence. New Englanders, we have observed, drew upon their own Puritan history. Hamilton may well have whetted his revolutionary instincts on Presbyterianism, virtually smuggling

99. Schachner, *Alexander Hamilton*, 1–10.
100. Schachner, *Alexander Hamilton*, 17, 23, 25, 27, 30.
101. Schachner, *Alexander Hamilton*, 30–33.

them into Anglican King's. Hamilton first encountered the Rev. Hugh Knox on St. Croix in 1772. An Ulster Scot and strongly partisan New Side Presbyterian, Knox had graduated from Princeton, and took a particular interest in Hamilton. Knox had personal connections to powerful Presbyterians in New York, and helped get Hamilton located at a Presbyterian academy in Elizabeth Town and prepared to enter Princeton. Hamilton demanded to enter as a sophomore at that college, but President Witherspoon denied him the privilege. So Hamilton went over to King's. He brought there no prior attachments to Anglicanism and surely found in that city anti-Church expressions aplenty that reinforced the Presbyterian piety that Knox had instilled in him.[102]

Hamilton's speech surprised the New York public. But he soon gave them another reason to notice him. The background here is the initiative taken by Samuel Seabury to make the case, comprehensively and urgently, for loyalty to Great Britain. Seabury had become one of the Anglican stalwarts in the colonies. He came from New England originally, born in 1729, the son of the Rev. Samuel and Abigail Seabury, he the minister of the Congregational Church in North Groton, Connecticut. But shortly after Samuel's birth, his father converted to Anglicanism. That change may have owed something to his friendship with Timothy Cutler or to his Anglican in-laws. Samuel entered Yale in 1744 where he earned the B.A. At Yale and King's he also earned M.A. degrees. In the 1750s he pursued medical studies in England and Scotland. At age twenty-four Seabury received ordination into the Church by the bishop of London and thereupon took up a missionary field in New Brunswick, New Jersey. He would gain public recognition in the King's College controversy in New York City. He became a polemicist against the Presbyterians and fought to secure the Anglican grip his denomination held on the college. Then also he began to forge the powerful Anglican alliance that included Chandler, Inglis, Auchmuty, and Samuel Johnson, with Benjamin Nicholl and James Wetmore as well. All were transplanted New Englanders. In 1765 Seabury helped form the Anglican Convention and campaigned for an American bishop. He stated the case in the most direct way:

> The poor Church of England in America is the only instance that ever happened of an Episcopal Church without a bishop and in which no orders can be obtained without crossing an ocean of 3000 miles in extent. Without bishops the Church cannot flourish in America and unless the Church will be supported and prevail, this whole continent will be overrun with infidelity and deism, Methodism and New Light and with every species and every degree of Scepticism and Enthusiasm.[103]

Seabury published his *Free Thoughts on the Proceedings of the Continental Congress* following the events in Philadelphia in 1774. The long essay focused on the

---

102. Forrest McDonald, *Alexander Hamilton: A Biography* (New York: Norton, 1979), 10–12.

103. Bruce E. Steiner, *Samuel Seabury, 1729–1796: A Study in the High Church Tradition* (Columbus: Ohio University Press, 1971), 13–14, 34–37, 91–94, 105–6 (the quotation).

action taken by the Congress in calling for non-imitation, non-exportation, and non-consumption of British goods and manufactures. Seabury denounced the action as first of all unfair—to British business and to the inhabitants of Ireland and the West Indies. They had done nothing to provoke the British imperial measures against which Americans had reacted, Seabury said. Also, he warned, the Congress's actions could only further alienate the affections of colonists and the British people. Furthermore, Seabury believed that America could not gain by the measures called for. "Our malice will hurt only ourselves," he averred. The American economy, said Seabury, cannot go it alone. "You are obliged to buy many articles of clothing," he told his readers; "you cannot make them yourselves." Seabury was not shy about making himself appear a friend of the poorer Americans. "The lower classes of people," he cautioned, "are to be deprived of their daily bread, by being thrown out of employment by the non-exportation agreement." Seabury tried to portray the Constitutional Convention as a vehicle of repression, "slavery." And he protested, "If I must be enslaved, let it be by a King at least and not by a parcel of upstart lawless Committeemen. If I must be devoured, let me be devoured by the jaws of a lion, and not gnawed to death by rats and vermin."[104] Seabury signed his publication "A. W. Farmer."

In his next offering, in November, Seabury dealt with more strictly legal matters. He called his piece *The Congress Canvassed*. All patriots' cant about "liberty and the rights of Englishmen," he said, have their worst effects in denigrating the authority of the British Parliament over the colonies. For in that Parliament, Seabury insisted, Americans secure their personal and property rights. Seabury also called illegal the whole process by which the colonies had each selected their own delegates to the Philadelphia convention. "The assemblies have but a delegated authority themselves. They are but the representatives of the people; they cannot therefore have even the shadow of [a] right to delegate that authority." So why should Americans bend to the authority of the Continental Congress? Seabury asked. If they will not acknowledge the right of Parliament to tax them, why should they yield to the clearly more dubious authority of this convention?[105]

The eighteen-year-old student at King's decided he had read quite enough of Seabury after this publication, and he now prepared a systematic reply of his own. There emerged perhaps the most comprehensive personal debate of the American Revolution era. Hamilton issued *A Full Vindication of the Measures of the Congress* in December 1774. The next one, *The Farmer Refuted*, came from him in February 1775. We shall consider the two together, although the first addressed economics mostly and the other had its greater focus on politics.

Hamilton's reply to Seabury first expressed the economic nationalism for which Hamilton would be later known. Instead of deprivation from the boycott,

104. Samuel Seabury, *Free Thoughts on the Proceedings of the Continental Congress* in *Letters of a Westchester Farmer*, 44–46, 49, 50, 54–55, 57, 61 (the quotation).

105. Samuel Seabury, *The Convention Canvassed*, in *Letters of a Westchester Farmer*, 73, 79 (the quotation), 87.

as feared by Seabury, Hamilton saw opportunity. For even complete cessation of the American trade, Hamilton said, "would not be so terrible as he pretends. We can live without trade of any kind." Hamilton cited American sources of cotton, wool, flax, hemp, and other items. Above all, he wrote, here was the possibility for American manufacturers to arise and grow. Hamilton assured his readers, "If by the necessity of the thing, manufactures should once be established and take root among us, they will pave the way, still more, to the future grandeur and glory of America." Hamilton thus spoke to American hopes, but to American vengeance, too. Against the contentions of Seabury he boasted that Great Britain would pay a great price for loss of American trade. "The revenues of Great Britain would suffer a vast diminution," he said.[106]

Hamilton gave much attention to the question of law and authority. He made his essays a virtual argument for independence by his analysis of the imperial structure. He contended that America owed allegiance to the king but none to Parliament. In his second essay Hamilton offered an impressive historical and legal brief, centering on textual analysis of the several colonial charters. He announced his thesis: "We hold our lands in America by virtue of charters from British monarchs, and are under no obligations to the lords or commons for them." Of the king: "He it is that has defended us from our enemies, and to him, alone, we are obliged to render allegiance and submission." How did Hamilton intend to use this argument? He insisted that Parliament derives its authority from the electors and from none other; and it is coextensive with that source. But as such, its authority cannot reach to any beyond that electorate. "It follows therefore," wrote Hamilton, "that all its authority is confined to Great Britain." Hamilton also affirmed that those patriots who decried British tyranny and protested their "enslavement" had the matter right. For "the only distinction between freedom and slavery consists in this: In the former state, a man is governed by the laws to which he has given his consent, either in person, or by his representative: In the latter, he is governed by the will of another." Hamilton, like all the patriots, had heard the theory of "virtual representation." Mere "sophistry," he said.[107]

In *The Farmer Refuted* Hamilton espoused a natural rights theory. By this time he had read Seabury's rejoinder to his first piece and spoke directly to him. He chastised Seabury for his inattention to natural rights. "Ignorance of them in this enlightened age cannot be admitted, as a sufficient excuse for you," he wrote. Sarcastically Hamilton recommended to Seabury the books of his own King's College education—Pufendorf, Burlemaqui, Locke, Grotius, and Montesquieu.

106. Alexander Hamilton, *A Full Vindication of the Measures of the Congress, etc*, in *The Papers of Alexander Hamilton, Volume I: 1768–1778*, ed. Harold C. Syrett (New York: Columbia University Press, 1961), 55–56, 63.

107. Hamilton, *Full Vindication*, 47 (quotation); *The Farmer Refuted*, in *The Papers of Alexander Hamilton, Volume 1*, 91–92, 95–96 (quotation). Hamilton added, "I will go farther, and assert, that the authority of the British Parliament over America, would, in all probability, be a more intolerable species of despotism than an absolute monarchy" (p. 100).

Then he charged that Seabury had drawn his doctrine from Thomas Hobbes. The two, said Hamilton, concurred in the matter of man in a state of nature. "He held, as you do," charged Hamilton, "that [such a man] was then perfectly free from all restraint of law and government." No virtue pertains in such a state and, Hobbes said, it must emerge as the artificial product of social intercourse. Hamilton accounted for Hobbes's falling into this "absurd and impious doctrine" by reason of his ignoring an overseeing deity. The Anglican divine had thus made a fatal error in adopting Hobbes. But "good and wise men," Hamilton responded, have in all ages embraced a different view. "They have supposed that the deity, from the relations we stand in to himself and to each other, has constituted an eternal and immutable law, which is indispensably obligatory upon all mankind, prior to any human institution altogether."[108]

"This," wrote Hamilton, "is what is called the law of nature." Ready for Hamilton in his intellectual duel with Seabury was the 1771 American printing of William Blackstone's *Commentaries*. His studies of the common law supplied for the collegian the freshest formulation of natural rights ideology, and Hamilton quoted Blackstone liberally on the law of nature: "Being coeval with mankind, and dictated by God himself, [it] is, of course, superior in obligation to any other. It is binding over all the globe, in all countries, and at all times. No human laws are of any validity, if contrary to this; and such of them as are valid, derive all their authority, mediately, or immediately, from the original." Hamilton had executed a clever end run here in thus using one of the great champions of parliamentary supremacy against the American Loyalist who was pleading against Hamilton for just that notion. Hamilton perceived, though, that if Seabury succeeded in using Hobbes to posit an original social anarchy that required the authority of the state as its check, he sealed his case for parliamentary ascendancy. But the doctrine of natural rights, countered Hamilton, with its divine origin and sanction, became the check against the original anarchy. The state has as its primary purpose to honor those rights and from it to derive its laws. "Hence also," wrote Hamilton, "the origin of all civil government, justly established, must be a voluntary compact, between the rulers and the ruled, and must be liable to such limitations as are necessary for the security of the *absolute rights* of the latter." Citing Blackstone again, Hamilton avowed that society exists to protect individuals in their absolute rights. Parliamentary law, as now exercised in England, he urged, subverts natural rights. It dissolves the social contract.[109]

---

108. Alexander Hamilton, *The Farmer Refuted*, 86–87.

109. Hamilton, *Farmer Refuted*, 87–88. Hamilton biographer Karl-Friedrich Walling concludes that Hamilton's conception of natural rights "is clearly Lockean in character." But Hamilton gave it a slight twist. He saw natural rights less as privileges than as opportunities, or the guaranties for those not born to privilege, such as himself, to realize their natural potential. This notion approximated a pursuit of happiness, "but it is a very Hamiltonian kind of happiness, based on the possibility of rising from obscurity to greatness." (*Republican Empire: Alexander Hamilton on War and Free Government* [Lawrence: University of Kansas Press, 1999], 25–26).

Hamilton's words seem radical indeed. He relied on natural rights in his two pieces more than had Jefferson in his *Summary View of the Rights of British Americans.* And they may surprise people who know the later Hamilton and his often expressed but thoroughly overstated contempt for democracy. Hamilton spoke from a New York perspective. He could decipher the texts of other colonies' charters, but New York had none of its own. So he made an ultimate appeal that transcended the legalisms of charters and spoke to the natural law that God dispensed. On the other hand, as Hamilton scholar Gerald Stourzh points out, Hamilton's radical natural rights ideas differed from the social radicalism of the democratic ideologues in revolutionary America. His radicalism did not lead to social leveling. It did little to undue the authority of George III himself. And it did not make him favor the arbitrary violence of the mob. He would prove as much in saving Myles Cooper from one. And when the mob ransacked Rivington's printing press, Hamilton denounced its actions. His words, in a letter to John Jay, confirm his conservative Whig thinking:

> In times of such commotion as the present, while the passions of men are worked up to an uncommon pitch there is a great danger of fatal extremes. The same state of the passions which fits the multitude, who have not a sufficient stock of reason and knowledge to guide them, for opposition to tyranny and oppression, very easily leads them to a contempt and disregard of all authority.[110]

Qualifications aside, the Seabury–Hamilton debate starkly differentiates the colonial political mind from the British. Seabury had no trouble with the idea of subordinated colonies. The Roman Empire, he said in reply to Hamilton, flourished mightily under such an arrangement. In fact, the concept of natural rights seemed wholly alien to Seabury, especially insofar as it led, with Hamilton, to the right of political representation. "The right of the colonies to exercise a legislative power, is no natural right," wrote Seabury. "They derive it not from nature, but from the indulgence or grant from the parent state," to whose "permission" the colonies owe their very existence. Nor could Seabury fathom Hamilton's distinctions of authority as exercised by king on the one hand and Parliament on the other. "If we obey the laws of the King, we obey the laws of Parliament," Seabury told Hamilton. Hamilton's contention to the contrary, he said, merely reflected "the ridiculous absurdities of American whiggism."[111]

And principles aside, too, the debate registered personal animosities generated by political commitments. Seabury's third piece showed that Hamilton had rattled him. He faulted Hamilton's writing style. He lapsed into rhetorical overkill, saying of the Continental Congress delegates that "they *talked* like mad-

---

110. Gerald Stourzh, *Alexander Hamilton and the Idea of Republican Government* (Stanford, Calif.: Stanford University Press, 1970), 13–15, 23–24, 176 (the quotation). It should be noted that Rivington had published Hamilton's essays.

111. Samuel Seabury, *A View of the Controversy Between Great-Britain and Her Colonies,* in *Letters of a Westchester Farmer,* 111–12.

men; they *acted* like madmen; they *raved* like madmen; they *did everything* like madmen." Seabury succumbed to distemper. He addressed his rival: "I fear neither your answers nor your threats. The first committee-man that comes to rob me of my tea, or my wine, or molasses, shall feel the weight of my arm; and should you be the man, however lightly you may think of it, a stroke of my cudgel would make you reel, notwithstanding the thickness of your skull."[112]

And so it went. Seabury wrote one more piece, and along the way others joined in. Inglis and Cooper coauthored a retort to the anonymous patriot. Cooper had no idea who he was and expressed disbelief when informed it was his own King's College student. Others expressed their wonder that an eighteen-year-old collegian had produced such disquisitions. Patriots praised the collegian and condemned the Loyalist. Some of them vented their wrath directly. When Seabury's *A View* hit the streets the Sons of Liberty burned whatever copies came into their hands. All the while Hamilton, for his part, actually dreamed of war. When a New Yorker formerly in the British army formed an American company of college students and other young men from the city, Hamilton eagerly joined. They would rise every morning before classes in spring of 1775 and go to the churchyard of St. George's Chapel for drill. "With the näive enthusiasm of youth they accoutered themselves in gaudy uniforms, emblazoned grandiose inscriptions on their attire and adopted a high-flown name." They called themselves "The Corsicans."[113]

The year 1776 was another eventful one for New Yorkers. Within a week of the signing of the Declaration of Independence in Philadelphia, patriots took to the streets. Down came the large equestrian statue of George III that stood on the Bowling Green—more bullets for the revolutionary army. The next morning the enthusiasts marched to the city jail, seized the keys from the sheriff, and liberated the prisoners. Loyalists fled the city, mobs often right on their heels. The Provincial Assembly also acted. It issued an edict forbidding any prayers for the king in church services. The move directly nullified a traditional component of Anglican worship. Church leader Inglis believed that the main animus of the rioters was the Church of England itself. Writing later to the SPG Inglis blamed Presbyterians for forging a secret alliance with the Continental Congress. He had heard nothing but revolutionary politics coming from the New York Presbyterian pulpits.[114]

This official of King's College experienced the consequences of a Tory identity in the summer of this year. "I have frequently heard myself called a Tory and a traitor to my country, as I passed the streets," wrote Inglis, "and epithets joined to each which decency forbids me to set down. Violent threats were thrown out against us, in case the king were any longer prayed for." He described how on one

---

112. Samuel Seabury, *A View of the Controversy*, 104, 120 (quotation), 106 (quotation).
113. Lydekker, *Life and Letters of Charles Inglis*, 146; Schachner, *Alexander Hamilton*, 38, 40; Ranlet, *New York Loyalists*, 49.
114. Kammen, *Colonial New York*, 370; Lydekker, *Life and Letters of Charles Inglis*, 154–58.

Sunday a band of some one hundred patriots stormed his service, "with drums beating and fifes playing—their guns loaded and bayonets fixed." Inglis complied with a directive of the Committee of Safety to have the king's arms taken down in the area churches. The Anglicans eventually suspended their services. Rebel officers, Inglis reported, demanded the keys to Trinity Church so that Dissenter preachers might take it over. Auchmuty had fled New York, and Inglis became head minister the next year. Inglis decided to hide the keys from the rebels, for "I could not bear the thought that their seditious and rebellious effusions should be poured out in our churches." The patriots despised Inglis. In 1778 the Provincial Congress drew up a list of persons whose property was to be confiscated and who, if found, were to be executed. Inglis made the list.[115]

In September New York City saw the worst. The British army, which had gathered on Long Island, now prepared to take the city. Inglis, who had fled to seek the army's protection, rode back into New York with it. They came in overwhelming strength. The Battle of Harlem Heights gave the British control of the city; they would hold it until war's end as New York provided the British army its logistical center throughout the revolution. Now the patriots had to flee. But they vented their wrath on the way out. They plundered Inglis's house. A fire struck the city, for which each side would forever blame the other. Trinity Church burned, only the shell of its walls and steeple remaining. Inglis and others ran to King's College and threw water on the roof, sparing it a similar fate. Few students remained by then. In April the Committee of Safety had ordered the college be made a house for American soldiers. Now the British took over the college building. King's College, or what little was left of it, sat out the revolution, still a Loyalist institution.[116]

The patriot triumvirate from King's all served in the war. Hamilton did so for the duration and with great distinction. He became a trusted aid to George Washington. When the general led the American troops into Princeton, Hamilton, the story long held, fired the shot that disfigured the portrait of George II in Nassau Hall.[117] In 1777 both Jay and Morris returned to New York for some important business. Here, as in all the colonies, they answered the charge of the Continental Congress to form a new state constitution.

Both Morris and Jay had held out to the last against independence, but when the die was cast they committed to it. At the convention, however, these two from King's College gave different meanings to the conservative Whig positions they held. Ostensibly, Morris was the more conservative. Barely twenty-five, he had nonetheless given permanent shape to his ideas. He believed that property and commerce underscore social stability and progress. Government

115. Lydekker, *Life and Letters of Charles Inglis*, 164–66, 191.

116. Kammen, *Colonial New York*, 270; Lydekker, *Life and Letters of Charles Inglis*, 167–68; Humphrey, *King's College*, 153–54.

117. Schachner, *Alexander Hamilton*, 55. It is not entirely clear that it was indeed Hamilton who fired this shot.

must protect both. He accepted political liberty for all, but not unlimited liberty for any. Unlike Hamilton he seldom invoked natural rights. To society he ascribed a higher priority than the individual. Human beings must live in a society, Morris asserted, and can enjoy only those rights that experience had proven necessary for its preservation.[118]

At the New York meeting, however, Morris provoked his colleagues in surprising ways. On one issue he provoked John Jay in particular. Jay proposed that Roman Catholics should not enjoy civil rights without swearing a first loyalty to the state uncompromised by another loyalty to a foreign authority, that is, the pope. Morris assaulted this provision and made every maneuver he could do defeat it. He then came back with a qualified but nonetheless expansive statement of religious liberty: "The liberty of conscience hereby granted, shall not be so construed as to excuse acts of licentiousness, or justify practices inconsistent with the peace or safety of this State." Jay's original exclusionary provisions eliminated, the amendment won unanimous approval.[119]

Morris also tried to commit New York to ending slavery. He pressed on the convention a powerful resolution: "And whereas a regard to the rights of human nature and the principles of our holy religion, loudly call upon us to dispense the blessings of freedom to all mankind . . . it is therefore most earnestly recommended . . . that in future ages, every human being who breathes the air of this State, shall enjoy the privileges of a freeman." Jay supported Morris in this matter (though because of his mother's death he had to leave the convention and could not vote on it). However, their group constituted a minority. The convention defeated the motion by a vote of thirty-one to five.[120]

Finally, Morris wanted to restrict the popular vote in the new constitution. And he wanted an executive branch so strong that the governor could exercise the veto liberally over the legislature. In 1777, that idea was reactionary, and it got nowhere among the conventioneers. Instead, they adopted a motion introduced by Jay that gave the governor very limited power.[121] Thus Conservative Whiggery, within a broad consensus, could mean different political values and priorities. But the careers of Hamilton, Jay, and Morris would converge again in the next two decades. The history of these years in the young nation would demonstrate that King's College had supplied it with three of the most powerful advocates and practitioners of the Federalist party ideology.

The College of Philadelphia entered the revolutionary years in schizophrenic mode. Its provost, William Smith, championed the Church of England and had worked for its gains and influence in the college. Vice Provost Francis Alison had won a reputation for his learned defense of the Presbyterian standards. He

---

118. Mintz, *Gouverneur Morris*, 72–73.
119. Monaghan, *John Jay*, 94–95; Mintz, *Gouverneur Morris*, 75 (the quotation).
120. Mintz, *Gouverneur Morris*, 76; Monaghan, *John Jay*, 95.
121. Mintz, *Gouverneur Morris*, 74.

defended the Old Light position and had tried to give it a theological presence at the college. The years after 1764 would both confirm and enhance the standing of each man as a stalwart of his denomination. The business of academe readily spilled over into the business of imperial politics. No college would experience more directly than the College of Philadelphia the intervening hand of the state legislature. In 1779, the full force of the American Revolution, and the internal revolution that attended it, became starkly visible in Pennsylvania.

The political background informs this story. The Quaker, or Assembly party, still prevailed in 1765. It drew its strength from the eastern Quakers and from German pietists whom the party had carefully cultivated. Benjamin Franklin and Joseph Galloway provided the leadership. The Assembly party had long sought to seize power from the proprietors, the Penns, and in 1764 formalized that effort in a petition to the Crown to make Pennsylvania a royal colony. In this effort, the Quakers drew support from others in the colony who also wanted more autonomy. The rival Proprietary party resisted the effort. This faction had its cohesiveness in the patronage of the Penns, who created a network of provincial placeholders. They constituted an Anglican elite who could nonetheless, for the while, draw support from Scotch-Irish Presbyterians. The French and Indian wars brought into open conflict the animosities of the Pennsylvania frontier groups against the pacifist policies of the Quakers. The Scotch-Irish did not have a large representation in the legislature, however, and conservative elites dominated both parties. Pennsylvania was slower than the other colonies to embrace the cause of independence.[122]

Provost William Smith did not welcome the Stamp Act and lent his voice to a small group in the assembly that denounced it. Smith made his views known to the SPG as he denounced Parliament's efforts to "take money out of our pockets." He believed Parliament lacked wisdom and right in imposing these taxes, and he upheld the right of representation by the colonies. Smith also appealed to the protections of the original charters and "the inherent rights of Englishmen." He furthermore warned that "a people planted, and nursed, and educated in the high principles of liberty" would not readily submit to such abuse. Smith wondered why England would wish to risk "an alienation of the affections of a loyal people" and even the loss of business by such shortsighted action. With patriotic notions so emphatically conveyed, we must wonder how it came about that in 1775 Smith had become one of the most reviled of men in the eyes of Pennsylvania's American revolutionaries.[123]

The reason lies in Smith's ambitious religious politics. None knew them better than Franklin. As we have seen he brought Smith to the college on the great

---

122. Douglas M. Arnold, *A Republican Revolution: Ideology and Politics in Pennsylvania, 1776–1790* (New York: Garland Publishing, 1989), 17–19; Wayne L. Bockelman and Owen S. Ireland, "The Internal Revolution in Pennsylvania: An Ethnic-Religious Interpretation," *Pennsylvania History* 41 (1974): 140, 144.

123. Horace Wemyss Smith, *Life and Correspondence of the Rev. William Smith, D.D., Volumes I and II* (1879; New York: Arno Press, 1972), 1:385.

hope that it would pioneer in America as a nonsectarian institution. But Smith quickly allied with the proprietors and turned to make the College of Philadelphia a stronghold of Anglicanism, which the Penns had embraced. He made himself a visible public Anglican as well. At three Anglican conventions held in the early 1760s Smith presided at each. He was a watch guard of Anglican interests, as his correspondence with England reveals. Smith repeatedly lamented the poor condition of the Anglican colonial ministry. He sent his own graduates to England for ordination to help remedy the situation. And he served as Anglican vigilante in the colonies, always keeping an eye on the "enemies" of the Church and reporting their doings. Thus in 1768 Smith wrote to the secretary of the SPG warning that "the Presbyterians from one end of the continent to the other are attacking the Church." The issue? Once again, American bishops.[124]

Smith had not taken the lead in this matter, nor did he welcome the initiative of the Anglican convention of 1766, held, as we noticed, in New York City. The prospect of an Anglican bishop in the colonies, Smith well knew, would greatly raise the animosity against the Church. Smith observed the reactions to Chandler's *Appeal*, citing "the malevolent set of writers" who had taken to the newspapers to issue their "shameful misrepresentations." Smith wished that "our side had not given any cause," but felt compelled nonetheless to defend the Anglican churches. He added that "I am determined now to contribute my mite" to defend them.[125]

But another person resolved to stop the bishop movement. He was Francis Alison. So the College of Philadelphia presents an extraordinary situation in which its two leaders engaged in the religious politics of the day as opposing polemicists. Alison, to be sure, did not need the bishop issue to induce his anti-Anglican feelings. He already smarted from Anglican designs at the college[126] and now saw the bishop issue as all of a piece. At the same time that the Anglicans held their 1766 Convention, Presbyterians met, also in New York, and in greater numbers, at the meeting of the Synod of New York and Philadelphia. Alison, in poor health, did not attend, but did arrange to have an overture read on his behalf before the assembled Presbyterians. Alison stated, "I am greatly for an union among all the anti-Episcopal churches." He said that Provost Smith "told me in plain terms, that they were determined to have one, or more bishops" and that he would get the Lutherans and Quakers to support them. Alison wrote about bishops, "what we dread is their political power, and their courts, of which [native-born] Americans can have no notion adequate to the mischiefs that they introduce." Alison raised the specter of a new ecclesiastical tyranny over the

---

124. *Life and Correspondence of Smith*, 1:406, 412, 414.
125. *Life and Correspondence of Smith*, 1:414.
126. Later in 1769, such was Alison's despair of the college situation and the Anglican control of it that he looked to Princeton as a bulwark against episcopacy. The next year he worked with other Presbyterians to secure a charter for an academy in Newark, Delaware (Bridenbaugh, *Mitre and Sceptre*, 185).

colonies, and so dire was the threat, he believed, that "a firm union against episcopal encroachments" must result. "Every lawful method," he urged, "should be
used to keep free from that yoke of bondage."[127]

Alison did not take on political issues as a rule. But he did denounce the
Stamp Act and rallied Presbyterians against it. In 1768, using the pseudonym
"Centinel," Alison insisted that Americans had rights equal to English citizens,
but also noted that Americans differed from the English to the extent that one
government could no longer unite them. He thus urged political autonomy for
the thirteen different colonies. Alison directly linked the secular politics and the
ecclesiastical. Thus, he believed, the bishop issue merited the attention of the
Stamp Act Congress because it threatened both "our civil and religious liberties." Alison joined energetically with Ezra Stiles in the Plan of Union to resist
Anglican ambitions. He concurred in the necessity of the committees of correspondence, to be established around the colonies, to monitor and thwart the
Anglican designs. Alison also took up his pen in the cause. In New York City,
the "American Whig" fought the bishop scheme, and in Philadelphia the "Centinel" led. Alison, John Dickinson, and George Bryan contributed the pieces to
this series of anti-Anglican statements.[128]

Provost Smith found the Centinel pieces insufferable. He had in fact already
entered the fray by publishing a series of opinions called "The Anatomist," essentially a defense of Chandler's pamphlet against its many critics. Alison in turn
produced several issues of "The Remonstrant" to confront "The Anatomist." Alison outsold Smith by a fair measure. In June 1768 Smith presented the first of
two issues of the "Anti-Centinel." A literary warfare thus raged, and it contributed a noteworthy share of the kulturkampf in revolutionary America. Here
is Carl Bridenbaugh's assessment of this contest: "Above all, the Dissenters were
rich in talents. The New York-New Jersey [Anglican] clergy, with only occasional assistance from their ablest penmen, Provost Smith, really could not compete with Livingston, Alison, and their bench of able controversialists in literary
competence, ecclesiastical learning, and forensic skill."[129]

The bishop issue raised Presbyterian self-consciousness. Presbyterians had
mostly repaired their differences—Old Light and New Light—in 1758, and now
in the mid-1760s they emerged as a political force. A "Presbyterian party," so-
called, brought new radical Whig voices to Pennsylvania politics. Charles
Thomson provided the main leadership here. Although he was not a product of
the College of Philadelphia, he was a former student of Alison and later taught
at his school. Thomson was born in Ulster, in a town halfway between Belfast
and Londonderry, in 1729. For reasons unknown his father decided to emigrate

---

127. Bridenbaugh, *Mitre and Sceptre*, 272–73.
128. Robson, *Educating Republicans*, 137; Bridenbaugh, *Mitre and Sceptre*, 299.
129. Douglas Sloan, *The Scottish Enlightenment and the American College Ideal* (New York: Teachers College Press, 1971), 94; Bridenbaugh, *Mitre and Sceptre*, 274, 299–301, 306 (the Bridenbaugh
quotation).

in 1739. His wife had died the previous year. The father died shortly after arriving in Pennsylvania and Charles was entrusted to the care of a blacksmith family. He soon set out on his own. He found his way to Newark, Delaware, and entered the New London school run by Alison. Charles stayed with the Alison family. Here he had a heavily classical education, for which teaching Alison was renowned, and here he found a great love for the *Spectator*. As an excellent classical student, Thomson caught the attention of Franklin and became a tutor at the Pennsylvania Academy in 1751. The next year his former mentor Alison joined the school as its new head. When the academy was elevated to the College of Philadelphia in 1755 Thomson resigned. Its seems most likely that he did so because William Smith came on board as the new provost. We do not know exactly when this enmity began—that between Thomson and the man he called "that designing, subtle, mortal Dr. Smith"—but it became intense.[130]

Thomson eventually went into business and became a Philadelphia merchant. He had not pursued politics very much, but the Stamp Act of 1765 roused him to action. He saw in the act an overreaching plan on the part of the British to put the colonies under foot. He wrote a letter to Franklin decrying the deprivation of "those rights, those distinguishing and invaluable rights of Britons." Thomson became the prime organizer of the Philadelphia opposition to the Stamp Act. He formed a personal alliance with fellow Presbyterian John Dickinson, who penned his famous "Letters from a Farmer in Pennsylvania" after Philadelphia received the news of the Townshend Acts in 1767. In the city newspapers Thomson urged that residents undertake "the glorious fashion of wearing none but American manufactures," this in "the cause of liberty and their country." When Thomson observed the synod meeting in 1766 he fully identified with Alison's campaign against the bishop. Finally, by 1768 Franklin saw the hopelessness of the royal colony project for Pennsylvania, and his resigning from that project created an alliance between him and Thomson. They lived almost next door to each other.[131]

Benjamin Rush also provided a major personality for the radical faction. The Presbyterian influences on Rush came from his mother, who sent him to his uncle Samuel Finley's academy. His earliest social views reflected the moral judgment of New Light preachers; in 1761 he referred to Philadelphia as a "seat of corruption, and happy are those who escape its evils." He denounced the young men of that city as "devoted to pleasure and sensuality." In 1765 Rush experienced first hand the preaching of George Whitefield, which reinforced the listener's Calvinist persuasion. That year Rush took the extreme oppositional view on the Stamp Act, faulting those like the Quakers and Franklin who reacted in a tepid manner. After studying medicine in England and Scotland, Rush returned to Philadelphia.

---

130. Boyd Stanley Schlenther, *Charles Thomson: A Patriot's Pursuit* (Newark: University of Delaware Press, 1990), 1–24.

131. Schlenther, *Charles Thomson*, 58–59 (the quotation), 64, 73–74, 77, 80, 83; Joseph E. Illick, *Colonial Pennsylvania: A History* (New York: Scribner, 1976), 257.

With other intellectuals like David Rittenhouse, he became a stalwart republican, but with every bit the moral judgment of the religious influences that had nurtured him. Rush earned much of his lasting reputation for his work in medicine. He joined the Medical College of the College of Philadelphia in 1769, but his continued political commitments would take him to his signing of the Declaration of Independence in 1776 and beyond to his work for the Constitution of 1789. We have a useful testimony of the radical Whig mind in Pennsylvania in a letter Rush wrote to Patrick Henry after independence. Rush saw the ills of America as all rooted in the British nexus. "I tremble to think of the mischiefs that would have spread through this country had we continued our dependence on Gt. Britain twenty years longer. The contest two years ago found us contaminated with British customs, manners, and ideas of government."[132]

A few years of relative calm prevailed in Philadelphia in the early 1770s. Then one day in May 1774 Paul Revere rode his horse into the city. He had traveled from Boston with news of the closing of its port by the British. He wanted advice from Philadelphians. In response a large crowd gathered at the City Tavern. The meeting voted to extend its sympathy to the Bostonians and to have them know that it considered them to be "suffering in a general cause" and that "we shall continue to evince our firmness in the cause of American liberty." Provost Smith was voted onto a committee to meet the next day, May 21, to draft a lengthy letter to the Bostonians. Smith did the writing. His letter conveyed the moderate feelings of the committee. It did not endorse Boston's suggestion of non-importation and non-exportation, or at least not just yet. It preferred a petition to the Crown, and it hoped it might appeal to the better sentiments of the English leadership, the "many wise and good men in the mother country." Smith stayed on top of the city politics. He made another address at the end of June when a meeting of freeholders more strongly denounced the British action in Boston. He urged that "order and decorum" prevail. He cautioned against "any heated or hasty resolves" and called for the "temperate and enlightened zeal of the patriot" as the standard for the day. Finally, Philadelphia responded to Boston's query about the advisability of a general congress of the colonies. It agreed to send delegates to the first Continental Congress, and Smith joined Dickinson, Thomas Reed, James Wilson, and others to draft the instructions for Pennsylvania's representatives to that meeting.[133]

These events began to recast Pennsylvania politics. First, they made clear that the Quakers would give little support to the larger American cause. Several of them expressed their disapproval of Bostonians' excessive actions in destroying the hated tea. Quakers would oppose any economic retaliation against England.[134] The moderation of Smith and his group and the reluctance of the Quak-

---

132. Paul F. Lambert, "Benjamin Rush and American Independence," *Pennsylvania History* 39 (1972): 443–49 (the quotation).

133. *Life and Correspondence of Smith*, 1:491–98.

134. Schlenther, *Charles Thomson*, 103; Illick, *Colonial Pennsylvania*, 273.

ers gave an opening for an expanding radical movement. The year 1774 proved critical. Since 1770 Thomson had gone to work organizing committees and associations in every county of Pennsylvania. Rallying behind him there emerged a new political voice—that of the mechanics and other workers. They urged non-importation, which the merchants had abandoned, and seized the radical lead. Now they pressed to exercise more political muscle, too. This shift accompanied another one. Scotch-Irish Presbyterians soon dominated the radical wing, contributing even some of the city's respectable commercial and professional leaders. Quaker merchant Henry Drinker therefore could only lament the city elections in fall 1774. "The lower class of people," he complained, "were generally mustered by the Presbyterian party" and he cited particularly "that inf[amou]s C. Thomson fellow. To what a shamefully depraved state we have arrived," he added.[135]

The next year the Continental Congress met again in Philadelphia. On May 10, 1775, that body left the State House and marched together over to the College of Philadelphia and attended the commencement exercises of that year. They took their seats, and thereupon the governor entered, followed by the trustees, Smith, Alison, and the professors. Respectable citizens from the city occupied the gallery, which was filled, as the splendor of the occasion would warrant. Speeches from the students followed. One came from William Moore Smith, the eldest son of the provost. His topic: the fall of empires. His theme: empires fall as citizens lapse into luxury, allured by the imports from distant places.[136]

The next month in Christ Church, Provost Smith delivered the most decisive sermon of his career. What he said attracted wide notice. All present expected Smith to address the immediate imperial crisis. And he did. He reviewed the history of colonial and British relations, celebrating many years of splendid cooperation that had helped promote the rising glory of America. Smith emphasized that the British, too, had gained immensely from the relationship—"our wealth was poured in upon them from ten thousand channels." He cited the record of colonial response to British appeals for help—"we left them not alone, but shared their toils and fought by their side." But they have now turned against us, he said. And unjustly. Smith charged that England had violated American liberties, for we have "never sold our birth-right." The liberties that Americans hold are inviolable, Smith insisted. "These are the principles we inherited from Britons themselves."[137]

Smith spoke to his Anglican congregation as an Anglican leader. He wanted all of Philadelphia to hear his message, though, for he intended to say that the

---

135. Illick, *Colonial Philadelphia*, 92, 94; Bockelman and Ireland, "The Internal Revolution in Pennsylvania," 141–42; Robert F. Oaks, "Philadelphia Merchants and the First Continental Congress," *Pennsylvania History* 40 (1973): 151–52 (the quotation).
136. *Life and Correspondence of Smith*, 1:500–1.
137. *Life and Correspondence of Smith*, 1:507, 509–10.

colonial Church of England would not turn against America. "A continued submission to violence is no tenet of our church," Smith proclaimed. Nor would
Smith uphold nonresistance or a pacifist posture in the face of British oppression.
"The doctrine of absolute non-resistance," he asserted, "has been fully exploded
among every virtuous people. The free-born soul revolts against it." He went on:
"God, in his own government of the world, never violates freedom." And, he
said, "you are now engaged in one of the grandest struggles, to which freemen
can be called." Indeed, Smith delivered a remarkable address when we consider
his prominence in the Anglican denomination, more known for its loyalism than
its patriotism. Silas Deane perceived its significance: "As the Doctor has been
called a high churchman, and one that had a bishopric in expectation, I hope his
thus publicly sounding the pulpit alarm on the subject of liberty will be an example to the Church clergy elsewhere, and bring them off from the line of conduct which they have hitherto ingloriously pursued."[138]

In view of the fact that Smith's patriotic appeal won him little favor in his
own city, it is instructive to notice the reaction it got in England. The *London
Magazine* denounced him: "Dr. Smith, though an Episcopal clergyman, appears
to be as zealous a friend to the liberties of America, and as warm against the measures of [the British] administration, as any person whatsoever." The aged John
Wesley decried Smith's radical notions:

> Dr. Smith supposes the Americans have a right of granting their own money: that
> is, of being exempt from taxation by the supreme power. If they contend for this
> right, they contend for neither more nor less than for independency. That they con-
> tend for the cause of liberty is another mistaken supposition. They have no liberty,
> civil or religious, but what the [Parliament] allows. Vainly do they complain of un-
> constitutional exactions, violated rights, and mutilated charters.[139]

Of course, Smith was also thinking politically. He perceived the danger that
would come to the American church if it were perceived to be unpatriotic. He
spent no little effort urging that consideration on the home officials of the
Church. He explained to the bishop of London why he honored the request of
the Continental Congress for observance of a fast day and why he gave the sermon to honor the event. What Smith truly wanted was moderation on all sides,
earnest discussions, and any mediation that could avert open conflict. He never
called for nor endorsed American independence.[140]

The radicals did, though. On May 20, 1776, they seized the day. A large
gathering materialized at the State House, and some four thousand people endorsed radical proposals. They denounced the assembly, which had prevented

---

138. *Life and Correspondence of Smith*, 1:512, 513, 517–18 (Deane quotation). Smith spoke again
in July and sought to define a middle way. His efforts served only to raise patriot animosity against
him (Robson, *Educating Republicans*, 35).
139. *Life and Correspondence of Smith*, 1:520–23.
140. *Life and Correspondence of Smith*, 1:524–25, 527, 531–33.

the Pennsylvania delegation to the Continental Congress from endorsing independence. In July came the news of Jefferson's declaration, an event that "appeared to transform Pennsylvania from a placid province into an emotional
state." To be sure, that situation introduced a radical shift in Pennsylvania history, too, one that would profoundly affect the college. A new religious/ethnic
group came into power. Quakers and Anglicans declined significantly in the assembly. That change signified a decline in English domination, too. Presbyterian Scotch-Irish and German Lutheran numbers increased the most. Of even
greater consequence, the new legislature looked like ordinary citizens, a walking white male democracy. An Anglican minister said of the new body, "some
of them are so obscure that their very names have never met my ears before."
This truly radical shift left some of the original patriots dumfounded and troubled. Rush had earlier in the year helped Thomas Paine get his *Common Sense*
into print. Now a teacher at the medical college, he saw an unlearned group
coming into power and a legislative tyranny in its wake. Charles Thomson concurred. He saw obscure men being elevated too rapidly and too far and grieved
that "the affairs of this state [have been thrown] into the hands of men totally
unequal to them."[141]

These skeptics had even more to worry about when the convention met in
July to draft the new Pennsylvania state constitution. The radical campaign to
choose the delegates included broadsides from the Committee of Privates with
the admonition "choose no rich men, and few learned men as possible" for the
convention. Voters virtually followed suit. And the convention proceeded to
write the most radical constitution in America. It reflected not only class but religion. University of Pennsylvania historian Edward Potts Cheyney saw in the
creation of the document the long influence of Whitefield and the moralistic
Protestants that grew from his heady preaching. It drew also from radical republican ideologies. There resulted a puritanical effort to inscribe morality and
virtue into law. The new constitution thus declared, "Laws for the encouragement of virtue, and prevention of vice and immorality, shall be made and constantly kept in force." William Smith for one had argued that moral elevation
comes only from education and nurture, not from the dictates of the state. Pennsylvania's new government also reflected the reaction against the proprietary history of the colony. "Government," said the new constitution, "is . . . not for the
particular emolument or advantage of any single man, family, or set of men." The
constitution expanded the base of decision making, beginning with the electorate itself (no financial or property requirements). It prevented plural office-
holding. A unicameral legislature had the greatest power in the new structure

---

141. Illick, *Colonial Pennsylvania*, 301, 302, 310 (first quotation), 314; Ann D. Gordon, *The College of Philadelphia, 1749–1779: Impact of an Institution* (New York: Garland, 1989), 254–55 (Anglican quotation); Schlenther, *Charles Thomson*, 138 (Thomson quotation). For more on the ethnic-
religious transformation in Pennsylvania politics see all of Bockelman and Ireland, "The Internal
Revolution in Pennsylvania," 125–56.

while a Supreme Executive Council (SEC) had only the limited authority the constitution gave to that branch of government.[142]

The conditions in revolutionary Pennsylvania affected the College of Philadelphia in two important ways. First, they forced its closing. Here as in other colleges provincial troops moved into college buildings, and in this case as early as late 1775. The arrangement did not mix well with the academic norms, and in June 1777 the officers abandoned instruction altogether. In September the British moved into Philadelphia and they had their own designs for the college hall, classrooms, and yard. Alison left the college upon its closing, but the departure made him uneasy. Smith remained, and when General Howe moved his British troops in, Alison feared a conspiracy between them to take over the college; "I am not willing to trust them," he wrote in a letter. The British occupied Philadelphia into May 1778. When they left the city Loyalists departed with them. The college reopened in January 1779, also the year of Alison's death.[143]

The constitution was not long in place when the radicals who wrote it began to move against the college. At the end of August 1777 Howe was advancing toward Philadelphia. The Supreme Executive Council that the constitution had created moved against political suspects. It took its lead from the Continental Congress, which had called for the apprehension of all persons whose general conduct and words suggested a disposition averse to the patriotic cause. The council drew up a list of forty-one such individuals. It named many Quakers, and it named William Smith. It did show some deference toward "men of reputation" and asked for some "tenderness" toward them. Many, Quakers especially, suffered a worse fate than Smith as a result. Officials did not take him into custody and he had apparently only to give a promise that he remain at home and be available to the call of the Executive Council if needed. The Battle of Brandywine, which gave the British their access to the city, liberated Smith to resume his normal life. He chose to leave the city, however, and sat out the British occupation, and the closing of the college, near Valley Forge.[144]

But the animus against the college did not end at the provost's office. The Scotch-Irish Presbyterians, following their electoral victory, now acted more self-consciously as a political group. They had people like John Bayard, Thomas McKean, and Sam Bryan in key posts. When the Constitutionalists (the radical party so named because they now defended their constitution against widespread hostility toward it) looked at the college they saw a board of trustees stocked with old proprietary partisans and rank Loyalists. In fact, the board's whole modus operandi defied the democratic ideals of the radicals. Since the beginning

---

142. Edward Potts Cheyney, *History of the University of Pennsylvania, 1740–1940* (Philadelphia: University of Pennsylvania Press, 1940), 118; Gordon, *College of Philadelphia*, 253–54; Illick, *Colonial Pennsylvania*, 307–9.

143. Cheyney, *University of Pennsylvania*, 116–17; Gordon, *College of Philadelphia*, 258; Sloan, *Scottish Enlightenment*, 95.

144. *Life and Correspondence of Smith*, 1:572–73.

of the college the board had been a vehicle of political patronage with family connections providing the continuity of personalities who controlled it. The revolution made matters only worse in the eyes of the Constitutionalists. They saw Loyalists on the board retreat to the British lines when the fighting broke out, or embark to England itself. Of other trustees one could say that they had at most a lukewarm acceptance of the new government. So the legislature acted against them. Four trustees were jailed or paroled when the British threatened to enter the city.[145]

The departure of the British from Philadelphia in spring 1778 gave the Constitutionalists the opportunity for another move against the college. In November the Scotch-Irish leader Joseph Reed won election as president of the SEC. Bryan was vice president. At this time the assembly instituted a loyalty oath to the state, required of all citizens. Any who did not sign it by the end of the next year would be barred forever from political office. This move provided the context for the college and the Constitutionalists' actions against it. The new constitution had called for establishing "one or more state universities." The radicals realized that they already had an institution they could make to fit the bill. In February 1779 a committee took on the task of examining all aspects of the college and the academy and reporting to the assembly. The trustees met the next month and prepared a lengthy case in their defense, Smith doing the critical work. They tried in particular to show that the College of Philadelphia had only by historical accident come under the control of Anglicans, but that in fact Presbyterians dominated the ranks of masters and tutors.[146]

It probably mattered not at all what Smith and the trustees did. The investigating committee came back with a stinging report on the college. Its words convey the radicals' contempt. "The principal institution of learning in this state," it said, was "founded on the most free and catholic principles, raised and cherished by the hand of public bounty." But, by a change in 1764, it had made itself a virtual ally of Britain and had imposed on its officers and faculty an effective test of allegiance to that nation. The next sentences left little doubt as to what action the assembly would take. "We cannot think the good people of this state can, or ought to, rest satisfied, or the protection of government be extended to an institution framed with such manifest attachment to the British government and conducted with a general inattention to the authority of the State." Change was imminent. [147]

And it came sooner rather than later in part because of the impolitic behavior pursued by the trustees. The revolution seemed to have changed nothing in their thinking. From 1776 on they elected to their board men known for their

---

145. Gordon, *College of Philadelphia*, 252, 257; Cheyney, *University of Pennsylvania*, 119; Bockelman and Ireland, "The Internal Revolution in Pennsylvania," 149.

146. Bockelman and Ireland, "The Internal Revolution in Pennsylvania," 155; Cheyney, *University of Pennsylvania*, 120–22; Gordon, *College of Philadelphia*, 263.

147. *Life and Correspondence of Smith*, 2:22; Cheyney, *University* of Pennsylvania, 122–23.

opposition to the new state constitution. Most were solid patriots, to be sure, individuals like Francis Hopkinson and Robert Morris, but they publicly fought the Constitutionalists. They continued to do so into the summer of 1779, in this case electing the Scotch-born, brilliant legalist James Wilson—a patriot, but also lawyer for the proprietors in actions against the assembly.[148]

The assembly had prepared a bill to change the college and in November 1779 stood for election while the bill was still under consideration. Members supportive of the trustees lost, while most of the committee that drafted the bill returned. On November 25 the bill passed 39 to 5 and became law four days later. The new legislation stated in its preamble the importance of education and the proper interest of the state in nurturing it. It considered "seminaries of learning" as a blessing to the public. It was not a populist or anti-intellectual document. (Thomas Reed had received a master's degree from the college.) The act instead addressed a political situation. It inaugurated a new era for the college by changing the board. All the existing trustees were dismissed and another group came in to replace them, still twenty-four in number. Now, however, the trustees would have in their ranks the senior minister of each Christian denomination in the city. Also, prominent civic leaders would also serve. The trustees could elect new members from this group, but subject to the veto of the legislature. The college now also had a new name: the University of Pennsylvania.[149]

So in a sense the new University of Pennsylvania looked back to the original ideals of the College of Philadelphia. The act of 1779 sought to assure that no religious group would dominate the institution. Benjamin Franklin may have had more clearly secular notions in mind than did the legislature that assured representation of many religious groups, but the authors of the legislation clearly wanted to undo and move beyond the religious politics that had corrupted Franklin's original goals. We have seen earlier how Franklin suffered personally from the intense sectarian warfare that described Pennsylvania politics and the College of Philadelphia. So it was fitting that, taking his seat on the new board of trustees for the University of Pennsylvania, we find the new state's most prominent citizen—Benjamin Franklin.[150]

In New England, all four colonial colleges became patriot schools. All had roots in the Calvinist tradition. Even the school that had moved furthest from it, Harvard, drew from the Puritan past a historical memory that inspired revolutionary sentiments. Yale men had the more recent consistent Calvinism of the New Divinity and the renewed Old Light identification of an Ezra Stiles to provide religious foundations for radical politics. Rhode Island College and Dartmouth moved less easily into revolutionary mode, but politics, not intellect, explains that difference.

148. Gordon, *College of Philadelphia*, 260, 267.
149. Gordon, *College of Philadelphia*, 275–77; Cheyney, *University of Pennsylvania*, 124–25.
150. Cheyney, *University of Pennsylvania*, 124.

In the Southern and Middle Atlantic Colonies, the five colleges became patriot schools. The two in New Jersey did so almost automatically. Queen's College emerged from the Americanist wing of the Dutch Reformed Church with a vigorous Calvinism, raised to emotional intensity in the religious Awakening, and identified with the American cause in the revolutionary years into which it was born. Princeton, the first school of the Awakening, could draw from both that source and the Scottish Enlightenment that John Witherspoon introduced to it after 1768. The other colleges all had either a formal or nominal Anglican identity. In each, patriot institutions came into being by imposition—from within or from without. William and Mary's weak Anglican core dissolved from the American loyalties of James Madison and from the American loyalties of alumni like Thomas Jefferson. King's became Columbia from the efforts of student patriots like Alexander Hamilton and the victory of American armies on the fields of battle. At the College of Philadelphia radical leaders triumphant in state politics, by careful design, created the University of Pennsylvania. A concluding postscript provides a larger meaning for these developments.

Postscript

From a certain perspective—their curricula—the American colonial colleges suggest a stark and unexciting uniformity. One could attend Harvard in 1680 or Dartmouth in 1775 and confront a required four-year program that ranged from the classic languages and literature to natural philosophy (science) to moral philosophy, with additional exposure to mathematics, logic, and rhetoric. Of course, one could find critical differentiations. Students at Harvard and Yale, in accordance with their reformed traditions, studied the works of William Ames well into the eighteenth century. Anglican colleges like William and Mary and King's had no reason to run their students through that regime. Then, too, the colleges had their own informal curricula. Occasionally an exceptional teacher like William Small at William and Mary could introduce the modern intellectual world to an ambitious student like Thomas Jefferson. After midcentury, students at many of the colleges were forming their own literary societies and making their own entry into the modern world of ideas. All colonial graduates, however, could speak a common cultural language, assured by the dominating tradition of the college curriculum over a century and a half.

But the higher education scene in the colonial era is one of contest, of intellectual warfare both within and between the nine institutions. Such was the case because the colleges always looked out for their own particular publics. Indeed, those publics created them. The colleges came into being, usually, when a religious denomination, or faction within it, had acquired sufficient self-consciousness and a particularized intellectual tradition of its own to give it institutional expression by way of a college founding. Harvard followed readily from the long struggle of Puritans in England and quickly became the New England expression of an identity forged in warfare against rival Anglicanism. But it also spoke for a particular set within English and American Puritanism. The College of New Jersey emerged from New Side Presbyterians who had contested with opposition in their own denomination and with the established power of Anglicans in the Southern and Middle colonies. The Dutch Reformed who created Queen's College came out of a party within that denomination that had a special sense of their Americanness. They had participated in the religious Awakening and had sought to introduce English-language ritual into their worship. Likewise within the New England Congregationalists a New Light and Separatist party emerged. They met the resistance of the Standing Order that supported Harvard and Yale. Some of these Dissenters became Baptists. Rhode Island College gave form to the self-awareness of that religious group and its affiliates in other colonies.

These identities gave the colleges their pluralistic character. They grew amid the rich and varied expressions of Protestantism, in Europe and the American colonies, in the period examined here. Those expressions often took on polemical form; more often they yielded a literature marked by learning, subtle argumentation, and scholarly nuance. Readers will perhaps judge that many of the documents analyzed in the course of this narrative abound in technicalities, narrow doctrinal disputations. They were conveyed by religious tract and pulpit sermon. But these textual productions also spoke for a particular group of people who sought an institutional identity for themselves. The colleges served that purpose. We have noticed on many occasions that individuals who best expressed the intellectual constructions that identified a Protestant group emerged as presidents of the colleges that the group created—Increase Mather at Harvard, Jonathan Dickinson at the College of New Jersey, Samuel Johnson at King's, Thomas Clap and Ezra Stiles at Yale. Even before they assumed their presidential offices, Dickinson and Johnson engaged each other—New Light Presbyterian against Arminian Anglican—on various points of theology and church polity. Creation of Princeton and King's gave institutional expression to these disputations.

And yet all the colleges aspired to be more than just a particularized institution. That interest returns us to the prevailing uniformity. Whatever their religious identity, college leaders wished a connection to the larger intellectual life of Western civilization. All the schools had recourse in their four-year curricula to the root foundations of the West in the classical components in their programs of study. Of course, a training in this realm of culture gave one the marks of gentlemanly prestige and respectability. The classics also gave the colleges a measure of the same. They assured also that these schools would not be narrowly sectarian. And in the graduates they produced none of the colleges served only their denominations. They produced lawyers, physicians, politicians, and businessmen. Colleges, born of denominational identities, in turn reshaped those denominations. They had liberalizing and modernizing effects on them. John Witherspoon at Princeton supplies the best example.

The colleges also evolved to become expressions of American nationalism. That institutions given to an education in ancient literature and Christian teachings should so evolve may seem curious. And, of course, in intellectual history, this matter is one of the most difficult. How did a colonial college education produce the array of patriots that we earlier observed, in only a partial listing? We do not have an abundance of empirical evidence to show that one course, or one author, created a Jefferson, an Adams, or a Madison. Personal experience, or even simple prejudice, could lead one to oppose England and champion American causes as much as could any intellectual spark. But even in such cases learning informed the passions. College students and college graduates could draw upon a literature, mostly from the ancients, but fortified by English Whig writers, that supplied them with republican persuasions and patriotic rhetoric.

One would not describe the results as an American ideology as such. We have seen many variations, different emphases, and contrasting personal experiences in the ways that American patriots made use of their collegiate learning. Thus the New England graduates, at Harvard especially, often revisited their own Puritan history of the sixteenth and seventeenth centuries to give historical meaning to their current struggles. Yale people drew upon the New Divinity with which their school was associated and formulated their case for independence. Baptists at Rhode Island College could use their own subjugation in New England to make the case for freedom. Ideology never escaped its institutional problematics. Dartmouth might have been a school of patriots; we have seen how political complexities prevented it from being so. Here politics trumped intellect. But intellect could trump politics, too. William and Mary, King's, and the College of Philadelphia all had Anglican leadership. They all found in their midst a subversive patriot group, of faculty or students, and they changed their institutions.

"American intellectual culture," then, provides a better reference than "ideology" in describing the legacy of the American colonial colleges. Products of these institutions who led the colonies into revolution faced the pressing necessity of defining their purposes and justifying their actions. It was a challenge, but an opportunity also. These leaders had vast intellectual resources on which to draw. American political thinking thus became richly synthetic. However variant the synthesis, though, one is at pains to imagine the American Revolution and the creation of the new republic apart from the intellectual culture fashioned in these years. Those who founded the colonial colleges did not generally speak in nationalist terms. They created programs of studies that took their students back to the ancient world. They filled their libraries with Christian literature, books on modern philosophy and science, and Whig political theories. In the middle eighteenth century the collegians who studied them created new documents of American nationhood.

Bibliography

ORIGINAL SOURCES

Colonial Imprints

For many of the original publications cited in this study I have used the *National Index of Imprints through 1800*. Every historian of colonial America knows this invaluable collection. The work of Clifton K. Shifton and James E. Moody, under the sponsorship of the American Antiquarian Society in 1969, it contains boxed microcards of nearly fifty thousand individual imprints. I have accessed this collection through the University of Wisconsin-Milwaukee Library holdings.

Collections and Anthologies

Anderson, Wallace E, ed. *Jonathan Edwards: Scientific and Philosophical Writings*. Works of Jonathan Edwards, John E. Smith, general editor. New Haven, Conn.: Yale University Press, 1980.

Boyd, Julian P., ed. *The Papers of Thomas Jefferson*. Princeton, N.J.: Princeton University Press, 1950– .

Breward, Ian, ed. *The Work of William Perkins*. Appleford, England: The Sutton Courtenay Press, 1970.

Bushman, Richard L., ed. *The Great Awakening: Documents on the Revival of Religion, 1740–1745*. New York: Atheneum, 1970.

Butterfield, L. H., ed. *John Witherspoon Comes to America: A Documentary Account Based Largely on New Materials*. Princeton, N.J.: Princeton University Press, 1953.

Commager, Henry Steele, ed. *Documents of American History*. New York: Appleton-Century-Crofts, 1948.

Cragg, Gerald R. *The Cambridge Platonists*. New York: Oxford University Press, 1968.

Heimert, Alan, and Perry Miller, eds. *The Great Awakening*. Indianapolis: Bobbs-Merrill, 1967.

Hosfstadter, Richard, and Wilson Smith, eds. *American Higher Education: A Documentary History*. 2 vols. Chicago: University of Chicago Press, 1961.

Hunt, Gaillard, ed. *The Writings of James Madison*. 9 vols. New York: G. P. Putnam's Sons, 1900.

Hutchinson, William T., and William M. E. Rachal, eds. *The Papers of James Madison, Volume I, 16 March 1751–16 December 1779*. Chicago: University of Chicago Press, 1962.

Klein, Milton M., ed. *The Independent Reflector*. Cambridge, Mass.: Harvard University Press, 1963.

Labaree, Leonard W., ed. *The Papers of Benjamin Franklin*. 35 vols. (to date). New Haven, Conn.: Yale University Press, 1960.

Lovett, Robert W., ed. *Publications of the Colonial Society of Massachusetts: Harvard College Records, Part V, Documents, 1722–1750*. Boston: Colonial Society of Massachusetts, 1975.

McGiffert, Michael, ed. *God's Plot: Puritan Spirituality in Thomas Shepard's Cambridge*. Rev. and exp. Amherst: University of Massachusetts Press, 1994.

McLoughlin, William, G., ed. *Isaac Backus on Church, State, and Calvinism: Pamphlets, 1754–1789*. Cambridge, Mass.: Harvard University Press, 1968.

Miller, Perry, ed. *The American Puritans: Their Prose and Poetry*. Garden City, N.Y.: Doubleday Anchor Books, 1956.

Miller, Thomas, ed. *The Selected Works of John Witherspoon*. Carbondale: Southern Illinois University Press, 1990.

Rodgers, John, ed. *The Works of John Witherspoon*. 3 vols. Philadelphia: William W. Woodward, 1800.

Sandoz, Ellis, ed. *Political Sermons of the Founding Era, 1730–1805*. Indianapolis: Liberty Fund, 1991.

Schneider, Herbert, and Carol Schneider, eds. *Samuel Johnson, President of King's College: His Career and Writings*. 4 vols. New York: Columbia University Press, 1929.

Sloan, Douglas, ed. *The Great Awakening and American Higher Education: A Documentary History*. New York: Teachers College Press, 1973.

Smith, Horace Wemyss, ed. *Life and Correspondence of the Rev. William Smith, D.D.* 1879; New York: Arno Press, 1972.

Syrett, Harold C., ed. *The Papers of Alexander Hamilton, Volume I: 1768–1778*. New York: Columbia University Press, 1961.

Vance, Clarence H., ed. *Letters of a Westchester Farmer*. White Plains, N.Y.: Westchester County Historical Society, 1930.

SECONDARY SOURCES

Adair, Douglass. *Fame and the Founding Fathers: Essays by Douglass Adair*. Edited by Trevor Colbourn. New York: Norton, 1974.

Ahlstrom, Sydney E. *A Religious History of the American People*. New Haven, Conn.: Yale University Press, 1972.

Akers, Charles W. *Called Into Liberty: A Life of Jonathan Mayhew, 1720-1766*. Cambridge, Mass.: Harvard University Press, 1964.

Anderson, Wallace E. "Biographical Background." In *Jonathan Edwards: Scientific and Philosophical Writings*, ed. Wallace E. Anderson, Works of Jonathan Edwards, John E. Smith, general editor. New Haven, Conn.: Yale University Press, 1980.

———. "Immaterialism in Jonathan Edwards' Early Philosophical Notes." *Journal of the History of Ideas* 25 (1964): 181–200.

Arnold, Douglas M. *A Republican Revolution: Ideology and Politics in Pennsylvania, 1776–1790.* New York: Garland Publishing, 1989.

Bailyn, Bernard. *The Origins of American Politics.* New York: Knopf, 1968.

Bain, Robert A. "The Composition and Publication of *The Present State of Virginia, and the College.*" *Early American Literature* 6 (1971): 31–54.

Bedini, Silvio A. *Thomas Jefferson: Statesman of Science.* New York: Macmillan, 1990.

Bender, Thomas. *New York Intellect: A History of Intellectual Life in New York City, from 1750 to the Beginning of Our Own Time.* New York: Knopf, 1987.

Bercovitch, Sacvan. *The American Jeremiad.* Madison: University of Wisconsin Press, 1978.

Beverley, Robert. *History and Present State of Virginia.* 1705; Indianapolis: Bobbs-Merrill, 1971.

Birdsall, Richard D. "Ezra Stiles versus the New Divinity Men." *American Quarterly* 17 (1965): 248–58.

Bockelman Wayne L., and Owen S. Ireland. "The Internal Revolution in Pennsylvania: An Ethnic-Religious Interpretation." *Pennsylvania History* 41 (1974): 125–59.

Bonomi, Patricia U. *A Factious People: Politics and Society in Colonial New York.* New York: Columbia University Press, 1971.

Branson, Roy. "James Madison and the Scottish Enlightenment." *Journal of the History of Ideas* 40 (1979): 237.

Brant, Irving. *James Madison: The Virginia Revolutionist.* Indianapolis: Bobbs-Merrill, 1941.

Breen, T. H. *The Character of the Good Ruler: Puritan Political Ideas in New England, 1630–1730.* New York: Norton, 1970.

Breitenbach, William. "The Consistent Calvinism of the New Divinity Movement." *William and Mary Quarterly* 3rd Series, 41 (1984): 241–64.

Bridenbaugh, Carl. *Mitre and Sceptre: Transatlantic Faiths, Ideas, Personalities, and Politics, 1689–1775.* London: Oxford University Press, 1962.

Bridenbaugh, Carl, and Jessica Bridenbaugh. *Rebels and Gentlemen: Philadelphia in the Age of Franklin.* New York: Oxford University Press, 1962.

Brobeck, Stephen. "Revolutionary Change in Colonial Philadelphia: The Brief Life of the Proprietary Gentry." *William and Mary Quarterly* 3rd Series, 33 (1976): 410–34.

Broderick, Francis L. "Pulpit, Physics, and Politics: The Curriculum of the College of New Jersey, 1746–1794." *William and Mary Quarterly* 3rd Series, 6 (1949): 42–68.

Brodie, Fawn. *Thomas Jefferson: An Intimate History.* New York: Bantam, 1974.

Bronson, Walter C. *The History of Brown University, 1764–1914.* 1914; New York: Arno Press, 1971.

Brumsted, J. M. "Revivalism and Separatism in New England: The First Society of Norwich, Connecticut as a Case Study." *William and Mary Quarterly* 3rd Series, 24 (1967): 588–612.

Bushman, Richard C. *From Puritan to Yankee: Character and the Social Order in Connecticut, 1690–1765.* New York: Norton, 1967.

Butler, Jon. *Awash in a Sea of Faith: Christianizing the American People.* Cambridge, Mass.: Harvard University Press, 1990.

Buxbaum, Melvin H. "Franklin and William Smith: Their School and Their Dispute." *Historical Magazine of the Protestant Episcopal Church* 39 (1970): 361–82.

Carlton, Charles. *Archbishop William Laud.* London: Routledge and Kegan Paul, 1987.

Caspari, Fritz. *Humanism and the Social Order in Tudor England.* Chicago: University of Chicago Press, 1954.

Cheyney, Edward Potts. *History of the University of Pennsylvania, 1740–1940.* Philadelphia: University of Pennsylvania Press, 1940.

Collins, Varnum Lansing. *President Witherspoon.* 2 vols. in 1. 1925; New York: Arno Press, 1969.

Collinson, Patrick. *The Elizabethan Puritan Movement.* Berkeley: University of California Press, 1967.

———. *The Religion of Protestants: The Church in English Society, 1559–1625.* Oxford: Oxford University Press, 1982.

Come, Donald Robert. "The Influence of Princeton on Higher Education in the South before 1825." *William and Mary Quarterly* 3rd Series, 2 (1945): 359–96.

Conforti, Joseph A. "Samuel Hopkins and the New Divinity: Theology, Ethics, and Social Reform in Eighteenth-Century New England." *William and Mary Quarterly* 3rd Series, 34 (1977): 572–89.

Cragg, G. R. *From Puritanism to the Age of Reason: A Study of Religious Thought within the Church of England, 1660–1700.* Cambridge: Cambridge University Press, 1950.

Cremin, Lawrence A. *American Education: The Colonial Experience, 1607–1783.* New York: Harper & Row, 1970.

Cross, Arthur Lyon. *The Anglican Episcopate and the American Colonies.* 1902; Hamden, Conn.: Archon Books, 1964.

Crowe, Charles. "The Reverend James Madison in Williamsburg and London, 1768–1771." *West Virginia History* 24 (1964): 270–78.

Curtis, Mark H. "Hampton Court Conference and Its Aftermath." *History* 46 (1961): 1–16.

———. *Oxford and Cambridge in Transition, 1558–1642: An Essay on Changing Relations between the English Universities and English Society.* Oxford: Oxford University Press, 1959.

Davies, Horton. *Worship and Theology in England: From Cranmer to Hooker, 1534–1603.* Princeton, N.J.: Princeton University Press, 1970.

Davis, Richard Beale. *Intellectual Life in the Colonial South, 1585–1763.* 3 vols. Knoxville: University of Tennessee Press, 1978.

De Jong, Gerald F. *The Dutch Reformed Church in the American Colonies.* Grand Rapids, Mich.: Eerdmans, 1978.

De Wetering, John Van. "Thomas Prince's Chronological History." *William and Mary Quarterly* 3rd Series, 18 (1961): 546–57.

Dever, Mark E. *Richard Sibbes: Puritanism and Calvinism in Late Elizabethan and Early Stuart England.* Macon, Ga.: Mercer University Press, 2000.

Diggins, John P. *The Lost Soul of American Politics: Virtue, Self-Interest, and the Foundations of Liberalism.* New York: Basic, 1984.

Doelman, James. *King James I and the Religious Culture of England.* Cambridge: D. S. Brewer, 2000.

Drummond Andrew L., and James Bulloch. *The Scottish Church, 1688–1843: The Age of the Moderates.* Edinburgh: The Saint Andrew Press, 1973.

Editor. "Early Presidents of William and Mary." *William and Mary College Quarterly Historical Papers* 1 (1892): 63–75.

Ellis, Joseph J. *The New England Mind in Transition: Samuel Johnson of Connecticut, 1696–1772.* New Haven, Conn.: Yale University Press, 1973.

Emerson, Everett. *Puritanism in America, 1620–1750.* Boston: Twayne Publishers, 1977.

Eusden, John D. "Introduction" to William Ames, *The Marrow of Theology*, edited by John D. Eusden. Boston: Pilgrim Press, 1968.

Ferling, John. *John Adams: A Life.* Knoxville: University of Tennessee Press, 1992.

Fiering, Norman. *Jonathan Edwards's Moral Thought and Its British Context.* Chapel Hill: University of North Carolina Press, 1981.

———. "The First American Enlightenment: Tillotson, Leverrett, and Philosophical Anglicanism." *New England Quarterly* 54 (September 1981): 307–44.

———. *Moral Philosophy at Seventeenth-Century Harvard: A Discipline in Transition.* Chapel Hill: University of North Carolina Press, 1981.

Fincham, Kenneth, and Peter Lake. "The Ecclesiastical Policy of King James I." *Journal of British Studies* 24 (April 1985): 169–207.

Fincham, Peter. *Prelate as Pastor: The Episcopate of James I.* Oxford: Oxford University Press, 1990.

Fleming, Thomas. *New Jersey: A Bicentennial History.* New York: Norton, 1977.

Flower, Elizabeth, and Murray G. Murphey. *A History of Philosophy in America.* 2 vols. New York: Putnam, 1977.

Foster, Stephen. *The Long Argument: English Puritanism and the Shaping of New England Culture, 1570–1700.* Chapel Hill: University of North Carolina Press, 1991.

Fowler, William M., Jr. *Samuel Adams: Radical Puritan.* New York: Longman, 1997.

French, Allen. *Charles I and the Puritan Upheaval: A Study of the Causes of the Great Migration.* Boston: Houghton Mifflin, 1955.

Gaustad, Edwin S. "Society and the Great Awakening in New England." *William and Mary Quarterly* 3rd Series, 11 (October 1954): 566–77.

Gaustad, Edwin Scott. *The Great Awakening in New England.* New York: Harper and Brothers, 1957.

Genuth, Sarah Schechner. *Comets, Popular Culture, and the Birth of Modern Cosmology.* Princeton, N.J.: Princeton University Press, 1997.

Gerlach, Larry R. *Prologue to Independence: New Jersey in the Coming of the American Revolution.* New Brunswick, N.J.: Rutgers University Press, 1976.

Gibbs, Lee W. "Introduction" to William Ames, *Technometry.* Philadelphia: University of Pennsylvania Press, 1979.

Godson, Susan H., et al. *The College of William and Mary: A History, Volume I, 1693–1888.* Williamsburg, Va.: King and Queen Press, 1993.

Goen, C. C. *Revivalism and Separatism in New England, 1740–1800: Strict Congregationalists and Separate Baptists in the Great Awakening.* New Haven, Conn.: Yale University Press, 1962.

Gordon, Ann D. *The College of Philadelphia, 1749–1779: Impact of an Institution.* New York: Garland Publishing, 1989.

Graham, Louis. "The Scientific Piety of John Winthrop." *New England Quarterly* 46 (1973): 112–18.

Grasso, Christopher. *A Speaking Aristocracy: Transforming Public Discourse in Eighteenth-Century Connecticut.* Chapel Hill: University of North Carolina Press, 1999.

Green, V. H. H. *Religion at Oxford and Cambridge.* London, SCM Press, 1964.

Griffin, Edward M. *Old Brick: Charles Chauncy of Boston, 1705–1787*. Minneapolis: University of Minnesota Press, 1980.

Guild, Reuben Aldridge. *Early History of Brown University, Including the Life, Times, and Correspondence of President Manning, 1756–1791*. Providence, R.I.: Snow and Farnham, 1896.

Gunderson, Joan R. *The Anglican Ministry in Virginia, 1723–1766: A Study of a Social Class*. New York: Garland Publishing, 1989.

Hornberger, Theodore. *Scientific Thought in the American Colonies*. Austin: University of Texas Press, 1945.

Hall, David D., ed. "Introduction," in *The Antinomian Controversy, 1636–1638: A Documentary History*. Middletown, Conn.: Wesleyan University Press, 1968.

Hall, Michael G. *The Last American Puritan: The Life of Increase Mather, 1639–1723*. Middletown, Conn.: Wesleyan University Press, 1988.

Hanna, William S. *Benjamin Franklin and Pennsylvania Politics*. Stanford, Calif.: Stanford University Press, 1964.

Hawke, David Freeman. *Benjamin Rush: Revolutionary Gadfly*. Indianapolis: Bobbs-Merrill, 1971.

Hedges, James B. *The Browns of Providence Plantations: The Colonial Years*. Cambridge, Mass.: Harvard University Press, 1952.

Heimert, Alan. *Religion and the American Mind: From the Great Awakening to the American Revolution*. Cambridge, Mass.: Harvard University Press, 1968.

Herbst, Jurgen. *From Crisis to Crisis: American College Government, 1636–1819*. Cambridge, Mass.: Harvard University Press, 1982.

Hill, Christopher. "Parliament and People in Seventeenth-Century England." *Past and Present* 92 (August 1981): 100–24.

Hindle, Brooke. *David Rittenhouse*. Princeton, N.J.: Princeton University Press, 1964.

———. *The Pursuit of Science in Revolutionary America, 1753–1789*. 1956; New York: Norton, 1974.

Hiner, Ray Jr. "Samuel Henley and Thomas Gwatkin: Partners in Protest." *Historical Magazine of the Protestant Episcopal Church* 37 (1968): 39–50.

Hockman, Dan M. "William Dawson: Master and Second President of the College of William and Mary." *Historical Magazine of the Protestant Episcopal Church* 52 (1983): 199–214.

Holifield, E. Brooks. *The Covenant Sealed: The Development of Puritan Sacramental Theology in Old and New England, 1570–1720*. New Haven, Conn.: Yale University Press, 1974.

Howell, W. S. *Logic and Rhetoric in England, 1500–1700*. New York: Russell and Russell, 1961.

Humphrey, David C. "Colonial Colleges and English Dissenting Academies: A Study in Transatlantic Culture." *History of Education Quarterly* 12 (1972) 184–97.

———. *From King's College to Columbia, 1746–1800*. New York: Columbia University Press, 1976.

Ingersoll, Elizabeth A. "Francis Alison: American *Philosophe*." Ph.D. diss., University of Delaware, 1974.

Isaac, Rhys. "Religion and Authority: Problems of the Anglican Establishment in Virginia in the Era of the Great Awakening and the Parsons' Cause." *William and Mary Quarterly* 3rd Series, 30 (1973): 3–36.

———. *The Transformation of Virginia, 1740–1790*. Chapel Hill: University of North Carolina Press, 1982.

Jardine, Lisa. "Humanism and the Sixteenth-Century Arts Course." *History of Education Quarterly* 4 (1975): 16–31.

Kammen, Michael. "A Character of William Smith, Jr." In William Smith, Jr., *The History of the Province of New York, Volume One: From the Discovery to the Year 1732*, edited by Michael Kammen. Cambridge, Mass.: Harvard University Press, 1972.

———. *Colonial New York: A History*. New York: Scribner, 1975.

Kelley, Brooks Mather. *Yale: A History*. New Haven, Conn.: Yale University Press, 1974.

Ketcham, Ralph. *James Madison: A Biography*. New York: Macmillan, 1971.

Kirtland, Richard B. *George Wythe: Lawyer, Revolutionary, Judge*. New York: Garland Randall Publishing, 1986.

Klein, Milton M. *The Politics of Diversity: Essays in the History of Colonial New York*. Port Washington, N.Y.: Kennikat Press, 1974.

Knight, Janice. *Orthodoxies in Massachusetts: Rereading American Puritanism*. Cambridge, Mass.: Harvard University Press, 1994.

Kuklick, Bruce. *Churchmen and Philosophers: From Jonathan Edwards to John Dewey*. New Haven, Conn.: Yale University Press, 1985.

Labaree, Leonard W. "The Conservative Attitude toward the Great Awakening." *William and Mary Quarterly* 3rd Series, 1 (1944): 331–52.

Lake, P. G. "Calvinism and the English Church, 1570–1635." *Past and Present* 114 (1987): 32–75.

Lake, Peter. *Anglicans and Puritans? Presbyterian and Conformist Thought from Whitgift to Hooker*. London: Unwin Hyman, 1988.

Lambert, Paul F. "Benjamin Rush and American Independence." *Pennsylvania History* 39 (1972): 443–49.

Landsman, Ned C. *From Colonials to Provincials: American Thought and Culture, 1680–1760*. New York: Twayne Publishers, 1997.

———. "Witherspoon and the Problem of Provincial Identity in Scottish Evangelical Culture." In *Scotland and America in the Age of Enlightenment*, edited by Richard B. Sher and Jeffrey R. Smitten 29–45. Edinburgh: University of Edinburgh Press, 1990.

Le Beau, Bryan F. *Jonathan Dickinson and the Formative Years of American Presbyterianism*. Lexington: University Press of Kentucky, 1997.

Leinitz-Schurer, Leopold. "A Loyalist Clergyman's Response to the Imperial Crisis in the American Colonies: A Note on Samuel Seabury's Letters of a Westchester Farmer." *Historical Magazine of the Protestant Episcopal Church* 44 (1975): 107–19.

Lippy, Charles H. *Seasonable Revolutionary: The Mind of Charles Chauncy*. Chicago: Nelson-Hall, 1981.

Lively, Bruce Richard. "William Smith, the College and Academy of Philadelphia and Pennsylvania Politics, 1753–1758." *Historical Magazine of the Protestant Episcopal Church* 38 (1969): 237–58.

Lockeridge, Kenneth A. "Social Change and the Meaning of the American Revolution." *Journal of Social History* 6 (1973): 403–39.

Lockwood, Rose. "The Scientific Revolution in Seventeenth-Century New England." *New England Quarterly* 53 (1980): 76–95.

Lowrie, Ernest Benson. *The Shape of the Puritan Mind: The Thought of Samuel Willard*. New Haven, Conn.: Yale University Press, 1974.

Malone, Dumas. "Jefferson Goes to School in Williamsburg." *Virginia Quarterly Review* 33 (1957): 481–96.

Mayer, Henry. A Son of Thunder: Patrick Henry and the American Republic. Charlottesville: University Press of Virginia, 1991.

McCallum, James Dow. Eleazar Wheelock. 1939 New York: Arno Press and the New York Times, 1969.

McCosh, James. The Scottish Philosophy, Biographical, Expository, Critical, from Hutcheson to Hamilton. New York: Robert Carter and Bros., 1875.

McDonald, Forrest. Alexander Hamilton: A Biography. New York: Norton, 1979.

McLachlan, James, ed. Princetonians, 1748–1768: A Biographical Dictionary. Princeton, N.J.: Princeton University Press, 1976.

McLoughlin, William G. Isaac Backus and the American Pietistic Tradition. Boston: Little, Brown and Company, 1967.

———. "Massive Civil Disobedience as a Baptist Tactic in 1773." American Quarterly 21 (1969): 710–27.

———. New England Dissent, 1630–1833: The Baptists and the Separation of Church and State. 2 vols. Cambridge, Mass.: Harvard University Press, 1971.

———. Rhode Island: A Bicentennial History. New York: W. W. Norton, 1978.

———. Soul Liberty: The Baptists' Struggle in New England, 1630–1833. Hanover, N.H.: University Press of New England, 1991.

Meyer, D. H. "The Uniqueness of the American Enlightenment." American Quarterly 28 (1976): 165–86.

Middlekauff, Robert. Franklin and His Enemies. Berkeley: University of California Press, 1996.

———. The Mathers: Three Generations of Puritan Intellectuals, 1596–1728. New York: Oxford University Press, 1971.

Middleton, Richard. Colonial America: A History, 1585–1776. 2nd ed. Cambridge, Mass.: Blackwell, 1996.

Miller, John C. Samuel Adams, Pioneer in Propaganda. 1936; Stanford, Calif.: Stanford University Press, 1960.

Miller, Perry. Errand into the Wilderness. 1956; New York: Harper and Row, 1964.

———. Jonathan Edwards. N.p.: William Sloane Associates, 1949.

———. The New England Mind: From Colony to Province. Cambridge, Mass.: Harvard University Press, 1953.

———. The New England Mind: The Seventeenth Century. Boston: Beacon, 1939.

Mintz, Max M. Gouverneur Morris and the American Revolution. Norman: University of Oklahoma Press, 1970.

Monaghan, Frank. John Jay: Defender of Liberty. New York: Bobbs-Merrill, 1935.

Moore, James. "Hutcheson's Theodicy: The Argument and the Contexts of A System of Moral Philosophy." In The Scottish Enlightenment: Essays in Reinterpretation, ed. Paul Wood, 237–60. Rochester, N.Y.: University of Rochester Press, 2000.

Moran, Susan Drinker. "Thomas Shepard and the Professor: Two Documents from the Early History of Harvard." Early American Literature 17 (1982): 24–42.

Morgan, Edmund S. American Slavery/American Freedom: The Ordeal of Colonial Virginia. New York: Norton, 1975.

———. The Gentle Puritan: A Life of Ezra Stiles, 1725–1795. New York: Norton, 1962.

Morgan, John. Godly Learning: Puritan Attitudes towards Reason, Learning, and Education, 1560–1640 Cambridge, Mass.: Cambridge University Press, 1986.

Morison, Elizabeth Forbes, and Elting E. Morison. New Hampshire: A Bicentennial History. New York: Norton, 1976.

Morison, Samuel Eliot. *Builders of the Bay Colony*. Boston: Houghton Mifflin Company, 1930.

———. *The Founding of Harvard College*. Cambridge, Mass.: Harvard University Press, 1935.

———. *Harvard College in the Seventeenth Century*. 2 vols. Cambridge, Mass.: Harvard University Press, 1936.

———. *Three Centuries of Harvard, 1636–1936*. Cambridge, Mass.: Harvard University Press, 1942.

Morton, Richard L. *Colonial Virginia, Volume 1: The Tidewater Period, 1607–1710*. Chapel Hill: University of North Carolina Press, 1960.

Murdock, Kenneth Ballard. *Increase Mather: The Foremost American Puritan*. Cambridge, Mass.: Harvard University Press, 1925.

Noll, Mark. *Princeton and the Republic, 1766–1822: The Search for a Christian Enlightenment in the Era of Samuel Stanhope Smith*. Princeton, N.J.: Princeton University Press, 1989.

Norton, David Fate. *David Hume: Common-Sense Moralist, Skeptical Metaphysician*. Princeton, N.J.: Princeton University Press, 1982.

Oaks, Robert F. "Philadelphia Merchants and the First Continental Congress." *Pennsylvania History* 40 (1973): 149–68.

Olson, James S. "The New York Assembly, the Politics of Religion, and the Origins of the American Revolution, 1768–1771." *Historical Magazine of the Protestant Episcopal Church* 43 (1974): 21–28.

Parker, David L. "Petrus Ramus and the Puritans: The 'Logic' of Preparationist Conversion Doctrine." *Early American Literature* 8 (1973): 140–62.

Patrides, C. A. "Introduction" to *The Cambridge Platonists*, edited by C. A. Patrides. Cambridge, Mass., Harvard University Press, 1970.

Patton, Glenn. "The College of William and Mary, Williamsburg, and the Enlightenment." *Journal of the Society of Architectural Historians* 29 (1970): 24–32.

Pearson, A. F. Scott. *Thomas Cartwright and Elizabethan Puritanism, 1535–1603*. Gloucester, Mass.: Peter Smith, 1966.

Pelikan, Jaroslav. *The Christian Tradition: A History of the Development of Doctrine*. 5 vols. Vol. 4: *Reformation of Church and Dogma (1300–1700)*. Chicago: University of Chicago Press, 1984.

Peterson, Merrill D. *Thomas Jefferson and the New Nation: A Biography*. New York: Oxford University Press, 1970.

Pettit, Norman. "Editor's Introduction" to *Jonathan Edwards, The Life of David Brainerd*, edited by Norman Petit, The Works of Jonathan Edwards, John E. Smith, general editor. New Haven, Conn.: Yale University Press, 1985.

———. *The Heart Prepared: Grace and Conversion in Puritan Spiritual Life*. New Haven, Conn.: Yale University Press, 1966.

Pilcher, George William. "The Pamphlet Warfare on the Proposed Virginia Anglican Episcopate, 1767–1775." *Historical Magazine of the Protestant Episcopal Church* 30 (1961): 266–79.

———. *Samuel Davies: Apostle of Dissent in Colonial Virginia*. Knoxville: University of Tennessee Press, 1971.

Pomfret, John E. *Colonial New Jersey: A History*. New York: Scribner, 1973.

Pope, Robert G. *The Half-Way Covenant: Church Membership in Puritan New England*. Princeton, N.J.: Princeton University Press, 1969.

Porter, H. C. Reformation and Reaction in Tudor Cambridge. 1958; Hamden, Conn.: Archer Books, 1972.

Potter, Janice. The Liberty We Seek: Loyalist Ideology in Colonial New York and Massachusetts. Cambridge, Mass.: Harvard University Press, 1983.

Prall, Stuart E. Church and State in Tudor and Stuart England. Arlington Heights, Ill.: Harlan Davidson, 1993.

Randall, Willard Sterne. Thomas Jefferson: A Life. New York: HarperPerennial, 1994.

Ranlet, Philip. The New York Loyalists. Knoxville: University of Tennessee Press, 1986.

Richardson, Leon Burr. History of Dartmouth College. Hanover, N.H.: Dartmouth University Press, 1932.

Rivers, Isabel. Reason, Grace, and Sentiment: A Study of the Language of Religion and Ethics in England, 1660–1780. Volume I, Whichcote to Wesley. Cambridge: Cambridge University Press, 1991.

Roche, John F. The Colonial Colleges in the War for Independence. Millwood, N.Y.: National University Publications, 1986.

Roosevelt, Theodore. Gouverneur Morris. Boston: Houghton, Mifflin and Company, 1888.

Rossiter, Clinton. "Richard Bland: The Whig in America." William and Mary Quarterly 3rd Series, 10 (1953): 33–79.

Rouse, Parke, Jr. James Blair of Virginia. Chapel Hill: University of North Carolina Press, 1971.

Rupp, George. "The Idealism of Jonathan Edwards." Harvard Theological Review 62 (1969): 209–26.

Roth, David M. Connecticut: A Bicentennial History. New York: Norton, 1979.

Schachner, Nathan. Alexander Hamilton. New York: D. Appleton-Century Company, 1946.

Schlenther, Boyd Stanley. Charles Thomson: A Patriot's Pursuit. Newark: University of Delaware Press, 1990.

Schmidt, Leigh Eric. "Jonathan Dickinson and the Making of the Moderate Awakening." Journal of Presbyterian History 63 (1985): 341–53.

Schwartz, Hillel. "Arminianism and the English Parliament, 1624–1629." Journal of British Studies 12, No. 2 (1973): 41–68.

Sher, Richard B. Church and University in the Scottish Enlightenment: The Moderate Literati of Edinburgh. Princeton, N.J.: Princeton University Press, 1985.

———. "Witherspoon's Dominion of Providence and the Scottish Jeremiad Tradition." In Scotland and America in the Age of Enlightenment, ed. Richard B. Sher and Jeffrey R. Smitten, 46–64. Edinburgh: University of Edinburgh Press, 1990.

Shifton, Clifford, ed. Sibley's Harvard Graduates: Biographical Sketches of Those Who Attended Harvard College. Vol. 11. Boston: Massachusetts Historical Society, 1960.

Scott, Jack. "A Biographical Sketch." In John Witherspoon, Lectures on Moral Philosophy, ed. Jack Scott. Newark: University of Delaware Press, 1982.

Silverman, Kenneth. A Cultural History of the American Revolution. New York: Thomas Y. Crowell, 1976.

Skemp, Sheila L. William Franklin: Son of a Patriot, Servant of a King. New York: Oxford University Press, 1990.

Sloan, Douglas. The Scottish Enlightenment and the American College Ideal. New York: Teachers College Press, 1971.

Smylie, James H. "Madison and Witherspoon: Theological Roots of American Political Thought." American Presbyterians 73 (1995): 155–63.

Solberg, Winton U. *Redeem the Time: The Puritan Sabbath in Early America.* Cambridge, Mass.: Harvard University Press, 1977.

Sprunger, Keith L. *The Learned Doctor William Ames: Dutch Backgrounds of English and American Puritanism.* Urbana: University of Illinois Press, 1972.

Shriver, Frederick. "Hampton Court Revisited: James I and the Puritans." *Journal of Ecclesiastical History* 33 (1982): 48–71.

Staloff, Darren. *The Making of an American Thinking Class: Intellectuals and Intelligentsia in Puritan Massachusetts.* New York: Oxford University Press, 1998.

Stearns, Raymond Phineas. *Science in the British Colonies of North America.* Urbana: University of Illinois Press, 1970.

———. *The Strenuous Puritan: Hugh Peter, 1598–1660.* Urbana: University of Illinois Press, 1954.

Steiner, Bruce E. *Samuel Seabury, 1729–1796: A Study in the High Church Tradition.* Columbus: Ohio University Press, 1971.

Stourzh, Gerald. *Alexander Hamilton and the Idea of Republican Government.* Stanford, Calif.: Stanford University Press, 1970.

Stromberg, Roland N. *Religious Liberalism in Eighteenth-Century England.* London: Oxford University Press, 1954.

Tanis, James. *Dutch Calvinistic Pietism in the Middle Colonies: A Study in the Life of Theodorus Jacobus Frelinghuysen.* The Hague: Martinus Nijhoff, 1967.

———. "Reformed Pietism in Colonial America." In *Continental Pietism and Early American Christianity,* edited by Ernest Stoeffler. Grand Rapids, Mich.: William B. Eerdman's, 1976. 34–73.

Taussig, Harold E. "Deism in Philadelphia during the Age of Franklin." *Pennsylvania History* 37 (1970): 217–36.

Thompson, C. Bradley. "Young John Adams and the New Philosophic Rationalism." *William and Mary Quarterly* 3rd Series, 55 (1998): 259–80.

Thomson, Robert Folk. "The Reform of the College of William and Mary, 1763–1780." *Proceedings of the American Philosophical Society* 115 (1971): 187–213.

Tolles, Frederick B. *Meeting House and Counting House: The Quaker Merchants of Colonial Philadelphia, 1682–1763.* New York: Norton, 1948.

Trinterud, Leonard. *The Forming of an American Tradition: A Re-Examination of Colonial Presbyterianism.* Philadelphia: Westminster Press, 1949.

Tucker, Louis Leonard. *Puritan Protagonist: President Thomas Clap of Yale College.* Chapel Hill: University of North Carolina Press, 1962.

Tully, Allan. *Forming American Politics: Ideas, Interests, and Institutions in Colonial New York and Pennsylvania.* Baltimore: Johns Hopkins University Press, 1994.

Tyacke, Nicholas. *Anti-Calvinists: The Rise of English Arminianism, c. 1590–1640.* Oxford: Clarendon Press, 1987.

———. "The Rise of Arminianism Reconsidered." *Past and Present* 115 (1987): 201–16.

Upton, L. F. S. *The Loyal Whig: William Smith of New York & Quebec.* Toronto: University of Toronto Press, 1969.

Valeri, Mark. "The New Divinity and the American Revolution." *William and Mary Quarterly* 3rd Series, 46 (October 1989): 741–69.

Vance, Clarence H. "Introductory Essay." In *Letters of a Westchester Farmer,* edited by Clarence H. Vance. White Plains, N.Y.: Westchester County Historical Society, 1930.

Warch, Richard. *School of the Prophets: Yale College, 1701–1740.* New Haven, Conn.: Yale University Press, 1973.

Werge, Thomas. *Thomas Shepard*. Boston: Twayne Publishers, 1987.

Wertenbaker, Thomas. *Princeton, 1746–1896*. Princeton, N.J.: Princeton University Press, 1946.

Wilderson, Paul W. *Governor John Wentworth and the American Revolution: The English Connection*. Hanover, N.H.: University Press of New England, 1994.

Wills, Garry. *Explaining America: The Federalist*. New York: Penguin, 1981.

———. *Inventing America: Jefferson's Declaration of Independence*. Garden City, N.Y.: Doubleday, 1978.

Winship, Michael P. "'The Most Glorious Church in the World': The Unity of the Godly in Boston, Massachusetts, in the 1630s." *Journal of British Studies* 39 (January 2000): 71–98.

Woolverton, John Frederick. *Colonial Anglicanism in North America*. Detroit, Mich.: Wayne State University Press, 1984.

Ziff, Larzer. *The Career of John Cotton: Puritanism and the American Experience*. Princeton, N.J.: Princeton University Press, 1962.

Index

About the Author

J. David Hoeveler is professor of history at the University of Wisconsin at Milwaukee. His books include *The New Humanism* (1977) *James McCosh and the Scottish Intellectual Tradition* (1981), *Watch on the Right* (1991), and *The Postmodernist Turn: American Thought and Culture in the 1970s* (1996).